MW00856212

LOVETT'S LIGHTS on ACTS

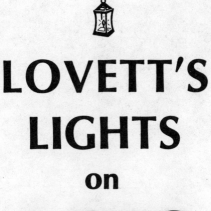

LOVETT'S LIGHTS on ACTS

WITH REPHRASED TEXT BY

C. S. Lovett

M.A., B.D., D.D.

author of
DEALING WITH THE DEVIL
LATEST WORD ON THE LAST DAYS
SOUL-WINNING MADE EASY

director of Personal Christianity

Published by

PERSONAL CHRISTIANITY
Baldwin Park, California 91706

ISBN 0-938148-28-1
1982 EDITION

DR. LUKE

ILLUSTRATED BY LINDA LOVETT

© C. S. LOVETT 1972

No part of this book may be used or reproduced in any manner whatsoever without written permission of the copyright owner except in the case of brief quotations in articles and reviews.

PRINTED IN THE UNITED STATES OF AMERICA

PREFACE

"I appeal to Caesar. . .!"

That did it! The apostle Paul would now go to Rome. The Palestinian authorities had no choice but to put him aboard a ship and send him to the Emperor. But Paul didn't go alone. His personal physician and traveling companion was allowed to go with him. When they arrived in the capitol, they found the emperor in no hurry to hear the case. What was Dr. Luke to do with all that spare time?

In the past, when Paul had been imprisoned, Luke made good use of his time. When the apostle was held in Caesarea for two years, he began to put together a history of Christianity. He had been taking notes on his journeys with Paul as well as collecting data from many who were eyewitnesses to events in the life of Christ. Numerous accounts concerning the Lord had begun to appear, but apparently they weren't reliable enough to suit Dr. Luke. So he undertook to compile a trustworthy history of the Lord's earthly life and the establishment of His church on earth (Luke 1:1-4).

Luke was a Greek, a Gentile. His home was in Macedonia. He was already a Christian when he met Paul and became his traveling companion. He was a scholar, beautifully educated and easily able to check sources and examine records. He was qualified to interview eyewitnesses and set down the facts after he had verified them. He wrote in flawless Greek. Not only was it the literary language, it was his native tongue.

During Paul's first imprisonment at Rome, which extended over several years, Luke completed his two-volume history. Apparently he had also become acquainted with a member of the Roman nobility by the name of Theophilus. For a reason unknown to us, he dedicated his two-volume work to him. He may have called it, "Theophilus' letters number one and number two." We can't be sure, because Luke himself gives us no title for his work. Scholars have since called volume one of his history, "The Gospel according to Luke." His second volume, bearing the same dedication to his friend Theophilus, scholars have since named, "The Acts of the Apostles." Most modern teachers regard them as a single work, referring to them as Luke-Acts. It can be shown that the opening verses of the Gospel are really the dedication of the entire two-volume work.

The church fathers, in arranging the New Testament, separated Luke's two volumes. His first roll (the Gospel) they placed with Matthew, Mark, and John. His second roll (Acts) they placed between the gospels and the epistles to make it serve as a bridge. The epistles would be isolated without this book to connect them with the gospels. Much that is in Paul's epistles will be less meaningful without the background of his journeys as reported by Luke. The Book of Acts picks up the story exactly where the Gospel leaves off.

LUKE'S TWO-PART HISTORY OF THE LORD JESUS

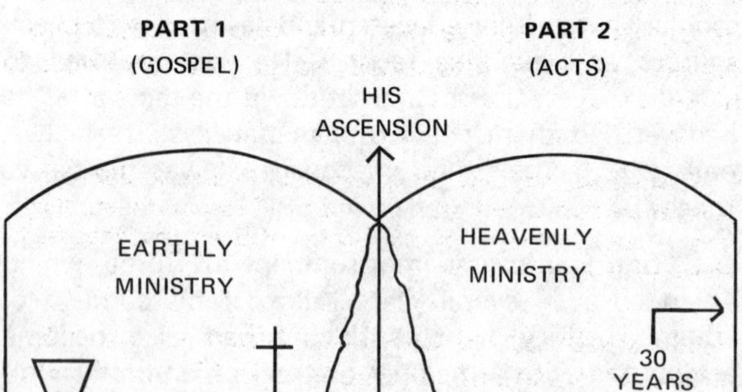

In his first volume (the Gospel) Luke tells of Jesus' earthly ministry from His birth to His ascension. His second volume continues the history of Jesus after His ascension and carries it on for some thirty years. The latter is an account of the Lord's SPIRITUAL ministry as Christianity spread from Judea to Rome. It ends with the great apostle Paul proclaiming the Gospel in the heart of the Roman Empire. The events will not be seen in their true light unless readers understand that the experiences of the apostles are an extension of Jesus' own ministry.

Luke confines himself to facts. He does no preaching. He doesn't have to. The facts speak eloquently by themselves. There is no way to account for the survival of Christianity, if it is not a supernatural movement. The church had no wealth in those early days, certainly no military might. There was no political power behind it. When you think of the unfavorable conditions under which it developed, you wonder how it ever got started. Its founder was a discredited Jew and His followers were insignificant nobodies.

But there was something unique about it. Those who got involved were utterly TRANSFORMED. Christianity not only survived, but spread because people were CHANGED as they came in contact with the unseen Christ. We read how two of these transformed nobodies astonished those who challenged them:

> **"Now when they saw the boldness of Peter and John and perceived that they were unlearned and ignorant men, they marveled; and they took knowledge of them that they had been with Jesus" (Acts 4:13).**

What happened to those two fishermen to make them so outstanding? Luke tells us in his history. He will show how the church began at Pentecost—the day the Lord returned in the Spirit to indwell His disciples. He will also show how receiving the Spirit transformed them into outspoken evangels. It was Pentecost that made ordinary people supernatural agents for Christ on earth. Without Luke's record we would never know the Holy Spirit came precisely as Jesus promised. Apart from his account, we would have no idea what happened when the disciples began to carry out the commission.

Dr. Luke felt he could best interpret the spiritual history of the Lord by showing how He worked in the lives of two of His apostles, Peter and Paul. Others are mentioned, but these are the heroes. No doubt they should be taken as **representative** of the rest. Surely the Lord used them all in a mighty way. Thus, the first 12 chapters feature the apostle Peter, while the last 16 focus on the ministry of the apostle Paul to the Gentiles. Luke closes his history with Paul still in prison, enjoying unhindered freedom to preach the Gospel. One thing is clear, Christianity is NOT a movement carried on in memory of a dead Founder, but one which is energized by His presence as its LIVING LEADER!

CSL

INTRODUCTION

ACTS—JESUS' BIGGER JOB!

JESUS DISAPPEARS. . .!

Imagine yourself the editor of the Jerusalem daily newspaper in the days of the disciples. Picture the desperation of the newsroom trying to keep pace with events. Ah, but think how circulation would zoom with all those shocking headlines hitting the streets:

JESUS ARRESTED!

JESUS FOUND INNOCENT!

JESUS CRUCIFIED ANYWAY!

JESUS RISES FROM THE GRAVE!

JESUS APPEARS TO DISCIPLES!

JESUS DISAPPEARS!

JESUS APPEARS AGAIN!

JESUS DISAPPEARS AGAIN!

JESUS RE-APPEARS!

JESUS DISAPPEARS ONCE MORE!

. . .and on and on, because the Lord appeared and disappeared again and again in the 40 days that followed His resurrection.

Then at last the public would weary of your headlines. You know how it is in the news business when things become commonplace. Why even today some

TV stations will not televise a space launch anymore. The event is no longer sensational.

But Jesus' disappearances were vital

The Lord wasn't trying to make headlines. He was performing a delicate task. He was trying to get His disciples familiar with the idea that even though He was out of sight, **He was still alive.** By means of frequent appearances and disappearances, He was teaching them BY DRAMA to live by faith in the fact that He was still alive, **though absent from view,** He kept it up until their faith was ready for the day when they wouldn't see Him again—physically—and still be able to trust in the fact that He was alive and doing as He said He would.

But why was that so important? The Lord had a job for His disciples which required them to be convinced He was alive though they didn't see Him in the flesh again. And He used the method of appearing and disappearing to bring them to a solid conviction about it. **And it worked!** When they finally saw Him for the last time, **and knew it was for the last time,** they were ready to wait for His return in the Spirit.

WHAT WAS THE JOB HE HAD FOR THEM?

What was the task that required this conviction about His return? The disciples were going to go into the building business—the church building business. That didn't mean they were to go around building churches. He called the 12 for the building of ONE church, His body. He told them about it, though they didn't realize the 3½ years He spent with them was to get them ready for that particular job.

> **"And I say unto you that you are PETER and upon this Rock I WILL build My church; and the gates of hell shall**

not overpower it. I WILL give you the keys of the kingdom of heaven; and whatever you shall bind on earth shall have already been bound in heaven, and whatever you shall loose on earth shall have already been loosed in heaven" (Matt. 16:18,19).

We observe the Lord's church was to be built in the FUTURE. It hadn't been built yet. It was something He HIMSELF was going to do at a future time–and He was going to use them in the process. That's why He called them. The Twelve were not selected simply as buddies or pals to keep the Lord company. He had this job for them. They were going to build the Church–with Him!

Before Jesus departed from His body on the cross (died), He gave forth this shout–**"It is finished!"** But what had He finished, exactly? He hadn't built His church yet, and that was the work He had planned for His disciples. Ah, He had finished the foundation work. All by Himself He put down the foundation for the church He was going to build. That's **all** that was finished at Calvary.

"For no man can lay a foundation other than the one which is laid, which is Jesus Christ" (1 Cor. 3:11 NAS).

It is common to think of the cross as the END of Jesus' ministry. Well–laying the foundation is not the end of any building job. It is only the beginning. When Jesus cried, "It is finished," He meant the foundation work, that which He had to do **by Himself** was finished. Now it would be possible to get on with the actual building itself, the work which He longed to share with His disciples.

NOTE: Jesus foundation work for His church consisted of His 3½ years of personal ministry in the flesh. During that time He performed those preparatory tasks which only He could do: (1) He revealed to the world what God is like as a

PERSON. The personality of Jesus is precisely that of the Father in heaven. (2) He accomplished the atonement. Since He was the only perfect sacrifice, He alone could die for our sins. And since His church was going to be composed of blood-washed sinners, it required His death before sinners could be made clean. During the 3½ years He also selected and taught His disciples. Thus, His cry from the cross. . ."It is finished," is as though He were looking on the foundation work done and saying. . ."There now, that's done!" Actually it was only preliminary to the construction of His church.

With the cross behind Him, the Lord could roll up His sleeves and wade into the bigger task of raising the church on the foundation He had laid. His greater ministry lay beyond the cross. Why? The part He was to play in the building of His church couldn't be done while He was in the flesh. His disciples were to operate in the flesh, while He operated in the Spirit. They were to take His place on earth, performing the human part, while He supplied the supernatural power. Consequently, the building of His church was going to be. . .a supernatural job!

THE CHURCH–A SUPERNATURAL CREATION

If I take the keys from my pocket and hold them up, you can see them. You can hear them jingle as I shake them. They are physical. If I give them to you, you would have access to my house. You would be able to admit yourself along with anyone else you cared to bring along. But my physical keys open physical doors only.

The Lord was not referring to physical keys when He spoke of giving the "keys of the kingdom" to the disciples. Instead it was the **authority** to admit souls into heaven. He was speaking of the supernatural business of bringing people into His church. The disciples would perform the physical part, that is **speaking** to lost souls. When people accepted the invitation to Christ, He would apply the atonement to their souls and bring them into His invisible church. The disciples were not authorized to invite men and women into a physical building, but into heaven itself.

How would this be possible? The Lord Jesus had ALREADY done the necessary loosing and binding work Himself. He did that by His cross. Now men and women could be saved or lost, depending on whether they wanted to be "loosed" or remain "bound" in Satan's grasp. The disciples were given the authority (keys) to tell people their sins were either "retained" or "forgiven" depending on what they did about the invitation to Christ (John 20:23).

Gathering souls into an invisible body has to be mysterious business. You don't get acquainted with it overnight. As humans, we are familiar with physical things only. It was not easy for Jesus to teach them about a supernatural creation. Yet, that's what His church is—an invisible body. That's why Jesus spent so long teaching His disciples. It wasn't easy to shift their thinking from physical to spiritual things. Day after day He tried to move their minds to matters of the Spirit. Much of what He told them was necessarily beyond them at the time. He said so:

"I have more to say to you, but it is all beyond you right now" (John 16:12).

Nonetheless He wanted to get as much in their minds as He could. Even though they didn't understand it, He knew they would comprehend it later when He returned in the Spirit as their indwelling Teacher:

"Now I have told you all this while I am still here with you, but My Replacement, the Holy Spirit, Whom the Father will send in My behalf, will be your Teacher. He will recall

to your minds all that I have said to you and make it plain" (John 14:25, 26 Lovett's Lights).

Jesus' frequent appearings and disappearings were geared to getting the disciples to think beyond the flesh. It was not an easy task. They did not have the Holy Spirit to explain things to them. Even so, the Lord insisted on having at least three mysteries stored in their minds before His final disappearance:

1. **His return in the Spirit to indwell believers.**

2. **His greater work of building His church, using His disciples.**

3. **The Spirit-baptism method of adding members to His church.**

If we are to understand the book of Acts, we must lay hold of them too. This book is Dr. Luke's way of showing how the Lord kept His Word to His disciples and brought these mysteries to fulfillment. Inasmuch as the Lord Jesus did return in the Spirit to be the INTERNAL Teacher, we can expect Him to explain the mysteries to us too. Once He does, we may no longer wish to call this book the "Acts of the Apostles," but the "Acts of Jesus operating in the spirit."

Now to consider the three mysteries:

1. Jesus' return in the spirit to indwell the believers.

From time to time the Lord would tell His disciples He was going to go away and they would not see Him again. Their hearts would sink. They couldn't stand the thought of being in this world without Him. Then He would use their distressed feelings to clothe the truth of His return in the Spirit.

"I am not going to leave you bereft of My presence, so that you are as orphans in this world. To the contrary, I am coming back to you" (John 14:18 Lovett's Lights).

Then He would comfort them with more mysterious words:

"If you love Me, you'll treasure and obey My commands. And I will ask the Father to send My Replacement to befriend you and be with you forever! I'm referring to the Spirit of Truth Whom the world cannot receive because it can't see Him and doesn't know Him. But you know Him, for He is with you right now and shall be IN you" (John 14:15-17 Lovett's Lights).

As He proceeded it got even more mysterious:

"In that day (when the Replacement, the Spirit of Truth comes) you will know that I am in My Father, you in Me, and I in you!" (John 14:20 Lovett's Lights).

What a fantastic thing to say! But did the disciples get it? No. Few today appreciate what He was saying and what it means in their lives. He was speaking of a new relationship with His disciples that would be closer and more intimate than anything they could imagine. He was coming back to be INSIDE them to share their very thoughts, and ambitions and sorrows. The new relationship was going to be so close it would be like two people living in one body. . .using the same mind.

NOTE: Fortunately we live in the day of television. We can understand how such a thing is possible. Men come close to doing this very thing in the physical realm. Consider how a man in a TV studio brings his presence to the viewing audience. The studio transmitter sends his unseen image to the surrounding area. By means of carrier waves, he can enter into every home with a TV set tuned to his station. The Lord, in heaven's studio, can reproduce His presence via the Holy Spirit (radio waves) in every heart that will turn to Him. If men can infinitely reproduce their presence

by means of circuits and transistors, surely the God of glory can bring His literal presence into each life by means of His Holy Spirit. As there is no limit to the number who can tune in a TV station, so is there no limit to the number who can receive Christ in the Spirit.

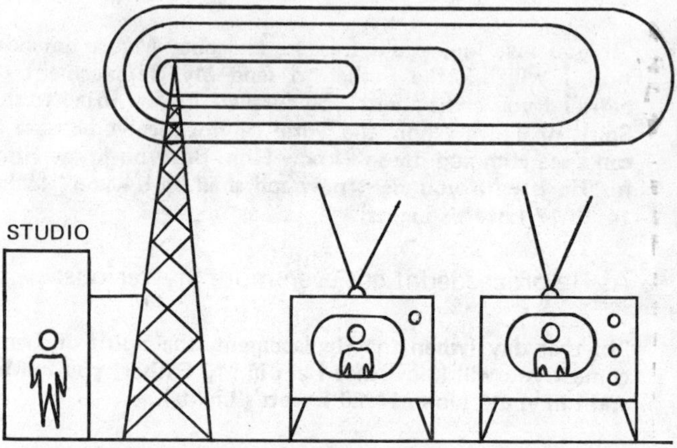

CHRIST IN HEAVEN'S STUDIO BROADCASTS HIMSELF IN THE HOLY SPIRIT.

While the indwelling of Christ is a mystery, it is nonetheless a FACT. It is now a fulfilled promise. Yet, it was something that could not take place as long as Jesus remained on earth in physical form. Why? The fulness of the Godhead was in Him bodily (Col. 2:9). He was simply NOT AVAILABLE in that form. You can't stuff bodies inside each other. And if you could, Jesus had only ONE body. Therefore, only one person could be saved by that method.

In order for Jesus to be **available** as the Holy Indweller, it was necessary for Him to make the transition from flesh to spirit. Once He did that, everyone could HAVE Him—**and all there is of Him.** This is why the Lord had to disappear. As long as He stayed on earth in human form, there was no way for this mystery to come to pass:

"It is expedient for you that I go away: for if I go not away, the Comforter (My Replacement) WILL NOT come to you; but if I depart, I will send Him to you" (John 16:7 Lovett's Lights).

The Lord Jesus coached His disciples a long time to bring them to the place where they were willing to trade His physical presence for His spiritual presence. We're not faced with that choice. We live on this side of the ascension and know the Lord Jesus via the Spirit only. If we could trade His spiritual presence for His physical presence, there might be some Christians who would do it. Why? They do not understand the advantage of His indwelling and the intimacy it makes possible.

Now let's turn to the second mystery the Lord gave His disciples:

2. Jesus' greater work of building His church, using His disciples.

As long as Jesus was confined to a body, He couldn't do anything about building His church. He could do the FOUNDATION work, as we said earlier, but He couldn't put one soul into it until He made the transition from flesh to Spirit. Since that is a spiritual work, it too lay beyond the cross. One can almost sense the Lord's eagerness to get out of the body and be about this BIGGER work He came to do.

In one place He complained of feeling restricted as long as He was in a body (Luke 12:50). When you come right down to it, Jesus' earthly ministry was God in a "straitjacket!" He was anxious to be done with the physical part (1. revealing the Father, 2. accomplishing the atonement) so that He could get out of the body and on to the more joyous work that was set before Him (Heb. 12:2). His eagerness shines through this mystery as He dropped it on His disciples:

"In all truth I tell you that whoever believes in Me will be able to do what I do—nay, he will be able to do even GREATER THINGS because I go to My Father" (John 14:12 Lovett's Lights).

Now anyone studying the earthly miracles of our Lord might wonder, how could a person do anything GREATER? But human minds always consider greatness in physical terms. One could look upon the raising of Lazarus to judge that no one could do anything greater. Or again one might consider how Jesus healed entire cities and wonder what could be greater. But the Lord Jesus considers the salvation of a soul to be a far GREATER work than healing the sick and raising the dead. Why? It is an ETERNAL work—whereas even the greatest physical miracle is NOT eternal. Those who are healed, get sick again. Even Lazarus, who was raised from the dead, died again. There was nothing **eternal** about any of Jesus' supernatural miracles on earth.

It is a far greater thing, in the Lord's eyes, to win a soul and bring that one into His church than to be able to duplicate all the miracles He did on earth. The bringing of the first soul into His church made the raising of Lazarus a puny task by comparison. So, it is no wonder the Lord is excited about His church—it is His greater work. It becomes our greater work when we do it with Him.

Once the Lord got out of the body to operate in the Spirit, not only could He get closer to His disciples to enjoy the intimacy for which He longed, but He could work THROUGH THEM. It was FUN for the Lord to be inside His disciples and start building His church by using their lips and feet. By indwelling the thousands that would come to Him, He would be able to multiply His own JOY thousands of times. The thrills and excitements that would come to each Christian as he moved in His might, would also be

His OWN! That's how God gets His kicks! And He has been enjoying the adventure for nearly 2000 years!

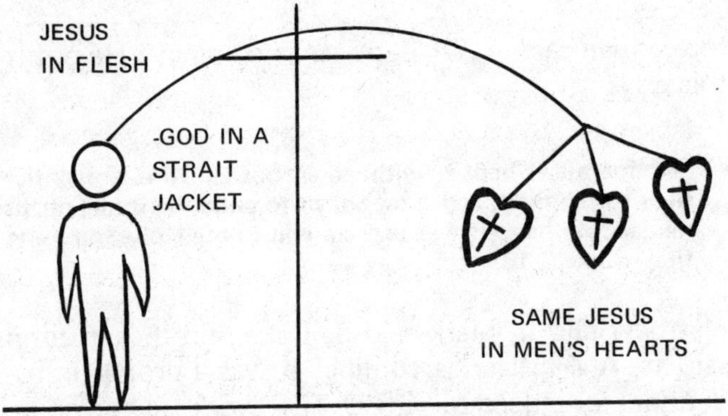

The Lord could have elected to build His church some other way. He chose instead to work THROUGH His disciples. Therefore, since the building of the church was HIS greater work, we find ourselves doing GREATER THINGS as we work with Him. His greater work becomes our greater work. If we can understand how Christ works through us to build His church, we're ready for the next mystery He planted in His disciples:

3. His church was to be built by spiritual baptism.

When Jesus began His public ministry, He didn't arrive on the scene one day to announce:

"Hey world! Here I am! Your God and Savior has arrived!"

It wasn't like that at all. He was properly introduced. A man named John the Baptist was given the task of presenting the Lord Jesus to the world, and to His own nation in particular. Months before the Lord appeared on the scene, John the Baptist began to herald His coming. But He didn't make the announcement people might have expected. He didn't say. . .

"The Messiah is coming!"

Instead He said. . ."A Baptizer is coming!" He put it this way:

"As for me, I baptize with water; but He Who is mightier than I is coming, and I am not fit to untie the thong of His sandals; He himself will baptize you in the Holy Spirit and fire" (Luke 3:16).

Matthew said it, Mark said it, Luke said it, and John said it—**A Baptizer is coming!** It was a proper introduction, for indeed the GREATER work He had come to do was the building of His church by BAPTISM.

NOTE: The references to "Spirit and fire" can be interpreted as Savior and Judge. The Spirit saves souls and fire judges the flesh. Throughout Scripture, fire represents the judgment of God. Notice too that the Lord is the ONLY Spirit-Baptizer. This is a work that HE HIMSELF was going to do. During His earthly ministry He never baptized a soul. The Holy Spirit was careful to put into the record (John 4:2) that the Lord Himself didn't baptize with water. One can imagine the resulting confusion should the Spirit-Baptizer be seen baptizing with water. Yet, the Lord permitted His disciples to continue the water baptism of preparation. Until the cross was completed, and He shifted to spirit, all such work was merely preparatory anyway. The Lord has reserved to Himself the spiritual baptism of souls into the church which is His body.

The word "baptism" is taken from the dye industry. It is a word which describes the act of placing clothing into a vat of dye. Carried over to spiritual things, it means "to place into or immerse." Applied to the greater work of the Lord Jesus, it means the placing of souls into the church. Immersing a man's body in a tank of water is a physical thing, but placing his soul into the invisible church, is wholly spiritual. That's what the Lord had come to do.

But how does it work in practice? First, there is the disciples' part. They are commissioned to SPEAK to people about the risen Christ. As they speak, the Lord Who lives within them goes into action also. He bears witness to the words that are spoken and the listener's heart BURNS within him. Without any external evidence he knows what he is hearing about Christ is true. Why? The witness in his own heart says it is true.

Then, should the man accept the witness he feels in his heart and be willing to act on the invitation of Christ, a twofold miracle takes place.

1. As he opens his heart to Jesus, the Lord comes via His Spirit to indwell him. Christ actually comes into his life and takes up residence within the man's body (1 Cor. 6:19). He becomes a temple or dwelling place for God in the Spirit. The apostle Paul insists this is the case, ". . .if any man have not the Spirit of Christ, he is none of His!" (Rom. 8:9).

2. In that same moment a second blessed thing happens: He is simultaneously "baptized" (placed into) the church, the body of Christ. The apostle Paul is just as insistent about this part of the miracle: "For by one Spirit have we ALL been baptized into one body. . ." (1 Cor. 12:13). It is this second half of the miracle that actually brings salvation. We are thus delivered (that's what salvation means) from Satan's kingdom to escape his fate—hell. For in that second. . ."God hath delivered us from the power of darkness, and hath TRANSLATED US into the kingdom of His dear Son" (Col. 1:13).

As soon as this twofold event takes place in a person, the Lord's mysterious words are fulfilled in that man:

"In that day you shall know that I am in My Father, you in Me and I in you!" (John 14:20).

NOTE: No one can FEEL himself being placed into the body of Christ. Spirit-baptism is a miracle which cannot be examined by the senses. The Lord has so designed us that we have no AWARENESS of what takes place in the spirit-world. We have no sensation of being moved or shifted or exalted into the kingdom where we literally "SIT TOGETHER in heavenly places in Christ Jesus" (Eph. 2:6). While the second part of the miracle of "baptism" cannot be felt, the first part can. When Christ comes to indwell us, there is instant PEACE between us and God. Peace is a feeling. We are immediately aware of His love for us and His presence. But the MECHANICS of being shifted from Satan's kingdom to Christ's is something we must take by faith on the basis of His word. We absolutely have no awareness of it.

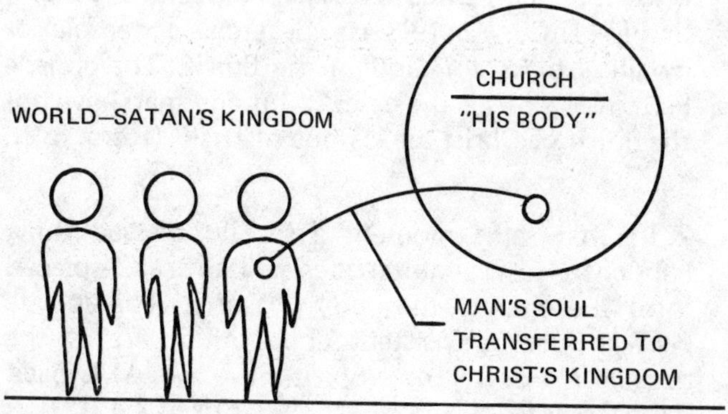

That's how Christ is building His church today. Once we understand these three mysteries, we will be able to appreciate the way He goes into action when we come to the second chapter of Acts. Even more wonderful is to consider that even to this day He hasn't stopped. The Lord is still:

1. Coming to people in the Spirit to indwell believers.

2. Engaged in the bigger work of building His church, using His disciples.

3. Adding members to His church (body) by Spirit-baptism.

Since His GREATER WORK hasn't ceased, we have the privilege of doing it with Him. Inasmuch as this was the JOY, yes even the FUN that was set before the Lord, it can also be our fun and joy to do it with Him. God designed us as fun-loving people. Coming to Christ does not eliminate our passion for excitement and adventure. Instead it increases our capacity for thrills. That's why He gave us the Great Commission. We're all invited to participate in the BIGGEST and most THRILLING task God has ever undertaken. . .

THE BUILDING OF HIS CHURCH.

(Matt. 18:18,19)

—C. S. Lovett

acts

(Jesus' Greater Work Through His Apostles)

1 1. Dear Theophilus: In my first book I dealt with all the things Jesus did and taught as He began His work, 2. right up to the day He was taken up into heaven. And how, before He ascended, He commanded His chosen disciples in the power of the Holy Spirit.

BEGAN. Luke's first letter (book) to Theophilus, his gospel, covered the span of Jesus' earthly ministry, yet it was only the beginning of the Lord's work. He BEGAN something, but as yet He hadn't finished it. Thus the Lord's human life was only introductory to a greater work which lay beyond His ascension. Luke cleverly ended his gospel in such a way, a reader would pant for the rest of the story. Some MSS. read, "...and He was carried up into heaven," (Lu. 24: 51). The last part of Luke pictures the disciples joyously returning from the ascension to await the coming of the Spirit. With the ascension common to Luke and Acts, it becomes the turning point where the gospel ends and Acts begins. One must always have the ascension in mind if he is to understand rightly the true nature of Christ's church on earth. What takes place in the visible world, as set forth in the book of Acts, originates in the invisible world as Jesus carries out His greater ministry in the Spirit.

COMMANDED. Jesus wouldn't return to the Father (the spirit-world, i.e., "God is Spirit"–Jo. 4:24) until He made sure the disciples understood their commission. It was urgent that they obey Him, for He had no other plan for building His church. Should they disobey Him, the "greater work" would NOT be done. We note that His commands, as were all His words uttered from a physical body, were anointed by the Spirit.

Why? In His flesh, Jesus was as **dependent** on the Spirit of God as we are now. All He said and did was by the Spirit (Matt. 4:1, 12:28; Heb. 9:14). However, after He returned in the Spirit to be IN THEM, He could lead them in carrying out those commands on a Spirit-to-spirit basis. Before the Lord ascended, He lived and worked in ONE body. After His ascension, He would live and work in MANY bodies. It was absolutely essential to His plan that the disciples do exactly as He told them. Now they were ready to listen. For 3½ years they were immune to His teaching, believing He was about to usher in the kingdom. Hence He makes sure His orders are clear before He leaves them for the last time.

"What did the Lord do in the interval between His resurrection and ascension?"

3. During the forty days which followed His crucifixion, the Lord presented Himself to His apostles many times and in ways which provided unquestionable proof that He was alive. Not only was He seen by them, but He used the occasions to speak to them about the kingdom of God.

PROOF. Had the disciples any doubt as to the literal resurrection of Jesus, it would have rendered them powerless for their mission. Before the Lord's post-resurrection appearances, they were inclined to doubt He had risen. Thomas especially, refused to believe it until he had seen and felt Him. So the Lord made no less than ten appearances during the forty days prior to His ascension. They were NOT seances with a shadowy figure billowing about making sounds. He returned in the SAME body and allowed them to examine it in broad daylight. On one occasion He was seen by more than 500 people (1 Cor. 15:6). He ate and drank with them and even held teaching sessions in which they were allowed to question Him about the kingdom. These appearances provided the apostles with immovable conviction, they never again questioned the fact of His resurrection. Instead, it became the basis of the "good news" they proclaimed.

4. On this particular occasion, when they were all together sharing a meal, He gave them a further command. They were not to leave the city of Jerusalem, but wait there until the Father had kept His promise. "I have already told you about this," said Jesus, 5. "for John used to baptize in water, but you will be baptized in the Holy Spirit in a few days."

WAIT. The natural sentiment of the disciples was to flee the hatred within the city of Jerusalem. But Jesus ordered them to stay there and await His return in the Spirit. Why? Was it because He couldn't be received anyplace else? No. The Spirit can be received anywhere, a truth He confided to the woman at the well (John 4:21). God wanted the earthly church to START AT JERUSALEM. In the very place where His Son was so hated, the Savior's grace was to flood forth. In the very city where He was despised, His glory was to be displayed in power by the conversion of thousands and by signs and wonders. The disciples' commission read... "Beginning at Jerusalem..." (Lu. 24:47). Jesus' plan called for the gospel to go forth from Jerusalem, thence to the uttermost parts of the earth. It is HIS city, His world headquarters on earth. Therefore they had to be in that city when the Spirit came so the Lord could begin the church according to His own plan.

TOLD YOU. There was nothing new about Jesus' reference to the coming of the Spirit. He had instructed them in great detail about the coming of His Replacement. Five famous passages in John chs. 14-16 explain precisely the Lord's words here. (See also my introduction to this volume.) The promise was foreshadowed by John the Baptist who introduced the Lord as the coming Baptizer. Since it was almost time for John the Baptist's words to be fulfilled, Jesus said..."In a few days you will be baptized in the Holy Spirit." The church would start at Jerusalem and they'd be among the first ones baptized into it. God's Spirit was to proceed like a torrent from heaven. He had promised the event by His O.T. prophets (Joel 2:28; Zech. 2:10). They spoke of it as an outpouring of God's Spirit to picture

His availability, but Jesus makes it clear that it is a baptism. He is the Baptizer building His church by baptizing (placing) people into it.

SPIRIT. In every place where the Holy Spirit is spoken of, we should bring our minds to see Jesus Himself. Why? The Holy Spirit IS the Spirit of Jesus (Acts 16:6,7). Yes, we distinguish between the 2nd and 3rd Persons of the Trinity for the sake of theology, but the terms "Spirit of Christ" and "Holy Spirit" are practically synonymous. We must not divide the Godhead so sharply that a big difference is made between the presence of Christ and the presence of the Spirit in a believer. He is indwelt by Christ in the Spirit. The King James translators used a word not found in the Greek to cover this phenomenon—GHOST. They saw the Holy Spirit as Christ's Ghost and coined the phrase... "Holy Ghost." The insertion of "ghost" was not a matter of middle age superstition, but an excellent device for picturing Christ's return in the Spirit. (See my notes under John 7:39.).

"What thought struck the disciples when Jesus said they would be baptized in the Spirit in a few days?"

6. This brought their minds to one conclusion and they asked Him, "Lord, does this mean you are going to restore the kingdom to Israel here and now?" 7. To which He replied, "The dates and events the Father has scheduled by His own authority are none of your business."

RESTORE. This is Jesus' last interview with His disciples. His words about Spirit-baptism cause their minds to leap once again to thoughts of political power. Again they bring up the idea of Israel being restored as the ruling world power per O.T. promises. For 3½ years Jesus tried to shift their minds from a political kingdom to His spiritual kingdom which is "not of this world" (Jo. 18:36). But the disciples wouldn't let go of the ancient dream. Scripture justified it (Isa. 1:26; Jer. 23:6-8; Hos. 3:4,5; Zech. 9:9,10). It was only human to think of the high positions they would hold were it to come to pass. On earlier occasions they had argued over who would be the greatest among them when the kingdom was ushered in. But this is the last thing Jesus wants on their minds. He wants them dedicated to the task of building His invisible church, not curious about an earthly kingdom.

BUSINESS. One feels the Lord is upset with them. He may not have been, but He silences their impatience about the kingdom with strong words, which have the force of..."Let the future alone." God does not want His people occupied with future events on earth. It has ever been His purpose to CONCEAL, that we might have the joy of DISCOVERING. Nothing is ever new to God. He never knows any surprises, but He doesn't mean for us to be denied that privilege. Each day is to be new for us **because** we do not know the future. Instead, we are to accept the future by faith from the hands of our loving "Father." If we concentrate on making the present one of OBEDIENCE, the future is guaranteed to be glorious. Oh that modern prophecy lovers and date setters would heed Jesus' reproof. What a job they could do for Him if they would forget the future and get on with the task at hand. God is concerned with TODAY, not tomorrow.

8. "It is enough that you are going to be empowered when the Holy Spirit comes upon you. Then you shall be witnesses for Me in Jerusalem, throughout all Judea and Samaria, yes, even to the ends of the earth."

EMPOWERED. If it's power they want, it's power they'll get—but not the kind they think. Instead of political power that would see Israel exalted as the empress of the world, they are going to receive a supernatural power that is "out of this world." They will have the ability (in Christ) to do things in the spirit-realm (Matt. 16:18,19). They are going to be able to release captives from Satan's kingdom and TRANS-

PLANT them into Christ's (Col. 1:13). No military force can do that. It can't capture the minds of men, let alone their hearts. Ah, but spiritual power is unseen and works by faith. Therefore in initial stages at least, it must be accompanied by evidences (miracles) to confirm its presence in the disciples. The miracles would be **supportive only,** however, for their function is simply to validate the greater spiritual power. The disciples forgot all about political power once they tasted the spiritual power of Pentecost. There is a tendency today, however, to forget about spiritual power and focus on miracles instead.

HOLY SPIRIT. The King James version again uses the term GHOST to show that it is Christ Himself Who comes to indwell the disciples. He is the One Who empowers believers for spiritual work. How? By performing the unseen part as they speak to lost souls. The disciples will utter words of invitation, but those words will be anointed by Jesus. Then, as men and women respond to the disciples' invitation, the Lord Himself baptizes them into His church. He is the Baptizer (Mk. 1:8; Luke 1:33). Spirit-baptism is His method of building His church (See introduction). If the disciples fail to speak, or withhold the invitation, no spirit-baptisms can occur. The Lord has actually given them the "keys of the kingdom," and He limits His action to their obedience (Matt. 16:18). He means to work through His agents **exclusively**. Just as the Lord went about speaking in the Father's power, so will the disciples be backed by Jesus' power as they go into the world. Their words will also be "spirit and life," because Christ is in them (John 14:20). Once their baptism takes place and Christ indwells them, they will be ready to take His HUMAN place in the world. They will **replace** Him.

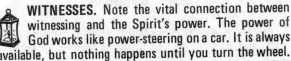

WITNESSES. Note the vital connection between witnessing and the Spirit's power. The power of God works like power-steering on a car. It is always available, but nothing happens until you turn the wheel. So with the Christian. He always has the Spirit, but nothing happens until he begins to witness for Jesus. Any talk of having power apart from obedience to the Great Commission is a contradiction—the two go together. Spiritual power is best defined as that which takes place in OTHERS when witnesses speak about Christ. The power is NOT found in the speaker, but displayed in the **results.** The witness speaks and Christ ACTS!—that's why this book is Acts of Jesus Christ—through His Apostles. The disciples were told to WAIT in Jerusalem, because Christ had not yet returned in the Spirit to indwell them. They could speak, but no results would follow until He was in them to do the work. When HE did arrive, what took place were the ACTS of Christ as the disciples spoke in His Name!

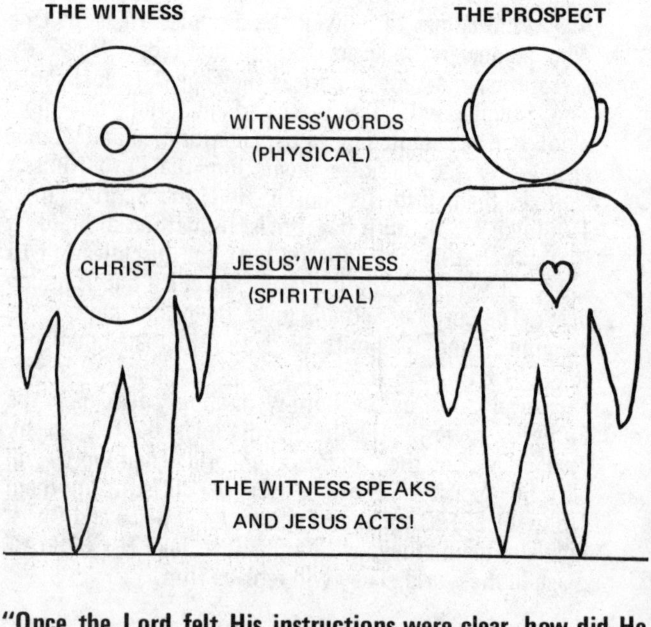

"Once the Lord felt His instructions were clear, how did He make His departure?"

9. As soon as He said these words, He began to rise into the sky. The disciples watched until a cloud received Him out of their sight.

RISE. Jesus led His disciples from Jerusalem out to Mt. Olivet where He gave them these last minute instructions concerning their commission as witnesses (Luke 24:50,51). Then came His final good-bye. But this time it is different. His former disappearances were instantaneous, whereas this one is gradual. They watch it happen. Now they know it is the last time they'll see Him. That's why He departs in this fashion. He is acting out a disappearance for them. It was a literal accommodation for their earth-bound minds. Actually it had nothing to do with His return to the Spirit, for the spirit-world is not related to space. There is no way to ascend to anyplace but more space. A physical ascent is meaningless except as a disappearance-drama for the eyes of men. His return to the spirit-world could be illustrated today by switching off a light bulb and asking, "Where did the light go?"

CLOUD. It was not by accident that a cloud was used to receive the Lord, for it is the SIGN of the Son of Man (Matt. 24:30). Thus we have three great events connected with Jesus and the cloud: (1) His transfiguration where He talked with Moses and Elijah about the way He would exit this life (Matt. 17:5). (2) His ascension described here. (3) When He comes again in glory..."You shall see the Son of Man coming in clouds with power and great glory" (Mk. 13:26). This may be the shekinah cloud which hovered over the tabernacle in the days of Moses and indicated God's presence with His people (Ex. 40:34). If so, the disciples were granted a further witness that Jesus was received into a "theophany" which represented the divine presence. Thus, both the ascent and the cloud would dramatize the fact that Jesus departed into the presence of His Father. I suspect the cloud may have had a peculiar luminescence, so that the disciples would connect it with the presence of God.

"Wow! The disciples must have been spell-bound at such a sight!"

10. And while they were still staring into the sky, watching the Lord's departure, two men dressed in

white suddenly appeared beside them. 11. "Men of Galilee," they said, "why are you standing here scanning the sky? This same Jesus who has been taken up from you into heaven, will one day return in the very same way as you have seen Him go!"

MEN. Jesus is gone! Henceforth they are to know Him no more after the flesh (2 Cor. 5:16). Lest there be any doubt about that, God sent two angels to make it clear: (1) they confirmed that Jesus did actually go into heaven, (2) but they also announced that He will one day return in exactly the same manner. The disciples already had His promise of a SPIRITUAL return to be IN them, but this was different. The angels speak of another PHYSICAL return of the Lord. Who were these two men? We don't know. Perhaps they were the same ones who rolled the stone from His tomb and spoke to Mary. Maybe they were Moses and Elijah who spoke with Him atop the Mt. of Transfiguration? It's what they are saying that counts, not who they were. Is it not supposed to be that way with all of God's messengers—even today?

RETURN. These angels give us a lot to go on. They tell us the glorious return of Christ will be: (1) visible: the disciples actually witnessed His departure; (2) unexpected: the disciples didn't know this was to be their last meeting with Him; (3) His personality will be unchanged: the same Jesus is to return; (4) in clouds: I think it will be clouds of saints (I Thess. 3:13, Heb. 12:1); (5) bodily: our bodies are scheduled to be changed to conform to His (Phil. 3:20,21); (6) to the same Mt. Olivet: prophecy says it will be the same mount (Zech. 14:4); (7) glorious and magnificent: if the ascent of the **humiliated** Christ was spectacular, the return of the **glorified** Christ will be breath-taking! About 2000 years have passed since His departure. As did the disciples, we too enjoy Jesus' indwelling presence. The Holy Spirit is to us a "guarantee" that we will share the Lord's earthly inheritance (the kingdom) with Him (Eph. 1:14). Thus we are assured of being a part of the descending host when He comes in glory (I Thess. 3:13).

Until that day, however, His indwelling in us is our "hope of glory!" (Col. 1:27).

"Did the disciples carry out Jesus' order after He ascended?"

12. Then they left the Mount of Olives and returned to Jerusalem which was less than a mile away. 13. On entering the city, they went directly to the upstairs room where they had been lodging. The party consisted of Peter and John, James and Andrew, Philip and Thomas, Bartholomew and Matthew, James the son of Alpheus and Simon the Zealot, and Judas the son of James. 14. Besides these, the brothers of Jesus were also present, plus a number of women including the mother of Jesus. The entire group gave themselves continually to prayer, having only one thing on their minds—the Lord's promise of the Spirit.

RETURNED. His introduction finished (vss. 1-11), Luke is now ready to begin Part II of Jesus' history. Filled with wonder by the ascension, the disciples return to Jerusalem in obedience to the Lord's word (Luke 24:49). They go immediately to an upper room (probably akin to a banquet room in a modern hotel) where an extended prayer meeting gets under way. They will stay together until the Lord returns in the Spirit to begin building His church. Luke starts with a run-down on the people present at this great prayer meeting. Since the apostles are the focal point of the Lord's church, he lists them first. The list here is essentially the same as that in his gospel with some slight variation in order. Bartholomew is the same as Nathanael. Judas (not Iscariot) was also called Thaddaeus. It was common in those days to have both Greek and Aramaic names.

PARTY. Besides the apostles there were three other groups of people present: (1) **Jesus' brethren.** Apparently they became convinced He was the Messiah and are now unquestioned believers. Formerly they challenged Him to prove Who He was, refusing to believe in Him (John 7:5). The most outstanding one was James (not the apostle). Note how they are spoken of separately from the apostles. None became an apostle. (2) **The women.** Some of the apostles were married and their wives followed them from Galilee. Jesus' mother is included among them. Note that no particular homage is paid her. She is seen here for the last time and is simply listed as a disciple. (3) **Numerous other disciples.** These made up the rest of the 120 who watched Jesus ascend. The entire group returned to the city to wait on the Lord.

"Did they do anything besides pray?"

15. After the prayer meeting had been going on for several days, Peter stood up and addressed the group. About 120 of the brethren were assembled on this occasion. 16. "My brothers," he said, "The Holy Spirit, speaking through David, prophesied concerning the man who guided those who arrested Jesus. What happened to Judas came about in fulfillment of Scripture. 17. He was one of our group and called to be an apostle as surely as we were."

ASSEMBLED. Luke does not mean to imply that all of Jesus' disciples were in Jerusalem participating in the prayer meeting. The Lord had many more disciples in other parts of the country, particularly in Galilee where He spent most of His earthly ministry. Paul mentions an occasion when the Lord was seen by more than 500 of the brethren at one time after His resurrection (1 Cor. 15:6). So, only a small number of His disciples are a part of this meeting. Luke is not interested in reporting on the masses of Jesus' followers elsewhere, but only in showing how the gospel proceeded from Jerusalem to Rome. His history will not even tell us much about the apostles other than Peter and Paul. His main purpose is to show how the Lord Jesus started His church and caused it to flourish to the capital of the Roman Empire.

PETER. The prayer meeting continues for some days. Things are a little too quiet for Peter. He's not one to sit around for long without action. A little over 40 days ago he denied the Lord. The Master graciously healed the trouble between them that morning on the beach. Yet, even that same morning, Jesus had to rebuke him for poking his nose into someone else's business (John 21:22). Now he's at it again. A man doesn't change much in 40 days. Running true to form, he seizes the initiative, insisting the group conduct a little business while waiting for the Lord to come and take charge of His church. Peter is going to help the Lord out. Remember, he still has only his old nature. As yet, he has not been born of the Spirit (John 3:5). He may think it is church business, but there is no church yet. It will not be born until the Spirit comes. Even so, he will propose the group fill the vacancy among the twelve apostles caused by Judas' defection. He feels justified, having found some Scripture which supports his suggestion.

"Say, Dr. Luke, what did happen to Judas?"

18. Somehow the money Judas gained by his treachery was used to secure him a field. He fell headlong into that field bursting open so that all his insides poured out. 19. All the people in Jerusalem heard about it, so they named the place "Hakeldama," which means, "The Field of Blood."

FIELD. Luke is speaking here, not Peter. He has interrupted Peter's speech to explain to Roman readers what happened to Judas. When Luke visited Jerusalem with Paul, he learned the details of Judas' death and enters them here. According to Matt. 27:7, the priests bought this field with the money Judas flung back in their faces, but not until after Judas had gone out and hanged himself. The best explanation seems to be that Judas' suicide attempt was a failure. The rope broke and he died as the result of a violent fall which was so great, it caused him to burst open. Likely he fell from a height. It must have been a gory mess. It has been

speculated that the priests bought the very spot on which Judas died, turning it into a "potter's field" for burying aliens.

20. "Well," continued Peter, "David says this in the Psalms:

'Let his homestead be a desolate place and let no man dwell in it' (Psa. 69:25).

(and again...)

'Let another take over his office' (Psa. 109:8).

21. So now we need a man to take Judas' place. It must be someone, however, who has been with us throughout the earthly ministry of the Lord, 22. from the time John baptized Him right up until the day when He was taken from us into heaven. We need such a man to join with us as a witness to Jesus' resurrection."

NEED. Peter feels the number TWELVE is somehow sacred and should be restored. He wants the apostolic group complete again. Of course, this is his own idea. He has no leading of the Lord to do anything but WAIT. The Master has not yet returned in the Spirit to direct His disciples. It would have been much safer to wait until he was Spirit-led, than to take matters into his own hands. But that is not like Peter, even though he didn't know what lay ahead. So he took the initiative, backing his action with Scripture. Whether it was really necessary or not is another matter. This is the same Peter who drew the sword to help the Lord at His arrest. And again the same Peter who said, "I'm going fishing," when the Lord told them to wait in Galilee (Matt. 28:10, John 21:3). No real damage was done, but it is unwise to undertake any action for God apart from the leading of His Spirit. Jesus had already told them, "Without Me ye can do nothing" (John 15:5). But Peter is going to try it anyway.

HOWEVER. There is no way for Peter, or anyone else in the group to know the heart of another disciple, as did the Lord Jesus. Therefore, theirs can only be a HUMAN judgment. Peter lays down the qualifications: (1) it must be one of the 120 then present, (2) who was in the company of the apostles from the time of Jesus' baptism to His ascension. The purpose of the apostles, **as Peter saw it,** was to bear witness to Jesus' resurrection. Since they were on the waiting side of Pentecost, they couldn't really know what Jesus had in mind for His apostles when He picked them. If the twelve were merely to be resurrection witnesses, and nothing more, then Peter's suggestion was harmless enough. But if God had more in mind for His apostles, then Peter was out of order.

"Wouldn't they have to use purely human methods at this point?"

23. Then two names were placed in nomination by the group: Joseph, who was called Barsabbas (also known as Justus), and Matthias. 24. Then they offered this prayer: "Lord, since you know the hearts of men, show us which of these You have chosen 25. to take Judas' place, inasmuch as the traitor abandoned the apostleship and went to his own place."

NAMES. Peter convinced the group that Judas should be replaced right then and there. They also accepted his statement on the qualifications. So two men were chosen, but neither history nor the N.T. speaks of either of them again. Because of this, it is felt this election was wholly out of order, that Paul was God's replacement for Judas. When you listen to the claims of Paul, you get the feeling he was God's choice (Gal. 1:11-17). If, however, the purpose of the 12 was to bear witness to Jesus' earthly ministry, then Paul was totally unqualified. But if Jesus chose His apostles on the basis of what HE SAW in them, and how they would perform AFTER being filled with the Spirit, then Paul was as well qualified as Peter (Gal. 2:7-9). Paul had one great qualification which no appointee could match—

he was commissioned DIRECTLY by the risen Lord. Besides, if Jesus had been in a hurry to name one of their group, as Peter insists, He could have easily appointed him during the 40 days prior to the ascension. There was ample opportunity. So there is no excuse for Peter's big rush—especially when Jesus told him to WAIT!

SHOW US. The disciples ask God for a sign or indication from heaven. They are to be commended for wanting Him to make the final choice. However, He was forced to choose (if indeed He had anything to do with it at all) between the two men they picked. In speaking to the Lord, they acknowledge that INSIGHT into a man's heart is the vital thing in selecting an apostle. That alone should have told them not to meddle. This is how Jesus made all of His choices. He read the hearts of those He picked (John 1:48). No one in the room had that kind of knowledge and therefore were not qualified to name the nominees. After Pentecost, when Peter was indwelt by the Spirit, he seemed to possess something of that kind of knowledge (Acts 5:3). How much better had he curbed his impetuousness a few more days.

"How did they finally determine who should succeed Judas?"

26. After this, they drew lots to decide between the two names. The lot fell to Matthias and so he was considered equal in rank with the other eleven apostles.

LOTS. This is an O.T. method for reaching decisions. Usually the lots were placed in a vase and shaken like dice. Whichever fell out first was the decision. The disciples felt they were honoring God by letting Him choose in this fashion. It is true, the old covenant was still in force when this was done, but their call was to a new covenant. They are not authorized to do things by O.T. methods. They were expressly told to wait and do "greater things" when indwelt by the Lord Himself. They have no authority to operate under the Law, when they have been called as ministers of the

New Covenant. After Pentecost, the LOT-METHOD is never heard of again. Once Jesus returned in the Spirit, the disciples didn't need to resort to clumsy, fleshly ways for knowing the Lord's will. Jesus was in them to guide them, even as His Father was in Him to guide Him. It would be entirely out of order for anyone to use this passage as justification for casting lots today. The disciples themselves were out of order in doing it. Those who "put out the fleece" are in the same category.

2

1. **Then**—at an hour well into the day of Pentecost, the believers were all together in one place, when...

PENTECOST. This is a Greek name for a Jewish feast. It is an untranslated word meaning, "fiftieth." The Hebrew "Feast of Weeks," or "Day of the First Fruits," as it was also called, came seven weeks after the Passover. It was one of the three great annual festivals held in Jerusalem, the other two being the Passover and the Feast of Tabernacles. All males, no matter where in the world they lived, were required by the Law to attend these feasts (Ex. 34:22,23). Consequently the city of Jerusalem was filled with devout Jews on this day of Pentecost. It was a Sunday, fifty days (counted inclusively) after the resurrection of the Lord.

ONE PLACE. Was this the upper room? Who knows? The size of the crowd has led some scholars to speculate it might have been one of the 30 large rooms in adjoining buildings of the temple. Luke does observe they were "continually in the temple, praising God" (Luke 24:53). His point is that they were ALL together. I take that to mean the 120. It is true that on this day the rest of Jesus' disciples from Galilee would be in the city for the feast. And they could total above 1000. However, it appears doubtful they would be joined to the 120. The privilege of being the first to receive the Spirit seemingly belongs to those who were with the Lord when He ascended and obeyed His command to **remain in the city.** In my opinion, only the 120 are referred to here, and the place is the upper room which had become their headquarters.

2. Suddenly a roaring noise **descended** out of the sky! It resembled the blast of a violent gale. The sound filled the entire house where they were sitting.

NOISE. The Lord's final words had prepared the disciples to expect something big, but they couldn't anticipate this! The abruptness was startling, heralding the supernatural. A sound came down upon them with a deafening roar. It may have been like a localized sonic boom. The supernatural noise focused on a single house, rather than sweeping in the usual horizontal fashion. There was NO wind, only the SOUND which resembled the blast of a gale. In a way, it was as though God rapped for the disciples' attention. They were arrested at once. If we put the emphasis on the words, "out of the sky," we have a visual aid of the Lord's return in the Spirit. He was faithful to His promise. With His coming trumpeted by the sound, the electrified disciples were ready for the next breathtaking event.

"Wow! What a terrific way to get people's attention! Did that mean something bigger was coming?"

3. **Then**—what might be described as tongues of fire appeared and began distributing themselves, so that they touched every person present, coming to rest on each one.

FIRE. If the first supernatural event engaged their ears, the second captured their eyes. The substance was NOT fire. It was a luminous material which neither singed nor burned. As the dazzling substance moved into the room, the disciples watched in awe. They were within arm's length of the glory of God. This may have been the Shekinah at close range. Indeed the Lord was returning in Spirit. This visible manifestation symbolized His presence. It too was a visual aid. Since we are studying the work of Christ, we interpret these phenomenons as outward symbols of Jesus' activity in the Spirit. The disciples were seeing a physical enactment of an unseen miracle just then taking place. The essence of the flame-like tongues is unimportant. What they DID should occupy our attention.

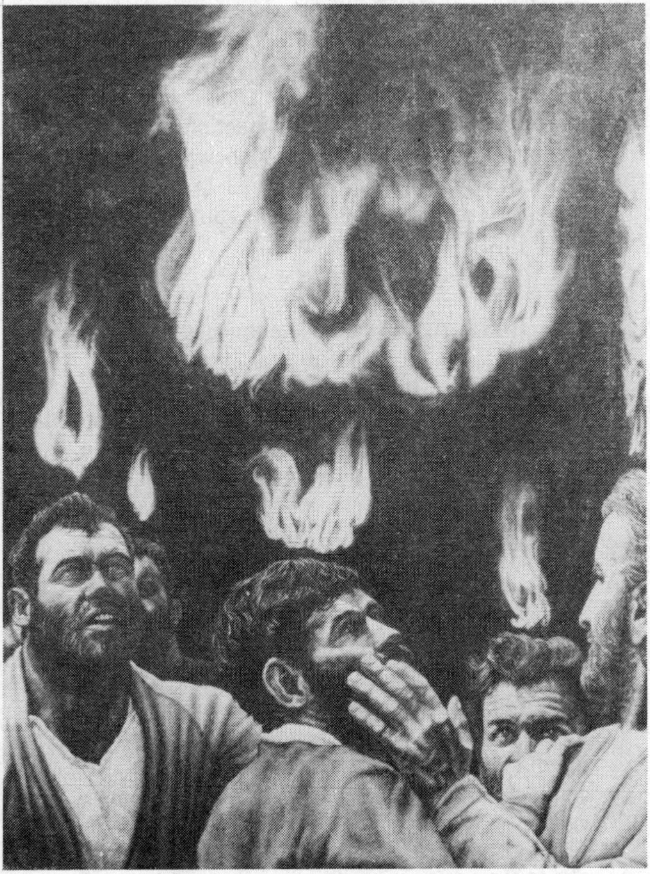

© Linda Lovett 1976

DISTRIBUTING. Then the dancing "bonfire" did a remarkable thing. It began to break itself into individual flame-like tongues. I suspect it reproduced itself again and again, miraculously, as did the five loaves and two fish. They too, as you recall, were broken up and distributed until all were filled. The feeding of the 5000 prefigured Pentecost. Now in this room, the substance began to multiply itself in the same way, and individual tongues were distributed to each of the disciples. What did this mean? It symbolized the diffusion of Christ in the Spirit. It revealed how each Christian could have the ONE Christ. The physical phenomenon accompanied the actual event, providing a dramatic visual aid of what was happening. In our day we have television to illustrate how someone's presence can be reproduced infinitely (see introduction). Apart from this phenomenon the disciples had no way of grasping the distribution of the infinite Christ in the Spirit. Omnipresence was a truth beyond them. But they could understand this. They saw it happen.

REST. As the flame-like tongues came to rest, this was the moment of new birth for each of the disciples. In that same second each received the Lord. They now had His righteousness by **impartation,** rather than by the O.T. method of **imputation** (Rom. 4:3). They had O.T. salvation before Pentecost, but now they have N.T. salvation which is the EXPERIENCE of receiving Christ's nature by regeneration (2 Pet. 1:4). Each had ALL there was to have of Christ. The promised Replacement had come to be IN THEM (John 14:16-18). Two things happened in a flash: (1) each received the Lord, (2) each was baptized into Christ. Thus, He was IN THEM and they were IN HIM with both events occurring simultaneously. I am persuaded that the most spectacular event of Pentecost was this distribution of the flaming substance (Shekinah?), demonstrating the coming of Christ to each believer. This, of course, would explain why the phenomenon has never been repeated. It was a onetime occurrence, as was the SOUND which heralded His **spiritual descent** from heaven.

"Once the disciples knew the Lord had returned to be in them, they must have exploded with joy!"

4. And they were all filled with the Holy Ghost and began to speak in languages they didn't know, for the Spirit was giving them the ability to make such utterances.

FILLED. I purposely retain the King James' word "Ghost," to show this is Christ in the Spirit (Jesus' Ghost). Once the disciples were aware of Jesus' return to be in them, they experienced the **internal** witness of the Spirit (Rom. 8:16). The pressure of His presence caused an eruption of joy! At once they were filled with the Spirit. But what is this filling, exactly? It is the exaltation of one's soul to the place where he is obsessed with joy over his indwelling Lord. This filling was due to their AWARENESS of what was happening. Thus the **filling was a thrilling.** Anyone obsessed with the joy of Jesus is filled with the Spirit. The thrill (filling) can wear off, as do all thrills, while the indwelling of Christ remains an unchanged fact. Thus there can be many fillings, whereas there is but one spirit baptism into Christ. The disciples, too full to sit still, rush from the room overflowing with joy. This particular filling was the **by-product** of their **awareness** of the spiritual baptism.

SPEAK. There is no way to be full of Christ (the Spirit) and remain silent. With Jesus' indwelling presence confirmed outwardly (sight and sound) and inwardly (the Spirit's witness), the disciples can't contain themselves. Their joy is boundless. As they begin sharing with the gathering spectators, a third phenomenon occurs. They find themselves speaking in languages they hadn't learned. Now they know Jesus is in them, for HE is doing this. They are thinking in Aramaic, but Jesus is reshaping their words into foreign languages. This miracle is for their benefit, proof that He is working through them as promised. As the multiplied tongues in the room (flame-like) pictured the **diffusion** of Christ, the multiplied tongues of the disciples manifest His working through them. They started to speak as they normally would (in Aramaic), but Jesus took their words and miraculously reshaped them into other dialects. Here was another visual aid showing HOW He means to build His church. While this phenomenon was primarily for the day of Pentecost, Luke will show it occurred on two other occasions (Acts 10:46; 19:6). We will discuss those as we come to them.

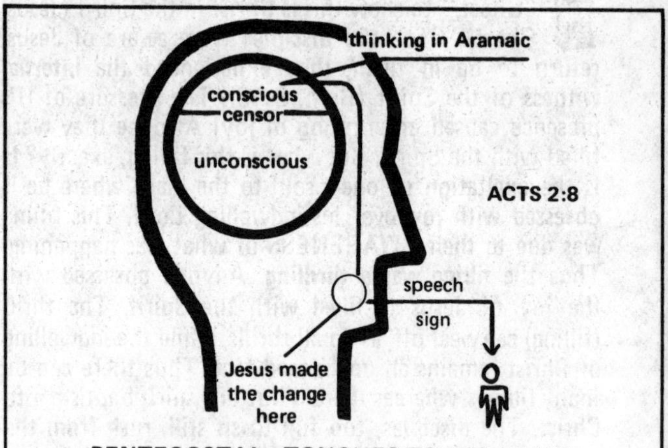

PENTECOSTAL—TONGUES TOWARD MEN

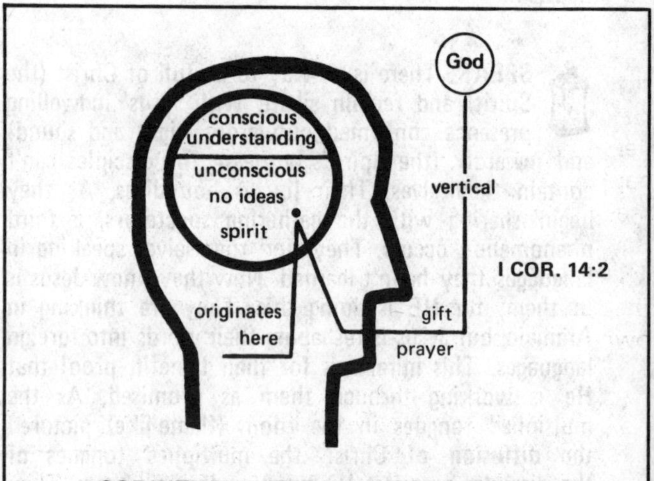

CORINTHIAN—TONGUES TOWARD GOD

UTTERANCES. The miraculous speech of Pentecost should not be confused with the GIFT of tongues which later appeared in the Corinthian church. The Pentecostal speech was NOT a gift, but an ENABLEMENT of the Spirit. It lasted only as long as the Spirit gave the ability. It was a temporary enduement. There is a big difference between the Pentecostal and Corinthian tongues. No one could understand the Corinthian tongues, for they required still another gift for the interpretation. Paul acknowledged the "gift of tongues," which operated at Corinth, but imposed severe checks on its use (1 Cor. 12:3ff.; 14:2ff.). The "gift" suffered such abuse it was necessary for him to apply censure and restraint. On the other hand, the Pentecostal tongues were INSTANTLY RECOGNIZED by people from many lands. Even so, the miracle of speech was SECONDARY to the message, for this was Jesus, Himself, speaking through His disciples. Hearts were gripped by His words, for "never spake a man like this man!" (John 7:46).

"To whom were the disciples speaking in these various dialects?"

5. At this time, Jerusalem was filled with devout Jews staying over for the feast. They had journeyed to the city from every country in the world. 6. When they heard the noise, they came running to see what was happening. Then, as each of them heard the disciples' message in his own language, they were awestruck. 7. Bewildered, they asked, "What's coming off here? These are all Galileans, aren't they? 8. How is it then, that each of us can hear them speaking to us in our own native tongue?"

GALILEANS. The Galileans couldn't disguise their speech, for the Galilean dialect employed strange guttural sounds. Peter was betrayed by his dialect, you recall, as he warmed himself by the fire in the high priest's courtyard (Jo. 18:25). Here now were guttural

Galileans in fluent command of the languages of the known world. Normally the disciples spoke in Aramaic only, knowing possibly some Greek and Hebrew as well. But now the crowds were hearing the dialects of Asia-Minor, Italy, Egypt, and Persia, right down to their provincial peculiarities. All who heard were Jews or Jewish converts. As yet the disciples do not realize the gospel is for non-Jews as well as Jews. That truth, however, is implied in the phenomenon of **every** tongue.

NOISE. The blast-like sound which filled the house was heard by those on the outside who rushed to investigate. The King James reads, "when this was noised abroad," as if rumors alone brought the first crowds. Later versions have corrected this to show it was the sound blast that brought them running. Then they were met by the super-heated disciples gushing forth words of praise and telling what great things God was doing in them. The crowds were shocked for three reasons: (1) hearing these words in their own language, (2) the unbelievable nature of the truths uttered by the disciples, (3) the exuberant, almost uncontrolled joy of the believers. It is of course true, that the amazing ability of the disciples to speak in many languages would cause reports to spread through the city, gathering a massive crowd in time.

"Did these Jews really come from every country in the world?"

9. "With us here today are men from the East—Parthians and Medes, Elamites and those who dwell in Mesopotamia. Then there are those from the borders of greater Judea. The North people are here from Asia Minor—Cappadocia, Pontus and Western Asia, as well as 10. Phrygia and Pamphylia. From the South have come those of Egypt, Libya, and Cyrene. We even have visitors from Rome, both Jews and Proselytes. 11. Besides those, there are Cretans and Arabs here too—and yet, we all hear them speaking in our own language, telling what great things God has done!"

WE ALL. At this time, godly Jews lived all over the world, scattered there by the dispersions which began seven centuries before. It was part of God's plan to scatter Jews so they could later be a blessing to the Gentiles. Of course, it was a punishment too. Now the scattered Jews had come to Jerusalem for the Feast of Pentecost, inasmuch as it was celebrated at the temple. Luke gives us a list of 15 countries to show that Jewish communities had been established throughout the known world. By checking the four compass points, we see that Luke is referring to Jews from nations in all directions. The reference to Judea should not be limited to the immediate province, but include the borders of the former Judean empire as it extended from the Egyptian frontier to the River Euphrates. The Roman church may owe its origin to the visitors who heard the gospel in Jerusalem this day and carried it back to the Imperial City.

LANGUAGE. It takes months to acquire a foreign language. So to be found speaking in a dozen different dialects instantly has to be miraculous. It was in this fashion that the 120 became instant linguists. See again how the pentecostal enablement varies from the GIFT of tongues which flourished at Corinth 20 years later. Paul describes the Corinthian tongues as the language of PRAYER (1 Cor. 14:2,14). Prayer operates **vertically**, whereas the pentecostal languages were manward, i.e., operated **horizontally.** The pentecostal ability lasted only so long as the Spirit gave utterance, but God's gifts are irrevocable, owned for a person's lifetime (Rom. 11:29). This gift didn't have a significant place in the churches other than at Corinth. See that the gift of interpretation would provide the meaning of someone's prayer, and would NOT be a message from God.

"How did the crowds react to the disciples' words?"

12. The crowd was stunned by all this. Amazed and perplexed they kept asking one another, "What in the world can this mean?" 13. Others, however, ridiculed

the disciples and made fun of them. "These people are drunk," they said, "that's what this is all about."

DRUNK. Some in the crowd were godly, others were not. The devout ones had honest questions after hearing the amazing words of the disciples. "What does this mean," is their reverent inquiry. Those who were not impressed by Jesus speaking through His disciples, attributed the whole affair to drunkenness. The Galileans were notorious drinkers. However, it was not the "tongues," which produced the ridicule, for they heard the disciples perfectly. It was their behavior. The exaltation of their souls must have produced such a high state of excitement it brought on behavior resembling drunkenness. Perhaps we shouldn't judge these men too harshly when we consider the antics of the disciples. Especially when we note that Peter doesn't rebuke them at all when he explains the situation (vs. 15). He merely corrects their mistaken interpretation of the event. The devout ones were led to see past the disciples' behavior to wonder if God were involved in what was going on.

"The situation seems to demand some kind of an explanation, doesn't it?"

14. Whereupon Peter, acting as the spokesman for the Eleven who were by his side, stepped forward to speak to the crowd. Raising his voice so all could hear, he called for attention, "Fellow Jews! Listen to me, all of you, particularly those of you who live in Jerusalem. Pay close attention as I explain what is happening. 15. These men are not drunk, as you suppose, for it is only nine o'clock in the morning."

PETER. The scene has shifted to a place where a crowd of thousands has gathered, probably in the outer court of the temple. It was the only place large enough for such an assembly. The ecstatic words and actions of the disciples have been attributed to drunkenness. Peter can't let that go by. He rises to defend his brethren. But it is a different Peter who speaks now. Christ is IN him. His calmness is remarkable.

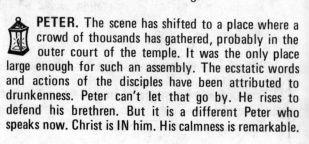

His manner is self-possessed and sober. He is NOT ecstatic, but speaks with carefully chosen words. He addresses the crowd in Aramaic, the language of the country and one which all his hearers could understand. Peter adopts the 3rd person and refers to "these men," so as to identify himself with his audience. He asks the Jerusalemites to listen most carefully, for they did not have the advantage of understanding the foreign languages and dialects.

NOT DRUNK. One might expect Peter to wade into the scoffers accusing them of blasphemy, but he doesn't. He is dignified, refraining from any kind of slander against them. Instead he acts as if the charges had been made in jest, for there is a tinge of humor in his own words. He answers the charge by observing that it is only nine o'clock in the morning. The third hour of the day (8 to 9 a.m.) was one of three periods of daily prayer. It was also the time of the morning sacrifice and worship. According to well-established custom, the Jews were not to eat or drink anything until after this hour. Therefore, the charge of drunkenness has to be groundless. Peter didn't have to labor this point for the faces of the disciples probably shown more like angels than drunks. There is little fear that the world will accuse modern Christians of being drunk. There now seems to be a fear of holy intoxication. Few are willing to get that involved with the Spirit of God today.

16. "To the contrary, what you are seeing and hearing is an event that was predicted by the prophet Joel:

17. 'Here's what will happen in the last days,' says God, 'I will pour out My Holy Spirit upon all mankind, and your sons and daughters shall prophesy, and your young men shall see visions and your old men shall dream dreams, 18. yes, even upon My servants will I pour out My Spirit, whether men or women, and they shall all prophesy.' "

PREDICTED. Peter turns to the Scriptures to explain what is happening. He speaks in Aramean, for by now the foreign "utterances" have ceased. Their purpose was accomplished as soon as the 120 understood Jesus was working through them. What you are seeing and hearing, says Peter, is not due to the influence of alcohol, but the arrival of a DAY promised by God through His ancient prophet Joel (Joel 2:28-32). Peter is not explaining the miraculous speech only, but the wild joy and amazing words the disciples are saying. God foretold such a day, said Peter, now it is here. Beginning with this day, ALL men could have the Spirit of God. No longer would it be limited to a chosen few, as was the case in O.T. times. Receiving the Spirit would now be as simple as turning your cup right side up in a rainstorm. The receiving of Christ was meant to be that easy for everyone. The "last days" begin with the first coming of Christ and will end at His second coming. We are still in the last days, already 2000 years long.

POUR OUT. The prophet Joel used farmer talk in speaking of the Spirit's coming. It would be like rain, he said, falling freely on everyone without regard for age, sex, or rank. Men, women, children, and even servants could receive Him, for there was to be no distinction. The imagery of rain is most apt for picturing the coming of Christ in the Spirit. The outpouring speaks of His AVAILABILITY. It is another way of expressing the idea of His omnipresence. All during the last days, says Peter, anyone can be saved, for Christ has come in the Spirit and anyone can receive Him. Jesus is the "gift of God" (Rom. 6:23). The gift of the Spirit is the gift of Christ. As full of the Spirit as he was, Peter was yet unaware that this promise included the Gentiles. He still has to learn this from the Lord (Ch. 10).

DREAMS. With the coming of the Spirit, every Christian enjoys the privilege of spiritual illumination. There's a sense in which the light in his mind is "turned on" so that he can behold the things of God. Dreams and visions are part of the spiritual spectrum in which all believers participate. Joel's quote goes beyond the unveiling of Scripture and divine communications. It speaks of the privilege of fellowship with God in the sanctuary of the imagination. The anointed imagination allows one to give reality to the unseen Lord making fellowship with Him possible (1st Jo. 1:3). True, we see Him "darkly" as through a veil, but it is nonetheless real. We are the temples of God. His throne is located in our hearts and we come before Him in the true sanctuary, the illumined imagination. God is no longer interested in outward forms of worship, desiring instead that we come to Him in the Spirit. Thus He is "closer than breathing, nearer than hands and feet."

PROPHESY. A peculiar gift came with receiving Christ—the ability to prophesy. The humblest Christian enjoyed this gift. It was God speaking through a man, not only of future things, but of a godly walk and holy discipline. Hearts burned as Christians spoke of Jesus. Listeners felt God's all-seeing eye. Because the speaker's message was understood, Paul ranked it as the greatest of all gifts (1 Cor. 14:1). The BURNING HEART of the listener, as he received inspired words from a Christian, was its chief characteristic. This gift, the "flame" of the early church, soon died out as men preferred the more showy gifts of healing and tongues. In spite of Paul's warning, "despise not prophesying," the ability to prophesy fell into disuse and vanished from the church before the end of the First Century (1 Thess. 5:20). On the day of Pentecost, however, it was going full blast and hearts were convicted in wholesale fashion. Oh that we had this gift in operation today!

19. 'And I will cause wondrous things to occur in the sky and on earth—blood and fire and billowing clouds of smoke; 20. the sun will be turned into darkness and the moon as red as blood before the awesome day of the Lord arrives. 21. In the meantime, everyone who cries out for mercy in the Lord's Name shall be saved...' "

AWESOME DAY. Joel's prophecy spells out precisely the terminal points of the "last days." There is a time span between verses 18 and 19, one which is now 2000 years long. While the beginning of the last days was marked by great joy and spiritual blessing, the end of that age is to be characterized by destruction and disaster. Many are looking for a repeat performance of Pentecost, but it won't come. The days will grow increasingly troublesome and faith will all but vanish from the earth. John's description of God's day of wrath in Rev. 6:12 is also based on this same prophecy in Joel. The slaughter in the earth will be fantastic (Rev. 14:20). Only the return of the Lord will end the carnage (Matt. 24:22,29,30). Likely atomic warfare is pictured here, for the mushroom cloud could indeed blot out the sun and redden the moon. We know it can produce rivers of blood.

MEANTIME. During the interval between Pentecost and Christ's visible return, anyone can be saved by inviting Jesus into his heart. However, this "age of grace," will end abruptly with Christ's physical return in glory. For then He will come "in flaming fire taking vengeance on them that know not the gospel" (II Thess. 1:8). He will no longer be available in the Spirit. No one will be able to receive Him then as they can now, for the church age, the age of the Spirit, will have ended. In the meantime, God continues to pour out His Spirit on all men. Those expecting a second outpouring of Christ before the close of this age overlook the fact that He is still being "poured out" right now. Men can have all there is in Christ right now if they will accept it by faith. But a day is swiftly approaching when that privilege will come to a sudden halt.

"Is Peter going to advise the Jews they crucified their own Messiah?"

22. "All you men of Israel! Jesus the Nazarene was a man who came to you fully accredited by God. His credentials were the miracles and wonders and signs which God did through Him. These things were not

done in secret, but occurred in your very midst, as you well know. 23. This same man, you put to death. However, when He was handed over to you and you used the heathen government to crucify and murder Him, it was by God's permission. You were following a fixed plan carried out according to the will and foreknowledge of God."

ACCREDITED. The most astonishing event of history was the arrival of the Son of God in the world. He was the Messiah of Israel. Peter, after dealing with the scoffers, proceeds to tell the Jews that Jesus of Nazareth was their own Messiah. If they could be convinced of that, their agony of conviction would be awful. So he begins by calling their attention to Jesus' credentials which certified He came from God. He produced all the signs of the Messiah. There was no way for the Jews to deny His credentials. His works were extraordinary, performed by the thousands in broad daylight before their eyes. That He was a man from God could scarcely be challenged, and they knew it.

YOU. Peter begins to bear down when he says, "You put Him to death." He makes it clear the Jews were FULLY responsible. They merely used the Roman authorities to carry out their vicious deed. The plot to kill Jesus was conceived by Jewish leaders who stirred the populace to demand that Pilate should "crucify Him." The nailing to the cross by the soldiers was only incidental to their plot. Then, as if anticipating the objection that it would be impossible to crucify the real Messiah, Peter says their wicked act was according to God's eternal plan. The sufferings of Jesus came about in fulfillment of many O.T. prophecies. In saying this, Peter does not mean to reduce their guilt. He will say nothing about God's plan for removing their guilt until his audience is deeply convicted and cries out for relief. It is God's genius that the free will actions of His enemies fit His prearranged plan. His foreknowledge, of course, makes it possible.

24. "But God raised Him from the dead, putting an end to the terror of death, for it was impossible that death should keep Him in its grasp."

BUT GOD. The Jews passed the death sentence upon Jesus, but God reversed their decision and raised Him from the dead. It is not necessary for Peter to develop the fact that Jesus was raised. It was an unquestioned fact—the great topic of conversation throughout the city. It had happened but seven weeks before and the tomb was not far away to remind them of it. Peter, therefore, spends no time proving Jesus was raised. It is only necessary for him to show that it had taken place according to the plan of God. If he could prove that, then devout Jews would know they had crucified their own Messiah. But that's what seemed so impossible to them. If He were the Messiah, how could anyone kill Him?

IMPOSSIBLE. Then Peter tells them something which really was impossible—that death should have a permanent claim on the Messiah. Why? The Scriptures foretold His resurrection. He also said He would rise again. But more importantly, He was LIFE Himself. Death cannot swallow life any more than darkness can swallow light—it is the other way around. Jesus vanquished the terror of dying by His own experience (1 Cor. 15:45; Heb. 2:15). Death should no longer terrorize Christians once Jesus passed through it unharmed. It's as though He says, "There's nothing to it, so don't be afraid!" His resurrection abolished the mystery of death, revealing it to be a harmless experience. He proved that physical death has no effect on a man's soul. That truth removes death's terror instantly.

"Knowing the Jewish reverence for the Scriptures, shouldn't Peter make his point from the Old Testament?"

25. "David was speaking of Jesus when he said this:

'I enjoy the Lord's presence continually, for He is with me always, strengthening Me. Therefore I know I will not be shaken from My stand.

26. This makes My heart glad and My tongue joyful. Even My flesh is assured of safety in death,

27. For You will not leave My soul in Hades, nor allow Your Holy One to suffer decay.

28. Inasmuch as You have revealed to Me the plan of life, I know it is Your will for Me to keep on enjoying Your presence and be filled with gladness (after death).' "

DAVID. Peter does not refer to the empty tomb or the Centurion's testimony, but goes directly to the Scriptures. He quotes King David whom the Jews regarded as a man anointed to speak for God. No one was better loved by the Jews. David describes someone whose soul goes into Hades (the place of the O.T. dead) while his body went into a grave. However, he does not stay there long enough for his body to suffer corruption, but is returned to life (see page 197, under "cave" in my commentary on John's gospel). The "plan of life" was so clearly revealed to this person, he knew he would continue to enjoy God's presence after death. None listening would claim that David had been returned from the grave. The reference then, had to be someone other than David, some "Holy One" God had promised to raise from among David's descendants.

29. "Brethren, allow me to speak frankly about the patriarch David. He died and was buried. No one can deny that, for his tomb is here with us today and his body is still in it. Therefore he couldn't have been referring to himself. 30. But he was a prophet. Beyond that, he knew that one of his own descendants would later rule from his throne, for God had sworn this to him with an unbreakable oath. 31. When he said that

His soul would not be left in Hades and neither would His body be allowed to suffer corruption, he was looking ahead to the resurrection of the Messiah. 32. And now we are all witnesses to the fact that God has raised up again, this same Jesus of whom we speak."

PATRIARCH. It's not hard for Peter to prove that the 16th Psalm didn't apply to David. Everyone was familiar with his tomb just South of the city. Peter wisely referred to David as the patriarch (that is, the founder of the royal line from which the Messiah was to come) so that he too venerated King David along with the others. No one in the crowd believed David was risen from the tomb. His corpse had been allowed to decay. Since King David was also a prophet, he was especially endowed to speak of the future. On top of that, God had solemnly promised him that the Messiah would be one of his descendants. Therefore, it follows David was prophetically speaking of the Messiah and not himself, when referring to the resurrection of the Holy One. Peter could easily claim that Jesus was the One David was referring to, for He was raised from the grave and all the disciples were eyewitnesses.

"The Jews must have been spellbound. Their love for the Scriptures could only lead them to one conclusion."

33. "And now, exalted by the right hand of God, He has activated the Father's promise to bestow the Holy Spirit. Therefore what you are seeing and hearing is the result of the outpouring of His Spirit. 34. David, himself, was not the one who ascended into heaven, yet he did tell us:

> **'The Lord said unto My Master, Sit on My right hand, 35. While I make your enemies a footstool under your feet.' "**

EXALTED. One reading these lines might envision Jesus sitting beside God in heaven, ruling from a secondary throne. But this is NOT the case. There is NO seat beside God's throne. The term, "right hand," refers to God's majesty and power. The expression to SIT at God's right hand, is an idiom which means, "RULE with My authority and power." We have a kindred saying ourselves, "my right hand man." But we do not mean someone constantly at our elbow. Joseph was exalted to Pharaoh's "right hand," but he spent his time collecting grain in the fields, not in the palace. Similarly, Jesus is not seated anywhere, but ruling in the hearts of men. Our hearts are to be His throne. The expression refers to His RULE in the Spirit. The day of Pentecost was the day He began to rule in the Spirit, and He does so with the authority and power of God. "Footstool," refers to an O.T. custom whereby kings symbolically placed their feet upon the necks of vanquished foes.

ACTIVATED. As long as Jesus operated in the flesh, He did not operate in the Spirit. He made that clear (John 16:7). When He shifted from His earthly ministry to operate exclusively in the Spirit (His ascension), it was God's plan for Him to return as the Holy Ghost. What men saw and heard on the day of Pentecost, were signs that Jesus had returned as the Indweller and Baptizer. Again the term, "outpouring," refers to the availability of Christ. In these "last days," He is available to everyone, like rain from heaven. We should also note that this spiritual operation of Christ as the Holy Ghost is temporary. It is to last only until His enemies are "put under His feet," i.e., when Christ has triumphed over all. To this agrees the apostle Paul who states that the mediatorial role of Christ will one day end (1 Cor. 15:27,28).

LORD. Again Peter turns to the Jew's favorite Scriptures and quotes from the 110th Psalm, a passage he once heard Jesus use against the Pharisees (Matt. 22:44). He has already made it clear that David couldn't be the resurrected one, for he was still in his tomb. That argument has been clinched. But neither can David be the exalted one referred to here, for it is clearly stated that it is David's Lord who is so elevated. Observe how the Psalm actually reads: "The

Lord (YHWH, God) said unto my Lord (Adonai, Messiah), sit on My right hand..." When David speaks of his "Lord," he cannot be referring to himself. But whom? Ah, God's Mediator, the Messiah. Therefore, says Peter, David is speaking of Jesus, for He is the One Who was raised from the dead. Consequently, He is the One Who has been exalted and has sent forth this glorious effusion of Himself (via the Spirit) upon men.

36. "Let every man in Israel know for certain that God has made this Jesus, Whom you crucified, both Lord and Messiah."

LORD AND MESSIAH. Peter's argument is irresistible, with only one conclusion. Israel, both as a nation and individual Jews, is guilty of the enormous crime of slaying her own Messiah. See the contrast between what they did to Him and what God did with Him. They slew their Messiah, but God raised Him and exalted Him, not only as the Messiah, but gave Him a title far above that—"LORD." Peter's use of this word (Lord) refers to the ineffable Name of God which the Jews would not pronounce, YHWH. They substituted the word Adonai (Lord) in its place. Thus Peter is saying that Jesus' exaltation raised Him to the same level as the One Who spoke to Moses from the burning bush. As a man, Jesus was simply the Messiah of Israel. But as the exalted One, He is none other than the God Who appeared to Abraham and called Israel into existence. Peter declares that the One they crucified is now the ruler of the universe and not just the king of the Jews. Imagine this uneducated, but Spirit-filled fisherman boldly indicting his nation. He is a miracle himself!

"Were these Jews ready for such news?"

37. When they heard this, their consciences burned, for they were cut to the heart. And they said to Peter and the other disciples, "What shall we do now,

brethren?" 38. "Repent," answered Peter, "each one of you must be baptized in the name of Jesus Christ, so that you may have your sins forgiven. Then you will receive the gift of God, the Holy Spirit."

REPENT. Peter's message struck home. If Jesus was truly the Messiah, what guilt could be greater than that of killing Him? So they cried out in anguish. Incredible as it may seem, Peter says it still isn't too late. However, they must repent of this evil they have done and acknowledge Jesus for Who He really is. The word repent means to change one's mind or attitude FROM something TO something else. It is an act of the WILL, and not a matter of feelings, though sorrow can produce it. Peter advises them a change of heart concerning Jesus of Nazareth will bring God's forgiveness for their sin. But it cannot be the **same kind of repentance** they gave John the Baptist. That was phony, else they would have received Jesus when He appeared. This time they will be required to testify publicly that they believe Jesus is the Messiah of Israel to show that their repentance is genuine. If their repentance is **indeed** genuine, God will not only forgive them, but grant them the gift of the Spirit.

BAPTIZED. This is for Jews ONLY, specifically those guilty of publicly shaming and crucifying their Messiah. Since they denied Him openly, Peter demands they acknowledge Him openly. He requires the Lord's method of identification, i.e., the long established custom of Jewish water baptism. It was done in a public place with the phrase, "In the name of Jesus of Nazareth" said over them. Such a public acknowledgment would result in the loss of all things precious to Jews. Done in the face of the Sanhedrin and the mobs which hated Christ, it was solid evidence they had really changed their minds about Jesus. The baptism was identical to that of John the Baptist, only this time they had to mean it. The price was too high for phonies to participate. The outward act certified the inward revolution of mind which made them eligible for the gift of God. Jewish baptism differs from Christian baptism in that it occurs BEFORE salvation, indicating repentance. Christian baptism occurs AFTER salvation indicating one has ALREADY received the gift of the Spirit (Christ).

RECEIVE. While repentance does secure forgiveness, forgiveness by itself is not enough. Men also need eternal life which is **in Christ** only. This is why we not only have the bread at Communion (forgiveness), we also have the cup (life). Repentance (the change of mind) and salvation (receiving God's gift) are two separate matters. Repentance makes a man eligible for salvation. Upon genuine repentance (turning from his former attitude about Christ) he may receive the gift of Christ, the Holy Ghost. Everything God offers man is IN Christ (Eph. 1:3). The gift of the Spirit is Christ Himself. We should further distinguish between the gift of the Spirit (Christ) and the GIFTS of the Spirit, the Lord's impartation of spiritual faculties to His servants. Some have erroneously assumed the gift of the Spirit (Christ) comes by laying on of hands (Ch. 8:17). If so, it is remarkable that Luke says nothing of it here.

"Were these Jews aware of the great privilege granted them this day?"

39. "For this great promise of God was made to you and your children, and to all those far away, as many as the Lord our God shall call to Himself."

PROMISE. Peter says it was God's intention that the gospel should come to them specifically. They are the very generation and remnant of His people to whom the spiritual advent of Christ was promised. Now it has come to pass. This is their big moment. But it was not only a local promise. It extends into the future, including generations of Israelites not yet born.

Peter, of course, isn't aware of the scope of his words. Unknown to him, God included the Gentiles in those "far away" people. The gospel invitation is for everyone called of God. But whom does God call? "Whosoever will" respond to His wooing via the invitation to receive Christ. However, until men hear the gospel, there is NO wooing. It is impossible for one to believe "on Him of whom he has not heard" (Rom. 10:14).

40. With such words as these and many others besides, Peter pleaded with his listeners. He begged them, saying, "Escape from the fate of this wicked generation!" 41. Many of them eagerly took his words to heart, and when all who believed his message were baptized, the number of souls won to the Lord that day was about three thousand. 42. These joined the apostles for fellowship, meeting with them constantly that they might be taught by them and participate with them in the meals and the prayers.

PLEADED. This is Christ in action, speaking through Peter. He is now starting to build His church (Matt. 16:18). He sees the hopeless impenitence of the Jewish nation and begs all who will listen to escape the fate of that unbelieving generation. The results are wonderful. About 3000 joyously respond to Peter's words giving evidence of their repentance by baptism. We assume they received the Spirit of Christ immediately and were saved. More were won in a single day than Jesus secured in His years of public ministry. Thus the disciples were already performing "greater works" than they had seen Him do (John 14:12). The Lord's church, His spiritual house, was off to a grand start (Eph. 2:22). The 120 disciples had a full day baptizing converts. The disciples thrilled to the way their words touched hearts as Jesus spoke through them. We have only a summary of Peter's words here, though it seems unlikely any critical parts are left out.

FELLOWSHIP. The first Christian community was made up of sincere Jews who defied the temple authorities and their nation to step out for Christ.

As soon as they were saved, they wanted to know more about their new-found faith. "Souls" were added, not just "names." The Lord continued to teach them through His apostles. In time the teaching took the form of the N.T. Scriptures. They ate their meals together, placing special emphasis on the breaking of the bread which now symbolized Christ's death. We are more ceremonial about it today, but the early Christians were childiike in their simplicity of honoring Jesus every time they broke bread together. This continued until abuses and persecutions made it unrealistic to have it as a part of the common meal. They also had appointed times for prayer together, attending even the public Jewish prayers as well (Ch. 3:1).

43. A great sense of awe swept over everyone, which was intensified by the wonders and signs performed by the apostles in Jerusalem.

AWE. The conviction produced by Christ's preaching through Peter didn't pass away. The people had the dread feeling that God was so close they could feel His hand upon them. This impression was reinforced by the miracles of the apostles which they performed not only on that day, but in the days ahead. What those miracles were we will learn shortly. A holy wonder pervaded the place, resulting in more believers being added to the fellowship. The Lord trained His disciples for the use of miraculous power in the days of His earthly ministry. He had sent them on preaching missions with the power to heal sicknesses and cast out demons (Lu. 9:1,2,6). While miracles do not produce faith, they are a convincing testimony to the presence of God. It should be noted that with all the miracles Jesus did during His 3½ year ministry on earth, it didn't produce enough faith to survive His death. Not even the Twelve retained their convictions about Him.

"With Jesus' presence so manifest, that first fellowship must have been fantastic!"

44. All those brought together by their faith in Jesus remained in close fellowship, sharing all they had

with each other, 45. even to the point of selling their belongings and real estate that they might minister to those who had need.

SHARING. Once these Jews were saved, God's love burned in their hearts as the Holy Ghost (Christ) continued to manifest Himself (Rom. 5:5). It was an amazing demonstration of what the Spirit of Christ could do for mankind. The sense of love was so great they pooled their property so they could remain together as a community. This is not the communist approach which says, "All of your property is mine," but the Christian approach which says, "All of my property is yours." This first community of Christians was a miracle, falling into the same category as the apostles' miracles. It belonged to the introduction of Christianity. It was not meant to be permanent, anymore than the apostles' miracles. As long as the fire of spiritual unity burned hotly, the communal plan worked. However, once it began to wane, serious difficulties set in (Chs. 4:32-5:11). There is no mention of the practice of communal living in any other church in the N.T.

46. They continued to worship together as a group, meeting in the temple daily. They also took their communal meals together by going to each others' houses. With great gladness did they eat their food, enjoying each other with a childlike spirit. 47. All the while, they continued to praise God and enjoy the goodwill of the people. Each day the Lord added to their fellowship those who were being saved.

TOGETHER. In the weeks that followed Pentecost, the believers met regularly in the temple. Apparently they used Solomon's portico which ran along the East side of the outer court. Here they held their public meetings and witnessed to the crowds which gathered. Then, by households, they adjourned for their communal meals which had to be eaten in private homes. The doctrine and order of the first church was extremely simple: loving one another and witnessing for Christ. The rich were happy because they could give, the poor were happy to receive. All were happy in Christ. There was no pride, no big show, no hypocrisy. They were beautifully childlike as they trusted each other and cared for each other. The common people were impressed with what they saw, for the transformation was obvious. As yet no real trouble has developed between the infant church and the temple authorities.

SAVED. As the disciples witnessed for Christ, the indwelling Lord bore witness to their words. They worked and HE worked. Even so, note how He is the One Who adds to His church. He is the Great Baptizer, the church's Builder. Souls were placed in the body by spiritual baptism (Jesus' part) as they responded to the spoken invitation (the disciples' part). If this were simply a group of people who believed that Jesus of Nazareth was the Messiah, it never would have survived to cover the world. The church was a supernatural organism acquiring its vitality from the fact that Christ Himself (via His Ghost) indwelt the believers so that their souls glowed with His love. Then, as they spoke about Him, other hearts burned too. In this way, the gospel passes from one person to another with people coming alive as they believe God's Word and receive Christ in the Spirit. The day of Pentecost was only the beginning of Christ's "greater work." It started with the "remnant" of Israel, and spread throughout the world. The Lord continues to add to His church and will do so until the last living stone is in place (1 Peter 2:5).

"Could you give an example of the miracles the apostles performed?"

3

1. Sometime after this, Peter and John were going up into the temple to participate in the three o'clock hour of prayer. 2. As they approached the "beautiful gate," they noticed a lame man sitting there. Inasmuch as he had been crippled

from birth, it was customary to carry him along and set him down at this gate where he might beg from those going into the temple. 3. Now when this man saw Peter and John about to enter the inner court, he began to beg from them.

PRAYER. The apostles continued to live as faithful Jews, observing the set times of prayer in the temple, i.e., 9 a.m., 12 noon, and 3 p.m. As yet they do not understand how Christ's indwelling has made them the "temple of the Holy Spirit," superseding the Jerusalem temple and its ordinances (1 Cor. 6:19). Peter and John now appear as inseparable friends. They were close companions even before Pentecost. On this afternoon, they are about to enter the temple's inner court when they encounter a beggar, who was born crippled, lying at the entrance. We can suppose this gate received the most traffic, and he counted on the people to express their piety with gifts to him. He was a familiar sight. He had been doing this a long time inasmuch as he was over 40 years old (Acts 4:22).

4. Peter and John eyed the man sympathetically. Then Peter spoke, "Look here!" 5. The lame man looked toward them eagerly as if expecting to receive something from them. 6. But Peter said, "I don't have any money, but I do have something else to give! In the name of Jesus Christ the Nazarene—WALK!"

LOOK. Peter and John could have looked the other way. That's what most did. But their indwelling Lord prompted them to take a personal interest in this man. So they stopped, just as Jesus had stopped at this very gate (perhaps?) to heal a man born blind (See under John 9:1). The disciples now stand in the Master's shoes ready to do as He did. As they call to him, the beggar becomes expectant. It was unusual to have people call to him. Something in their eyes makes him think he's about to receive money. Then Peter, aware that one doesn't need money to serve the Lord, says he has a gift for him. Peter mentions a name the man has heard before—Jesus of Nazareth! But what could be the gift? In that name Peter gives a command—"WALK!" The gift was healing for his body. Everything the man had heard about Jesus raced through his mind. He had been a healer. Was it possible to receive such a gift from One Who had been crucified?

© Linda Lovett 1979

WALK. The man just sat there. He knew what Jesus' NAME meant. According to Jewish custom, it was the equivalent of Jesus Himself. Acting in the authority of that name, Peter commands a lifetime cripple to rise and start walking. Yet, he is acting as the representative of someone ALIVE, not dead. Peter has made the offer. He gave the command by faith, though as yet there is no evidence Jesus is going to heal the man. Therefore, Peter is the one who must act FIRST. Why? Jesus has limited Himself to the actions of His servants. Operating in the Spirit, Christ cannot work until Peter does. Peter knew it would be by Christ's power the man would be healed, yet he said..."I GIVE." Not only does Christ give, but I give. By faith Peter acts and Jesus works. That's the way it was when Jesus was in the flesh. He acted, and His Father did the works. The faith of the lame man is NOT involved. Thus, this is not faith-healing, which involves the faith of the sick person, but the **power to heal.** It is Peter's faith we are seeing in operation here. He has authority over the crippled man's disease.

7. Then, grasping the man by the right hand, he helped him up. As he did so, the man's feet and ankles became strong instantly, 8. so that he actually leaped to his full height and began to walk! Then he went into the temple with them, sometimes walking, sometimes leaping, all the while giving praise to God as he went.

INSTANTLY. Peter makes his move, reaching forth his hand to help the cripple respond to his command. The upward pull of Peter's hand, the surge of strength in his ankles, must have germinated the seeds of faith in this man. As power came to his legs, perhaps with a snap, he leaped up the rest of the way. What a complete miracle! Imagine a man who had never even learned to walk, running and leaping at once! The man's soul is flooded with joy and gratitude. He doesn't run away, but goes into the temple to praise God with the apostles. How many who are healed use their healing for the glory of God? Luke reported nine cured lepers who didn't even say thank you (Luke 17:17). It is told that Thomas Acquinas happened upon Pope Innocent II when he was counting money. "See Thomas," said the Pope, "The church can no longer say silver and gold have I none." Thomas answered, "Yes, and neither can she say, 'rise and walk in Jesus' name!" There had been an obvious trade of spiritual power for money.

"Wow! How did this affect the people who saw it!"

9. Everybody saw this man walking and praising God; 10. and when they realized he was the same person who used to sit begging at the Beautiful Gate, they were rocked with wonder and astonishment at what happened to him.

ASTONISHMENT. As in the case of the man born blind, there was nothing obscure about this miracle (John 9:1 ff.). The crowds knew this man. They had seen him begging at this gate year after year. It could not have been a trick of magic. Besides, was not the blind man healed at the temple gates the previous December? Jesus' power to heal was no secret. The crowd takes note that Peter and John did not heal in their own name, but in that of Jesus of Nazareth. That was the shocker. Nothing was more obvious to them than the fact that the SAME POWER by which Jesus healed cripples during His earthly ministry was somehow still in their midst! Therefore, the healing of this man was more than a miracle—it was a SIGN. Jesus was not dead, but working through His disciples. That a lame man should "leap as a deer," was one of the expected signs of the Messiah (Isa. 35:6).

11. All the people came running to Solomon's portico where the man was still clinging to Peter and John, and they were filled with wonder and amazement at what they saw. 12. Now when Peter saw how awed the people were, he seized the opportunity and spoke to the crowd:

> "Men of Israel, why are you so surprised? Why do you stare at us as if we had made this man walk through some power or virture of our own?"

PORTICO. With the prayer time and sacrifice over, Peter and John emerged from the inner temple via the Beautiful Gate. The healed man has attached himself to them, actually holding on to them with his hand. He senses the presence of God in these men. The three of them make their way Eastward to the portico of Solomon. This was the only remaining part of Solomon's great temple that was not destroyed by Nebuchadnezzer. Bearing Solomon's name, it was distinguished from all other porches or colonnades in the temple area. Here an astonished crowd gathered, convinced of one thing—a great miracle had been performed.

Thus, for the second time, Peter has an amazed audience eager for an explanation. The real purpose of the miracle is now clear. It was NOT for the salvation of the lame man, but to draw crowds to which Peter might address the call to repentance.

OPPORTUNITY. See how Peter does not address the stunned crowd as an unruly mob, but as an assembly of devout people. "Men of Israel," was a coveted title in which the Jews delighted, for it separated them from Ishmael and Esau. The crowd is staggered at the sight of the healed man and rightly so. They all knew him by sight. Peter censures them slightly for assuming he was healed by the apostles themselves. He could sense the admiration fixed on them, wondering what great power was in them, or what holiness made them worthy of God's power. The point of the miracle was to draw attention to Jesus, but this escaped the people. It didn't occur to them to connect it with Jesus. That was now Peter's job. He has an excellent opportunity since this large crowd was ready to hear anything he had to say. Also, the healed man was there to provide visible confirmation.

13. "It is the God of Abraham, Isaac, and Jacob, the God of our fathers Who has done this to honor His Servant Jesus, Whom you brought to trial and rejected in Pilate's presence. Even when Pilate was eager to free Him, 14. you disowned the Holy and Righteous One. You demanded that Pilate release to you a murderer instead, 15. and killed the Author of life. But God raised Him from the dead and we are eyewitnesses to that fact, for we saw Him after He was raised."

GOD. What a temptation for a man who earlier wanted to be greatest in the kingdom (Luke 9:46). Here was a chance to be credited with the work of God. But see the change in Peter. Listen to his honesty. We didn't heal this man, says the apostle, God did. The God of our fathers produced this miracle through us. Yet, it wasn't for the benefit of this lame man, but for the honor and glory of Jesus. It is the same Jesus, he says, whom you denied, preferring a murderer in His stead and then killed. Now, from His exalted role as God the Spirit, Jesus is working through His disciples. He is again performing the same signs He did in His earthly ministry. Note Peter's contrast of the Jews' treatment of Christ with what God did with Him. This was his favorite technique for bringing conviction. He had the authority inasmuch as he was an eyewitness.

SERVANT. When Peter calls Jesus God's Servant, the Jerusalem crowd would instantly think of the "Suffering Servant" of Isaiah 52 and 53. The ancient prophet predicted God's Servant would suffer, but afterwards be exalted. Peter uses another familiar term from the O.T. when he says they disowned the "Holy and Righteous One." They knew that was the Messiah's name. Then see how he compounds their guilt by tracing their actions step by step to the crime, using contrasts, to pinpoint the awfulness of their deed. Pilate, a pagan, was ready to free Jesus, but they wanted Him sentenced. They asked for a murderer, a taker of life, rather than release the "Holy One," Who was the Giver of life. What a paradox that Peter should offer them life through the One they killed. The "Author of life," here and in Heb. 2:10 denotes Christ as the source of salvation.

16. "Now consider this man whom you all know by sight. It was the name of Jesus that healed him. However, it was by faith that we offered him healing. Therefore, it was faith in the name of Jesus that restored him to perfect health in the presence of you all."

FAITH. Peter impresses upon his listeners that the power to heal this man resides in Jesus, for again, the Jewish use of the NAME of Christ meant Jesus Himself. Peter makes it clear that the name is not a magical formula to be used without faith, for apart from faith, even Jesus' name is powerless. So the man was not healed by the mere use of Jesus' name, but through FAITH in that name. This was important, for sorcerers and exorcists employed NAMES for healing and hexing people in those days. By faith in Jesus name, says Peter, the apostles were invested with the power to perform miracles, with the miracles themselves signs of the Messiah. The point of the miracles was to prove the power of the crucified Christ was still in their midst, and now operating in His servants because of their faith in Him. The definite article in Gk. makes it read, "the faith," as it pertained to the disciples, not the cripple.

"How will Peter woo the crowd after such a harsh condemnation?"

17. "And now, my brothers, I am well aware that you, like your rulers, didn't realize what you were doing. 18. And since God long ago announced through the prophets that His Messiah should suffer, these things came to pass in fulfillment of His Word."

BROTHERS. After his stabbing statements, Peter softens his words as he moves to the invitation. With sincere love, he calls them "brothers," admitting they committed their crime in ignorance. Likely he is thinking of Jesus' words from the cross, "Father, forgive them, for they know not what they do" (Luke 23:34). Because of that prayer they can be forgiven no matter how great their guilt. See how their ignorance, like that of the apostle Paul, does not cancel their guilt. It merely explains why they acted as they did. Their guilt is actually compounded when you consider they should have known better. O.T. prophecy in general was dominated by one theme–the Messiah, His birth, works, suffering, and death. Had not the murder of the Messiah been a part of God's plan, they would have been left without hope. As it is, they can now be forgiven.

19. "Now you must repent and turn back to God so that He can wipe out your sins, then you will be

ready to receive that spiritual renewal which comes through the presence of the Lord."

REPENT. If the Jews will change their minds about Jesus (repent) and adopt God's attitude toward Him, He will wipe out their sins—including the terrible one they committed in demanding His death. Then all the benefits of the Messiah's death will be theirs. See the two phases of salvation presented here: (1) the forgiveness of sin, which is insufficient by itself, (2) the regeneration (renewal) of their hearts via Christ's indwelling presence. Observe the place Peter gives to repentance. He is not extreme, yet he insists they must change their minds about Jesus. Then they will be eligible for the "spiritual renewal" that comes with the Lord's presence. The Gk. for "wipe out" sins is the same as Col. 2:14, where it is pictured as the obliteration of a document.

20. "If you will do that, then God will send Jesus back to you, for He is your appointed Messiah. 21. However, He must remain in heaven until the final restoration of all things even as God announced through His prophets long ago."

SEND. Keep in mind that Peter is addressing the "whole house of Israel." He is asking the entire NATION to repent. It is still the pentecostal season, and Jerusalem is packed with devout Jews from about the world. He wants the nation to reverse its decision made at the Passover, and with one accord, acknowledge Jesus as the Messiah. Israel refused the offer of forgiveness as a nation, though some individual Jews did repent. The **national** rejection of Jesus continues to this day. As it was, the Gentiles turned to Jesus in increasing numbers, while fewer and fewer Jews repented and were saved. Israel's hardness of heart brought blessing to the Gentiles (Rom. 11:11).

UNTIL. Peter's words appear to indicate the Lord's return is conditioned upon Israel's repentance **as a nation.** If the suffering and death of the Messiah were due to Israel's ignorance and betrayal, then the Messiah's delay could also be due to Israel's continued rejection. Should this be the case, it provides a strong argument for the evangelization of the Jews **as a nation.** On the other hand, there is Scripture which suggests that the Messiah's return is needed to produce Israel's national conversion. Either way, the great restoration and parousia (kingly visit) of the Lord promised in the O.T., are related to Israel's repentance as a nation. This could be a significant verse for fixing the time of the rapture of the church.

RESTORATION. At this point in God's program only the SOULS of His people have been redeemed, nothing else. The apostle Paul says all of creation is waiting for its redemption (Rom. 8:18-23.) It will not come about until Jesus returns from the spirit-world (heaven) to establish Israel as His earthly kingdom as He promised David. This event of which the prophets spoke, is the future hope of Israel. When Jesus comes again, He will do everything the Jews expect of Him, including His reign over mankind. There will also be a great renovation of the physical world, with changes in the animal kingdom ("the lion shall lie down with the lamb") and the weather. In those days, the "desert will blossom like a rose." Until that day arrives, the Lord Jesus must continue to rule from the hearts of men, for all things are not yet subject to Him (Heb. 2:8).

"Can Peter back up such a remarkable claim?"

22. "Did not Moses say:

> **'The Lord your God will raise up for you a Prophet like myself, and He will come from among your own people. Listen carefully to everything He says to you. 23. Anyone who fails to heed that Prophet shall be excluded from among God's people and destroyed.'**

24. With one voice, all the prophets from Samuel onwards, predicted these days would come to pass.

They have all spoken of that which we're seeing today."

MOSES. Peter goes back to Moses to show how Christ has always been the burden of prophetic truth. In citing Deut. 18:15-19, he reveals how the first of the great prophets looked forward to the day of Christ. All of Moses' successors, including Samuel, who spoke directly to David about the kingdom, foretold the advent of Jesus. Long before Christ arrived, these verses came to be associated with one particular prophet who would speak for God as did Moses. The resemblance between Moses and Jesus in terms of intimacy with God and as heads of new covenants is striking. In the light of all that Peter has said so far, only one person has any claim to being that prophet–Jesus.

EXCLUDED. The latter part of Moses' prediction is extremely severe. Giving heed to the prophet was to be a life or death matter. Those refusing to heed His words would be excluded from the kingdom of God. When the Prophet finally arrived in the world, God said on one occasion, "This is My beloved Son. Listen to Him!" (Matt. 17:5). Inasmuch as "all have sinned," all men are under sentence of death. They are like people drowning in a river. However, they are not there because God became angry and threw them in the water. They are already in the river because of sin, and perishing because they refuse the help God sent through His Son. Sinners are certain to perish if they will not heed the words of God's Prophet, the Lord Jesus. This feature makes Christ the only "WAY" to God.

25. "You are the heirs of all those promises which God made through the prophets. You come under the covenant which God made with Abraham and reaffirmed to our fathers when He said. . .

'All the families of the earth shall be blessed by your offspring.'

26. When God raised up His Servant, it was to you He sent Him first. He did it to bless you by getting each one of you to turn from his evil ways."

HEIRS. Peter tells his listeners they are the heirs of God's promises through the prophets. They are the ones who were alive when God's Word to Abraham was fulfilled. God promised to bring forth from Abraham an heir who would bring blessing to all mankind. And now that heir (Jesus) had arrived. He came to the Jews first, for they were Abraham's natural offspring. Since He was raised up in their midst, the blessing was extended to them first of all. It is not only the raising of Jesus from the dead that is intended here, but His arrival in the world as Abraham's Seed. He came to deliver them from sin, but they rejected Him, preferring one who could deliver them from the Romans. Now Peter says He has been raised again, and they have a fresh opportunity to receive God's pardon if they will seize it. If they refuse, they forfeit all their rights as heirs of Abraham and the prophets.

"Could they get away with such bold preaching on the temple grounds?"

4

1. Before Peter and John had finished speaking to the people, they were interrupted by the arrival of some chief priests, along with the captain of the temple guard and other Sadducees. 2. It infuriated them to have Peter and John teaching the crowds like this, proclaiming that Jesus' resurrection proved people do rise from among the dead.

PRIESTS. Word reaches the temple authorities that two of Jesus' followers have performed a great miracle on the temple grounds and are using it to prove to the crowds that He had risen from the dead. So the chief priests, accompanied by the chief of the temple's Levitical guard (the captain was himself a chief priest), and other Sadducees, hasten to the scene to put a stop to it. The Sadducees, the dominant party of the Sanhedrin at this time, denied any kind of a bodily resurrection. Neither did they believe in spirit-beings. The teachings of these two men were intolerable to them, for should the resurrection of Jesus be true, it would wipe out the basis for the Sadducee party in Israel. The Levites (also Sadducees) were indignant that these unauthorized men would dare to invade the privileges of the Levitical priesthood and teach the people. Thus it was the Sadducees who moved first to silence the apostles.

3. So they arrested them. But since it was toward the end of the day, they held them in custody until the following morning. 4. Meanwhile, many of the people who had listened to their preaching joined the believers, bringing their number to about five thousand, not counting the women.

ARRESTED. The first persecution of the new church came as the arroused Sadducees set about to silence the apostles. Armed with authority, they seized them and placed them in confinement. Their teachings, if widely accepted, could put an end to the Sadducees' power. However, since the apostles didn't begin their preaching till after the 3 o'clock sacrifice, it was now too late in the day to convene a lawful meeting of the Sanhedrin. The matter would have to wait until morning. Fortunately Peter had said enough. So even though they were imprisoned, their message continued to spread. The Lord used their words to draw many to Himself, so that the number of believers increased even though the apostles were momentarily silenced by the Sadducees.

5. In Jerusalem the next day, there was a regularly scheduled meeting of the Jewish leaders, the elders, and the teachers of the Law. 6. Included among them were Annas the high priest, Caiaphas, John, Alexander, and all who belonged to the high priest's family.

MEETING. It so happened that on this day there was a regularly scheduled meeting of the full Sanhedrin with the Sadducee party especially well represented. Annas, the defacto high priest (a Sadducee), was there with all of his kinsmen. The Sanhedrin, composed of about 70 members, sat in a semi-circle with the president's chair (high priest) at the head. By now, this august body is alert to the business at hand. The actions of the apostles constitute a very grave threat. Just eight weeks before, they had sentenced Jesus to death. They thought they were rid of Him for good. Now it appears they are going to have a great deal more trouble because of Him.

ANNAS. Annas was the high priest in Israel for 9 years beginning with his appointment in A.D. 6. He was later deposed, but he had gained such a foothold while in office that he continued to be the power in Israel, even though his son-in-law, Caiaphas, was the **legal** high priest. Likely he was the richest man in Israel, controlling all the temple traffic (money changers, etc.). He may have even sat in the president's chair at this meeting, despite the fact that his son-in-law held the job by Roman appointment. The **people**, however, regarded him as God's high priest. Besides Caiaphas, five of his sons and one grandson occupied the high priest's office, so that Annas remained the power behind the throne until the revolt of A.D. 66. The John mentioned here was Annas' son and was high priest in A.D. 36. We have no information on Alexander.

7. And they brought in the prisoners and made them stand before them. "By what power did you do this?" demanded the council, "What name did you use?" 8. Then Peter, with the awareness of the Holy Ghost filling his being, answered:

"Rulers and elders of the people. 9. If it is because we have done a good deed to a cripple that we are on trial here, and you want to know how he was healed, 10. here is our answer to you and all the people of Israel: it was done in the name of Jesus of Nazareth, the Messiah—the same One you crucified, but Whom God raised from the dead. This man stands here in your presence completely healed in His name!"

WHAT NAME? The council has convened. The members are in their places. Peter, John, and the healed man are brought from their cell and placed in the midst of the semi-circle. We can assume the president asked the questions on behalf of the council. The questioning (we have only a summary here) shows the council is not interested in the apostles' preaching as much as in the NAME they used to produce the miracle. The question assumes the healing was done. It cannot be denied with the healed man standing right there. What remains is to discover HOW it was done. The Sanhedrin suspects it was due to some diabolical influence. That's why they press for the NAME used in the formula. In those times, people believed in exorcism (casting out demons) for healing.

ANSWERED. It would be expected that these uneducated Galileans would be intimidated and overwhelmed by this august body of rulers. Peter knows these men have the power to condemn him, just as they condemned his innocent Master eight weeks before. But he has been prepared. The Lord had told him what to do on such occasions. . ."Take no thought of how you shall answer for the Holy Ghost shall teach you what to say" (Lu. 12:11,12). Peter was ready to experience the fulfillment of those instructions. If the council wanted to know by what name this was done, he'd tell them, and without fear—Jesus of Nazareth, the Messiah. Note how he considers he is speaking to the entire nation through its rulers. The power to heal this man, says Peter, resides in Jesus.

FILLING. Peter senses the Holy Ghost is about to speak through him. He sets himself to let the Lord use him, even as He used him at Pentecost to speak to the crowds. The obsession returns. Peter is once more caught up in the thrill of declaring Jesus. Again, that thrilling is the filling. Of course, it is Peter who speaks, but his words are inspired by the Spirit. That is, the Spirit thinks and Peter speaks—in exciting cooperation. The grammar of the Gk. text shows this filling was occurring right at that moment. A different Gk. form is used to denote a Spirit-filled man. When "Spirit-filled" is used as an adjective, it refers to someone really "turned on" for Christ. When it speaks of a person as "being filled," it is referring to an action then taking place. Peter is here **being filled** as the awareness of the Lord's presence and desire to use him, floods his being. He is caught up in the thrill of Christ!

"Was it the Sanhedrin's question that stirred Peter to such boldness?"

11. "This same Jesus is the Stone which Scripture says was 'rejected by the builders, but later became the most important stone in the building.' You are the builders who rejected the Stone. 12. Know therefore, that there is no salvation in anyone else! Among all the names under heaven, His is the only one given to men for salvation."

STONE. After telling the council the name he used was that of Jesus of Nazareth, he shifts to the attack. Taking one of the earliest Messianic Scriptures, he shows how David had prophesied 1000 years before that the rulers of Israel, "the builders of God's house," would reject the Stone which God had selected (Psa. 118:22). The rejected Stone has a name—Jesus! This same Stone, says Peter, has been raised up by God and given the place of honor (keystone) in His house (the church). Peter says this 1000 year old prophecy has been fulfilled by this very council. If the rulers refuse this name (Stone) a second time, they will be guilty of leading their nation into judgment. As it is, Israel still has a chance to repent. Note how Peter says there is only one way to God, and that by the name (person) of Jesus. He refutes those who say, "I believe all religions lead to God."

"How did the Sanhedrin react to Peter's daring attitude?"

13. When the rulers observed the amazing boldness of Peter and John, noting that they were untrained laymen, they were shocked. Only then did they get the connection and recognize them as having been with Jesus. 14. Even so, there was no way for them to refute Peter's statement, for the healed man was standing there with them.

RECOGNIZE. Jesus had no human credentials when He began His ministry. He had no diplomas from the schools of religion, no letters from the high priest, neither was He licensed by the Sanhedrin. Yet, everyone was shocked at His learning, for no one could match His handling of the O.T. Now Peter and John are manifesting the same boldness and astute handling of the Scriptures. Then it dawned on them—"These men were with Jesus! They must have received their strange power from Him!" Were not Jesus (His Ghost) in these fishermen, they would have cringed in terror. Instead, they dare to accuse their rulers of a terrible crime against God. It was obvious they received this audacity from their Master too. How else could untrained laymen be so fluent and fearless before this great body?

REFUTE. The mouths of the rulers are stopped by the same wisdom with which Jesus answered them eight weeks before. It seems they are not to be rid of Him after all, for now His threatening presence appears in these disciples. Just as Jesus' words were backed by mighty miracles, so are those of His disciples. With the healed man present, the rulers cannot deny that he was healed in Jesus' name. Today we do not have physical miracles to back the Gospel, but we do have the miracle of transformed men. It takes superhuman power to convert the worst of men into saints. People will always debate Christianity, but the most conclusive evidence for Christ is a Christian. So long as the Gospel is demonstrated in godly lives, the claim of Christ is unanswerable.

15. So they sent them from the council chambers while they discussed the matter among themselves. 16. "What are we going to do with these men?" they asked. "There's no denying they have performed a tremendous miracle, besides everyone in Jerusalem knows about it. 17. However, we might be able to keep it from spreading any further if we warn them it will go hard with them if they do it again."

WARN. The council is baffled. The prisoners are escorted outside while the leaders try to figure out what can be done. No law had been broken by the healing, and the miracle had made the apostles popular with the people. But they can't permit them to go on telling everyone how they crucified their own Messiah. The Sadducees would not want them teaching that Jesus had risen from the grave, a truth they now seem powerless to deny. If they could have refuted it, they would have done so on the spot. The public is apparently ready to believe Jesus is alive, for as yet, the authorities have not produced His dead body. The healing of the man seemed to confirm that He had indeed risen.

18. So they called them back in again and told them that under no circumstances were they to speak or do any teaching about the name of Jesus. 19. But Peter and John were ready with their reply: "We will leave it for your consciences to decide whether we should obey God or you. 20. As for us, we cannot possibly refrain from telling of the great things we have seen and heard."

REPLY. Summoning the prisoners back into the chambers, the council commands them not to mention the name of Jesus again, publicly or privately. But the "ignorant" fishermen are supplied with divine wisdom. "We will obey God rather than men," they say, cleverly knowing that if the council were faced with the same choice, that is what it would say. If you were in our shoes, they are saying, would you obey God or man? Your own consciences must surely agree that we are obliged to speak the things God has shown us. Peter is remembering the Great Commission, that it was a direct command. The prohibitions of men don't carry any weight when they conflict with God's commands. To obey men in such a case would amount to unfaithfulness to God.

"That sounds like open defiance. How will the council react?"

21. After more threats, the council let them go. They were at a loss to know how to punish them in the face of aroused public opinion. All of the people were praising God for what happened, 22. inasmuch as the man on whom this miracle of healing had been performed was over 40 years old.

THREATS. What a sight! Imagine 70 or more of Israel's greatest leaders confounded by two laymen, uneducated fishermen at that. The council is confused. First, they have the men removed. Then, they admit their helplessness to each other. All agree their only weapon is threats. So they command silence from men who are aflame with the thrill of Christ! What a spot to be in. To have ignorant fishermen use Scripture and logic against them was humiliating indeed. If the Sanhedrin thought this ban on Jesus' name would work, they were quickly disillusioned. Peter fearlessly says they will not keep quiet. Note the change in Peter. Some weeks before he cowardly denied all knowledge of Jesus, now look at him! He's invincible before the enemy. That's what Christ's Spirit does for a man.

OPINION. Despite Peter's open defiance, the council does nothing but repeat its threats. Public opinion was such they feared to act. Peter's appeal to their consciences didn't help any. The council is powerless to crush these nobodies from Galilee. They hesitated to stir public indignation, for the crowds clearly believed the miracle was wrought in the power of God. The frustrated council turns them loose.

It was a bad mistake. Now it appears the authorities fear the disciples' power and were afraid to persecute them. This greatly encouraged the Christian colony. On the day of Pentecost, multitudes were convicted by Peter's words and came to Jesus. But here, in the council chamber the same facts stated in the same power bring not one person to Christ. Why? The power of the Spirit never overrules the will of man. His working merely brings out what is already in the heart (Heb. 6: 7,8). In this case, bitterness.

"Surely that seemed like a great victory for the Gospel?"

23. Just as soon as they were set free, Peter and John returned to their friends and reported all that the chief priests and elders had said to them. 24. When the believers heard it, they joined together as one man to offer this prayer:

"O great and sovereign Lord, You are the Maker of heaven and earth and the sea, and all that is in them."

RETURNED. While the apostles were on trial, the baby church went to prayer. Peter's wisdom and their deliverance came as a result. Once released, the apostles rushed to their friends with good news. Now it is clear that the two groups, the church and Israel's hierarchy, are headed for deadly conflict. In a sense, the apostles made fools of the Sanhedrin and that could only lead to trouble. Beyond this, Peter and John were released under the most dire threats. For the moment, the church continues as a Jewish sect. The believers worship in the temple and meet in the synagogues. As yet they are not called Christians, but "followers of the way." That is, they follow that way of life taught by Jesus.

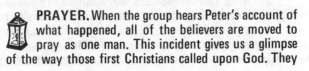

PRAYER. When the group hears Peter's account of what happened, all of the believers are moved to pray as one man. This incident gives us a glimpse of the way those first Christians called upon God. They do not address Jesus, even though they know He lives within them. They continue addressing their prayers, as they did in the synagogues, to God, using the traditional language of the Hebrew Scriptures. Their ground of confidence is the power of God as the Creator of heaven and earth. They approach Him on the basis that His power is now operating in their behalf. From their prayer we gather they sense danger and distress lie ahead of them. But surely the power of almighty God is greater than the power of an enraged Sanhedrin. That will be the basis of their boldness.

25. "By the Holy Spirit You spoke these words through the mouth of Your servant David:

> **'Why did the Gentiles rage, and the people cherish such foolish dreams? 26. See how the kings of the earth align themselves, and how the rulers join together against the Lord and against His Messiah.'**

27. For it is a fact that in this very city Herod and Pontius Pilate met together, along with the Gentiles and the people of Israel to make common cause against Your holy Servant Jesus, Your Messiah. 28. However, they were merely fulfilling that which Your power and wisdom had already decreed."

DECREED. The persecution of the disciples, brings to mind the opening verses of the 2nd Psalm, which the Jews had come to ascribe to David. David looked forward with astonishment to a time when the Gentiles (Pilate and the Romans), the people (Israel), the kings (Herod), and the rulers (Annas and Caiaphas) would gather as a deadly combine against God's Messiah. The disciples look back to see how the crucifixion of Jesus by this confederacy was according to the plan of God. And how it was overruled by God's sovereign power when He raised Jesus from the dead. Now the disciples are being persecuted, as was their Master. However, if all human powers combined are not enough to frustrate the plan of God, then what can keep the disciples from carrying out God's will? Since they have been released by the Sanhedrin, they regard their enemies are also under God's control, and that their arrest was part of God's plan. They know they are God's servants as surely as was Jesus.

29. "And now, O Lord, take note of their threats and enable us, Your servants, to declare Your word boldly. 30. And as we do, stretch forth Your hand to heal. Grant that signs and wonders might be performed through the name of your Holy Servant Jesus."

BOLDLY. Delivered from the hand of the rulers, the disciples reason that the combined powers of men are futile against God. Thus they ask Him to do two things: (1) restrain the rulers from carrying out their threats, (2) grant supernatural powers enabling them to perform signs as they preach the gospel. Having God bind your enemies and simultaneously give you power to perform signs, should make even the shiest Christian bold. Some reader might look at these passages and say, "Why can't we be like that?" Ah, we're at the other end of the church age, the close of the gospel era. In these days of apostasy, there is neither the holding back of the enemy nor supernatural signs. With the approach of the tribulation period, it is more likely to be true that "he that endureth unto the end shall be saved." A man may have his hands full hanging on to his faith. What signs do appear are more likely to be from the enemy than from God. Satan will counterfeit the return of Jesus, masquerading as an "angel of light," hoping to "deceive the very elect" (2 Cor. 11:13-15; Matt. 24:24).

WONDERS. The disciples had no N.T. Scripture. No one had gotten around to writing down the teachings of Jesus. So they needed credentials to prove they were His representatives, that their words were actually His words. The Jews required a sign as proof a person spoke for God (1 Cor. 1:22). Since the

Jewish people were accustomed to thinking of Jesus as the Healer, the same sign (healing) was used to prove that Christ was speaking through His disciples. In the interval between the first announcements of the apostles and the giving of the N.T. in writing, God used wonders (mostly healings) to confirm His truths. Thus wonders and the apostles went together in those days, i.e., ". . .they went forth and preached everywhere, the Lord working with them, and CONFIRMING THE WORD with signs following" (Mk. 16:20). Once the Holy Spirit canonized the N.T. writings, wonders were no longer necessary. He Himself certifies His own word by the internal witness to men's hearts.

JUDAISM	CHRISTIANITY
tradition	signs
1400 years old	brand new

SIGNS. The church needed help in getting started. It was hard for Jews (to whom the gospel first came) to see how a tiny new movement started by a crucified Carpenter-rabbi, and composed of fishermen and peasants, could REPLACE the giant of Judaism. For 1400 years God made Judaism the custodian of His revelation and the only access to Himself. Now, all of a sudden, a handful of uneducated people claim that the great Israeli program founded by Moses, is no longer His instrument of revelation. They said it was replaced by life in Christ Who was raised from the dead and operated in the Spirit. Such a message was fantastic, ridiculous. It needed heavenly confirmation—at first, anyway. Thus, signs and miracles were the credentials of Christianity until it became clear that God had set aside Judaism. With the destruction of Jerusalem in 70 A.D. it was very clear. The use of signs had all but disappeared by then.

"Did God honor that request?"

31. When they ended this prayer, the place in which they had gathered rocked to and fro. Immediately they were filled with the Spirit and began to speak forth God's Word with boldness.

ROCKED. The disciples didn't have to wait for an answer. It came immediately and directly. As on the day of Pentecost, God used physical phenomenon to communicate His intentions. The swaying building was His reply. That did it. The thrill of Christ again surged through the believers. They were once more raptured with joy in the Lord. As the **awareness** of His presence flooded their beings, they were **filled** with the Spirit. The same obsession which gripped them on the day of Pentecost, returned. Unable to contain themselves, they rush from the place to declare God's Word. Note the absence of tongues. The language confirmation is not needed now. They **know** Jesus is in them. See again how the filling is separate from the baptism into Christ. That can occur but **once**, whereas there can be **many** fillings. The baptism is the beginning of the new life, while fillings are but rapturous events in that life. The shaking building pictured the effect the gospel was to have on people and nations in the days ahead.

"How was the communal experiment working by now?"

32. The entire body of believers was united as one mind and one heart. Not one of them regarded any of his possessions as his own, but considered everything the property of the fellowship. 33. The apostles enjoyed great power as they testified to the resurrection of the Lord Jesus, and all the brotherhood basked

in the favor of God. 34. There was not a needy person among them, for those who owned farms or houses, sold them, 35. and gave the money to the apostles to be shared as the different ones had need.

SOLD. Luke is not merely repeating the words which he used at the close of chapter two. The spirit of oneness still exists among the believers, showing up most clearly in the matter of private property. Each person put his assets at the disposal of the fellowship. Landowners converted their holdings to cash for easier distribution. For a time, not a single person suffered want, though it is known that there was considerable poverty in Jerusalem in those days. The apostles received the money, but probably delegated the task of distribution while they preached the gospel. As they declared the Word, God honored their request for signs and wonders. Dr. Luke wants us to picture this scene, with its amazing oneness, as he prepares to contrast the attitudes of Barnabas and Ananias.

"Any specific examples of those who sold their property?"

36. Now at this time there was a Levite from Cyprus by the name of Joseph. The apostles renamed him, Barnabas, an Aramaic name which means "Son of Encouragement." 37. This Barnabas owned a tract of land and sold it and laid the sales price at the apostles' feet.

BARNABAS. Luke cites Barnabas as an example of the generous spirit, not because his gift was necessarily the largest contribution made, but because we are to meet him later as Paul's missionary companion. He was born on the island of Cyprus, 60 miles off the coast of Syria, and belonged to the tribe of Levi. By this time, Levites could own land. The generous spirit of Joseph was so inspiring, the apostles nicknamed him, "The man who encourages others." That is the meaning behind the Aramaic word, Barnabas. Likely this disposal of his business affairs left him free to devote his life to the gospel. It should be noted that no believer HAD to sell his property. The program was voluntary, with love for each other the only motivating force. This is a most important observation when we consider the next man.

"With whom did Dr. Luke wish to contrast Barnabas?"

5 1. But there was another man named Ananias, who with his wife Sapphira, sold a piece of property. 2. Secretly they retained a part of the purchase price. With the full knowledge of his wife, Ananias brought the remainder of the sales price to the apostles, pretending it was the total amount received.

BUT. Satan isn't happy to see Christians united. So he looks for a weak spot. He had no trouble finding one because those earliest Christians weren't perfect. Luke records an event which keeps us from overestimating the oneness and sanctity of that first Christian body. When Barnabas sold his estate, he gave all the proceeds to the Lord. He was greatly praised for his action by the others. When Ananias and Sapphira saw his halo and fame, they became jealous. Then it was that Satan inspired them to do as Achan did when Israel was starting out as a conquering nation (Joshua 7:10-26). The sin of covetousness caused them to perform a lie in order to appear great in the eyes of men. The story of Ananias is to the book of Acts what the story of Achan is to the book of Joshua.

RETAINED. No one was under obligation to sell his property. And after selling it, he was still not obliged to give any or part of the proceeds to the apostles. Actually it was nobody's business what Ananias and Sapphira did with their property or the money derived from its sale. The evil was in wanting the church to think they were matching Barnabas' generosity. Therefore, their motives were the opposite of Barnabas'. Their sin was that of deliberate misrepresentation for the sake of religious pretense. Now Satan had a foothold. With these two believers under his influence, he had a good chance of breaking up the sweet communal program. There's no telling what else he could lead them to do once he had them in his pocket.

3. Whereupon Peter said to him, "Ananias, how could you let Satan capture your heart? He has lead you to lie to the Holy Ghost by misrepresenting the sales price. 4. Before you sold the land, was it not yours? And after it was sold, were not the proceeds still yours to do with as you pleased? Why then did you allow this evil to get started in your heart? You haven't lied to men—you have lied to God!"

LIED. Ananias sought to deceive the Christian community in an attempt to gain a reputation for generosity. Inasmuch as God's presence was so real in this fellowship, it amounted to an attempt to deceive God's Spirit. Empowered to detect the evil, Peter rebukes Ananias with words which describe the enormity of his crime. His lie was not in language, but in conduct. It was a sacrilegious fraud. These two believers professed to be God's servants, but they were being used of the devil. Satan was finally successful in causing trouble in the fellowship. As the "father of lies," the devil was the real author of Ananias' sin. Yet, it was always within Ananias' power to shun his suggestion. Satan cannot force anyone to sin. It should be noted that we do not see this kind of discernment being exercised today. Apparently this was a special working of the Lord through Peter.

HEART. Peter knew of Satan's subtlety. He had once been the devil's agent when he suggested the Lord avoid the cross (Matt. 16:23). Satan had flooded his heart too. He knew the devil planted the idea in Ananias' mind, using his jealous feelings to supply the motivation. Likely this man and his wife could give all sorts of reasons why their action was justified. Satan works that way. Perhaps, when the actual cash was in his hands, that was Ananias' moment of decision. As he began to scheme and plan the deception, he became more and more filled with the spirit of Satan (see under John 13:27). See—Christians can also become filled with the spirit of Satan. Note how Christ's Ghost and God are viewed as one by comparing vss. 3 & 4. A lie to the Spirit is a lie to God.

"How did Ananias react to this sudden exposure of his sin?"

5. The moment Ananias heard these words he collapsed and died on the spot. All who were within hearing distance of the incident were awestruck. 6. Immediately the younger men came in, and after wrapping his body, took it out and buried it.

AWESTRUCK. Peter did not mean for Ananias to die. But God used this deception as an exemplary case to teach the baby church of His holiness. He wanted His people to have a horror of sin. This was to stand for all time as an example of God's hatred of religious hypocrisy. So, as Achan was stoned, Ananias dropped dead on the spot. His "ghost," as the King James translators refer to it, departed from his body. He was removed from this life to be with Christ in the Spirit. The effect was immediate, filling the church with fear. If Ananias could be struck down for religious pretense, think what other sins of hypocrisy would be worthy of the same. It is a good thing for us this was an initiatory case to show God's feelings, for if He did that today, preachers and people would be dropping like flies.

BURIED. What really killed Ananias? The sudden exposure of his sin? The realization he had violated God's holiness? No doubt his guilt had already begun to weigh heavily. To have it all come out before the whole church, may have been too much for him. No matter what actually produced his death, it was divine action. We don't have to know the mechanics. No sooner did Ananias collapse, than the younger men of the Christian community came in to remove his body for burial. This was the custom in that climate where corruption sets in quickly and no red tape hindered the process. Besides, it would have been difficult for Peter to minister with a corpse on the floor.

"Wasn't Ananias' wife as guilty as he?"

7. About three hours later Ananias' wife came in completely unaware of what had happened. 8. "Tell me woman," said Peter, "did you sell your land for such and such a price?" "Yes," she replied, "that was the price." 9. Then Peter said to her, "How could you and your husband even think of tempting the Spirit of the Lord with something like this? Listen! Do you hear those men coming through the door? Well, they are just returning from burying your husband. Now they will have to carry you out too." 10. Immediately she collapsed at his feet and died. When the young men came in and found her dead also, they carried her out and buried her beside her husband. 11. Because of these things an awesome fear swept the church, extending even to those who merely heard about them.

WIFE. It may be that Peter was shocked when Ananias fell dead at his feet. If so, he has now had three hours to think about it. Perhaps the story of Achan came to mind and he realized God was dealing severely with this first sin in the church. He becomes convinced that Ananias' death was divine judgment. So when Sapphira comes in he says nothing to her about her husband, but gives her a chance to tell the truth. But she lies, revealing her part in the conspiracy. Peter expects her to share her husband's fate and boldly says so. In accusing the pair of putting the Spirit's forbearance to the test, it shows they knew what they were doing. It was a deliberate, preconceived act, therefore an insult to the omniscience of God.

FEAR. In obeying Jesus' prompting to deal with the pair as he did, Peter no doubt halted the progress of this sin in the baby church. Sin is the only thing which can silence the church's testimony. Persecution cannot. Modern Christians who give, expecting to receive in return, or ease their consciences, or make a display of their generosity, tread the path of Ananias and Sapphira. Fortunately God does not pronounce death for this offense today. However, it does not prevent a silenced testimony or the lack of power in one's life. The fear which spread through the baby church had a purifying effect and protected its development. It also secured a reverence for the apostles which was needed until the infant church reached a point of maturity. This is the first time the word church is mentioned in the book of Acts.

BURIED. Guilty partners in life, sad companions in death, the names of Ananias and Sapphira are remembered today as belonging to the company of Achan, Judas, and Demas. Standing as examples of what the "love of money" does to people, they are far removed from the list of martyrs who died for the cause of Christ. Perhaps it was God's mercy which took them from this life. Having yielded to Satan, they could have been used for further mischief in the Christian body. Instead of leaving them in Satan's hands "for the destruction of the flesh," God took them home (1 Cor. 5:5). With their bodies in the ground, they could no longer be the devil's instruments and were spared perhaps a worse fate.

"What was the effect of all this on the church?"

12. The apostles agreed they should keep on meeting
in Solomon's portico, where they continued to
perform many remarkable miracles in the sight of the
people. 13. This caused outsiders to keep their distance
from them, yet everyone held them in high esteem.
14. In spite of this public awe, more and more believers
were added to the group, for men and women kept
coming in increasing numbers.

MIRACLES. Having reported the first hostile act against the new church and the supernatural death of Ananias and Sapphira, Luke summarizes the happenings which followed. The apostles boldly decided to continue using Solomon's portico as a regular meeting place, for it accommodated large crowds. It was also convenient to the most popular entrance of the temple. The general atmosphere was again like that of Jesus' Galilean ministry, for the Lord continued to perform the same signs through His apostles. The crowds were expected to recognize the signs as those Jesus did during His earthly ministry. Thus they were evidence that He was alive and working through His apostles. The miracles also confirmed the authority of the Lord's apostles. It was intended that onlookers should behold the apostles' miracles and associate them with Jesus.

DISTANCE. With the deaths of Ananias and Sapphira, no phony believers were added to the fellowship. People were afraid to pretend in spiritual matters, once it was noised about that two people were slain for hypocrisy. So, for a time, the church was protected. On the one hand the Sanhedrin made no secret of its hostility toward the new church, and on the other, the apostles were covered with such great authority and power only the most genuine seekers dared to step out for Christ. This combination of awe, wonder, and fear served to screen out all who were not sincere. However, even with this highly selective screening device, many came to the Lord and the church continued to swell in numbers.

"What effect did the apostles' miracles have on the crowds?"

15. It reached the place where sick people were brought out onto the streets on cots and mats so that when Peter walked by them, at least his shadow would fall on some of them. 16. Crowds of people flocked in from the outlying villages around Jerusalem bringing with them their sick and those afflicted by demons, and every last one of them was healed.

SICK. Christianity is basically a healing religion. It was prophesied that Jesus would come as a healer. After He began His public ministry, He presented Himself as a healer (Lu. 4:16-20). He healed entire cities (Mk. 1:32-34). But the souls of men hold God's first interest. Why? No matter how fully a man's body is restored it must finally die, but the healed soul remains well forever. One is temporary, the other eternal. Thus spiritual healing must always have the priority over physical healing, for the temporal cannot take precedence over the eternal. However, the healing of men's bodies was a glorious sign of Jesus' work. What better way to symbolize the healing of a man inside a body, than healing his outside house? But to emphasize physical healing over spiritual healing, is to focus on the sign rather than the Person to Whom it points.

HEALED. Healing was the established sign of the Messiah to the Jews. Therefore to see men and women healed in wholesale fashion AFTER Pentecost, meant that the Messiah was STILL present and working through His apostles. It was Galilee all over again, with Jesus giving a REPEAT performance. The healings were miraculous, the same kind Jesus had done Himself. Not a single person was left unhealed. Everyone brought to the disciples was healed completely. So great was Jesus' working through Peter (and the others) that his shadow was as mighty to heal as the hem of Jesus' robe (Lu. 8:44). Here were the apostles displaying the total power of Jesus over sickness and demons. The crowds were expected to recognize this as a rerun of Jesus' work in Galilee, and understand HE was still alive and working through His servants (Matt. 4:23,24).

CROWDS. We don't have crowd healings today. The GIFT of healing is no longer needed as a SIGN to confirm the presence of Jesus in His servants. The Word and the Spirit are sufficient now. But are there not healings today? Yes, but of a different sort. We do not see supernatural miracles, i.e., arms restored, new teeth and eyes returned to empty sockets, and a bushy head of hair appearing on a bald scalp. Today's "miracles" are not the result of the GIFT of healing, but the ART of healing. There are "gifted" doctors, psychologists, and evangelists who know how to trigger the healing mechanism built into EVERY body. Today's healings rely on the body's power to heal itself, whereas the apostles had authority over men's bodies. Not everyone is healed by our modern evangelists, for their success depends on the cooperation (faith) of the victim. Today's evangelists are successful only as they are able to trigger the healing mechanism in others. A person with the true GIFT of healing could empty a hospital on a single visit.

"Sooner or later wouldn't the Sanhedrin have to act?"

17. Finally the High Priest and all of his associates in the Sadducee party could tolerate it no longer. Stirred by jealousy, 18. they had the apostles arrested and placed in the public jail.

ARRESTED. Their re-arrest was no surprise to the apostles. The Lord warned them they would be treated as He was. They saw Him taken out and crucified. They were prepared to expect no less. So with amazing courage they continued to bear testimony to Jesus in the temple precincts. It was the Sadducees who hated them most, since they preached the resurrection of the dead. Should that idea become popular, the Sadducees would lose their power. So, filled with jealousy, they rose up once again and swooped down on the apostles while they were preaching in Solomon's portico. This time they threw all of them in prison. When the Sanhedrin convened in the morning, they intended to take more drastic steps than on the previous occasion. Keep in mind the Sadducees dominated the Sanhedrin, though the bulk of the people were Pharisees.

19. But during the night an angel of the Lord opened the gates of the prison and lead the apostles outside. 20. "Go!" he said, "and take your stand in the temple. You are to continue telling people all about this new life!" 21a. Accordingly they proceeded to the temple at daybreak and began teaching once more.

ANGEL. When God delivers miraculously, it is for a purpose. The angel did not say, "Now run for your lives!" They were told to continue their work. The angel himself did not preach, for that task was given to Jesus' disciples exclusively. They possessed the "keys to the kingdom," whereas the angel had the "keys" to the jail. We don't know the identity of this heavenly messenger, but the walls, iron gates, and heavy chains were nothing to his touch. God is never without someone to do His bidding, even if He has to use heavenly agents. In ordering this arrest, the Sadducees acted in defiance of God. Now they were to see how futile their plans were. The haste of the apostles is noteworthy. They didn't dally in their obedience, but arrived in the temple area before sun up. What boldness! Imagine returning to the very scene of their arrest!

21b. Now when the high priest and his associates arrived at the temple to convene the Sanhedrin, which is the full senate of the nation of Israel, they sent orders to the prison to have the prisoners brought before them. 22. But when the officers arrived at the prison, they couldn't find them there. So they returned to the council with this report: 23. "The jail doors were all locked and the guards were all standing in their places, but when we opened the gates, no one was there!" 24. When the head of the temple police and the chief priests heard this, they suffered mild panic wondering to what proportions this whole business might grow.

PANIC. Before the High Priest and his followers could reconvene the Sanhedrin the next day, the apostles were back teaching in Solomon's portico. Finally the great assembly was in session ready to deal with the prisoners. The security chief was ordered to bring them to the council chambers. But when the officers reached the jail, the apostles could not be found. The doors were securely locked and the guards were still at their posts, yet the prisoners were gone. This was cause for alarm. If the apostles had the power to escape confinement, how could they be restrained from carrying their message to the people? Likely it was suspected the apostles had friends among the police, or even in the Sanhedrin itself. In any event, it now appeared the apostles had made fools of the Sadducees. This further contributed to their perplexity and distress. Such a thing put them in danger of losing their power.

25. But just then someone came in with word about the apostles: "Say! Did you know the men you put in prison are back in the temple teaching the people!" 26. With that, the chief of temple security took some officers to go get them. But they used no force, for fear of being stoned by the people. 27. When they brought them back into the council chambers, they had them stand before the Sanhedrin that the High Priest might question them.

NO FORCE. As soon as the security chief heard the apostles were still within his jurisdiction (he had charge of all temple discipline), he took some of his subordinates and fetched the apostles. Apparently he asked them to come with him. No force was used. Had the apostles elected not to accompany him, the crowd was ready to back their resistance. They could have chosen to avoid this meeting, but their arrest was in God's plan. This time their appearance was voluntary and not as prisoners. Perhaps this is why they were delivered from jail in the first place. Everything is on a different basis now. The apostles' escape was without flight. That, plus their great courage added to the confusion and perplexity of the Lord's enemies. The deliverance also brought new confidence to the apostles as can be seen from Peter's address to the council.

28. "Did we not give you strict orders," said the High Priest, "that you were never again to teach in this name! Now look what's happened—you have flooded all Jerusalem with your teaching. Obviously you intend to make us responsible for that man's death!"

ORDERS. The High Priest made three charges against the apostles: (1) they continued to mention Jesus' name after being forbidden to do so, (2) they had stirred up the entire city of Jerusalem, (3) they were trying to make the Sanhedrin guilty of shedding innocent blood. It should be noted that after Jesus was crucified ("hung on a tree"), the Jewish leaders regarded His name as accursed. Custom required that it never again be spoken. This is why they will not say "Jesus" in making their charges. Instead they refer to "this name" and "that man." Ironically, the Lord uses the lips of His enemies to declare that the apostles had successfully carried out the first part of their commission. Jesus told them to begin "in Jerusalem." Now it appears they have done the task. The High Priest says "all Jerusalem" is flooded with their teaching. If that is so, it won't be long before the next part of the commission gets underway.

"How will the apostles answer these charges?"

29. Then Peter, speaking for himself and the other apostles, replied: "We must obey God rather than men. 30. The God of our fathers sent Jesus, but you had Him killed and hung on a tree. 31. Then by His mighty power God raised Him up, exalting Him as a Prince and Savior, that He might lead this people of Israel to repentance and grant the forgiveness of their sins."

REPLIED. Speaking on behalf of the apostles, Peter repeats much of what he said to the Sanhedrin before. God sent Jesus as a Prophet, but they slew Him. What's worse, they disgraced Him. Peter mentions the extent of that disgrace. . ."hung on a tree" (Deut. 21:22). The Roman method of execution was crucifixion on a wooden cross. The Jewish method was by stoning. However, after a criminal was stoned, the Jews hung his body on a tree for the remainder of the day and commanded that his name be obliterated from the minds of the people. It was the worst form of disgrace. Peter is now referring to the wooden cross as a "tree." Thus the Jewish leaders disgraced Jesus awfully when they secured His crucifixion, hanging Him on a "tree," putting Him to open shame. Legally, He was "cut off" from Israel. Recall how, in rage, they once shouted, "Let this man's blood be upon us!" Now they are facing that solemn fact, for Peter is saying, His blood is upon you!

EXALTING. Once again Peter contrasts what the Jewish leaders did with Jesus against what God did with Him. They slew Him and dishonored Him, but God raised Him up, bestowing the utmost honor upon Him. Exalted to the rank of Prince, Jesus now is leading the Jewish people (via His Spirit) to repentance. As their Savior, He can secure the forgiveness of their sins. While the authority of the Sanhedrin was very great, it was less than that of the exalted Jesus. Therefore, says Peter we must obey the One Who has commissioned us, for His is the greater authority. God must be obeyed rather than man. What superhuman courage it must have taken to accuse the most **august** assembly of the land with the **worst** crime under heaven. Without fear, Peter blames the leaders for Jesus' death, and through them, the nation of Israel. This in spite of the fact they had the power to put him to death.

32. "What's more, we are witnesses to all this, and so is the Holy Spirit Whom God has given to those who obey Him."

WITNESSES. Peter tells the Sanhedrin that the apostles are more than eyewitnesses to their crime against Jesus and God's exaltation of Him, they are also commissioned to testify to such things. Peter next reveals the source of His boldness—the Holy Spirit (the indwelling Lord). He is aware that even as he addresses the council, the Spirit of God is simultaneously speaking to the rulers' hearts. The Sanhedrin is receiving more than a man's words, it is also being penetrated with the truth by God's Spirit. It is this awareness of the Spirit's role in witnessing that makes for Christian boldness. It is a divine partnership. The Christian speaks out for Christ, and the Spirit penetrates the prospect's heart. Peter declares that ALL who obey the gospel receive the Spirit. Why is this so? The Spirit of Christ has been poured out (like rain) upon ALL flesh (Acts 2:17). Those who obey the gospel receive Him. It's like obeying a command to turn your cup over in a rainstorm. As soon as you do, it's filled. There can be no second Pentecost, for Christ is still being poured out today, as we noted earlier.

"How would the Sadducees react to such words?"

33. Upon hearing these words, the council became so enraged it was ready to kill the apostles. 34. But then one of the rulers rose to his feet. He was a Pharisee named Gamaliel, a teacher of the law who was extremely popular with the people. He had the council put the apostles outside the chambers while he addressed the assembly.

GAMALIEL. Seated on the council was Gamaliel, the Rabban. He was the greatest law teacher of the day and grandson of the famous Hillel, founder of Israel's strongest school of religion. His title of Rabban, higher than that of Rabbi, was conferred on very few Jewish leaders. The apostle Paul, was one of his students (22:3). He may have been present at this meeting, for he was a member (26:10). Even though the Sadducees are enraged to the point of enacting the death penalty, they dare not take such action without the support of the Pharisees. It was dangerous politics to go around them. They were extremely popular with the people, though a minority on the council. Recognizing the apostles also had the favor of the crowds, this powerful Pharisee is about to give his advice in the matter. It must have tickled him to see the apostles making the Sadducees look foolish.

"Such a great man would surely have keen advice."

35. "Men of Israel," he began, "don't act too hurriedly in deciding what to do with these men. 36. Some time ago a fellow named Theudas appeared on the scene. He claimed to be somebody, as you recall, and managed to get about 400 people to follow him. But he was killed and all of his followers were scattered and nothing ever came of his movement."

THEUDAS. When the apostles had been escorted from the council chamber, Gamaliel addressed the Sanhedrin. He warned his fellow members against any rash action. He spoke as a Pharisee, for the Pharisees held that God needed no help from men in the execution of His plans. Since it was his belief that anything God didn't establish could not survive, he means to ask the council to refrain from taking any action at all. First, he cites the case of Theudas. We know nothing of this man historically, but he was probably one of the many insurgent leaders who arose in Palestine shortly after the death of Herod the Great in 4 B.C. This man's attempt ended in his own destruction after which his movement evaporated.

37. "Then later on, during the days of the census, along came Judas the Galilean. He too was successful in getting people to join his rebellion, but then he was also killed and all of his followers scattered. 38. So here is my advice—let these men alone. Let them do what they will, for if what they are planning and teaching is merely a human effort, it will be overthrown soon enough. 39. But if God is behind them, you will not be able to defeat them. Instead, you could find yourselves fighting against God."

ADVICE. Gamaliel feels he has laid the proper groundwork for the advice he wishes to give. He has cited two instances where movements have disappeared shortly after their leaders were killed. He suggests the same thing will happen to Jesus' followers. However, because unusual signs accompany this movement, he qualifies his advice. If it is not of God, he says, it will come to nothing. But should it prove to be of God, then the council risks fighting against Him. This notable leader is to be credited for acknowledging God as the Supreme Planner of history, but his advice holds true only in the long run. It sometimes takes centuries for God's will to be revealed in this way. It would be awkward to apply Gamaliel's principle that survival means divine backing on a short range basis, especially today when the cults are flourishing. In time, though, we know these cults will be defeated. If Gamaliel's pupil, Saul of Tarsus, was present, he was not one to take such advice. He was the kind who made history rather than waiting for it to reveal God's hand. He was a man of action. Later, when this same council acts to stone Stephen, Saul will shun Gamaliel's advice to participate in the forefront of the execution himself (Acts 7:58).

40. The council took his advice. After calling the apostles back into the chamber, they had them flogged. Then they let them go with a stern warning that they were never again to speak in the name of Jesus.

FLOGGED. That Gamaliel was speaking for the rest of the Pharisees, must have been evident to the Sadducees. Therefore, the council decided to accept his advice. They didn't have much choice. It would have been unsafe for them to execute the apostles without the support of the Pharisees. Still they weren't about to let them go without some kind of punishment. So they had them severely beaten. At least the Sadducees got some satisfaction out of that. The apostles had indeed disobeyed their gag order. This type of beating was regarded as particularly disgraceful. It left the victim bleeding and badly wounded. Most likely they received the "forty stripes save one," as per the instructions of Deut. 25:3.

"Wouldn't that tend to discourage the apostles?"

41. The apostles left the council chamber rejoicing that they had been counted worthy to suffer such indignity for the sake of Jesus' name. 42. And every day, both in the temple and in house after house, they kept right on teaching and preaching Jesus as the Messiah.

REJOICING. The apostles had stared into fierce faces in that council chamber. They heard the direst threats made against them. And those threats were backed by a healthy sampling of the Sadducees' sincerity—severe beatings. But far from being discouraged, they marched from the chamber with their faces beaming like children at a picnic. The Lord had warned them they would participate in His sufferings, now they had. Of course, what they suffered was nothing compared to what He had endured for them, but it was a start. Each time they had the privilege of suffering for Him, it filled them with great joy. Refusing to let any human power keep them from their holy mission, they kept right on preaching Christ in defiance of the Sanhedrin's order. They were ready to die for Him if necessary. That determination filled their souls with glory. It will do the same for any Christian with similar determination today. Note how the house-to-house method has been successful then even from the beginning.

6

1. During the period when the disciples were growing in number, a problem arose between the Greek-speaking Jews and those who were native Hebrews. Those who spoke Greek only, complained that their widows were not getting a fair share of the daily allocation of food.

COMPLAINED. Long before the church was founded at Jerusalem, there was a rift between those Jews who were born in Palestine and spoke Aramaic, and those born in Greek-speaking countries. The language difference made for tension between them. With so many Jews coming to Christ in those days it was natural that some of them would be Hellenists or Greek-speaking Jews. The church had been going for some time, perhaps months, when those feelings of tension erupted once again. This time it occurred among the believers themselves. While it may have been nothing more than a suspicion, the Hellenists complained that their "widows" were being disadvantaged because the distribution of the food was in the hands of the "Hebrews." This is the second bit of trouble Satan has been able to stir up in the church. It is not too hard to sow suspicion where there are natural differences in people.

"How will the apostles handle this complaint?"

2. So the Twelve summoned the whole body of disciples together to deal with the situation. "It wouldn't make sense," they said, "for us to neglect the Word to administer a food program, 3. so you brethren look among yourselves and choose seven men you can trust. Make sure they are Spirit-filled and show good common sense. Then we will put them in charge of this matter. 4. That way we can continue to devote our time to prayer and getting out the Word."

SUMMONED. Peter is undoubtedly the spokesman. He summons all the disciples remaining in the city for a meeting. By now a good many of the believers had returned to their own lands. The Feast of Pentecost has been concluded. Note that Peter does not say, "The charges are ridiculous," or "We'll appoint a committee to investigate." Instead he acts with wisdom. He knows how suspicion works. Besides the charges might possibly be true. However, unity is the important thing. He doesn't want Satan upsetting the church with a petty thing like this, so he acts as if the charges **might** be true and sets forth a plan to take care of it. The difficulty is trivial. Christian love prompts Peter to handle it generously. Satan can wreck a church with little matters. All he needs is a seed of suspicion. Then he blows it out of proportion so that division results and the work of the Lord suffers.

LOOK. See how Peter makes no attempt to control the affair. He puts it in the hands of the church without favoring any group. Neither does he dictate what selection should be made, stating only the kind of men required. The number seven might have been used because of its sacred associations. It is the **character** of the chosen officials that is vital here. Three qualifications are stated: (1) they were to be men with good reputations, people of integrity as well as trustworthy; (2) they were to be spiritually-minded, filled with the awareness of Jesus. It is this awareness (fulness) that makes us think, act, and speak as we should; (3) they were to show practical wisdom equal to the demands of the office. How helpful it would be if this precedent were observed in church appointments today.

PRAYER. Observe how the apostles were determined to give the priority to spiritual matters. They were aware of their call and how vital it was to stay close to Jesus in order to carry it out. It is the devil's trick to keep modern pastors busy doing good things in order to keep them from the best. The pastor of a successful church today has to be everything from a psychologist to a building contractor. Little time is left for prayer and digging into the Word. The apostles refused to be business administrators. They felt it wrong to neglect the spiritual for the temporal, hence the election of the deacons. They were willing to delegate a great deal of authority to others rather than allow themselves to be taken from the higher task of feeding men's souls.

"What did the assembly think of this suggestion?"

5. The whole assembly was pleased with the apostles' proposal, so they chose Stephen, a man full of faith and of the Holy Spirit, Philip, Prochorus, Nicanor, Timon, Parmenas, and Nicolas of Antioch, a gentile convert to Judaism who was now a Christian. 6. Then they presented them to the apostles, who prayed for them and commissioned them by the laying on of hands.

CHOSE. Luke gives us the names of the seven men. The most prominent is Stephen. Luke will devote half of this chapter and all of the next one to this man. His unusual faith and spiritual character made him outstanding, which accounts for the church choosing him first of all. All commentators agree that Philip is the same person who preached the gospel in Samaria after the death of Stephen. He is mentioned later where it is specifically stated he is "one of the seven" (21:8). The history of the other five is unknown to us. Luke strangely singles out Nicolas, giving his place of origin, Syrian Antioch. He wasn't even a Jew. Note that all of the names are Greek, which suggests they belonged to the complaining Hellenists. If they are, it reveals a generous spirit on the part of those Christians. Their great humility is seen in their eagerness to settle any problems.

HANDS. The selected men were presented to the apostles for approval. See how the apostles made the actual appointment to office. The commissioning was ceremonial. After praying for them they laid hands on them. This was an O.T. means for expressing identification, blessing, or the commissioning of successors. (Lev. 1:4, etc.) Done before the assembly, it amounted to appointing them as deputy apostles. That was a high office. The act was a sign only, it had no efficacy of its own. In no way did it impart anything of the Spirit, for these men were ALREADY "Spirit-filled" (vs. 3). It has been traditional to call these men deacons, limiting their function to financial matters. But they were also to minister the Word. Stephen will give a good account for himself as a defender of the faith. Philip will excel as an evangelist. Perhaps the best term for them is "ministers." The same Greek word is used in connection with the apostles. They were "deacons" of the Word.

7. After this, the Word of God enjoyed an even wider influence. The number of disciples gained in Jerusalem increased greatly, with a host of temple priests embracing the faith.

INCREASED. The apostles' quick handling of the food problem removed a dangerous threat. Where there is tension, the Lord cannot work through His people. God's business requires unity of spirit among believers. That's why Peter was willing to answer the Hellenists' complaint so generously. He knew the success of the church depended on maintaining the bond of peace (Eph. 4:3). Thus Satan suffered another defeat.

God stepped in to deal with the Ananias and Sapphira affair, but this time the apostles knew what to do. With the easing of tensions, the apostles and their deputies devoted themselves to increased preaching. The unity of spirit made the Word so effective the result was a vigorous expansion of the church. So great was their spiritual power, that many of the temple priests turned to Jesus.

PRIESTS. It sounds great to have the Word reaching into the temple with such power that a large number of priests embraced Christ. Actually it was a new threat. Though they turned to Jesus, they did not quit their temple jobs. With so many of them embracing the gospel, there was now the risk of the church being drawn into the temple program. That would be unhealthy. The church would then lose its identity as a new way of life. The Lord wanted His church utterly divorced from the ceremonies and rituals of Judaism. He wanted His people to look INWARDLY to Him. They were His temple now (1 Cor. 6:19). Christianity has nothing to do with the OUTWARDNESS of Judaism (Jo. 4:24). Therefore, it is time to cause a sharp division between the temple and the new church—and God has just the man for the job. We should note that these priests were those with common jobs about the temple. The chief priests remained the dedicated enemies of Christ.

"How would the Lord go about isolating the church from Judaism?"

8. Stephen, full of grace and power, was performing great miracles and signs among the people.

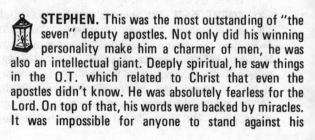

STEPHEN. This was the most outstanding of "the seven" deputy apostles. Not only did his winning personality make him a charmer of men, he was also an intellectual giant. Deeply spiritual, he saw things in the O.T. which related to Christ that even the apostles didn't know. He was absolutely fearless for the Lord. On top of that, his words were backed by miracles. It was impossible for anyone to stand against his wisdom. He was undefeatable, a powerhouse for Christ. This would explain why he was the first to be chosen as a "deacon." Next to Peter, he was the most popular Christian of that day. He is the one God has raised up to cause a break between the temple program and the church. It will be a sharp break. The break between the new Christians and the temple will be quite pronounced once Stephen's work is done.

PERFORMING. Stephen's ministry is remarkable. He won't last long. He will appear in the text for this brief moment, then he will be stoned to death. But this will not shorten his reward in any way. He will be like one of the workmen who went into the vineyard at the last hour (Matt. 20:8-10). It is in that parable of the vineyard that we learn that HOW LONG a person is on the job has no bearing on what he receives from the Lord. God needed a man to create a division between Judaism and the church. He used the great mind of this man to frame the last appeal to Israel, **as a nation**, to consider Jesus as the Messiah. His arguments were so irrefutable and unanswerable, that the furor they caused, produced the final break between Judaism and the church. The city of Jerusalem would now be turned against the Christians.

9. But there were those who opposed him. On one occasion some men of "The Freedmen" synagogue, which served the Cyrenians and Alexandrians as well as those from Cilicia and Asia, tried to debate with Stephen. 10. But the Holy Spirit inspired him with such wisdom they were no match for him.

SYNAGOGUE. In every major city throughout the world there were religious centers called synagogues. Here Jews would gather for the reading and exposition of their Scriptures. Jerusalem had many of these synagogues. Some accounts say several hundred of them. When Jews would come to the city for the annual feasts, they would collect in those synagogues which represented their native countries, and employed their languages and customs. "The Freedmen" synagogue appears to have been a large one serving those who were freed slaves or born free as Roman citizens in the countries named above. The language of this synagogue would be Greek, for the people were Hellenists. The mention of Cilicia suggests this may have been Paul's synagogue before he was converted. He came from Tarsus in Cilicia. Stephen, if he were a Hellenist, would have also used this synagogue.

DEBATE. In this "Freedmen" synagogue, Stephen stood up and delivered a penetrating testimony for Jesus. Then some of the members (Pharisees undoubtedly) took issue with him, attempting to dispute his words. But they were powerless before his Spirit-filled utterances. It is possible that Saul, the brilliant young rabbi trained by Gamaliel, was among those attempting to refute the gifted Stephen. If so, he felt the sting of defeat. We are not told the subject of the disputation. However, Stephen's answer in the next chapter leads us to understand it was the Messiahship of Jesus. The knowledge, eloquence, and healing miracles of Stephen undoubtedly provoked these unbelieving Jews to jealousy. Some may have even known him personally and were envious of his wisdom and charm.

"How did these defeated Jews handle their wounded pride?"

11. In retaliation they secretly bribed some men to perjure themselves and spread a false report: "We have heard this man say blasphemous words against Moses and against God!"

REPORT. Nothing makes the soul more furious than wounded pride. So, defeated in debate, the synagogue leaders take another course of action. They hire informers to spread the word that Stephen was saying blasphemous words against Moses and God. Blasphemy was punishable by death. Actually they didn't have to manufacture lies. They merely twisted what he said to make it appear in the worst light. This is a most subtle form of attack. A defense is complicated when truth and falsehood are entwined. It is likely true that Stephen said Jesus' words superseded those of

Moses. They did. Since Jesus also said that temple worship was to be discontinued in favor of "worship in spirit and in truth," similar statements by Stephen could be interpreted as an attack on God. To the average Jew, the temple was God's house. Stephen was apparently repeating much of what Jesus said about obsoleting the temple. Now it was being twisted to frame charges against him, even as his Master had been framed before him.

12. Armed with these accusations, the synagogue leaders were able to stir up the people of the city, the elders, and the teachers of the Law. Then they made their move against Stephen. After securing his arrest, they had him brought before the council. 13. There they presented more witnesses who declared, "This man refuses to stop speaking against this holy place and the Law. 14. We have heard him say that Jesus the Nazarene will destroy this temple and change the customs handed down to us by Moses."

ARREST. Stephen's words before the synagogue so inflamed the leaders they aroused the mobs and arranged for him to be brought to trial before the nation's highest tribunal—the Sanhedrin. Here he would be in a position to address the entire nation through its leaders. His words will be God's final invitation to Israel to repent and receive her Messiah. If she refuses, the curtain will come down on the first act of God's three part drama: (1) Jerusalem, (2) Samaria, (3) uttermost parts of the world. The Pharisees have now joined with the Sadducees. Stephen's words about the temple awakened their hatred. 'Till now they enjoyed watching the Sadducees squirm over the truth of Jesus' resurrection. Both parties are now ready to see Stephen silenced for good. The city is behind them, for the residents resented his words against the temple. The pilgrim traffic of the temple affected all those living in Jerusalem. To suggest its destruction would win Stephen a town full of enemies. The rejection of Stephen will end Phase 1 of the Great Commission.

DESTROY. Apparently Stephen not only repeated Jesus' words about destroying the temple and raising it up again in three days, but expounded their meaning. The Pharisees could easily have him quoting Jesus as saying, "I will destroy this physical temple in three days and replace it with a spiritual one." That would abolish the temple entirely. However, we know Jesus was speaking of the "temple of His body" (Jo. 2:19,21). At this time most of the disciples attended the temple services and were regarded as devout Jews by the Pharisees. But Stephen's preaching declared the wiping out of the whole temple system, replacing it with a spiritual program—life in the Spirit. Stephen's sharp mind had apparently grasped this truth before the apostles: therefore, he is the only one in trouble because of it. To the apostles, Christianity was still a part of Judaism and temple worship a vital obligation. Yet it was true. The gospel spelled the end of the sacrificial system and the ceremonial Law. There is no way to reconcile the OUTWARDNESS of Judaism with the INWARDNESS of salvation.

15. All those in the council chamber found they couldn't take their eyes from Stephen's face. They stared at him transfixed, for his features had taken on the radiance of an angel.

RADIANCE. Everyone attending the trial was eager to see how Stephen would handle himself in this situation. He was a man of great power. Would he be able to deliver himself from the mighty Council of Israel? Or would he be afraid? If they were looking for signs of fear on his face, they were disappointed. Instead they saw his features transfigured so that he took on the appearance of an angel. His radiance must have become brighter and brighter as the presence of the Lord became increasingly real to him. His look was that of a man beholding glory. His viewers undoubtedly sensed he was in the presence of God. If Saul was there to see those glowing eyes, we can be sure he never forgot the sight. Perhaps that inner light which glowed from Stephen's eyes burnt in his soul 'till at last he too knew what it was to stand in the holy presence of Jesus. The reality of Jesus was so great it overshadowed the presence of his enemies. Full of glory, Stephen is about to give us the longest address in the book of Acts.

7

1. Then the High Priest asked him, "Is this really so?"

SO. Caiaphas is no doubt the High Priest, the same one who presided over Jesus' trial. Jesus was arrested on identical charges and false witnesses were brought against Him, too. But when given a chance to defend Himself, the Lord said nothing. He was never convicted of anything; consequently Pilate found Him innocent. Because nothing came from the lips of the Founder of this new movement, the High Priest is hoping Stephen will say something which could be used to discredit the fast rising church in the eyes of the devout Jews. It is Christianity the Sanhedrin wants to stop, not just Stephen. The dedicated deacon is going to speak, but not to defend himself. Instead he will defend Christianity by showing it is the way God has always intended for His people to worship Him. Through Stephen, God is here giving Israel her last chance to repent **as a nation** before replacing Judaism with Christianity.

2. "Brethren and fathers! If you think God meant for our faith to be centered in this place, listen to me! Our glorious God appeared to our father Abraham when he was still living in Mesopotamia. It was before he migrated to Haran that the revelation which started our race was given to him. 3. Our race began back there when God said to him, 'Leave that country and all of your relatives and go to another land to which I shall direct you.' "

GO. The brilliant and learned Stephen will launch his argument exclusively from the sacred history of the Jews. He will use the one document they revere to show that his faith in Jewish history is as strong as theirs. His presentation will therefore be based on hallowed facts whose authority is acknowledged by all. He will review the origin of Israel from the call of Abraham to the building of Solomon's temple to show that God never at any time wanted a PERMANENT house for Himself on earth. It was ever God's intention to dwell in the hearts of His People as taught in Christianity. He will also show that from the beginning, the FORM of worship has constantly changed. So he starts off by observing that the cradle of the Jewish faith was not Palestine at all but a Gentile land beyond the great river in the East, the land of Mesopotamia (Iraq).

"Is Stephen saying that Judaism is not limited to Palestine?"

4. "It was God's call that caused him to leave the land of the Chaldeans and settle in Haran. Then, after his father died, God led him into this country where we are living today. 5. But how did he enter this land? As an owner or conqueror? No. He wasn't given an inch of this ground. Not a speck of it was ever his. Yet, God promised that one day it would be his and his descendants after him, though at the time this promise was made to Abraham, he had no children."

LAND. What made Abraham uproot himself from the land of his birth and journey to a strange place? It would have been madness had not the God of glory appeared to him in Person and summoned him. Stephen's point here is—anyone who really obeys God must "hang loose," that is, be without roots. The servant of God has to be ready to go anywhere, for God is NO respecter of **places.** Even while Abraham was floating about, he was in the center of divine blessing and protection. That in itself should prove that God's blessing is not a local matter. Stephen will ultimately say, there is no place on earth where God's favor can be localized, including the great temple built by Solomon, "for God does not dwell in houses made by human hands." Remember: Stephen is charged with blaspheming the temple.

6. "God further told Abraham that even his descendants would move to a foreign country where they would live as slaves for 400 years. 7. 'But after that time has passed,' God told him, 'I will pass judgment on the nation which enslaves them and they shall escape that place and come back and serve me here.' "

DESCENDANTS. The fact that PLACE had nothing to do with God's blessing was first exemplified in Abraham. He had no land other than by promise. And he was told that his descendants would have no land of their own either, that for centuries they would sojourn in a strange country. Yet all during that time they would still be God's chosen people. Thus, not only did Abraham have no land as his own, his children would have to leave the land promised to them and suffer as slaves for 400 years. The exile, however, would be temporary. In due time God would avenge them of their captors and bring them to worship Him in the promised land. The point? All during the time they have no place to call home, they are still the children of God, His favored people. This contradicts the idea that God's blessing was limited to Jerusalem.

8a. "And God gave Abraham a sign, a token of the agreement He had made with him. The circumcision ceremony was that sign, so Abraham circumcised Isaac on the eighth day after he was born."

CIRCUMCISION. While circumcision was practiced by the heathen nations in contact with Israel, only to Abraham and his descendants did it have spiritual significance. Note that it was GIVEN to Abraham, thereafter to become an essential part of the covenant itself. The circumcision ceremony was basic to the religion of the Jews. It was the doorway into Judaism. Therefore, Stephen is showing that the heart of the jewish religion was already functioning before there was such a thing as the "holy place." Having been charged with defaming the "holy place," he skillfully shows from the Jew's own history that before there ever was such a "PLACE," the essential conditions for the religion of Israel were already fulfilled.

"How did the patriarchs fit into Stephen's argument?"

8b. "Isaac became the father of Jacob, and Jacob the father of the twelve patriarchs. 9. But will you note how the patriarchs themselves opposed the purposes of God. They became jealous of Joseph and sold him as a slave into Egypt. But God was with him, 10. and rescued him from all of his afflictions. He granted him favor and wisdom in the sight of Pharaoh, King of Egypt, to the place where he made him governor of Egypt and in charge of all palace affairs."

PATRIARCHS. Stephen wants his listeners to see how soon the kicking against God's plan really started. Even when the nation was no bigger than 75 people, the founding fathers schemed against the program God was working out through Abraham. Their youngest brother, the noblest and best of them, they sold as a slave. Though Joseph was despised and forsaken by his brethren, God's hand was on him and raised him to the pinacle of greatness in Egypt. Despite the conniving of the patriarchs, God would see to it that the program He set in motion, when He brought Abraham from Ur of the Chaldees, would reach its proper conclusion with the coming of Christ. For that reason He manipulated the fortunes of Joseph and elevated him to the rank of Governor of Egypt. So then, as early as the household of Jacob, there was plotting against God's program. Stephen answers the charge that he has blasphemed the temple by showing how the Jews themselves have always plotted against the program of God.

"How did the Egyptian affair serve God's plan?"

11. "Then came the great famine which devastated all Egypt and Canaan and caused great suffering. Even our fathers faced starvation right here in the land. 12. But when Jacob heard that grain was to be had in Egypt, he dispatched our fathers there on that first trip. 13. It wasn't until they made the second visit to

Egypt that Joseph made himself known to his brothers and Pharaoh learned about Joseph's family. 14. Then it was that Joseph sent a message to his father Jacob inviting the entire family of 75 people to come to him in Egypt. 15. So Jacob went down into Egypt, where he and our fathers died. 16. Their bodies were afterwards carried back to Shechem and buried in the tomb which Abraham bought for a sum of money from the sons of Hamor in Shechem."

FAMINE. God used the famine to reunite Joseph with his family. When the suffering was intense in Canaan, Jacob sent his sons to Egypt to buy grain where Joseph's wisdom had garnered huge stores. They did not recognize Joseph on their first visit, says Stephen, but he did reveal himself to them on the second visit. The brilliant Stephen saw the parallel between Joseph and Christ and was even pressing that point. Truly One greater than Joseph was not recognized by his brethren when they saw Him for the first time, but will be acknowledged by them as their Deliverer when they see Him the second time. Luke has given us but a skeleton of Stephen's speech. Many details are left out. Some did not need to be stated, for the Jews were so familiar with their history the application was obvious to them.

DIED. God's Word to Abraham was partly fulfilled when his descendants went into that foreign land to dwell. The King James reads 70 persons, but the Septuagint (earliest Greek version of the O.T.) reads 75. Gen 50:13 tells us that Jacob was buried at Hebron (Mamre) rather than at Shechem (see also Gen. 23:19). But Joseph was buried there (Josh. 24:32). No doubt Stephen was making a point of the burials at Shechem to show that the bodies of the patriarchs were not on the sacred soil of Jerusalem, but in the hands of the hated Samaritans. Shechem was in Samaria. This could be another argument against the importance of PLACE in the program of God. Likely he was telescoping all the burials, but mentioning Shechem in order to stir his hostile audience. Samaria, however, is in the land of promise and it was an act of faith to have the bodies returned from Egypt to be buried there.

17. "Our national history continued with the nation growing steadily in Egypt. And when it was about time for them to depart from there in accordance with God's promise to Abraham, they had multiplied into a great number of people. 18. At last another king mounted the throne of Egypt who cared nothing for Joseph's memory. 19. This ruler viciously exploited our race, forcing our people to such hard labor they couldn't attend their children. Finally he decreed that every male child born to our people was to be cast into the river."

DEPART. The children of Israel did not leave the land of Egypt when the famine ended in Canaan. They were content to stay there and enjoy the hospitality of Pharaoh. A choice delta region had been set aside for them not far from the Egyptian court. There they grew to numbers estimated as high as 3 million people. But God wanted them in the promised land. So at an appointed time, He brought to power a new king who refused to recognize Egypt's debt to Joseph. Alarmed at the fast growth of the Israelites, he sought to repress it by forced labor and infanticide. Had not this anti-Jewish king come along, Abraham's descendants might never have thought of leaving Egypt. They were too comfortable there.

20. "About that same time Moses was born. He was an outstanding child, remarkably beautiful in the sight of God. For three months he was concealed in his father's house, 21. but finally he had to be cast out to die. However, it was done in such a way that Pharaoh's daughter found him and adopted him, raising him as her own son. 22. She saw to it that he was taught in all the wisdom of the Egyptians, so that he became skilled with words as well as a man of action."

MOSES. Moses' parents did their best to conceal their remarkable child. When at last they had to abandon him, they did it in such a way he was easily found by the king's daughter who raised him as an Egyptian prince. He received the best education the Egyptian court could provide. According to ancient historians, Stephen's words are an understatement of Moses' ability. One early writer claims Moses was the inventor of alphabet writing. Another says the Egyptians owed their entire culture to him. Philo reports him as skilled in arithmetic, geometry, music, philosophy, even poetry. While Josephus describes him as a man unique in wisdom, stature, and beauty, Moses disclaimed himself as a mighty orator. Therefore, his skill with words must refer to his logic and writing ability (Ex. 4:10).

"How will Moses figure into Stephen's argument?"

23. "Moses was almost forty years old when it occurred to him to visit the Israelites and see how things fared with his Jewish brethren. 24. He arrived in time to see one of them being badly mistreated by an Egyptian. He rushed to the aid of his Jewish brother and ended up avenging him by killing the Egyptian. 25. You see he took for granted his brethren would understand that God had raised him up to be their deliverer, but they didn't picture him that way at all. 26. The very next day he happened upon two Israelites fighting with each other. 'You shouldn't abuse each other this way,' he said to them, 'you are brothers.' 27. Whereupon the man who was in the wrong shoved him aside demanding to know, 'Who made you a ruler and judge over us? 28. Are you planning to kill me as you killed the Egyptian yesterday?' "

VISIT. God raised up two men to move Abraham's descendants out of Egypt. One was a cruel king who could cause them to become disenchanted with the country, the other was Moses who would lead them out. But the Israelites do not give up easily. They were to endure considerable suffering before they would be willing to break their attachment for Egypt. But Pharaoh was a fine instrument in God's hands. He did a good job of weaning them. Moses, raised in the palace and gifted by God, had all the qualifications—and the divine appointment—to deliver the Israelites. It is not unlikely that Moses (as did the Lord Jesus) began to suspect his role much before he was forty years of age. Apparently it was not until then that his convictions were strong enough to send him to Goshen, (the place where the Israelites were settled in Egypt) to present himself as their appointed deliverer.

UNDERSTAND. Moses visited his brethren with one thought in mind—offering himself to them as their deliverer. He was confident they would understand that God had raised him up and qualified him for the job. But of course they didn't. They wanted no part of him. Thus the chosen people set themselves to frustrate God's plan once more. Stephen is speaking to an audience that couldn't miss his point. They see at once how he is connecting the treatment Moses received when he first visited his brethren with that which Jesus received when He came to His brethren. He is saying, "If Moses, whom you revere so greatly, was once despised by the men of Israel, may it not be the same for Jesus? If Moses was once shunned as the deliverer from Egypt, may not Jesus be shunned as the Savior from sin? And if the continued rejection of Moses would have been ruinous for Israel, might not the continued rejection of Jesus be the same?"

"That must have shaken Moses!"

29. "Upon hearing those words, Moses panicked and fled to the land of Midian where he lived as an exile and became the father of two sons. 30. Then, after forty more years went by, an angel appeared to him in the flame of a burning bush in the desert region about Mount Sinai. 31. Moses was astonished at the sight. As he moved in for a closer look, he heard the voice of God saying to him, 32. 'I am the God of your fathers, the God of Abraham, Isaac, and Jacob.' This caused Moses to shake with such terror that he dared not look upon the sight any further. 33. But the Lord said to him, 'Remove your shoes for you are

standing on holy ground. 34. The suffering of My people in Egypt has been before Me continually. I have heard their cries and have come down to deliver them. Therefore, start packing—I have a job for you in Egypt.' "

FLED. Moses wasn't aware that others had seen him kill the Egyptian bully. When he found the knowledge was too widespread for comfort, he fled to a place in the Arabian desert just east of the Gulf of Akaba. There he sojourned in a strange place as did the patriarch Abraham, before him. He raised two sons, one of whom he named, "a sojourner there." This was to acknowledge that he himself had no place in that land. One day, after forty more years had gone by, he was working his flocks near the region of Mt. Sinai. Then—in that GENTILE territory—God appeared to him and called the ground HOLY. What made it holy? God's presence. Stephen mentions this to show once more that no spot on earth has any sanctity of its own. That place was holy only because God revealed Himself there. That, of course, is the central principle of the gospel. Men are holy now, for God lives in those who receive His Son.

JOB. The Lord revealed Himself as the God of Abraham, Isaac, and Jacob—not as the God of Moses. He said He was remembering His promise to the patriarchs and was about to intervene in behalf of their descendants. Stephen is hereby accusing the Sanhedrin of too much zeal for the levitical Law given by Moses. Moses was merely a cog in the machinery of which the patriarchs were the big wheels. The Sanhedrin is being reminded that Israel's origin did not date from Moses and the Law, or any of the levitical regulations given thereafter. The covenant between God and Israel dated back to the fathers, not Moses. The God Who appeared to Moses was ALREADY the God of the patriarchs and it was His promise to THEM that He was keeping. Moses was merely a part in the process of keeping that promise.

"In what other way did Stephen present Moses as a forerunner of Christ?"

35. "So now this Moses, whom the people of Israel rejected when they said, 'Who made you a ruler and judge over us?', God sent back to them to be just that—a ruler and judge. This time his commission was directly from God and he was aided by the Angel Who appeared to him in the burning bush. 36. Thus he led them out, performing signs and wonders in Egypt, in the Red Sea and in the wilderness wandering for forty years."

SENT BACK. Clearly Stephen is showing that Moses was a forerunner of Jesus the Messiah. The first time Moses went to his people, he was rejected, even as Joseph was rejected by his brethren. But the second time they saw Moses, they had no choice but to accept him. He came with too much power and authority. Moses' miracles were his credentials. It is not necessary for Stephen to supply all the details or make the application for his listeners. The Sanhedrin is painfully aware of Jesus' credentials. Many signs certified Him as God's Lamb and the Deliverer of His people. They see very clearly where Stephen's logic is leading. He is drawing a parallel between the way Moses was received by Israel and the way the Lord Jesus was received. He further hints the second coming of Christ when Israel will have no choice but to accept Him. His power and authority will be too great to refuse—as was Moses.

"How did Stephen show the Israelites' contempt for Moses, the Law, and the Land?"

37. "Did not Moses himself say to the people of Israel, 'God will raise up for you a Prophet very much like myself, and He will come from among your brethren as I did?' 38. Yes, this was the same Moses who lead the church of God in the wilderness; the one who served as the mediator between our fathers and the Angel Who spoke to him on Mt. Sinai; and the one who received the living word so it could be passed on to you. 39. And how did our ancestors receive him? They rejected him and repudiated his leadership. Wishing

themselves back in Egypt, they shoved him aside, 40. and said to Aaron, 'Make us idols that we might have gods before us. As for this Moses fellow, who brought us out of Egypt, we haven't any idea what has become of him.' 41. How much did the presence of God mean to them? Why they actually made a calf-shaped idol and offered sacrifices to it. How much did sacred customs mean to them? They held a feast in honor of this thing they made with their own hands."

DID NOT? Because Stephen intimated that Moses was only a forerunner of the Messiah, he was accused of speaking "blasphemous words" against him. Therefore, he quotes Moses to show that the Lawgiver himself said a Prophet greater than himself would one day rise from among the Jews. Stephen hadn't deprecated Moses, but the fathers of those listening to him had indeed spoken evil of him. They not only spoke words against that Prophet who was greater than Moses, they have repudiated the leadership of the Messiah Himself.

IDOLS. Stephen lists the sins of their ancestors, who, for all of God's kindness in sending a deliverer, longed for Egypt instead of the promised land. They were not satisfied with the invisible presence of God in their midst, but persuaded Aaron to make idols in Moses' absence. They preferred gods they could see to the God of the patriarchs. As far as the sacred customs were concerned, they preferred to sacrifice to an object made with their own hands. As far as the land was concerned, they were ready to abandon it before they inherited it. Neither Moses, the land, or the sacred worship of the God of Abraham meant much to the Jewish fathers in that day. Stephen is showing that long before the children of Israel entered the promised land, they had rebellious hearts. He means to show that his listeners are no less rebellious than their ancestors.

42. "Whereupon God turned away from them and gave them over to the worship of the host of heaven just as it is written in the book of the prophets:

'Was it to Me, o house of Israel, that you offered victims and sacrifices forty years in the wilderness? 43. No! It was the tent of Moloch you were carrying, and the star of your god Rephan, both of which were images you made to worship. I will also carry you beyond Babylon.' "

PROPHETS. All twelve books of the minor prophets were regarded by the Jews as one book. Stephen quotes from one of them, Amos, to show how God was well aware of the idolatrous nature of their hearts. True, they carried His tabernacle and followed His cloud, but secretly their hearts were inclined to idolatry. They were not worshipping Him ALONE. The making of the golden calf showed their hearts to be idolatrous from the beginning. Shortly after the Jews entered the promised land, they took up the worship of Moloch, an ox-head image with fire inside for consuming child sacrifices. Rephan, acknowledged as king of the heavenly deities, was the planet Saturn. Though God sent prophets to warn His people, He nonetheless let them suffer the consequences of their idolatry, the Assyrian and Babylonian captivities. Stephen is showing the unhappiness of the ancient people with a God they could not see. They insisted on having an image to worship and a holy place to gather. The reverence for the city of Jerusalem on the part of his listeners was in that same idolatrous tradition.

"Didn't the Israelites have some reminder of God's presence with them?"

44. "Now in the wilderness our fathers had a portable temple or tabernacle which served as a witness to God's covenant with them. It was constructed exactly as God wanted it, for Moses made sure it was fashioned according to the plan given him by the Angel in the Mount. 45. When God dispossessed the Gentiles, driving them out of the land before our fathers, under the leadership of Joshua, they brought the tabernacle with them. There it remained and was handed down to each succeeding generation until the time of David."

TABERNACLE. The Israelites did have a token of God's invisible presence. He Himself designed them a portable temple to symbolize His presence in their midst. Inside was a wooden box called the "Ark of the Covenant." It contained the tablets of the Ten Commandments. God wanted it extremely portable, easily put up and taken down. This feature pictured His own mobility when it comes to meeting His people. He is especially mobile when it comes to saving souls, for God must go to men—"There is none that seeketh after God." The Jews kept the tabernacle with them during those early days when they were taking possession of the land, a process which lasted until the time of King David. Stephen means to show how the Jews, though given a portable place of God's presence, rebelled against it in time, preferring a fixed site with a temple designed by man.

46. "David, who had won great favor in the sight of God, had a burning desire to build a more noble sanctuary for the presence of the God of Jacob. 47. But it was Solomon who actually built Him a house."

HOUSE. David was the darling of God's heart. God so blessed him in all that he did, he was able to bring peace to the nation. Then it was that David desired to erect a more stately sanctuary for the divine presence. But God gave the prophet Nathan a message for David. He was NOT to build the house. Instead God would make a house out of David, i.e., the "House of David," from which Jesus ultimately came. Stephen is subtly showing how Solomon, who was vastly inferior to David in the Scriptures, was the one given the **inferior** task. God promised a son of David would indeed build Him a house. Solomon's temple partly fulfilled that promise, but it was more truly fulfilled when Jesus came to build God a house made of people, His church (Eph. 2:21-22). Even Solomon said that God did not dwell in the temple he had built (1 Ki. 8:27). Stephen is not decrying Solomon's temple, but the fact that his fellow Jews were limiting God's presence to one place on earth, something He forbad David to do. It is remarkable how much church truth was known to Stephen. His knowledge approaches that of Paul.

"Was Solomon's temple really God's house?"

48. "Yet we are not to think of the Most High God as living in temples constructed by men, even as the prophet says:

> **49. 'Heaven is My throne, and the earth the footstool under My feet. What kind of a house would you build for Me?' says the Lord: 'and how could you enclose Me in it, 50. seeing all these things are items which I Myself have made?' "**

TEMPLES. Stephen's main argument is that God cannot be localized in a temple, a land, or a law. Israel's history proves that. God's dealings with His people have been progressive, continually unfolding. Stephen is saying that the Jerusalem temple was never meant to be any more permanent than the wilderness tabernacle. However, the Jews stubbornly believed God could be contained in a temple, with His presence limited to Jerusalem. This in spite of the fact their own prophets said it was impossible to contain God in anything made with human hands. Recalling that Jesus pictured the Holy Spirit as wind, see how capturing the wind in a room causes its power to vanish. Stephen climaxes his argument with Isa. 66:1 where in effect God says through the prophet, "Do you expect to imprison Me in a golden cage?" Wherever God is, there is His sanctuary. This is the end of Stephen's defense of Christianity.

"Will Stephen now drive home the application of his argument?"

51. "O what bullheaded people you are! Your hearts are as heathen as ever, and your ears continue to be as deaf to God as they are to me right now. Why must you be like your fathers in continuing to resist the Holy Spirit? 52. Can you name a single prophet your

fathers didn't persecute? They slew all those who came in God's name announcing the coming of the Righteous One. And now you have betrayed Him and murdered Him. 53. You are the ones who have disobeyed God's Law even though it was given to you by the hand of angels."

BULLHEADED. Stephen shifts to the attack with a surprise charge against his listeners. Some commentators feel his words created such a stir he was interrupted, and what we have here is his rebuttal to hostile words hurled against him. It is just as likely, however, that it was his strategy to attempt a penetration with stinging words. He has completed his argument using the nation's history as the basis. Now he presses the indictment. In calling them bullheaded, he merely repeats God's description of them (Ex. 33:5). He accuses them of being as indifferent to divine revelation as the heathen. He employs the same language Moses used to describe their fathers. Thus they are the children of their fathers in the way they spurn God's messengers.

MURDERED. No sooner was the Jewish nation formed than she began to reject the Law given her by angels. When Moses tried to administer that Law, the nation murmured against him continuously. Every time a prophet rose to accuse Israel of perverting the true worship of God, she killed him. Centuries later, still running true to form, she murdered the great Prophet Moses said would come. In her determination to slay Jesus, through Whom God spoke directly to the nation, Israel's rejection was more decisive than it had ever been before. Stephen places himself in the prophetic succession when he dares to accuse the Sanhedrin of hardness toward God. By murdering their own Messiah, says Stephen, they are merely finishing the job started by their fathers in the wilderness. Now their house is left desolate, their temple worship meaningless.

"Wow! That must have gotten some reaction!"

54. These words so infuriated the council members they ground their teeth in rage. 55. But Stephen, full

of the Holy Spirit, fixed his eyes heavenward and saw the glory of God and Jesus standing at the right hand of God. 56. "Look!" he exclaimed, "I see the heavens opened and the Son of Man standing at the right hand of God!"

RAGE. Stephen's word cut deep into their hearts. "Sawn asunder," is the exact expression in Gk. While his listeners unleash their fury, Stephen is fully calm. He is aware of God's presence. A Spirit-filled man is more occupied with Jesus than anything going on about him. Stephen perhaps enjoyed this vision all the while he spoke, for the people noticed how his face shone like that of an angel. As the crowd boils, Stephen exclaims what his inward eye beholds–the Son of Man at God's right hand. That does it. This was the most blasphemous thing he could say, as far as this audience is concerned. Only Stephen, besides Jesus Himself, used the "Son of Man" title. He was ahead of his time in grasping Jesus' real role in history. He understood that Christ had not only obsoleted the temple and Judaism, but He was Someone much greater than the Messiah of the Jews. The apostles, on the other hand, continued to participate in temple worship unaware of its obsolescence (Acts 3:1 etc.).

SON OF MAN. This was Jesus' title for Himself. The last time the Sanhedrin heard it, Jesus was on trial and uttered it to the high priest. He said they would one day see the "Son of Man sitting on the right hand of the power, coming in the clouds of heaven" (Mark 14:62). Then it was they charged Him with blasphemy. They knew what that meant, for Daniel had said the "Son of Man" would rule over all peoples and nations with an everlasting kingdom (Dan. 7:13ff). Now Stephen claims he sees Jesus as the "Son of Man," standing at God's right hand. This is too much. If they accepted Stephen's statement, it would mean they made a tragic mistake in the case of Jesus. Their alternative is to find Stephen guilty of the same blasphemy. But Stephen doesn't mind. He is too overwhelmed with the scene in glory. He sees the Lord STANDING as if to welcome him into the divine presence. It won't matter what happens to him next.

57. At this, the entire assembly exploded with passion. The people covered their ears and shouted thunderously to drown out his voice. Unable to restrain themselves, they moved as a man and rushed upon Stephen. 58. Seizing him, they hustled him from the city and began stoning him. The witnesses, who were also obliged to serve as executioners, left their robes in charge of a young man named Saul.

STONING. How are we to account for this incident, seeing it was illegal for the Jews to exact the death penalty without the Roman governor's permission? Likely Pilate was not in the city at the time, but in his palace at Caesarea. The Jews are in no mood to wait for a Roman hearing. In rage they act illegally. Besides, Pilate was a man given to expediency and the Sadducees were confident they could handle him. Stephen is rushed outside the city walls. The Jews refused to defile their sacred soil. The witnesses who testified against Stephen were required by law to participate in the execution (Deut. 17:7). They remove their long, flowing outer robes so that their arms might be free to hurl the stones. Saul is introduced as the custodian of the clothes.

59. And so they stoned Stephen, and as they did he prayed aloud, "Lord Jesus receive my spirit!" 60. Then, as his knees buckled under him, he cried with a loud voice, "Lord, do not hold this sin against them!" With that he fell asleep, 1a. with Saul standing by approving his murder whole heartedly.

PRAYED. Was Stephen present when Jesus was crucified? You'd think so from the way he prays. His words are reminiscent of the Lord's. . . "Father, into Thy hands I commend My Spirit." Yet there is a striking difference: Stephen commends his spirit to **Jesus,** not the Father. This is evidence of his faith in Christ's diety. His plea for the forgiveness of his executioners is also like that of his Master. But why not? The text has told us he was full of the Holy Ghost. A man filled with Jesus' Ghost must indeed act like Christ. Then come those unexpected words, "he fell asleep." Only for someone who was full of Christ's Ghost could this brutal death be referred to as peaceful sleep.

RECEIVE. Consider the lessons in Stephen's words, "Lord Jesus, receive my spirit!" He was aware that his spirit was a separate entity from his body. He makes this cry even as his body is being put to death. He understood then that he was NOT a body, but merely wore one like a suit. He was also confident that his spirit would survive after his body had been destroyed. But what does it mean when he commits his spirit to Christ? Will he somehow be engulfed in God's Spirit to lose his identity? Indeed not. He is simply saying, "Since I have no control over my exodus, I feel safe in putting my fate in Your hands." Note how Stephen's death shatters the popular notions that a good character saves a person from harm, and that deliverance from trial is the only way God deals with the saints.

SAUL. We have noted how Saul of Tarsus (Cilicia) was likely among those clamoring for Stephen's death. He must have seen the angelic glory on his face, heard him commit his spirit to Christ, and ask mercy for his executioners. Undoubtedly this had a profound effect on Saul (Paul). We might feel some sadness at the martyrdom of this great man, but if it contributed to the salvation of Paul it was worth it from God's point of view. Note Saul's approval of the murder.

He had to feel this way, for even at this stage he saw no way for Judaism and Christianity to coincide. At this point in his career, he was convinced that Christianity had to go if Judaism was to survive. But these feelings were useful. After his conversion, he felt just as strongly the other way. Once he saw how God had replaced Judaism with Christianity, he was just as determined to strip the gospel of all Jewishness. This is the theme of his letter to the Galatians.

8 1b. That very day a wave of violent persecution broke over the church at Jerusalem. All the believers, with the exception of the apostles, fled to the outlying districts of Judea and Samaria. 2. Even so, certain devout Jews took it upon themselves, that same day, to bury Stephen and see that a public lamentation was made over him. 3. But Saul, obsessed with the idea of stamping out the church, went from house to house, seizing both men and women, dragging them off to jail.

PERSECUTION. Stephen's death triggered a campaign of persecution against the church. Armed with temple authority, Saul spearheaded the drive to wipe out Christianity. He believed it threatened the survival of Judaism. Like a wild beast tearing at a carcass, he broke into private homes, dragging the occupants off to jail. He not only beat them (22:19-20), he had many of them slain (22:4,5). So furious were his actions, it compelled the believers to flee the city. From God's side, this was the Lord's way of beginning Phase II of His plan—"in all Judea and Samaria." Were it not for this, we don't know how long it would have taken for the church to move on its missionary obligation. The apostles stayed behind, apparently unthreatened by the persecution. The council may have withheld from Saul the authority to arrest or harass them, since they were conducting themselves in the temple as devout Jews. The main thrust of the inquisition was probably aimed at the Greek speaking Jewish Christians. They suffered the double prejudice of being both Christians and foreigners in the city of Jerusalem.

BURY. It was lawful to bury Stephen, but NOT lawful for a lamentation to be made over an executed criminal. Some "devout Jews" defied the Sanhedrin to see that public lamentation was made over him. If these were not Christians, then they were Jews who resented the illegal trial and execution sanctioned by the Sanhedrin. Had Stephen been legally tried by the Sanhedrin, with the death sentence approved by Roman authority, the people would not have dared to honor Stephen publicly. No doubt this lamentation "outrage" ignited Saul's obsession to wipe out the church. It must have infuriated him to see public honor given Stephen so that he died a hero rather than as a blasphemer. That same day Saul began entering private homes to decimate the Christians. But as always, the winds of persecution serve to fan the flames of truth. Saul's slaughterings merely sent the gospel where the Lord wanted it to go.

"Did that put an end to the Christian community at Jerusalem?"

4. Those who fled the city to escape Saul's wrath scattered throughout the countryside spreading the gospel as they went. 5. Philip, for instance, went down to one of the cities of Samaria and began preaching Christ to the people. 6. The crowds listened intently to what Philip was saying for they were impressed by the miracles which he did. 7. There were many in that city who were possessed by unclean spirits which came out of them, screaming as they departed. Many lame and paralyzed were healed as well. 8. As a result the city was filled with rejoicing.

PHILIP. "Deacon" Philip is the first reported as going with the gospel. With Saul's rage scattering the Christian community at Jerusalem, his administrative duties ended. So he goes to an unnamed city in Samaria to try his hand at evangelistic work. What better place? His Lord declared that region to be "white unto the harvest" (Jo. 4:35). As a Grecian Jew (a Hellenist), he would not be hindered by anti-samaritan feelings. The

Samaritans would welcome him since both he and they were snubbed by the Jerusalem Jews. At one time the Samaritans had their own temple at Mt. Gerrizim which ran in competition to the one at Jerusalem. But because they were a mixture of Jews and Assyrians (settled there in 722 B.C.), the Judeans looked on them as half-breeds. However, inasmuch as they revered Moses and awaited the Messiah, they were not regarded as Gentiles. Since the Lord had specified "Samaria" in the Great Commission, Philip felt comfortable about going to these people (1:8).

MIRACLES. Philip proclaimed the story of Jesus in this city and his words were backed by many miracles of healing. Two types of healings were performed—the casting out of unclean spirits and the restoring of paralytic and lame bodies. Thus he had authority over demons and disease, one being mental and the other physical. Recall how these were the same types of miracles performed by Jesus' disciples BEFORE He was crucified, when He sent them out to proclaim the kingdom of God (Lu. 9:1,2,6). The Samaritans were spellbound by Philip's miracles for many sick people were healed. On top of that, his words about the Messiah's coming made them ecstatic with joy. Yet, this wasn't the first time they had seen a miracle worker.

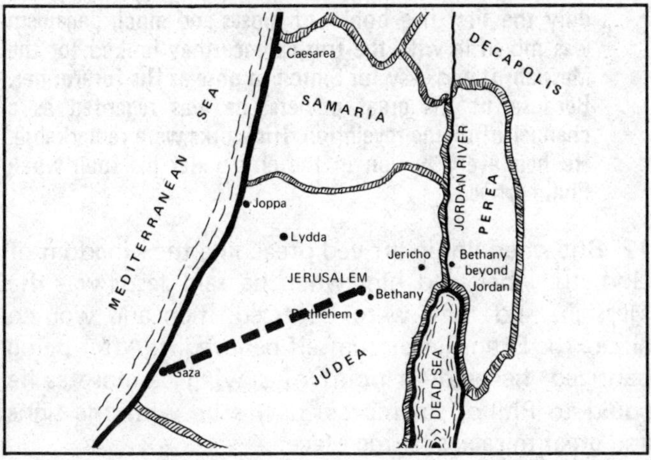

"Had they been exposed to a person with great powers before?"

9. Now in that same city lived a man named Simon. Long before Philip arrived, he had been charming the people with his magical arts. Claiming to be someone great, 10. he drew everyone to himself, from the highest to the lowest. The total populace acknowledged him as a representative of God, giving him the title, "The Great Power." 11. For a very long time he had managed to hold the people captive with his magic.

SIMON. From these verses we see this isn't the first time the Samaritans had beheld great powers in an individual. Long before Philip arrived, the city had been under the control of a magician named Simon. This man had come to their town bringing his secret wisdom from the East. His magic was no doubt similiar to that of the Egyptian sorcerers who battled Moses. He was probably a spiritist medium, able to reveal amazing things to the people about themselves. His contact with the spirit-world gave him access to demons who could supply him with secret information concerning the lives of the people. This made it easy for him to pass himself off as someone great. The Samaritans were vulnerable to his magic, because they were superstitious and fanatical about religious matters. Why? They had only the first five books of Moses and much paganism was mixed in with the truth. Since they looked for the Messiah, it was easy for Simon to pose as His forerunner. Because of his great powers, he was regarded as a channel of divine revelation. His works were remarkable. He had every person in the city under his spell when Philip arrived.

12. But when Philip arrived preaching the kingdom of God, they believed him when he said Jesus was the Messiah, and they were baptized, men and women alike. 13. Even Simon himself believed it. After being baptized, he made a point of staying as close as he could to Philip, so impressed was he with the signs and great miracles taking place.

BELIEVED. On the surface it sounds as if this entire town were saved through Philip's preaching. If true, it would have been a whopping success for his first time out as an evangelist. But he failed. These people believed all right, but not in Christ. They believed in Philip. They were already used to believing in a man on the basis of his remarkable works. They had accepted Simon as a "great power" from God because of his magic. And here is Philip with greater works, genuine miracles. It was natural for them to shift their faith from Simon to Philip. They did NOT shift from Simon to Christ. These Samaritans were like so many today who believe everything ABOUT Christ, but haven't RECEIVED him. They are professors, but not possessors. How do we know? Vs. 17 below tells us unmistakably they had not yet received the Spirit of Christ, and "if any man have not the Spirit of Christ, he is none of His" (Rom. 8:9b). The faith of these people was the same as that which Jesus shunned in the city of Jerusalem (John 2:23,24). It was faith based on seeing miracles, the kind that doesn't save. Even though they were baptized by a deputy apostle, they did not have Christ.

EVEN SIMON. Another key to the situation is that Simon is also said to believe. We learn from Peter in Verse 21 that Simon had no part in the salvation which came to many after the apostles ministered to them. What is more likely, is that Simon quickly recognized Philip's miracles as the real thing, and knew it would be futile to enter into a contest with him. His attitude was "If you can't lick 'em, join 'em." If he came to this conclusion early, he may have been the first to be baptized. In that case the town would have easily followed his example. He had everything to gain by playing along, posing as Philip's forerunner. He also expected to learn some of Philip's secrets by sticking close to him. Had Philip been able to read men's hearts, he would have recognized him as an imposter and cheat. But Philip was new in the evangelism business. He thought a whole town was saved. But that wasn't the case. We who live in a day when even whole churches are unsaved shouldn't be too shocked that a Samaritan village could mistake religion for Christ.

"How did the apostles react to the idea of the Samaritans receiving the gospel?"

14. When the apostles back in Jerusalem received the news that the Samaritans were embracing the Word of God, they sent Peter and John to visit them. 15. When they arrived, they found it necessary to pray for the people that they might receive the Holy Ghost, 16. for as yet He had not come to be in any of them. At this point, they had received nothing from God, having simply been baptized in the name of the Lord Jesus.

VISIT. A strange report reached Jerusalem. Philip, a Gk. speaking Jew (Hellenist) had taken the gospel to a city of despised Samaritans, and the entire town had embraced his word. The apostles felt obliged to check it out. Peter and John were sent to investigate. Obvious questions arose: (1) Were the Samaritans capable of sincere faith? (2) Did they actually receive the Spirit when they believed? (3) Did Philip himself know the Spirit's operation that well? Likely they were more suspicious because no confirming signs had been reported. Salvation was too serious a matter to be taken for granted. So the apostles went to make sure the work was done right. Later we'll find the apostle Paul checking on the work of Apollos, another Greek who spoke correctly about Jesus. But his converts were also unsaved due to an inaccurate understanding of the Spirit. They were saved only after Paul dealt with them (Acts 18:24-19:7).

PRAY. Peter and John must have sized up the situation instantly for they were experienced in working with the Spirit. They no doubt explained to the Samaritans the truth of Christ's indwelling and the difference between faith based on seeing miracles and a personal commitment to the Lord. Believing that He was the Messiah was not enough, they had to DO something about that news—receive Him as their PERSONAL Savior. It is what a person DOES with Christ that counts, not what he THINKS or believes ABOUT Him. Then they prayed for them. The Samaritans must have been startled to see them talking DIRECTLY to Jesus. Then it was they beheld the difference between believing **about Him** and **coming to Him directly**. If salvation came through believing **about** Jesus, even the demons would be saved (Ja. 2:19). This truth is so big that the Holy Spirit used an entire town to demonstrate it. Coming this early in the church's history it served as a vital lesson.

"When the Samaritans understood this, did they then receive Christ?"

17. Then Peter and John laid their hands on them and they received the Holy Ghost that same instant.

LAID HANDS. It seems strange to us, who receive Christ's Ghost without the laying on of hands, to see Him so intimately connected with the action here and again in the parallel situation in Acts 19:1ff. It was important here, for it betokened identification and fellowship. It was symbolical of blessing invoked and conferred. The 7 "deacons" were commissioned by this ceremony, you recall. In this case, it meant that the despised Samaritans were to be accepted into the fellowship on EQUAL TERMS with the Jewish Christians. What a work of grace was done in the apostles' hearts! See how they did this BEFORE the Samaritans received the Spirit. Thus it was also an act of faith on their part. We should not view this as a confirmation of Philip's work. His work was actually incomplete, else the Samaritans would have received the Spirit via his ministry.

SAME INSTANT. The imperfect tense in Gk. indicates the converts received the Spirit (Christ) in succession, rather than simultaneously. In which case it coincided with the laying on of hands. However, the laying on of hands and the receiving of the Spirit are separate matters. There is no hint anywhere in the N.T. that the imparting of the Spirit by this means is a gift. If so it would surely have been listed in 1 Cor. 12:4ff. Paul makes no mention of it in those places where he speaks of Christians being sealed, anointed, and given the earnest of the Spirit in their hearts (2 Cor. 1:21ff). Nothing indicates this was done on the day of Pentecost, to the Ethiopian eunuch, the household of Cornelius, nor to the Philippian jailor's family. Here it was used by the leaders of the Jerusalem church to make the despised outsiders of Samaria feel incorporated into the fellowship. The fact that the Spirit came into them simultaneously with the laying on of hands was for the apostles' sake. There could be no doubt in their minds that the Samaritans' experience was the same as their own.

RECEIVED. This is NOT another Pentecost, though expositors fondly call it that. Christ was poured out on ALL flesh (as the Holy Ghost) on the day of Pentecost. Though not so stated in the text, this event was undoubtedly accompanied by external phenomena. Why? To show that the Lord was IN the Samaritans. Every case of tongues in the book of Acts was a SIGN that the Holy Spirit was indwelling the believer. If foreign tongues were manifested, the apostles would instantly understand the Samaritan experience to be identical with their own. But there's another important need for signs. The tendency to consider Jerusalem as the headquarters of the Holy Ghost may have already developed. With similar phenomena occurring in Samaria, that notion is blasted. As the gospel proceeds from Jerusalem, Samaria, to the uttermost parts of the world, signs at each stage will show that Christianity has NO earthly headquarters. Christians are not to have any sacred city as did the Jews. Jesus dwells only in the HEARTS of His people. We are the headquarters of the Holy Spirit!

"What did Simon think of this new demonstration of power?"

18. When Simon noticed how the Spirit was bestowed the very moment the apostles laid their hands on the people, he offered them money, 19. saying, "Let me have this power too, so that people will receive the Holy Spirit when I lay my hands on them."

NOTICED. Simon the Sorcerer had formally identified himself with Christianity by submitting to baptism. But he wasn't involved with the Spirit. His scheming heart was immune to God's gentle wooing. When he saw the phenomenon accompanying the laying on of hands, he viewed it as a sorcery superior to his own. "At last," he thought, "I'm getting close to the secret of their power." Then it was he offered money to be let in on the "tricks of the trade." If only that same power could somehow be associated with HIS hands, what riches and prestige could be his! It is Simon's offer of money that assures us signs did attend the Samaritans' salvation. He would not have been willing to buy the unseen work of the Spirit, but the manifestations only. Without signs, his offer wouldn't make sense. Our modern word **simony** is derived from this man. It has to do with exploiting sacred things to make money. It appears that the works exhibited by the apostles were greater than those exhibited by Philip, for the magician made no such offer to him.

"Surely the apostles were wise to him?"

20. But Peter answered him, "Into hell with you and your money for thinking God's free gift is for sale! 21. It is obvious you have neither part nor parcel in this teaching, for your heart is not right before God. 22. However, if you repent of this evil, perhaps it is not too late for God to forgive the awful intention of your heart, if you ask Him. 23. For I see that you are saturated with the poison of envy and still bound in the chains of sin."

INTO HELL. Judas sold the Lord for money. Now here is Simon trying to buy the Holy Spirit with money. This is the second rebuke Peter has delivered concerning money and religious hypocrisy. Ananias also sought to use money to secure prestige and influence. See how Simon did NOT have the Spirit, else why would he try to buy Him? Those who have the Spirit know it (1st John 4:13). Peter may have been thinking of Judas when he perceived the evil of the magician's heart. He not only declared him an unsaved man, he consigned him to hell. He would not have said that of a born-again Christian. Simon was unsaved. The Gk. reads literally, "You have no part in the Word," i.e., the Word of salvation. Like the rich young ruler, he hadn't repented. He was still trusting in magic, thus he remained in the bond of iniquity. Though he "believed" Philip's message and was baptized, he still belonged to the devil. Not a few in our churches are in that same plight. But God is ready to save to the uttermost any who will seek His forgiveness.

24. Whereupon Simon exclaimed, "Please pray to the Lord for me that none of this harm of which you have spoken comes upon me!"

PRAY. Simon was probably a spiritist medium aware of the powers of the other world. That he has now incurred the scorn of these men with powers greater than his own, strikes terror to his heart. Some Gk. texts say he kept on weeping uncontrollably. He may have been unstable (mediums often are) and this accounts for the quick humbling of himself. He begs the apostles to pray for him—not that he would be forgiven, only that the dreaded consequences of his sin might be averted. His plea is humble enough, but there is no confession of sin, neither is there any thought of repentance. His only concern, like millions who dabble in religion, **is to escape punishment.** Note that he will NOT pray for himself. He would like to be forgiven by proxy, having no desire to face God in the matter of his sin. There are many today who want religious leaders to pray for them in this same way.

"Did Peter and John stay on after they had done their part?"

25. So when Peter and John had finished testifying and preaching in this village, they headed back for Jerusalem. On the way they stopped at many Samaritan villages to bring them the gospel also.

FINISHED. Peter and John may have been finished, but Philip wasn't. The two apostles did their preaching and testifying and departed, leaving it to Philip to ground the new converts. Even though his inexperience as an evangelist rendered him unable to distinguish between believing and receiving, he was nonetheless an able man. He was Spirit-filled, easily able to teach the things of Christ. The coming of the two apostles had done much for him. He would not be fooled a second time, for now he had been taught in a "live" situation. Peter and John are in no hurry to reach Jerusalem. They chose instead to work as missionaries along the way. They are eager to see the Lord's commission fulfilled in all of Samaria. Likely they found it a little strange thinking of the long-hated, half-jew Samaritans as members of the one family in Christ. But that's what happens when the love of God is shed abroad in men's hearts by the Holy Spirit (Rom. 5:5).

"Was Philip now qualified as an evangelist?"

26. Meanwhile, Philip was instructed by an angel of the Lord, "Arise and go south until you pick up the desert road that leads from Jerusalem down to Gaza."

INSTRUCTED. Philip's work in the village ends in an unusual way. New orders reach him via an "angel of the Lord," a strange expression Dr. Luke has used for the second time (see 5:19). This could have been by internal suggestion, but the "angel" idea leads us to think Philip heard distinguishable words. Hearing, of course, is done with the brain, for our ears merely transport vibrations. This seems to go beyond the usual prompting of the Spirit, for the instructions are quite precise. He is to go to a particular road, one which passes through a desert region and leads to Gaza. Gaza was about 60 miles S.W. of Jerusalem. At least two other roads led to it from Jerusalem. It was one of the 5 chief cities of the Philistines and is near the southern boarder of Canaan, about 3 miles from the Mediterranean. Going due south from Samaria, he would intersect this road.

GO. It is to Deacon Philip's credit that his ego wasn't crushed when two apostles came from Jerusalem to finish his work. He could have been very discouraged to find that his word, which brought such great joy to a village and saw all the people baptized, lacked the principal requirement for salvation, the Holy Spirit. But Spirit-filled men don't quit. Philip profited from watching Peter and John help the people receive the Spirit. We can be sure the next time he deals with a lost soul, he will do the job right. The Word of God reveals the mistakes of its heroes. Even Peter and Paul made mistakes and they were Spirit-filled apostles. Now that Philip has been more perfectly qualified as an evangelist, God can give him a wider ministry. It begins with the command to "Arise and go!"

27. So Philip did as he was instructed. Sure enough he found there an Ethopian eunuch of the court of the Candace, the queen of Ethiopia. This man was an important official, the queen's treasurer. He had been on a pilgrimage to worship at the temple in Jerusalem. 28. Now he was on his way home, driving along in his carriage and reading the prophet Isaiah.

EUNUCH. It was not uncommon in lands ruled by queens to have eunuchs serve as their royal officers. It's true this word in Gk. does not always mean an emasculated man, but in this case it appears likely. The man was a black, coming from the area of modern Nubia which is located in the upper Nile stretching from Aswan south to Khartoum. While sun-worship was the religion of his land, this man was somehow taught to worship the God of Israel. Because of his castration, he was probably not a full proselyte. Eunuchs were excluded from full religious privileges from early times (Deut. 23:1). Even so, this wealthy lord had taken to himself the covenant of Israel. Candace was a title given to queens of Upper Egypt, such as Pharoahs of Egypt and the Caesars of Rome were common names for those rulers. This was the man God had marked out for Philip.

READING. Philip, walking along the road on foot, observes the approaching carriage. Soon it overtakes him. He hears someone reading aloud in Greek. As a nobleman, the black official had available to him the O.T. in Gk. The Septuagint, a Greek translation of the Scriptures made in Alexandria, Egypt, was prepared for use by Jews throughout the region. The intelligent classes were taught the Gk. language. Invaribly such Scripture reading was done aloud, for the hand-lettered manuscripts were difficult to fathom unless each word was spelled out. Likely the nobleman was reading the scroll to his driver. Having just come from Jerusalem, he no doubt heard much about the crucifixion and resurrection of Christ, as well as the wonders of Pentecost. It could be he was determined to search the Scriptures for himself to see if these things were so.

29. The Spirit then said to Philip, "Go catch up with that carriage and stay close to it." 30. When Philip ran up to the carriage and heard the Ethiopian reading from the Prophet Isaiah, he said to him, "Surely you don't understand what you are reading?" 31. "No, I don't," he said, "And I don't see how I can without someone to teach me." Then he invited Philip into the carriage to sit beside him.

SPIRIT. As the carriage rolled past, Philip recognized what the nobleman was reading. Philip was, after all, a Greek-speaking Jew. Then he was seized by a compelling impulse (the Spirit's prodding) to catch up with the wagon and stay along side. It was the Scripture that drew Philip's attention. As he thought about it, it had to be connected with God's errand. The road was lonely. The passing of such a carriage had to be more than coincidence. It took more than human courage for Philip to approach this wealthy Lord in such a fashion. But God had arranged the meeting. Things work out well when we're lead of the Spirit, though the circumstances might seem forbidding at the time. Note how the angel of vs. 26 is here identified as the Holy Spirit.

UNDERSTAND. Philip's question wasn't actually rude. It was not at all likely that an Ethiopian (supposedly pagan), reading in Greek, (a foreign language to him) and studying Jewish ideas could possibly know what it was all about. That's what really prompted Philip's bold action. Consider this sight. The greatest man in Ethiopia riding home in the comfort and splendor of his carriage, while running alongside was a dusty, peasant-looking Philip. What could they possibly have in common? Then it was that Philip shouted to be heard above the horses. He called out his inspired question. The timing was perfect. The man didn't understand the Scripture he was reading. His humility is beautiful. He is not the least bit insulted. To the contrary he recognizes Philip as someone who might help him and invites him into the carriage.

"What exactly was the Ethiopian reading?"

32. The passage of Scripture the Ethiopian had been reading was this:

"He was lead as a sheep to slaughter;
As a lamb is silent while being shorn;
He did not make a sound;
33. He was humiliated, and justice was
denied Him. Who can adequately describe
the wickedness of His contemporaries?
For His life is cut off and He is gone
from the earth."

SCRIPTURE. The above passage is from Isa. 53:7. The quote is from the Gk. version (Septuagint). The words are hard to translate for they differ from the original Hebrew in a number of places. Also, as they appear in Gk., they are subject to alternate renderings. However the subject is clear—God's Suffering Servant. It is not likely that Isaiah himself grasped the real meaning of these words. Until Jesus appeared and died, this passage was very difficult to handle. No prophet in history had fulfilled it, certainly not the writer, Isaiah. It would be quite unlikely that anyone would associate it with the Messiah, for He was expected to come in great glory and establish His kingdom. It remained for Jesus to identify Himself as the Suffering Servant. He alone connected His own sufferings with this prophecy (Mark 10:45). Until Jesus spoke of Himself in this fashion, the passage remained closed to interpretation. This was why Philip was sure the black treasurer didn't understand what he was reading.

34. Then the official turned to Philip. "Tell me," he asked, "was the prophet Isaiah speaking of himself in this passage or was he referring to someone else?" 35. With that, Philip began to deal with him earnestly. Using this very passage as his starting point, he told him the good news about Jesus.

TELL ME. It seems impossible that anyone could visit Jerusalem, a city convulsed by Jesus' death and resurrection, and come away with no idea of what this passage was about. Yet is is clear from the text that the Ethiopian didn't understand it at all. However, the Holy Spirit was guiding his reading, for he was studying one of the most striking predictions of the Messiah's suffering in the O.T. Note how far God will go to help those who want to believe His Word. In this case He dispatched Philip from Samaria to keep this appointment on that lonely road. Philip not only explained the passage fully, but proceeded to unfold the whole story of Christ. Since there were no N.T. Scriptures as yet, he couldn't have chosen a better place to begin. The nobleman's response tells us that Philip made it clear to him that Jesus had died for him personally.

"You mean the Ethiopian was ready to receive Christ?"

36. As they rode along together they presently came to some water. "Hey look!" said the Eunuch, "here's water! What is there to keep me from being baptized right now?" 37. "Nothing," answered Philip, "if you really believe with all your heart." Whereupon the Eunuch replied, "I believe that Jesus Christ is the

Son of God." 38. With that he ordered the carriage to stop and together they went down into the water where Philip baptized him.

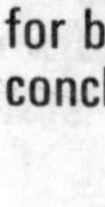

BELIEVE. Verse 37 is not found in the earliest texts. Most modern translations leave it out entirely or put it in the margin. However, I have elected to leave it in. It is in keeping with the story, showing how Philip made sure of the genuineness of the Ethiopian's faith. See how it is the Eunuch who presses for baptism, not Philip. Once before he was too rash in concluding people were saved. He doesn't want to make the same mistake twice. If this verse can be accepted as genuine, Philip has profited from his earlier mistake in the Samaritan village, and here he is seen extracting the Eunuch's declaration of faith BEFORE he baptizes him. Luke's report of this event lets us see Philip's improved skill. That the carriage was stopped by command, indicates the Ethiopian had at least one driver and possibly some attendants as well.

WATER. That Philip successfully explained the passage from Isaiah and clearly instructed the Ethiopian about Jesus is obvious. The man asks to be baptized the moment he spies water. Coming upon this water (location unknown) he wants to be baptized right away. He is headed for the Upper Nile where he might not find another Christian teacher or believer who could baptize him. So he wants it done while Philip is still with him. The eagerness of the Eunuch indicates what baffled him before is no longer a mystery. We cannot tell much about the depth of the water except to note that it was sufficient for them to enter it.

"Did they continue the journey together after that?"

39. When they came up out of the water, the Spirit of the Lord snatched Philip away and the Eunuch saw him no more. Even so, he proceeded on his journey, his heart filled with joy. 40. As for Philip, he found himself at Azotus. From there he toured all the Samaritan villages, preaching the gospel in every place until he came to Caesarea.

SNATCHED. Some commentators feel the catching away of Philip needs no miraculous explanation, that he came to this place on the impulse of the Spirit and departed the same way. They might be right. However, the sudden catching away of Philip seems to stand out in the Greek text as of the same order as that of Elijah (1 Ki. 18:12), and Ezekiel (Ezek. 3:14). The same Gk. word is used for the rapture of the saints in I Thess. 4:17. It probably isn't necessary to see Philip as flying through the air, but **transported instantly** so that he "found himself" at Azotus in the "twinkling of an eye." The timing was so arranged that it did not dampen the Eunuch's joy. He was probably so ecstatic that Philip's disappearance was either unnoticed or simply regarded as of the Lord. It may have even added to his wonder in Christ.

AZOTUS. Philip was now ready to serve the Lord as a qualified evangelist. He next appears at Azotus, the old Philistine city of Ashdod. From there he traveled north, visiting such cities as Lydda and Joppa as well as all the coastal cities. He preached the gospel in every place until he reached Caesarea, a city on the Mediterranean some 75 miles N.W. of Jerusalem. Here Philip settled down permanently. Some 25 or more years later we will find him there with his four prophetess daughters. It was his ministry to all the Samaritan villages that earned him the title of "evangelist" (21:8). He will not be mentioned again until Paul and Luke come to stay with him after returning from the third missionary journey. This closes the curtain on the Samaritan phase of the Great Commission.

9 1. Meanwhile Saul's rage against the Lord's disciples burned as hotly as ever. To carry out his threatened massacre, he went to the high priest, 2. begging letters of authorization to the synagogues at Damascus, that the rulers there might assist him in arresting all who followed in this new way. He planned to bring them back to Jerusalem in chains, both men and women.

SAUL. The story now shifts back to Saul and his crusade against the Christians. The first efforts to suppress them served only to scatter them, making them harder to watch. This moved Saul to secure the Sanhedrin's permission to hunt them down and return them to Jerusalem for trial. Luke means to contrast Saul's attitude here with that of Philip who was engaged in building up the church, Saul sought its demise. The Gk. pictures Saul panting like a tiger who has tasted blood. He is now obsessed. Those he sought were not

Damascus citizens, but refugees from Jerusalem. The high priest's decrees were binding on Jews are far away as Damascus, 130 miles N.E. of Jerusalem. The journey will take close to a week. (See map on page 161.)

WAY. The first Christians were called followers of the way. This was the earliest name given the new movement founded on the instructions of Christ. It is significant that it was not pictured as a religion, but as a way of life–a new style of living based on Jesus' teachings. It was this new way of life that infuriated Saul. He abhored it, because it stood in sharp contrast to the sterile, formal system of Judaism. He saw how the love and peace which attended the followers of Jesus threatened the existence of Judaism. It would indeed supersede Judaism if allowed to spread. Besides, Stephen's sermon made it quite clear that Christianity was meant to replace Judaism. The fact that the learned and popular Saul was not able to withstand the wisdom of Stephen no doubt triggered his rage in the first place. His hatred for the WAY continued to grow until it all but consumed him.

"Then Saul had committed himself to the destruction of the Christians?"

3. While he was still on the road to Damascus and approaching the city, a dazzling light from heaven suddenly flashed around him. 4. He fell at once to the ground. Lying there prostrate he heard a voice saying, "Saul, Saul! Why are you persecuting Me?"

LIGHT. Saul and his escort band had all but reached the Damascus walls when a fantastic thing happened. Above the searing glare of the noon-day sun (a brilliance unknown to Westerners), a light flashed around Saul of such intensity it caused him to fall to the ground. (There is no evidence he was on horseback). It was not lightning, but a revelation of the Lord. That this was a supernatural manifestation of Jesus should not be denied. Though operating in the Spirit, He used this light in such a way as to give FORM to the Holy Ghost. The light was more than a garment, for Paul tells us in other places that he SAW the Lord in this light. That fact is the basis of his claim to apostleship (1 Cor. 9:1; 15:8). Lying face down in the dust, the terrorized Saul hears a voice calling to him in Aramaic (common Hebrew). He doesn't even lift his head to see who it is, even though the Person calls him by name. So far, he has seen a FORM in the brilliance and now a Person speaks to him as he lies hugging the earth.

"Didn't Saul recognize the One Who spoke to him?"

5. "Tell me, sir, who are you?" he asked. The reply came, "I am Jesus, the One Whom you are persecuting. 6. Arise now and go into the city where you will be told what your work is to be."

SIR. This word reads "Lord," in the Gk. text, but it is clear that it meant nothing more than "sir" here in vs. 5. As yet, Saul does not know Who appeared in the brillance, neither does he know Who spoke his name. Hence his inquiry. Then came the soul-convulsing words. . ."I am Jesus. . ." He must have shuddered at that. Now he gets the connection. The One Who spoke is the same One he saw in the light. If Jesus is not dead, but speaking like this, then He has to be the Son of God. That truth made him grip the earth even harder. He didn't raise his head. The image he had seen in the light had already seared in his imagination. He never forgot it. Now he has a name to go with that figure–JESUS! The Lord said more to Saul but Luke did not record it here. The words found in the King James, "It is hard for thee. . .etc." to the end of vs. 6, are not found in any Gk. Mss. in existence. Neither are they found in the ASV or RSV. They were, however, a part of the scene as we know from Acts 26:14. The Lord had indeed been wooing Saul for a long time.

PERSECUTING. In a moment Saul met two soul-shattering truths: (1) that Jesus was God; (2) that He was also one with His people. He suddenly realized that every stone which struck Stephen was also against Jesus, that every chain he had fastened to the saints was also laid on Christ. He knew what was meant when the Lord said, "Why are you persecuting Me?" In persecuting His church, Saul had persecuted Jesus. It was realization of this terrible wrong that broke Saul. In trembling submission he said, "Lord what wilt thou have me to do?" (22:10). This time the word "Lord" has the meaning of "Master." The Lord didn't answer, knowing it would take three days for Saul to fathom what had happened. The discovery that he was fighting God instead of serving Him, brought moral convulsions to the striken Saul. It would be like reversing the Colorado River for him to shift from persecuting to serving Christ. Christians hurting each other wound the Lord. We can all be warned by these words.

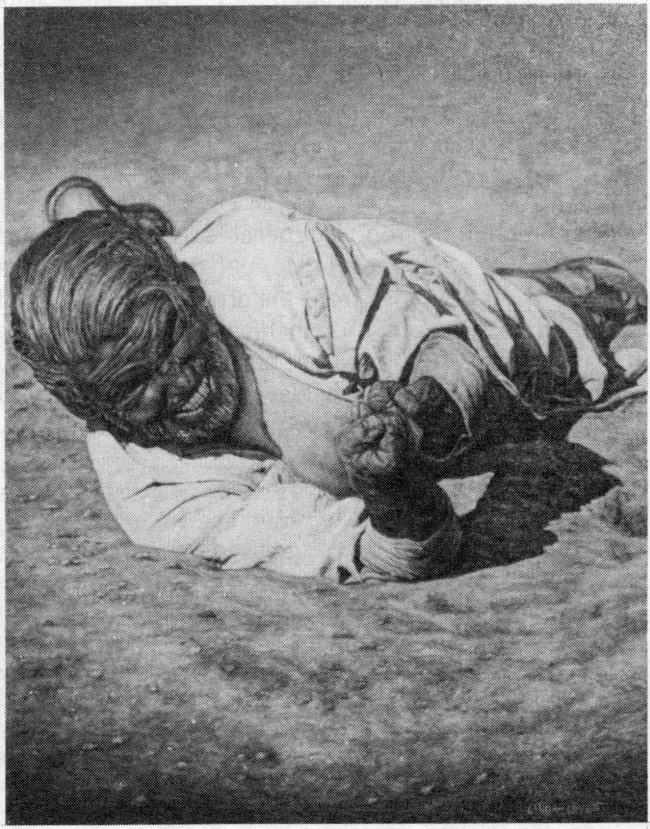

© Linda Lovett 1979

ARISE. The Lord takes command of Saul's life. The arrogant Jew is now broken, putty in Jesus' hands. To us this seems the opposite of the way God reaches souls today. Why this supernatural intervention which appears to overrule Saul's will? Why are not others humiliated and broken in this fashion? We must put this in the same category with the SIGHT/SOUND phenomenon of Pentecost. It was an outward dramatization of what was going on in the Spirit. The sight and sound experience of the Damascus Rd. is **typical** of every salvation experience. What God did outwardly with Saul, he does inwardly with each of us. We each hear His voice asking humiliating questions of our souls. Each of us feels the holy light of His word on our uncleanness, convicting us of sin. The manifestation was exceptional but those were exceptional days. There was but one Pentecost, only one Ananias and Sapphira incident, so only one Damascus Rd. experience. But all were representative of what occurs in the Spirit. Without such an experience it should be questioned whether a person is really born-again.

7. His companions stood by speechless, for they heard the sound of someone's voice, yet they couldn't see anyone. 8. As Saul rose from the ground he discovered he couldn't see even though his eyes were open. So his men took him by the hand and led him to Damascus. 9. For three days he remained blind during which time he went without food and water.

COMPANIONS. Luke's words indicate the soldiers accompanying Saul heard the voice, but saw no one. Some have taken this to contradict his words in 22:9 where he says they did not understand the voice of Him that spoke. The likelihood is that they all fell to the ground when struck by the intense light, but the men arose upon hearing SAUL speak to someone they themselves could not see. Saul remained on the ground until Jesus told him to rise. The others simply stood by trying to comprehend what was happening. The Lord's voice must have been after the manner of the crowd in John 12:29 which heard God's voice from heaven. That was a similar situation. (See my commentary on John, p. 211 under "Voice.") They heard indistinct sounds whereas Saul heard articulate speech.

BLIND. So brilliant was the shekinah flash all were blinded for a time. The soldiers recovered their sight quickly, but not Saul. His eyes were supernaturally darkened. He had rebelled so violently against the idea that Jesus was the Messiah, the discovery of his error produced a trauma that paralyzed his sight. Should a reader feel an actual layer of film was placed over his eye-balls, the technical language of Dr. Luke in vs. 18 would allow for it. At once the proud persecutor was helpless, shut up inside a world where all he could see was the FORM of the One Who had appeared to him in the flash. For three days he would be imprisoned in his thought world. There he would weigh his error in persecuting Jesus and get acquainted with Him. To serve Christ with the same furious passion with which he had served Judaism would take some shifting. God would give him time to make that shift. Shunning food and drink, Saul occupied himself with the transfer of his dedication.

"How did God deal with Saul next?"

10. Now there was at Damascus a disciple by the name of Ananias. He had a vision in which the Lord called to him, "Ananias!" The praying disciple quickly replied, "Here I am, Lord!" 11. And the Lord said to him, "I want you to go at once to Straight Street, to the house of Judas and ask for a man from Tarsus by the name of Saul. He is in prayer at this very moment, 12. and I have given him a vision in which he sees a man named Ananias coming in and placing his hands on him that he might see again."

ANANIAS. This is not the Ananias of Ch. 5, of course, but a devout Christian Jew who lived in Damascus. Likely the gospel had come to him from Galilee, or possibly at Pentecost. As he is in his home, a vision comes to him simultaneously with the vision given to Saul. Thus both men are prepared for each other. The Lord explains to Ananias why he must go at once. Saul even then sees him coming to minister to him. He is to be the answer to Saul's prayer. Therefore he must hurry. It is remarkable that not only is the name of the street given, but even Saul's host. Observe how not only are our external circumstances known to the Lord, but the very thoughts of our heads as well. Straight St. is one of Damascus' chief thoroughfares today.

"Was Ananias ready for this mission?"

13. "But Lord!" exclaimed the shocked Ananias, "I have heard much about this man and the terrible harm he has done Your saints at Jerusalem. 14. Why he has come to Damascus with authority from the chief priests to arrest all who call upon Your name!"

BUT LORD! Ananias hesitates to obey the divine command. Like Moses, who quaked at the thought of taking God's message to Pharaoh, he is reluctant to visit Saul (Ex. 3:11). Ananias learned from those who fled Jerusalem ahead of Saul that the persecutor had come with authority to seize Christians. Reports of Saul's cruelty had reached Damascus. He was already infamous for his fiendish devastation of the saints. This is the first time the word "saints" is applied to believers. It is here meant to designate ALL disciples, and is NOT a special title to distinguish a superior class of Christians. That Ananias gained his information from others indicates he is a resident of Damascus and not among those who fled Jerusalem.

15. "Go," said the Lord, "and do as I have told you. This man will not hurt you for he is My chosen instrument to make My name known to the Gentiles and their rulers, as well as to the people of Israel. 16. I, Myself, have yet to show him how much suffering he must undergo for My name's sake."

NOT HURT. The Lord overrules Ananias' protest by easing his troubled mind. He informs him that Saul will no longer afflict the church. No more will he cause those who bear Jesus' name to suffer. The reverse is true. Saul is now to suffer for the sake of that name. When Jesus says Saul is a chosen instrument, it is not to magnify the persecutor, but to help Ananias obey. He does not have to be afraid to go on this errand. Then the Lord gives the scope of Saul's future work. It is threefold. He is to declare the glory of Jesus to (1) the heathen, (2) their rulers, (3) and the children of Israel. Note that Israel is NOT excluded from his labors, though the order indicates the Gentile world is to be Saul's primary field of operation. Saul's subsequent history fulfilled all that Jesus said here, for he made the heathen world ring with the truth of the cross.

INSTRUMENT. We have come to the third greatest fact in God's redemptive program. The first was the advent of Christ from His incarnation to His ascension, the central epoch in all human history. Everything human is measured by it. The second fact was the spiritual diffusion of Christ at Pentecost, creating the dispensation of the Spirit. There Jesus became available to all men as the Holy Ghost. The third fact is this manifestation of Jesus to Saul whereby He salvaged him and made him an apostle. Nothing in subsequent history is comparable to it. In the next 30 years Jesus will work through this man to throw HIS ideas into the heart of the world with such force that paganism will be shattered and a new thing called "churches" will be established to multiply everywhere.

"Did Jesus' word about Saul allay Ananias' fears?"

17. So Ananias went to the house where Saul was. Upon entering, he laid his hands upon him, saying, "Brother Saul, I have been sent here by the Lord Jesus Who appeared to you on the road as you were coming here. It is His will that you regain your sight and be filled with the Holy Spirit."

BROTHER. Ananias goes without further hesitation. He enters the house going straight to Saul. Then come those vital words, "Brother Saul!" God has already revealed to Ananias that Saul is saved.

Otherwise he'd never call him brother. Thus he HAS received the Spirit **already.** But God means for him to be "filled." Then Ananias lays his hands on him. (Observe that this occurs AFTER salvation). In that moment they become Jesus' hands and Saul is commissioned as an apostle. It is not Peter or another apostle who does this, but a nobody named Ananias. There's no apostolic succession here. See how one doesn't have to be a big shot to do a big job for Christ. The touch of those hands tells Saul that all he beheld in the vision was true. With the actual contact of Ananias' hands, Saul's sight was healed. His heart leaps with joy and excitement. By the hands of a devout Jew, Jesus formally commissions Saul, even as the 7 deacons were confirmed and the Samaritans welcomed into the brotherhood. The physical touch symbolized the spiritual ordination.

FILLED. For three days Saul has been confined to the PRESENCE of the Lord. There in the sightless world he weighed all that had happened to him and became acquainted with Christ. That's where true fellowship with God occurs—in the sanctified imagination. But Saul was saved for more than fellowship. He was chosen for a mighty role in building Jesus' church. That meant he would have to SHIFT from the internal experience (the Spirit's presence) to external action (the Spirit's power) as he undertook his commission. When Ananias told him what he was to do, he felt destined to greatness in God (22:14,15). The magnitude of his call surged through him. The moment he felt the touch of Ananias' hands, all that he had heard was confirmed in a moment. He was turned on for Jesus that instant. That's when he was filled with the Spirit, for as noted before, the filling is a thrilling.

18. Immediately something like fish scales fell away from Saul's eyes and he was able to see again. Then he rose to his feet and was baptized. 19a. After that, he ate some food and was strengthened.

SCALES. The idea of falling scales is probably the SENSATION Saul felt when he was being healed. However, there is nothing to preclude actual scales (a medical term) from being attached to Saul's eyes. What is clear is that Dr. Luke means for us to understand this as a supernatural event. At the touch of Ananias' hand, Saul's sight returned. This miracle added to the joy already swelling within the new convert. Note the steps: (1) saved on the Damascus Rd., (2) 3 days in God's immediate presence, (3) commissioned to a worldwide ministry, (4) instantly healed. That should cause any believer to be filled with the Spirit. We again notice Saul's rapid change from a state of occupation with his **internal** experience to one of energetic action as he **moves out** to obey. By these steps, God was successful in shifting the **zeal** of Saul from Judaism to the call of Christ.

BAPTIZED. There is little of the human element in Saul's conversion. God Himself did most of the work. Ananias is God's immediate agent. We're not told HOW or WHERE he baptized Saul, whether from a bowl or a stream near Damascus. It was done swiftly, even before Saul took food or drink. Regarding it a command of Christ, he wanted to do it at once. Then he was ready for work. That he was Spirit-filled is obvious. See how completely the Lord turned his furious passion to the gospel—all within three days! Burning in his imagination was the vision of the One he'd met on the road. That vision, sealed during the three days, inflamed his desire to exalt Christ day and night. That's what it means to be Spirit-filled. Modern definitions fall short of what Paul meant when he commanded, "Be filled with the Spirit" (Eph. 5:18). Nothing is said of outward manifestations attending his being filled with the Spirit.

19b. Saul remained with the disciples in Damascus for a few days, 20. during which he immediately set to work proclaiming Jesus publicly in the synagogues. "He is the Son of God," Saul declared. 21. All who heard him were astounded. "Is not this the man," they asked, "who in Jerusalem was trying to destroy all those who called on this name? And didn't he come here for the express purpose of arresting them and taking them back to the chief priests?"

IMMEDIATELY. Saul couldn't wait to tell his people (the Jews) that Jesus was the Messiah. He was filled with the Spirit and highly zealous, but unfortunately he didn't have much organized knowledge. The **filling** of the Spirit is no substitute for being **taught** of the Spirit. In fact, the filling of the Spirit is wholly separate from Christian maturity. One can be Spirit-filled and totally unwise and immature. However, using what he had, he went at once to the synagogues to share his great discovery. There was no finer place for all synagogues provided for discussions. His theme was, "Jesus is the Son of God." Likely he used the same arguments that Stephen so effectively used at Jerusalem. He didn't have any arguments of his own as yet. He was trying his wings. But like Philip, he was an amateur evangelist and very green. His keen mind was quick to realize his lack of organization.

ASTOUNDED. We can understand the consternation of Saul's listeners. They were expecting this man to present his letters of authority. Instead he presents himself as a disciple of Jesus, declaring Him to be the Son of God! So shocked were they, they didn't pay much attention to what he said. Here was this well-known man declaring with all of his being, what a few days before, he was using all of his power to destroy. He had to be genuine, no imposter would dare such a thing. While the amazement was great, the results were missing. No souls are reported saved. The lack of results convinced Saul he needed to prepare himself. If faith in Christ was to replace Judaism, he needed a whole new theology for righteousness. He now has to fit Jesus into the O.T. Scriptures.

FEW DAYS. Saul didn't stay in amateur evangelism long. Within a few days he was off to the Arabian desert to begin a 3-year seminary course taught by the Holy Spirit. The task before him was not for a novice. He could see that now. True, he had the finest education a Jew could receive, but it wasn't enough. If Jesus was really the Son of God, then there were vast areas of theology he had to rethink before he could proceed with his call. Like Moses who spent 40 years with God in the desert, even though he owned the wisdom of Egypt, so now Saul needs this graduate work from God. When the three years in the wilderness are completed, Saul will return to Damascus and re-enter the synagogues with added power. Even so, 12 years will pass before he enters the full-time ministry at Antioch.

"After Saul was instructed by the Spirit, did he do a better job?"

22. As Saul's preaching became more forceful and convincing, he silenced the Damascus Jews with conclusive arguments that Jesus was indeed the Messiah. 23. And when all these many days had passed, the Jewish leaders plotted against his life. 24. But Saul was advised of their murderous plot and how they were watching the city gates day and night in hope of seizing and killing him. 25. So his disciples contrived to save him. One night they passed him through an opening in the wall and lowered him to the ground in a basket.

MANY DAYS. Saul had gone off into the desert with only the O.T. Scriptures. He returned with the truths of Romans, Ephesians, and Colossians roaring in his heart. He went back into the synagogues. This time it was a different Saul who confronted the Jews. He had a new ability, a new power. So great were his arguments and proofs from the Word, the Jews were unable to withstand his wisdom. He was now effective as a witness, reaching many souls throughout the city. From his letter to the Corinthians, we learn that these efforts provoked the ire of the ruler of the city (2 Cor. 11:32ff). This ruler and the Jewish leaders hatched a plot to kill Saul. Some of Saul's friends had apparently infiltrated the ranks of his enemies and discovered the plot. They arranged for his escape. We must assume that the "many days" mentioned by Luke refer to the end of the 3 year period, and that Saul went immediately to Jerusalem after this escape from Damascus (Gal. 1:17, 18).

DISCIPLES. The amazing force of Saul's personality is seen when we observe that he has secured disciples of his own. No doubt he attracted many of the Damascus Christians to himself. Convinced that the civil and religious authorities of the city have conspired to kill him, Saul allows his brethren (once his enemies) to effect his escape. They no doubt persuaded him it would be foolish to forfeit his life to a gang of unbelievers when the Lord had appointed him a ministry to the Gentiles. The description of Saul's escape agrees with the structure of ancient cities. They were protected by thick walls in which people had their homes. This was a window in a house overhanging the wall, or a window

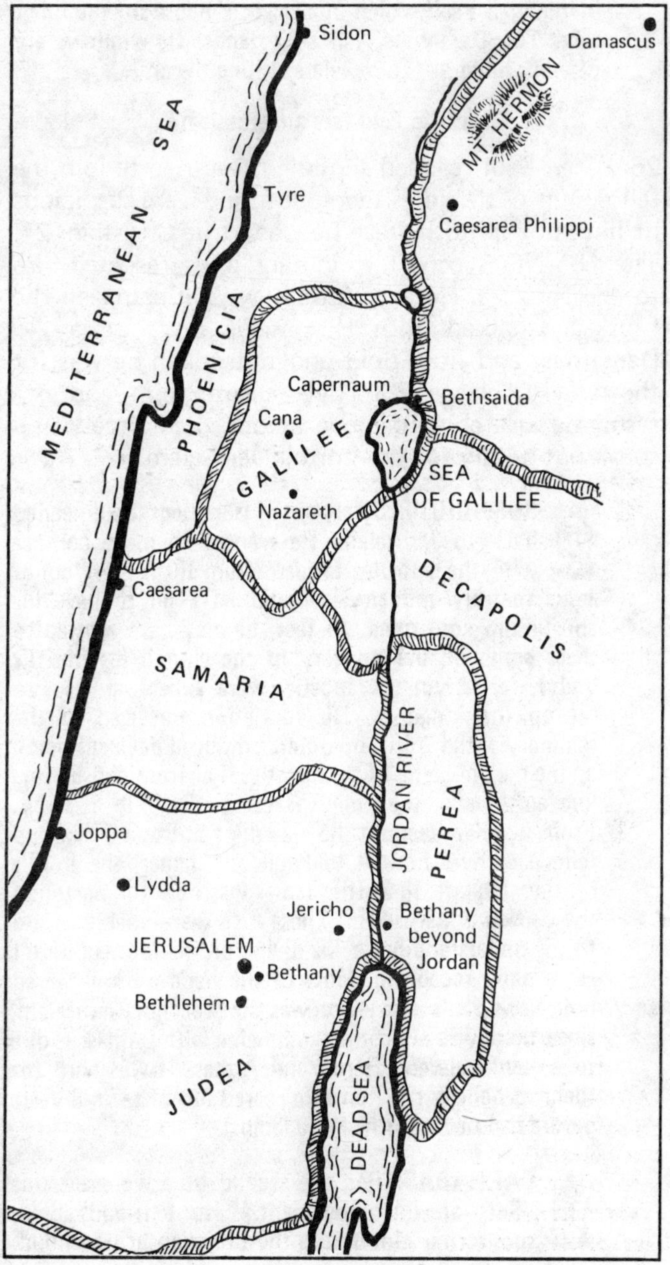
Sidon
Damascus
MT. HERMON
MEDITERRANEAN SEA
Tyre
Caesarea Philippi
PHOENICIA
Capernaum
Bethsaida
Cana
GALILEE
SEA OF GALILEE
Nazareth
DECAPOLIS
Caesarea
SAMARIA
JORDAN RIVER
PEREA
Joppa
Lydda
Jericho
Bethany beyond Jordan
JERUSALEM
Bethany
Bethlehem
JUDEA
DEAD SEA

in the wall itself which opened to a house on the inner side. The Damascus wall still stands. Its windows are often pointed out to travelers visiting the city.

"How did Paul fare at Jerusalem?"

26. When Saul reached Jerusalem, he tried to join the fellowship of disciples there, but they were suspicious of him, unable to believe he was a true Christian. 27. Then Barnabas took him in hand and presented him to the apostles. He explained how Saul had seen the Lord and talked with Him while on the way to Damascus, and how bold and outspoken he was for the name of Jesus. 28. They accepted him, and as a result he was able to move among them freely and speak out boldly for the Lord in Jerusalem.

SUSPICIOUS. Safely out of Damascus, Saul headed back to Jerusalem. He wanted to make contact with the apostles to learn from them more about Jesus' earthly ministry. He did NOT go to have his apostleship confirmed. In fact, he may have wanted to share some of the mystery of the church (as Christ's body), for as yet the apostles were expecting Jesus to set up the kingdom. His revelation, received in the seminary of the Spirit, no doubt produced deep suspicion on the part of some of the apostles. Far from considering him an apostle, they may have regarded him as a spy. From his own account, he was there but two weeks and fellowship was limited to Peter and James, the Lord's brother (Gal. 1:18-24ff.). James was now the pastor of the church at Jerusalem. These men were unable to add to his understanding or his divine ordination. He didn't get a good reception. Most of the believers still feared him. News of his conversion was slow reaching Jerusalem, since there was almost no commerce with Damascus due to a feud between Herod and Aretas. It was hard for them to believe the lion who roared out of town 3 years before had now returned as a lamb.

BARNABAS. For the second time we meet this "Son of Encouragement." He befriends Saul, sponsoring him before the Christian brotherhood.

Apparently they knew each other before. Barnabas' home (Cyprus) was but a few hours sail from Cilicia, Saul's home. Perhaps they had attended the university of Tarsus together. In any event, Barnabas' introduction permits him to move freely among the brethren. What a magnificent testimony to the great respect Barnabas enjoyed among the believers. There were old friends in Jerusalem who Saul longed to see. He wanted to tell them that Jesus was the Messiah. But when they learned of His defection from Judaism, they became unfriendly. What was once a dear and exciting city, is now a sad place for Saul. But that doesn't dampen his zeal or keep him from declaring Christ.

29. Among those to whom Saul openly declared the name of the Lord were the Grecian Jews. Because of his persistent arguing with them they were ready to take his life. 30. However, when his brethren heard of it, they took Saul down to Caesarea where they dispatched him to Tarsus.

GRECIAN JEWS. Saul's boldness was never more evident than in his return to the synagogues of the Greek-speaking Jews at Jerusalem. Likely he went back to the very synagogue where Stephen had confounded him and the other Hellenists. There he declared the same cause for which Stephen had died. It is obvious he had more zeal than wisdom, for he knew the spirit of this audience and how fierce an anger his arguments could kindle. He persists in pouring forth his irresistable arguments only to generate the same effect as did the sermon of Stephen—furious rage. Then the brethren stepped in to rescue him when he was about to be assassinated. Obviously the three years in the seminary of the Spirit had made Saul a sharp theologian, but they did not give him wisdom. His unwise use of knowledge took him into danger. Saul desperately needs wisdom if he is going to be useful to Jesus.

DISPATCHED. The Christians had to get Saul out of Jerusalem or the lid would blow off the city. This zealous convert is too hot for the town. Had he stayed, he would have doubtless followed Stephen to death, but the Lord had other plans for him. We learn later in Acts (22:17ff), how Jesus appeared to him in a vision and ordered him to leave. Even then Saul protested, wanting to stay, but the Lord repeated the command telling him flat out–"Go!" This of course made it easy for the brethren to get him to leave. So they escorted him to Caesarea where they placed him on a ship for Tarsus. He needed more time in God's seminary. During the next six to nine years at Tarsus, Saul was schooled, not in theology, but in wisdom. We now leave him in retirement until it is time to meet him again in Chapter Eleven.

"Did it ease the situation to have Saul hustled out of town?"

31. And so it was that the entire church throughout Judea, Galilee, and Samaria enjoyed a time of peace and became firmly established in the fear of the Lord. There was a steady increase both in numbers and spiritual strength due to the strengthening presence of the Holy Spirit.

PEACE. The persecution which erupted with the stoning of Stephen and was fired by Saul, gradually abated and at length ceased entirely. Serenity prevailed throughout the church. When Saul returned to Jerusalem, after his escape from Damascus, his activities threatened to re-kindle the trouble. Hence he was hustled to his home in Tarsus. Also, the Jews were content to let the church alone, for their hands were busy with another problem. Right at this time, the emperor Caligula wanted his statue erected in the Jews' temple. This thunder stroke kept the Jews occupied with little else for quite awhile. Note the mention of Christian congregations in the three provinces of Palestine. This is the only reference in Acts to churches in Galilee. Yet it was the place where Jesus labored most. It was also the home of the greater number of His apostles and disciples.

FEAR. The healthiest thing a Christian can do is fear the Lord. That doesn't mean to be afraid of Him as a Person, but fear to be out of His will. The presence of the Lord in those early disciples was so real their lives were filled with reverential awe. They lived in the "fear of the Lord." Their steps were regulated by His words. They sensed His watchful eye. We would call them "God-fearing men." As a consequence, the church stayed on course. By His Spirit, the Lord added new members to His body, seeing to it that all were edified. We can assume there was much inspired preaching in those days, and the hearts of listeners burned as the gift of "prophesy" operated full force. Phase II of the Great Commission appears fairly well completed. It is interesting that Luke, in spite of his limited space, pauses to summarize the church's progress. He considers this mention of it a vital entry in the record.

"Did this church expansion add to Peter's work load?"

32. And it came to pass that Peter, while making an official tour of all those churches, came to visit the saints at Lydda. 33. There he found a man named Aeneas who was paralyzed and had been bedridden for eight years. 34. And Peter said to him, "Aeneas! Jesus Christ heals you! Get up and make your bed!" With that he arose immediately. 35. All those dwelling in Lydda and Sharon came to see him, and their hearts were turned to the Lord.

TOUR. With peace coming to the church, Peter is free to make an inspection tour of the Christian groups throughout Palestine. It is possible he is retracing Philip's circuit. Philip has been doing a fine job establishing new churches. Peter has no reason to suspect Philip's work is deficient, but the chief apostle is responsible to make sure. Then he comes to Lydda. The Spirit leads him to a paralyzed man who has been bedridden for eight years. Nothing in the text indicates this man is a Christian. To the contrary, the Gk. expressions seem to present him as a stranger. His Aramaic name would have been mentioned were he a Hebrew Christian.

AENEAS. One cannot miss the similarity between this event and the healing of the paralytic who was carried to the Lord by four men (Mk. 2:3ff.). So closely do the details coincide, one is forced to conclude the SAME Jesus is the Healer in both cases. Jesus said to the paralytic, "Arise, take up your bed and walk!" To this man, the Lord says, THROUGH Peter, "Arise and make your bed!" Note how Luke makes no mention of the man's faith. Peter makes no inquiry at all. It appears we have another of those miracles intended as a SIGN to the people. Since the faith of the man is NOT involved, the Lord is apparently healing this man for the sake of drawing attention to HIMSELF.

GET UP! Peter was careful to see that the paralyzed man knew Who was healing him. He said to him, "Jesus Christ HEALS you!" The verb is in the present tense. He did not say, "Be healed," or "I have the power to heal you." Of course Peter's faith made it possible for the Lord to work in this fashion, but Jesus did it. Peter said so. The results were the same as when Jesus operated in the flesh. The man was totally cured at once. Not only was he cured, his strength was restored. After eight motionless years, he could make his bed. When the inhabitants of the Plain of Sharon heard of this healing (sign), they were drawn to Peter who gave them the Word. Thus the miracle drew them to the Word, and the Word brought them to faith, for "faith cometh by hearing, and hearing by the Word of God" (Rom. 10: 17).

"Did Peter remain in Samaria when he saw how widely God had opened the door for the gospel there?"

36. Now in Joppa there was a woman named Tabitha. In Greek she was called Dorcas, which means a gazelle. She was a Christian disciple whose life was filled with doing good to others, especially the poor. 37. It so happened at this time that she became ill and died. Then, in accordance with the custom, her friends came and washed her body, laying it in an upper room ready for burial. 38. However, when the disciples heard that Peter was at nearby Lydda, they sent two men to fetch him. "Come to us," they said, "as quickly as you can."

JOPPA. After Peter had been in Lydda some time, messengers come with word that he is needed in Joppa. In that town is someone else in whom he is to reveal the Lord's presence and power. Since Joppa was only 10 miles N.W. of Lydda, they no doubt heard of the miracle of the paralyzed man. When it was learned that Peter was so close by, two men were sent to fetch him. If Christ's power operated in him so mightily, it was hoped he might be able to do something. Joppa, a seaport town, was one of the oldest cities in the Mid-East with a history dating to the time of Jonah (Jonah 1:3). As often true of seaport towns, there was a mixture of Jews and Gentiles. This would account for Dorcas being mentioned by both of her names. The Jews would refer to her by her Aramaic name, Tabitha. The Gentiles would call her by her Greek name, Dorcas. 32 miles further north lies Caesarea, Philip's home.

DORCAS. Unlike Aeneas, Dorcas is introduced at once as a Christian. Her name, "Gazelle," was a favorite among the Jews. The slender and graceful gazelle was often used by Hebrews as an image of female loveliness. Dorcas appears as a deeply devoted disciple who loved the Lord so much, she sacrificed herself in the interest of others. A wonderful Christian lady, her life was filled with good works. She has so endeared herself to the Christians of Joppa, they were grief-stricken at her passing. Normally the Jews are in a hurry to bury their dead, but in this case they hopefully place the body in an upper room, just in case Peter is able to do something. Even so it is washed, the ceremonial preparation for burial.

"What would Peter do about a woman already dead?"

39. Peter went with them. As soon as he arrived, they took him to the upper room. Standing about weeping were all the widows, eager to show Peter the tunics and cloaks Dorcas had made for them while she was still alive. 40a. But Peter asked them all to leave the room, then he dropped to his knees to pray.

EAGER. The apostle did as requested, hurrying to Joppa with the men. As soon as he arrived he was conducted to the upper room where the corpse lay. Then the widows who Dorcas aided with her Christian giving and needlework, began assembling in the room. They came to display the garments she had made for them and to show their respect for her sacrificial life. In the presence of her corpse, they began exhibiting the tunics (undergarments) and the cloaks (gown-like outer garments) she had sewn with unwearied self-denial. Both the tunic and cloak are still worn in many places in the Mid-East by both sexes.

PRAY. Peter did not immediately address the corpse. Following the example of His Master in the case of Jairus' daughter, he asked the women to withdraw. It is possible that some were governed by idle curiosity, but the real reason was that he might devote himself to prayer. As yet he did not know whether it was the Lord's will to restore the deceased Dorcas to life. Surely he did NOT ask God for the power to raise her from the dead, but for an understanding of God's will. That's all he needed to know. Having the power to perform miracles wouldn't give Peter the right to step into a life or death matter. Whatever happens to this woman will be because the Lord wills it, not because Peter is a man of faith. Why? It is the Lord who will raise this woman, not Peter. Therefore he must determine the Lord's will before anything else. It isn't long before he knows what God wants him to do.

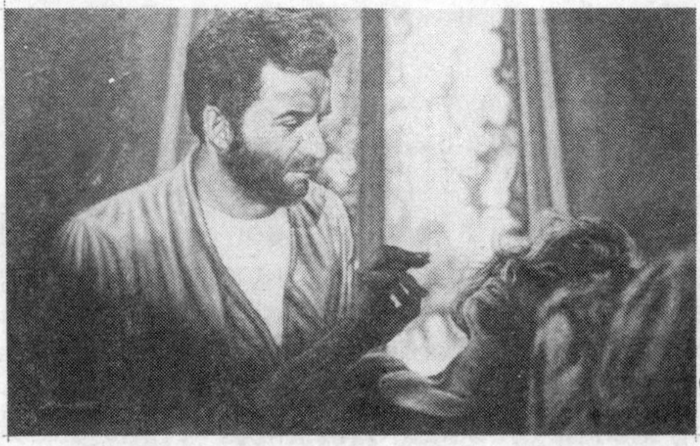

© Linda Lovett 1979

40b. Then turning to the body he said, "Tabitha, arise!" She opened her eyes and the moment she saw Peter, she sat up. 41. Taking her by the hand, he helped her to her feet. Then he called in the believers and widows and presented her to them alive. 42. The news spread quickly all over Joppa, and many learned to believe in the Lord. 43. Peter continued to stay on in Joppa for a long time after this, dwelling in the home of a tanner called Simon.

ARISE! Philip would have said, "Dorcas, arise!" He was a Greek-speaking Jew. But Peter would use her Aramaic name. He said literally, "Tabitha, cumi," (Tabitha, arise). It is fascinating that this short phrase differs only in **one letter** from the words of Jesus to Jairus' daughter, i.e., "Talitha, cumi!" (Little girl, arise). The similarity is so striking one cannot miss the fact that both events were performed by the same Person—Jesus. Recall that Peter was among those allowed to remain in the room when Jesus raised Jairus' daughter. Everything about the present scene is exactly as the Lord Himself had done: (1) removing the spectators, (2) addressing the deceased, (3) reaching with the hand to help. Nothing is more obvious than the fact that Christ did this miracle through His apostle. True, Peter's faith made it possible for the indwelling Lord to operate in this way, but it was Jesus' decision and power, not Peter's. Luke seems to be going out of his way to report another miracle which served as a SIGN to the people.

PRESENTED. Dorcas' eyes opened at once. She saw Peter and sat up. Helping her to her feet, he presented her to the waiting mourners. Luke doesn't tell us of their joy. Perhaps it was impossible to describe. In any event we should concern ourselves with WHY the Lord did this. It was not for Dorcas' sake, nor yet was it to cancel the grief of the Christian group. As He used miracles in the days of His flesh to attract attention to Himself and His message, so now does he use them to attract attention to the fact that He is still alive and working through His apostle. Because of this miracle, a multitude of people was drawn to Peter to hear the Word. Many believed the message and were added to the fellowship. Once more we are furnished with an incident which suggests the true title of this book is, "The Acts of Jesus Christ through His Apostles." The focus should remain on Jesus, as well as His apostles. So great was the opportunity created by this miracle, Peter found himself compelled to stay in the vicinity rather than return to Jerusalem.

SIMON. Since Peter was to be there some time, he located a place to live. He took lodging with another Jew who lived on the seashore. This man was a tanner by trade, an unclean business as far as Jews were concerned, for he handled unclean animals and dealt with dead and defiled carcasses. Were he not a Christian, Peter would never have stayed with him. He is still too much of a Jew for that. But that is precisely why Jesus wants Peter here. Phase III of the Great Commission is at hand. With the success of the gospel in Samaria, Peter is about to open the door to the Gentiles. But as yet he is wholly unprepared for the task. To him a Gentile is an unclean dog. So Peter's attitude has to be changed before Phase III can begin. God will keep Peter here in Joppa long enough to prepare his heart for a ministry to the Gentiles.

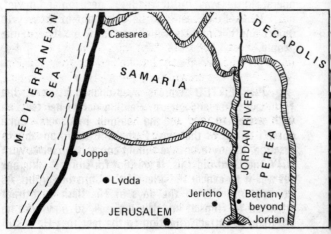

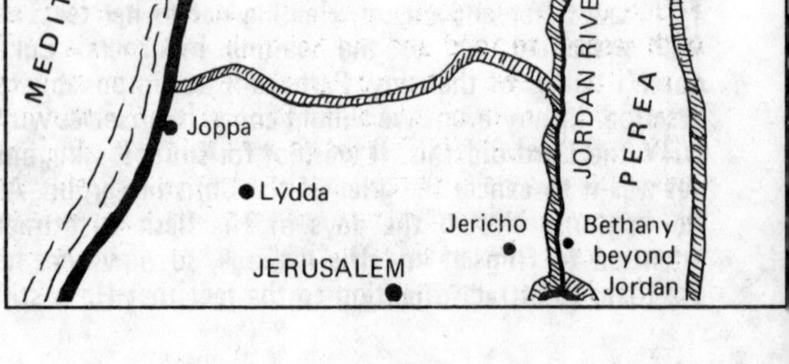

"How will God prepare Peter for the Gentile ministry?"

10 1. In Caesarea there was a man named Cornelius. He was a centurion in a Roman battalion garrisoned there, known as the Italian Cohort. 2. He was a deeply religious man, one who worshipped the true God, as did his entire household. He contributed generously to the Jewish poor people, and prayed continuously.

CAESAREA. This Gentile city on the Mediterranean coast was sometimes called Caesarea Palestine to distinguish it from Caesarea Philippi. It boasted a fine harbor and many splendid temples, palaces, and other buildings. It was the headquarters of the Roman governor of Palestine, since elements of the Roman army were garrisoned there. It was inhabited chiefly by pagans, but a few thousand Jews also lived there. Cornelius was an officer (captain?) who belonged to a battalion (cohort) made up of Italians, perhaps natives of Rome. There were 60 centurions in a Roman legion. Sometimes they were given special duty, as may have been the case with Cornelius. In any event, Luke seems to be emphasizing the fact that he was an Italian, perhaps for the sake of the Roman readers to whom he was writing. He was clearly a Gentile.

RELIGIOUS. Cornelius was deeply religious, yet NOT a Jewish proselyte. Like the Ethopian Eunuch (whose castration kept him from being a full proselyte), he had attached himself to the Jews' religion. No doubt he was drawn by the simplicity of worshipping one God, and the Jews' high moral code. He may have attended the synagogue and observed Jewish practices with respect to food and the Sabbath. But He was NOT a Jew for he was not circumcised. He was, however, as religious as a man could be. His life was filled with good works, yet he was NOT saved (Acts 11:14). In that, he represents many churchgoers today who are also religious but unsaved. It is interesting that the first Gentile with whom Jesus dealt was also a centurion. This could possibly be the same man.

3. One day, around three o'clock in the afternoon, he had a vision in which he clearly saw an angel enter his room and address him by name. "Cornelius!" said the angel. 4. For a moment he stared at the angel in terror. Then he said, "What is it, sir?" The angel replied, "God has taken note of your prayers and your giving, and they are recorded in heaven. 5. Now He would have you send men to Joppa to find a man named Simon, who is also called Peter. 6. He is staying with Simon the tanner, whose house is down by the beach."

VISION. Cornelius is deeply in prayer at the 3 o'clock Jewish hour of prayer when he has a vision of an angel coming into his room and speaking to him. The fact that it was a vision does not make it a deception. God can easily author a scene in one's imagination. It is not necessary for Him to use the eye-gate, for all sight has to be transmitted to the brain for interpretation anyway. All seeing is finally done in the mind. It is a simple matter for God to by-pass the optics and deal directly with one's imagination. See how no mention is made of any wings which poets and artists fondly attach to the heavenly visitors. As religious as he was, Cornelius was terrified. All of his good works did not ease his fears. Rightly so, for a heavenly visitor can bring nothing but terror to a sinner, despite all the sentimental talk about their beauty and cherub natures.

SIR? Cornelius cries out in fright. He is alarmed by the unexpected appearance of this dazzling (?) creature who calls him by name. "What is it, sir?" Or it could read, "What is it, my lord?" In the latter case, "lord" would be in the sense of a nobleman. The angel's reply was calculated to set him at ease. He tells him that God has taken note of all of his good works and they have been credited to his account in heaven. The language here is very O.T., for it speaks of his works as ascending like the smoke of an oblation. We conclude from this that God has been pleased to regard them as He might a Jewish offering. Evidently Cornelius has been asking God for more light or an understanding of salvation. The answer comes in the form of a command to send for Peter, no less than the chief apostle himself.

"How did Cornelius react to this vision?"

7. As soon as the angel visitor left him, Cornelius summoned two of his house servants and one of his orderlies, who was also a devout soldier. 8. He told them the story of what had happened. Then he sent them off to Joppa.

SENT. Obediently, Cornelius dispatches his servants to find Peter. But couldn't the angel have told him what he wanted to know? No. The gospel is to be preached by men who have been redeemed. Angels know nothing of that experience. Besides, Peter has been designated to open the door to the Gentiles, he has the keys to the kingdom. To this point, Peter's ministry has been confined to Israelites and the half-breed Samaritans. Nothing could be more repulsive to him than offering the gospel to Gentiles, uncoverted heathens—no matter how religious they were. Thus, Peter is not ready for the arrival of Cornelius' servants. So far, he is convinced there are only two classes of people in the world—Jews and Gentiles. To his mind, for a Gentile to be saved, he must first be circumcised, place himself under the Law, and become a Jew. As yet he knows nothing of how Christ's death destroyed the wall of partition between Jews and Gentiles, creating one body, the church. It will require divine intervention before Peter can bring God's answer to Cornelius' prayers. When he does, the door will be opened to the Gentiles.

"Is Peter prepared for a visit from Gentile messengers?"

9. The next day, as these men were approaching the city, Peter went up on the roof to pray. Since it was around noon, 10. he was hungry. While waiting for his meal to be prepared, he fell into a trance.

APPROACHING. Peter is not ready to welcome any Gentile messengers. And he definitely has scruples which would have to be overcome before he would think of returning with them to Caesarea. As an orthodox Jew, Peter wouldn't dream of entering the house of a Gentile, even if he were a God-fearing man. But God is about to change that. As Ananias and Saul were prepared for each other by means of visions, so now are Peter and Cornelius. The servants probably left Caesarea the evening before and are just completing the 32 mile journey. They are in the vicinity of Joppa when Peter goes to the housetop for his midday devotions. As a pious Jew, still deeply involved in the traditions of Israel, Peter prayed three times a day. The flat roofs of the dwelling were commonly used as a place to perform religious exercises in private.

TRANCE. Peter becomes hungry. This is understandable since it was around noon. He sends word down to Simon's kitchen to fix him some lunch. While he is waiting for it to be prepared, he falls into a trance. A trance is a state in which one's consciousness subsides and he occupies with things in his imagination. During that time the awareness of his surroundings is suspended. In such a moment when he is involved in an intense daydream, it is easy for God (Satan too) to interject a vision or appearance. So real is the vision about to come to Peter, that he will SEE, HEAR, and ANSWER, yet it will all take place in his mind. The fact that he is hungry explains why the vision centers chiefly in food. Peter may have been lying prostrate when he began his devotions, but with the passing of time, he dozes off into a trance.

11. He saw a parting of the sky and a huge, sheet-like object, slung by its four corners, gradually being lowered to the ground. 12. In it were all kinds of quadrupeds, reptiles, and birds. 13. Then a voice said to him, "Rise Peter, kill and eat!"

SHEET. What did Peter see before he closed his eyes; the awning above his head or a sail out on the Mediterranean? Whatever it was, God used it to form the vision in his imagination. He beholds a huge, sail-like object held fast by its four corners, being lowered from the sky to the ground. It contains all kinds of animal life. The animals are alive. Here is plenty of food for a hungry man. Then a voice says to Peter, "Kill and eat!" Peter is repulsed. Such a thing is an offense to an orthodox Jew. True, he had his pick of the creatures in the bag, but there were unclean animals in there and they contaminated (defiled) the clean ones with their presence. Besides, even the clean animals couldn't be killed without certain ritual. It wouldn't be kosher. No, the command is unacceptable to Peter.

"Would Peter dare refuse to obey a vision?"

14. "No Lord! I should say not!" replied Peter. "Never in my life have I eaten anything unclean or defiled!" 15. Then the voice came to him a second time, "What God has cleansed you must no longer regard as unclean." 16. This happened three times, then the whole bundle was yanked back into heaven.

NO LORD! What Peter had been told to do horribly violated his life style and Jewish conscience. Also, it was strictly forbidden by God's dietary laws of Leviticus 11. Peter has always rebelled when told to do something contrary to his nature. When the Lord wanted to wash his feet, he said "Never!" When the Lord said he would deny Him, he said, "Never!" So now, when he feels he has been told to do something out of order, he again says, "No!" How could the One Whose Law forbad the eating of anything but kosher food turn around and order him to eat it? Peter is baffled, "Surely God wouldn't contradict Himself!" But when he is rebuked by the reply, "What God has cleansed, etc.," he realizes he heard correctly. When it happened a third time, the matter was beyond the realm of coincidence. A change of some sort must be in the wind.

CLEANSED. If what Peter has just seen and heard is really true, it means God has cancelled the dietary laws. There is no longer any such thing as clean and unclean food. But has God contradicted Himself? No. What Peter doesn't understand is that God has CHANGED the program. Many of the things He commanded of Israel AS A NATION (including the dietary laws), were to keep them separated from the Gentiles. As long as Israel was the custodian of His revelation, He wanted that nation isolated from all others. The levitical laws served to accomplish it. But with the advent of the church, composed of BOTH Jews and Gentiles, those separating laws become obsolete. Peter is now meeting that truth. As he ponders the implications of the vision, it will occur to him that the meaning goes beyond articles of food. It will be quite a shock when he understands the animals shown him represent people. Hence the distinction between clean and unclean men is now at an end. This will become clearer to Peter as the circumstances unfold.

"That threefold vision must have left Peter baffled!"

17. While Peter was puzzling over the vision he had just seen, Cornelius' messengers, who had now found their way to Simon's house, appeared at the gate. 18. They called out, "Is Simon Peter staying here?" 19. Peter was still trying to fathom the meaning of the vision when the Spirit said to him, "Listen! There are three men here asking for you. 20. Hurry up and go downstairs. Don't hesitate to go with them for I Myself have sent them."

LISTEN! Peter is wide awake now, yet what he had seen in the vision did not vanish as does a dream. It lingered. He was meditating on it when suddenly the Lord spoke to him. As Philip was instructed to go south to the Gaza Road, so now Peter is instructed to go down to the men. God's timing is perfect. At the very moment when these men were knocking at the gate, Peter was being ordered to go to them. He is told that he shouldn't hesitate to go with them, for like himself, they were being divinely directed. The Spirit of Christ spoke to Peter by an internal communication. God does not need sound waves to fall on an ear drum to speak to a man. When it pleases him to do so, he can speak directly to one's mind where all sound waves are finally interpreted.

HURRY! Peter was on the roof, deep in thought, when the men made their inquiry. He did not hear them, he was too engrossed in the vision he had just seen. The Spirit interrupted his meditation to speak of the messengers. In that day, houses were usually constructed with two flights of stairs leading to the roof. One was inside the house. The other, made of stone, connected the roof directly with the street. Since Peter was told to hurry, he doubtless used the stone stairway. Even as he makes the descent to the street, he is still confused about the vision. He is soon to find out what it meant. The first clue will come when he learns the reason for the messengers' visit.

"Will Peter really go with these Gentiles to a Gentile home?"

21. So Peter went down and spoke to the men. "I'm the one you're looking for," he said, "what do you want?" 22. "We have come from the centurion Cornelius," they answered, "a man who worships the true God and keeps His Law, and has the respect of the Jewish people. He received a revelation in which a holy angel directed him to send for you. He asks that you come to his house and tell him whatever God would have you say." 23a. With that, Peter invited them in and gave them lodging for the night.

HOUSE. If Peter sounds abrupt, it should be remembered these are Gentiles knocking at the door of a Jewish home. That was in itself disturbing. But his tone will change. Consider what is happening to Peter. He has just been told to eat unclean animals because God has cleansed them. Now he is told to accompany these men to a Gentile (unclean) home. In doing so he would be defiled, that is, **ceremonially** unclean. After hearing their words concerning Cornelius, the whole situation seems related with his vision. Somehow there's a connection between the clean and unclean men. That, plus the fact he has been ordered to accompany them, convinces Peter of this. Peter's Jewish shell is beginning to crack. He invites the travel-weary servants to spend the night, purposing to go with them in the morning. At this point, we have Gentiles lodging in a Jewish house. That in itself was dramatic. Some tremendous changes are indeed taking place.

23b. The following morning Peter arose and departed with them, accompanied by some of the brethren from Joppa. 24. The day after that, he arrived at Caesarea. Cornelius, who was waiting for him, had gathered together his relatives and close friends.

ACCOMPANIED. After the night's rest, which the messengers obviously needed, Peter departed with them for Cornelius' home. The strangeness of the event prompted him to ask six of the Hebrew Christians of Joppa to go with him. Since he was certain to enter a Gentile home, he felt it would be wise to have responsible brethren witness what took place. If Peter had any doubt about the propiety of his going, it didn't slow him down any. He moved in haste as ordered. Accordingly they formed a small caravan of ten men, arriving in Caesarea the next day. There they found Cornelius awaiting their arrival. In anticipation of the meeting he had, by faith, invited relatives and intimate friends to gather at his home. Undoubtedly their congregation is all set to listen to Peter.

25. As Peter approached the house, Cornelius came out to meet him. He paid him great reverence by prostrating himself before him. 26. But Peter raised Cornelius to his feet, saying, "Stand up. I'm just a man no different from anyone else."

PROSTRATING. Certain of Cornelius' servants had no doubt been posted to watch for Peter's arrival. As he drew near the Roman's house, the excited Cornelius rushes out to meet him, showing him the utmost respect. Regarding Peter as a messenger of God, he humbles himself before him, according him divine honor. This act was somewhat natural due to the Roman practice of regarding certain men as gods, Caesar for example. Cornelius' prostration is an offer to worship Peter. But Peter wouldn't tolerate it for a moment. Reaching out his hand, he helps the centurion to his feet. He informs him, that he, like Cornelius is just another human being. What! A Jew just another human being—and just like a Gentile! In order for Peter to say there was no difference between them, he had to sweep aside 1400 years of tremendous difference. He was getting the message of the lowered sheet. He has already begun to practice what he learned.

27. Peter chatted with Cornelius as they entered the house, where he found, to his surprise, a large gathering of people. 28. Then he spoke to them:

"You know that Jewish regulations forbid a man like myself to associate with Gentiles or visit their homes. But God has shown me that I must not consider any man unclean or defiled. 29. That is why I didn't object to coming here when you asked for me. Now I need to know why it is that you sent for me."

SHOWN ME. What a sight, the pious Jew and a Roman centurion chatting like friends. God had performed a miracle, using two supernatural communications to arrange it. The biggest barrier to this meeting was Peter's Jewish prejudice against Gentiles. He had to be persuaded that God was abolishing the partition between Jew and Gentile. If the top apostle didn't understand this, likely none of the others would believe it. That's why he held the keys to the kingdom. That Peter has grasped the analogy between the **food** in the vision and **men**, is now clear. Told to call **no food** unclean, he now sees that instruction really applies to people. Before he will use the final key to the kingdom, he needs to understand the Gentiles are acceptable to God.

WHY ME? When Peter asks, "why did you send for me?" he is speaking to the large audience gathered in Cornelius' home. He is not challenging Cornelius' motives for inviting him. He wants to make sure the audience is of one mind, that it is a group of God-fearing people. He is qualifying his audience. Also, there are the six Jewish Christians who have come with him as witnesses. Perhaps that is why he speaks so frankly about the violation of strict Jewish custom in making this appearance in a Gentile home. Having cleared the air on that account, he wants them to tell him precisely what they expect of him. The messengers had already furnished him some details, so perhaps Peter is measuring their spiritual appetite. Do they mean business or are they merely spectators? Would modern preachers dare challenge their audiences in this fashion?

30. However it was Cornelius who answered:

"Four days ago I was here in the house saying my three o'clock prayers, when all of a sudden a man wearing shining robes stood before me. 31. 'Cornelius,' he said, 'God has taken note of your prayers and your giving and they are recorded in heaven. 32. And He would have you send to Joppa to invite Simon, who is also called Peter, to come to you. You'll find him staying with Simon the tanner whose house is down by the beach.' 33. So I sent for you at once, and you have been kind enough to come. Now we are all gathered here before God to hear whatever the Lord has instructed you to say."

ANSWERED. Cornelius first describes the vision he had seen three days previously. (The "four days" above are reckoned inclusively.) It occurred, he said, at that very same hour, the hour in which he is now speaking. He goes into detail about the angel's message, particularly the name of the city and Simon Peter's address. That should remove all doubt from Peter's mind as to the origin of the vision. Thus the mystery of the great sheet full of animals is clear. Peter was now aware that the great difference between Jew and Gentile, BEFORE GOD, no longer existed. The final clincher must have been Cornelius' words. . ."We are all here. . .before God. . .," indicating they enjoyed access to God without the benefit of Judaism. That confirmed the lesson he had learned at Joppa.

HEAR. Consider Peter's audience. The soil had already been prepared, for these people already believed there was but ONE God. They believed themselves to be in His sight, conscious of His presence. Men with God-consciousness sweeping their minds are not interested in secular or social matters. Neither do they care about theological speculations. They only want to hear what God is about to give them. See how their minds are unbiased, free of prejudice, wide open to ALL God has for them. Such a congregation had not come to listen and pass judgment, but to learn and ACT upon what they hear. We don't find audiences like that today. If we did, it is not likely they would put up with the trifling of some pulpits.

"Wow! What a promising situation for a gospel preacher!"

34. Then Peter began to speak:

"I am now convinced that God is wholly impartial, having no favorite race of people. 35. Every God-fearing man who seeks to do what is right, is acceptable to Him no matter to what race he belongs."

ACCEPTABLE. What a staggering thing for Peter to say! He always believed God WAS partial, that Israel was His favorite race. To him, Gentiles were dogs. He thought God felt that way too. In saying God has NO favorites, Peter sweeps away 20 centuries of Jewish prejudice. Next to the incarnation of Christ, the day of Pentecost, and the conversion of Saul, stand these words of Peter to the Gentile world. This is an epoch in human history. He does not mean that men are saved by fearing God and doing right, only that God will accept men for salvation **from any race.** Remarkable is it that

Peter is only now coming into this truth. Why? It is as old as Moses (Deut. 10:17). Peter knew this truth in theory, but it took the crisis of Cornelius to make it real to him. That room full of God-fearers was a shock. The very fact that he had been SENT to tell them how they might be saved, was proof they were acceptable to God.

"How will Peter go about sharing the gospel with these Gentiles?"

36. "First of all, you know that God sent the good news of salvation through Jesus Christ (the Lord of us all) to the children of Israel. 37. Also you must know the story of what happened all over the land of the Jews, from Galilee to Judea, right after John started baptizing. 38. Further, you are undoubtedly aware of the fact that God anointed Jesus of Nazareth with the Holy Spirit and with power. There was nothing secretive about it. He went about the country doing good, and in particular, healing all those who were dominated by the devil, for God was with Him."

YOU KNOW. Peter is aware that his audience is far from heathen. By reason of their residence in Caesarea in the Holy Land, and because of their spiritual hunger, they had to know a few things about Christ. So he begins by stating three facts he presumes to be familiar to them: (1) that the salvation message came first to the Jews, (2) they had to know about an event which occurred in their own land, (3) anyone with their spiritual interest couldn't possibly be ignorant of the Person of Jesus. He supposes them to know about a MESSAGE which had come to Israel, and an EVENT which took place in the land, and a PERSON Who had come from God. Peter could have spoken in Greek, but it is more likely that he spoke in Aramaic through an interpreter. Scholars agree we have no more than an outline of what Peter actually said.

39. "We are eyewitnesses of all that He did in the country of the Jews and in the city of Jerusalem,

where they murdered Him by hanging Him on a cross. 40. But God raised Him up on the third day, so that He was clearly seen again. 41. However, He did not appear to all the people, but only to those of us whom God chose beforehand to be His witnesses. We not only saw Him after He rose from the dead, we ate and drank with Him."

WITNESSES. Inasmuch as Peter's audience already has a knowledge of Jesus, it is only necessary for him to confirm the facts and the words of salvation with his own testimony. Cornelius and his friends, while familiar with the salvation message which had come to the Jews, did not know that the gospel of grace was for everybody, regardless of his nation. That's what they are going to learn from Peter. He proceeds first to explain how the apostles were actual eyewitnesses of all that happened throughout the ministry of the Lord. Undoubtedly we have only a summary of Peter's words here and must assume he provided many examples of the Lord's works of healing and power, such as we find in the gospels.

ROSE. The resurrection of Christ would receive the most attention, for that was the great sign given the world whereby people could know and believe that Jesus came from God. When Peter says the apostles "ate and drank" with the Lord, it is not only to prove that He didn't return as a bodiless spirit or phantom, but to speak of their intimacy with Him. They were with Him during much of the 40 days after His resurrection and could testify to its certainty. True, not everyone saw the Lord after He arose, but hundreds did—enough to make it an undeniable fact. The resurrection was the one great proof that Jesus was not only the Messiah of Israel, but Savior of the world. The audience in Cornelius' house felt the witness of the Spirit as this eyewitness unfolded the true story of Jesus.

42. "And He commissioned us to preach to the people and bear witness that He Himself, and no other, has

been ordained by God as the Judge of the living and the dead. 43. All of the prophets witness to Him with this testimony: everyone who believes in Him receives the forgiveness of sins through His name."

COMMISSIONED. Peter has reference to the 40 days after Jesus' resurrection during which He charged them to proclaim the kingdom of God to all men. Particularly were they to announce Him as the UNIVERSAL Lord. The Judge of the living and dead refers to all mankind of every age, so that He is the Judge of every soul who appears on earth. But it has only been within the last few hours that Peter has finally seen how the commission was to ALL men. He realizes now that Jesus is not only the Savior of the Jews, but of all those who place their trust in Him. He further realizes that this has been the general burden of the prophets, that the spirit of all prophetic testimony was salvation through faith in the NAME of this one Person, Jesus.

BELIEVES. Luke has skipped over much of what Peter said to this audience. But we've heard him before and can guess the details. It is the climax that is so suited to this Gentile congregation. ANYONE, regardless of nationality can now receive forgiveness of sins by believing in Jesus' name. This is what they had come to hear. This was a brand new message as far as Peter was concerned. Yet it wasn't the first time he had said such a thing. Though not aware of it at the time, the essence of his words here were contained in his message at Pentecost (2:39). He said it then under the Spirit's anointing. Only now is he aware of the UNIVERSAL Saviorhood of Jesus. How those words must have exploded in the hearts of his listeners.

FORGIVENESS. Notice how Peter's message here differs from his message at Pentecost. There he was addressing the NATION of Israel, asking for **national repentance.** Here he is addressing INDIVIDUALS, asking for **personal faith** in Jesus. The Pentecostal message was to JEWS ONLY. They were required to give evidence of their repentance by water baptism BEFORE they could be saved. Repentance is also needed in those at Cornelius' house. (There is no salvation without it), but it is not acknowledged by water baptism. To the contrary, we will see that water baptism is used to acknowledge salvation AFTER they have received Christ in the Spirit. The results of Peter's preaching show that water baptism has nothing to do with the forgiveness of sins. It is an outward testimony to the salvation already received.

"That must have sounded wonderful to those Gentiles!"

44. Even as those truths were coming from Peter's lips, the Holy Spirit fell upon all who were listening to the message.

MESSAGE. It was the Word that did the work in these Gentiles. Peter never finished his message. All these people needed to hear was that salvation could be theirs through personal faith in Jesus. Upon hearing that, they opened their hearts to Him. It was enough. The Lord, as the Holy Ghost, came into them at once. Every person in the room was saved. But that's to be expected. No one would have been there unless he was ready to receive the truth. Peter may have been leading up to the words, "repent and be baptized," but the Lord headed him off by manifesting the salvation experience **before** he could say anything more. Thus it appears the Spirit is dealing more with Peter than with the Gentiles. He's still being taught, learning something new and startling about water baptism. For the first time he saw people saved apart from being baptized in water.

FELL. Two expressions are used to indicate the coming of the Lord into these believers on this occasion. In the first instance it says the Holy Spirit "fell upon them" intimating that He came from above. Again it says He was "poured out" upon them (vs. 45). Both of these expressions mean the same. They refer to Christ's availability in the Spirit. People can receive Him as easily as getting a drink in a rain storm. All you have to do is turn your cup over. The Jewish doctors taught that the Holy Spirit would never come upon any heathen, nor on any Jew who lived in a foreign country. Now that notion is blasted before the eyes of Peter and the Jewish Christians who came with him. These Gentiles have received the Spirit along with outward manifestations to prove it.

"What manifestations attended the salvation experience of these Gentiles?"

45. The other Jewish Christians who had come with Peter were astonished to see the gift of the Spirit poured out upon the Gentiles also, 46a. for they heard them speaking in tongues and praising God.

ASTONISHED. How hard it is to shake off prejudice. But God was eager to help Peter and his Jewish companions do just that. In fact it was necessary for the expansion of the gospel. The phenomenon which attended the salvation of the Gentiles in Cornelius' house, was for the benefit of the Christian Jews, not the Gentiles. The signs furnished positive proof that these Gentiles had received the Holy Ghost. It would indeed take such a sign ("for the Jews require a sign–1 Cor. 1:22), to convince them that the Gentiles were also included in the blessings of Pentecost. Without such evidence, it is not likely they would have regarded them as genuinely saved. Had it been left for the inner spiritual changes to show up, as is the case with us today, there would have been plenty of room for doubt. As it was, the truth of Gentile salvation hits these Jewish Christians with such impact they are astonished.

TONGUES. With what tongues did they speak? Probably Aramaic, for the JEWS heard what they were saying. To have these Gentiles (likely Romans) speaking God's praises in fluent Aramaic, was an irrefutable SIGN that these Gentiles had received the SAME salvation as did the 120 at Pentecost. The tongues sign was for the Jews. The Gentiles didn't need any signs. They were filled with joy in the Holy Spirit. Peter no doubt intended to lay hands on these people as well, but that, too, was headed off by the Lord. Peter doesn't have to make these new believers feel welcome in the faith, God does it Himself. Thus Peter's lessons are coming thick and fast. Apparently this whole affair is for his benefit.

46b. Then Peter spoke up. 47. "Inasmuch as these people have received the Holy Spirit identically as we did, could anyone possibly object to their being baptized?" 48. So he gave orders for them to be baptized in the name of Jesus Christ. Afterwards, they begged him to stay on with them a few days longer.

IDENTICALLY. See how Peter draws a parallel between Cornelius' household and the 120 in the upper room? The languages spoken here were foreign tongues, not the ecstatic prayers of 1 Cor. 14:2. The unexpected appearance of these tongues has led some to call this a Gentile pentecost, as if it were another outpouring of Jesus. But Jesus was "poured out" on the day of Pentecost and is STILL being poured out today. It continues so that WHOSOEVER WILL can receive the Spirit in His fulness. There is no evidence that the wind-like, fire-like phenomena of Acts 2:2,3 were also present. The tongues were sufficient to convince Peter that these pagans had received salvation as suddenly and as completely as did those in the upper room.

RECEIVED. When Peter says WE, he means the original 120, not the 3000 who later believed on the day of Pentecost. The crowds were NOT saved instantly, there was a marked order in the pentecostal experience: (1) conviction of sin, (2) repentance, (3) faith in Jesus, (4) baptism, (5) receipt of the gift of the Spirit (salvation). But the Gentiles in Cornelius' home all received the Spirit in a second as did the 120. In Acts 11:17 Peter makes it clear they received the gift WHEN they believed, noting that God had cleansed their hearts through faith. This is why he felt it proper to order their water baptism. At last he understood the meaning of the words spoken to him in the vision of the lowered sheet, "What God has cleansed you must no longer regard as unclean." He knew that God had already washed these pagan hearts through faith, making them clean.

BAPTIZED. If no one could hinder the Spirit from coming upon these Gentiles, who then could forbid water (baptism) coming to them as well? That it was immediately commanded shows its importance. The receiving of the Spirit was obviously no substitute for it. Yet it was done in **response** to something God had already done. The application of water to the person's body pictured the soul cleansing that had already taken place. However, had these people been JEWS, the baptism would of necessity had to come first (see under 2:38).

"How did those at Jerusalem react to Peter's ministering to Gentiles?"

11 1. It wasn't long before the apostles and other brethren in Judea heard the news that the Gentiles had accepted the Word of God. 2. So when Peter returned to Jerusalem, those steeped in the tradition of circumcision took him to task. 3. "Why did you visit uncircumcised men," they asked, "and eat with them?"

NEWS. Before Peter could get back to Jerusalem, word of his astonishing behavior at Caesarea spread among Christian Jews like wild fire. The idea of mixing with Gentiles was opposed to all that Jews stood for, and to give them God's Word as he did, was scandalous. At Jerusalem the leaders of the church were waiting for him, ready to call him on the carpet for his actions at Cornelius' house. Instead of rejoicing that salvation had come to the Gentiles, they put him on trial, treating him like a criminal. He was forced to defend himself, an action which fails to support the modern Roman claim of pre-eminence for Peter.

CIRCUMCISION. At first, all Christians were of the circumcision tradition. Since they were all Jews, it was natural for them to view Christianity as an extension of Judaism. Consequently they were already circumcised before they came to Christ. They all believed that circumcision was an obligation never to be revoked. Thus, for a Gentile to become a Christian, it was deemed necessary for him to first be circumcised and then place himself under the Law of Moses. After that he was eligible to embrace Christ as his Messiah. At the time of the Cornelius affair there were no Christians in the Jerusalem church other than Jews and proselytes. Therefore, it is the entire church, along with its leaders, that has called Peter to question. This is not just a small party within the church. Later a party known as the "circumcision party," did develop. For many years these sticklers for Jewish orthodoxy vigorously resisted the idea of receiving Gentiles into the church without circumcision.

WHY? Peter's action in Cornelius' house had clearly violated strict Jewish rules. He not only ATE with these "unclean" people, an act that was totally forbidden, he had the audacity to call them believers. The church demands to know why. This act was like an earthquake to Judaism. It had the effect of tearing down the wall between Jew and Gentile—a separation they believed to be established by divine law. That wall had stood for 1400 years. They viewed Peter's action as opening flood gates. He had required nothing of these Gentiles in the way of moral standards or circumcision. Seemingly he brushed aside all Jewish procedure. They care more that Jewish rules were violated than having the precious Word go to lost souls. They feared the church would be swept by a tide of heathen. Should an influx of unclean people engulf the church, it would lose all of its Jewishness. This was an alarming prospect to thos who believed that Christianity was Jewish.

"Did Peter straighten them out?"

4. Then Peter told them the whole story point by point from the beginning.

5. "I was in the city of Joppa," he said, "and while I was praying I drifted into a trance and had a vision. I saw a huge sheet-like object, slung by its four corners, gradually being lowered out of the sky. It landed on the ground next to me, 6. so that I was able to look inside and examine what it contained. Inside that sheet were all kinds of animals, reptiles, and birds. 7. Then I heard a voice saying to me, 'Rise Peter, kill and eat!' 8. But I protested. 'No Lord!' I said, 'Never in my life have I eaten anything unclean or defiled!' 9. But again I heard a voice from heaven. It answered me, saying, 'What God has cleansed you must no longer regard as unclean.' 10. Three times this happened, and then the whole bundle was yanked back into heaven."

TOLD. How does Peter react toward those who would censure him for a noble work of God? He could have been contemptuous of them, even haughty, but he wasn't. He could have denounced them for their narrowminded prizing of rules more than people, but he didn't. Instead he is calm and generous, doing his best to justify his actions and conciliate his brethren. With great detail—far more than Luke gives us here—he tells the story point by point. His defense is a straight-forward narration of what happened.

11. "The amazing thing about it is, that at the precise moment when three men sent to me from Caesarea arrived at the house where we were staying, 12. the Spirit told me that I shouldn't hesitate to go with them. And these six brethren who are here with me now, accompanied me, and we went into the man's house together. 13. There he told us how he had seen an angel enter his house who stood before him and said, 'Send some men to Joppa, and have them find Simon, who is also called Peter, and have him brought here. 14. He will bring a message that can save you and your entire household.' "

AMAZING. Peter carefully points out the supernatural elements in the story. His listeners will be convinced only if they believe his actions were ordered by God. The sight of a huge sheet filled with animals and being let down from heaven had to be supernatural. Who would have the audacity to tell such a tale otherwise? See how he stresses the remarkable timing in the arrival of Cornelius' messengers, and the Spirit's admonition to accompany them without hesitation. Then, when Peter arrived in Caesarea, he found the situation to be just as the messengers had reported it to him. Cornelius was eager to learn how he and his household might be saved. The six Jewish witnesses who had accompanied Peter to Caesarea, were present to confirm his story.

15. "Well, I hadn't gotten too far into my message when the Holy Spirit fell on them just as He fell on us at the beginning! 16. At once I thought of how the Lord used to say to us, 'John baptized with water, but you shall be baptized in the Holy Spirit.' 17. Since it was very clear that God had given these Gentiles the very same gift He gave us when we believed on Him, who was I that I should argue with God or try to stay His hand?"

FELL. Peter's defense was NOT based on what he did, but on what GOD did. The climax of his argument is that God, per His own timing, baptized these Gentiles in the Holy Spirit. It happened even before Peter had finished his message. Peter doesn't even tell his Jewish brethren what the message was. It is as though Peter is saying, "I had very little to do with it. The whole thing was God's idea. He put it all together and who is going to argue with Him?" With the six Jewish Christians present to bear witness to what he said, Peter is content to rest his case. The events, as they unfolded, clearly showed it was God's will for these Gentiles to be saved. By presenting the Cornelius affair as something God had done, Peter's argument was irresistable.

BEGINNING. A staggering truth confronted the church at Jerusalem. The SAME Holy Spirit, with the same power and undeniable manifestations, had come upon the Gentiles just as He had descended upon the disciples at Pentecost. Peter was so convinced that these Gentiles had received the SAME baptism into Christ, he is reminded of the Lord's words concerning Spirit-baptism. "John baptized with water, but you will be baptized with the Holy Spirit. . ." The Jewish Christians are baffled. There was no tarrying, no laying on of hands, no circumcision—nothing. The Gentiles received the Holy Spirit when they believed. They didn't even get out of their seats. Yet the unmistakable SIGN of tongues forces the Jerusalem church to face the hard fact that salvation had come to these Gentiles, even as it did to them. Even so, salvation had been available to the Gentiles since the day of Pentecost (Ch. 2:39). They just needed someone to tell them.

"Would the Jewish Christians accept Peter's statement?"

18. And when they heard this, they settled down. They stopped their criticism and began to glorify God by saying, "Well then, it appears God has given these Gentiles an opportunity to turn to Him and receive eternal life."

STOPPED. There was no way for the Jerusalem church to counter what Peter had said. If God wanted Cornelius' household to turn to Him and be saved, that was His own business. So the church shifted from criticising Peter, to acknowledging God's right to save these Gentiles on His own terms. The grumbling was silenced for the moment, but 1400 years of national prejudice cannot be turned off like a faucet. It took a "Damascus Road" type experience to change Peter's mind. The rest of the church will die hard. Luke is sensitive to this matter, for the circumcision party will later try to block Paul's work when he begins preaching to the Gentiles. In theory, the church is here acknowledging the gospel is for the whole world, but the disciples will be in no hurry to put that theory into practice. This was a great fault in the Jerusalem church.

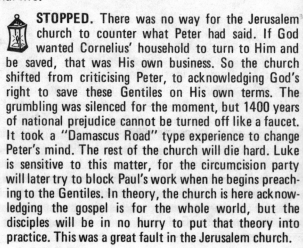

GLORIFY. It was a strange glory that came to God that day. The disciples were forced to admit the Gentiles were saved. God used tongues to convince the Jewish Christians He had opened the door to these Gentiles. ". . .with men of other tongues and other lips will I speak unto THIS people. . ." (1 Cor. 14:21). Nothing less would convince the unbelieving disciples. They were forced to acknowledge it, for they respected the SIGN of tongues. Even so, the rank and file church member resented it deeply. While the other apostles may have approved Peter's testimony, it would be a long time before the general hatred for the uncircumcised heathen would pass from the church. Most of the disciples likely believed this was an isolated case, that Gentile expansion should go no further. Consequently, Phase III of the Commission started without the willing submission of the church, even though it was marked by an undeniable SIGN of the Holy Spirit's approval. It remained for the apostle Paul to see that the Gentiles received God's invitation to salvation.

"Whatever became of all those Hellenistic Christians who fled Jerusalem?"

19. Meanwhile those who had fled the city of Jerusalem, because of the persecution triggered by Stephen, traveled as far as Phoenicia and Cyprus and Antioch, sharing the message with Jews only, and no one else.

MEANWHILE. Luke flashes back in his story to take up the account of what happened to those who fled Jerusalem (Acts 8:4ff). He had interrupted himself to tell of Saul's conversion, Philip's ministry to the Samaritans, and the Cornelius affair. In telling the story of those who fled northward, he is eager to show how they were used to create the great Gentile church at Antioch. The refugees moved first into the 130 mile stretch of the Mediterranean coast known as Phoenicia. Some likely settled in the towns of Tyre and Sidon. Some also returned to their homes on the island of Cyprus, but others made it as far north as Antioch. Among those would be Nicolas (the 7th deacon, Acts 6:5) for he was a "proselyte from Antioch." Note how they witness to Jews only. Some time will pass before they minister to Gentiles.

ANTIOCH. Located about 10 miles up the Orontes River, this was the capitol of Syria. Next to Rome and Alexandria, it ranked third in size and importance of all the cities in the Roman Empire. The climate was ideal, and a huge Jewish colony flourished there. The city was tolerant of all religions. It was a Gentile town, founded by Seleucius, who named it for his father, Antiochus. It became a free city in B.C. 64 when Syria was incorporated into the Roman Empire. Antioch was dominated by Greek language and culture, and was a mecca for the persecuted Hellenists forced to flee Jerusalem. The city is soon to enter a new phase in its history. It is about to become the center of Gentile Christianity.

20. But some of those believers, men of Cyprus and Cyrene, when they came to Antioch, began speaking to the Greeks as well, and they preached the Lord to them. 21. The Lord backed their ministry with such power, that a great number of them believed the Word and turned to the Lord.

GREEKS. In those places where the Hellenists had gone, after fleeing Jerusalem, they confined their witnessing to Jews only. But with the passing of time, a different breed of Hellenist arrived in Antioch from Cyprus and Cyrene. They were used to freedom and not nearly so strict in their Judaism as the Hellenists who were scattered earlier. Their more daring spirits, plus the free spirit of Antioch, prompted them to try a bold step—sharing Christ with the Greeks of that city. Evidently some of them were God-fearers (perhaps seekers) and it seemed only natural to tell them about Jesus. At this time many were looking for a divine Lord who could give them eternal life. Thus the city of Antioch was ripe for the gospel. Since it was so far from Jerusalem, the Jewish rules somehow didn't seem important any longer. The Greeks happily received the word of Christ.

BELIEVED. Without the sanction of the Jerusalem church, the gospel exploded with startling success in Antioch. The Holy Spirit backed the witness of the Hellenists and pagans began turning to the Lord in wholesale fashion. But why did Luke report the salvation of Cornelius BEFORE the Antioch affair? We don't know for sure. It is possible that more than 3 years passed between verses 19 and 20, and Peter had already used the "key of the kingdom" in Cornelius' house. However there is NO direct connection between the winning of Cornelius and this Gentile evangelization in Antioch. The Cornelius incident brought about formal recognition of Gentile salvation apart from Judaism, and pointed up the fact that Peter had the "keys of the kingdom." However, this was as far as the Jerusalem church cared to go. They were reluctant to do more than open the door.

"How did the Jerusalem church react to this turn of events?"

22. When news of what was happening at Antioch came to the attention of the church at Jerusalem, they sent Barnabas on a mission to investigate. 23. When he got there and saw how God was blessing the people, he was thrilled. He then began challenging the new converts to cling to the Lord with all of their hearts. 24. Being the good man that he was, full of faith and the Holy Spirit, a great many people were brought to the Lord as the result of his ministry.

INVESTIGATE. When the leaders of the Jerusalem church heard that a Greek (Gentile) church had been started at Antioch, they sent a delegation, headed by Barnabas, to check out this startling development. They couldn't have chosen a better man. He was himself a Hellenist (from Cyprus), and would be more sympathetic than any of the Christian Jews who had never been outside of Judea. When he reached Antioch, his unprejudiced heart was overjoyed at the sight of Gentiles receiving the Lord. True to his name ("Son of Encouragement"), he gave the Greek missionaries and converts all the help he could. His presence was so stimulating to the workers there that the number of converts increased sharply.

CLING. Barnabas laid stress on the PERSON of Christ. He urged the people to cling to Jesus rather than the teachings about Him. This is a vital distinction. There are many who are filled with knowledge ABOUT Christ, yet they do not know Him very well as a Person. There are those who work very hard FOR Jesus, but do not know the joy of working WITH Him. The goal of the gospel is **intimacy** with Christ. Christianity is FELLOWSHIP with the One Who made us. The religions of the world all ask men to **believe something,** whereas Christianity asks men to **receive Someone.** Occupation with Jesus is the heart of the Christian life. Thus Barnabas made a vital contribution to the new church at Antioch.

25. Then Barnabas went to Tarsus to see if he could find Saul.

SAUL. The church in Antioch was founded by laymen. Now it had reached the place where it needed a full-time leader. But it would have to be a man who saw the possibilities of this Gentile city and had the ability to exploit them for Christ. Also he would have to be one who could preach in Greek and understood the Greek culture. The unselfish Barnabas remembers such a man, Saul of Tarsus. He had introduced him to the brotherhood at Jerusalem. He had seen him risk his life for Christ while preaching to Greek-speaking Jews in Jerusalem. So instead of returning to the Jerusalem church with his report, he hurried off to Tarsus to see if he couldn't get Saul to come to Antioch. He knew the die-hard prejudices of the Jewish Christians at Jerusalem would be more apt to extinguish the revival fires at Antioch than fan them.

26. When he found him he brought him back to

Antioch. For a whole year after this, they stayed there ministering to the church together, teaching a multitude of new converts. It was there the disciples were first called Christians.

BROUGHT. Saul had fled to Tarsus for safety. There Barnabas found him and persuaded him to return with him to Antioch where they would labor together for a year. At last Saul stepped out onto the stage where his peculiar talents would be developed. We are not given the details of Saul and Barnabas' ministry, but they were so successful that Antioch became the world headquarters for the spreading of the gospel. Luke closes this section with a historical note. It was at Antioch that Jesus' disciples were first called Christians. The name was given to them by pagan Romans. It was not at first used in a good sense, but neither was it a term of contempt. It was simply the Gentile way of describing those who were always talking about Christ. In Greek the term means, "Christ-people."

MULTITUDE. The greatest growth and revival of the church have always come through persecution. When the disciples fled Jerusalem, they went as far north as Antioch. The Greek-speaking Christians began witnessing to the Gentiles in this great city and the gospel was just as appealing to the Greek as to the Hebrew mind. The town was ripe. It exploded under the ministry of Saul and Barnabas. So mighty was the revival which broke out, that the main scene of Christianity shifted from Jerusalem to Antioch. Within the year, the capitol of Syria became the world headquarters for spreading the gospel among the heathen.

"Wouldn't other Christians be attracted to this new world center?"

27. About this time some prophets came down from Jerusalem to Antioch. 28. And one of them, named Agabus, was moved by the Spirit to stand up and predict that a great famine was soon to come upon the world, which it did in the reign of Emperor Claudius.

PROPHETS. The fact that prophets moved into Antioch indicates the immense interest generated by this new center of evangelism. All we know of these prophets we read here and in 21:8ff, where Agabus is mentioned again. "Prophets" in the ordinary sense were gifted preachers, but these people had a special ministry of being able to predict future events. When it suited the Holy Spirit's purpose, these prophets were used of God to reveal things in the future. Their predictions, it would seem, were as much under the control of the Spirit as were the disciples' utterances (tongues) on the day of Pentecost. Consequently we should distinguish between the work of these prophets and the "gift of prophesy" referred to by the apostle Paul (1 Cor. 12:28; 14:29, Eph. 4:11). The "gift of prophesy" operated from the anointed, conscious intelligence of the speaker. Predicting the future has to do with superhuman announcements.

FAMINE. Historians tell us a number of famines occurred during the reign of Claudius, who was the successor of Caligula and held the Roman throne for thirteen years (A.D. 41-54). Scholars are of the opinion that the famine referred to here is one reported by Josephus as having occurred in A.D. 45. It affected most of Palestine and Syria. Even so, Agabus' prophecy was strictly fulfilled, for Italy itself and the other provinces of the Empire were afflicted with crop failures and famines during Claudius' reign. If the A.D. 45 date is correct, we have the first pinpointing of time in Acts. Luke, as all scholars point out, gives us very little to work with when it comes to a precise dating of the events he records in Acts. The Gk. word for "world," upon which the famine was to come, is the same from which we get our word "economy." Thus the reference is to the Roman Empire and not the earth's surface.

29. So the disciples decided to aid their Christian brothers living in Judea, with each contributing as much as he was able. 30. This they did entrusting the money to Barnabas and Saul who took it on to the church elders.

AID. It is not likely that the disciples acted on the word of Agabus immediately. They would hardly start raising relief for the entire Roman Empire. Undoubtedly they waited until word from Jerusalem revealed a need among the Jewish Christians there. As soon as that word came, the Antiochian disciples moved quickly to aid their brethren. The act testified to the genuineness of the Holy Spirit's work in their hearts. The Jewish Christians in Jerusalem would be in desperate straits, for they could not expect help from other Jews. They were outcasts. So, in the timing of God, their relief came from the Gentile believers in Syria. The departure of the relief party was probably not until after the events recorded in the next chapter.

MONEY. Consider how these new Christians, some of them perhaps not a year old in the Lord, gave as much as each "was able." They undoubtedly raised quite a sum of money. How thrilled Barnabas and Saul must have been to bear the gift to Jerusalem. What an effect it would have on those die-hard conservatives who challenged Gentile salvation. There could be no doubt as to the sincerity of these Antiochian Christians. When Saul and Barnabas arrived in Jerusalem they undoubtedly told the church of all that happened at Antioch. They used the relief funds as a means for uniting Jewish and Gentile believers in Christian fellowship. Note how the Gentile Christians graciously came to the aid of their suffering Jewish brethren, even though those same Jewish Christians were reluctant to see the Word of God come to them.

"Was everything peaceful in Jerusalem when Saul and Barnabas left Antioch with the relief fund?"

12 1. Right at this same time, King Herod took it upon himself to seize certain members of the church. 2. He arrested James, the brother of John, and had him beheaded. 3a. Then when he saw how this action pleased the Jews, he went a step further and arrested Peter also.

HEROD. This is Herod Agrippa I, the grandson of Herod the Great who slaughtered the infants after Jesus' birth. He was a half-Jew, raised in Rome. A favorite at the Roman court, he was given the title of king in A.D. 37 and made to rule over parts of southern Syria. Favored by the emperors Caligula and Claudius, more territories were added to his kingdom so that by A.D. 41 he ruled over all of Palestine, including Judea. To make himself popular with the Jews, he pretended strict observance of Jewish custom. In a display of Pharisaical zeal he executed James the son of Zebedee. This was the first of the apostles to be afflicted. He wasn't sure how it would set with the people, since the apostles were also strict observers of Jewish custom.

PETER ALSO. That the people were pleased with James' death, indicates a change in their attitude toward the apostles. They had been somewhat immune to attack after the stoning of Stephen. That's why they'd stayed behind at Jerusalem during the persecution (Acts 8:1). Their strict Jewishness kept them in favor with the crowds. But now Peter has engaged in the Cornelius affair, causing the church to embrace Gentiles. This action was very displeasing to the Jews who cherished their isolation from all Gentiles. Since the apostles approved Peter's action, they have now become the targets of Jewish displeasure. As soon as Herod detected this change of mood in the people, he moved quickly against the apostles as a means of enhancing his prestige. Now he dares to seize the chief apostle who had taken the lead in fraternizing with the Gentiles.

3b. The feast of the Passover was just starting 4. when Herod seized Peter and put him in prison. The apostle was held in tight security by four squads of soldiers who were rotated four times a day. It was Herod's intention to bring him out to the Jewish people for public execution as soon as the Passover ended.

SECURITY. Peter was arrested at the beginning of the seven day Passover holiday. Herod knew it would anger the Jews if he conducted any legal business during the holy days, so he kept him in custody under heavy guard. He was aware that Peter had once been delivered from prison (Acts 5:17-20). Of course he didn't know whether it was a supernatural deliverance or at the hands of friends. So extra pains were taken to prevent any escape this time. Four squads of soldiers (four men to a squad) took turns guarding him, with each squad on duty for six hours. A soldier was chained to each of Peter's wrists, while the other two guarded the prison doors. Herod purposed to slay Peter publicly immediately after the Passover.

"Wow! That must have shaken up the church!"

5. With Peter in prison under constant watch, the people of the church went to work bombarding heaven with a constant stream of fervent prayer.

PRAYER. After Paul had been hurried away from Jerusalem, the furor caused by his preaching in the Greek speaking synagogues died down and the church began to enjoy a time of peace. Great numbers were added to the fellowship. In time the church was threatened by ease and comfort. Then it was that God allowed Satan to begin this attack by Herod. He was satanically inspired to think he could advance his political fortunes by oppressing the church. Surprised by his success in the execution of James, he was moved to imprison Peter. To counter the softening influence of prosperity, God allowed this peril against Peter. The church went to its knees. Shocked by the death of James, the church is urgent in praying for Peter.

"Did Peter share their crisis feelings?"

6. On the very night before his scheduled execution, Peter was fast asleep between two soldiers. He was bound to them by two chains. In front of the prison door two more soldiers were keeping watch. 7. Suddenly the cell was flooded with light. An angel of the Lord appeared beside Peter. He jabbed the apostle in the side to arouse him. "Hurry! Get up!" he said.

The same instant the chains fell from Peter's wrists. 8. Then the angel spoke again, "Cinch up your loin cloth and put on your sandals." Peter complied. "Now throw your cloak around you and follow me," he commanded. 9. Peter went through the motions of following the angel, but he wasn't sure that what was taking place was really happening. He thought it was a dream or vision of some sort.

ANGEL. God harkened to the prayers of the saints. The angel was one of His answers, wondrous grace for Peter was the other. The brethren were no doubt praying that Peter would either be delivered or have the grace to bear the execution. What is Peter doing in death row on the eve of his scheduled execution while the saints were praying so fervently? Sleeping, and so soundly the angel had to jab him to awaken him. Some have attributed this deliverance to an earthquake, but that would have injured (at the very least, awakened) many. No, this was an angelic being on a superhuman mission. No human hands could have snapped those chains so silently. Note how they **fell** off. See also how the angel did for Peter only that which he couldn't do for himself. He could dress himself, but he couldn't extricate himself from the guards or leave the prison. With Satan powerless to hinder this escape in any way, even the guards were not aroused.

10. Thus they moved along, passing the first sentry, then the second. When they came to the great iron gate that led out into the city, it opened for them automatically! And so they walked out of the prison. After they had traveled the length of one street, the angel vanished, leaving Peter standing there by himself. 11. Then Peter realized what had happened. "I wasn't dreaming," he said. "It really happened. The Lord did send His angel to rescue me from Herod and all that the Jewish people had planned to do to me!"

WALKED. Peter obeyed the angel, perhaps like an automaton, thinking to himself it was all a dream. The guards seemed oblivious to them as they walked by. To see the two of them passing first one guard post and then another, and finally to have the great outer gate swing open by itself had to be dream stuff. When at last they had traversed the length of one street, Peter suddenly found himself alone. For a moment he is confused. He rubs his eyes. He pinches himself and takes a deep breath of the night air to make sure he isn't dreaming. No, it's no dream. Herod, of course, will be sure it was an inside job, but to Peter it is crystal clear that God had again intervened on his behalf. This story stands as a testimony to God's delivering grace and the power of earnest prayer. Those who seek a human explanation do themselves no favor.

12. After taking a moment to collect his thoughts, Peter headed for the house of Mary, John Mark's mother. A good many of the brethren were there, having gathered to pray for him. 13. When he knocked at the little door in the gate, a young maid by the name of Rhoda came to answer it. 14. When she recognized Peter's voice she got so excited, that instead of opening the gate to let him in, she ran back inside and reported that Peter was standing outside on the front porch. 15. "You're crazy, it can't be!" they said. Nevertheless, she kept insisting it was so. Then they began to reason, "It must be his guardian angel."

THOUGHTS. Peter needed a second to collect his thoughts. Such a thing doesn't happen every day. Once the angel departed from him, he was in a strange situation. He was a fugitive. Where would he go? When the guards awakened, the alarm would be spread and a search made. But that hasn't happened yet. So he decides to make a quick visit to Mary's house. There's some risk, for this is one place they'd surely look for him. This Mary appears to be a widow of sufficient wealth to own a place large enough for Christian assemblies. It is not impossible that her upper room is the place where Jesus kept the Passover with His disciples and made His pentecostal descent on the 120. In any event, Peter knows a large group is praying for him there and he hastens to let them know their prayers have been answered.

RHODA. Luke adds a touch of humor in reporting the excitement of the young serving girl. Less humorous is the fact that the believers, begging God for Peter's deliverance, could scarcely believe the answer to their prayers is standing outside the gate. They conclude the girl is either mad, or Peter's guardian angel has returned in the guise of Peter himself. They seem ready to believe that Herod had already killed Peter and now his ghost or angel (his spirit-counterpart) had come to say goodbye. In those days, people believed that one's guardian angel had the power to assume the bodily appearance of the person he protected. We learn from this not to be surprised at anything God might do when we pray earnestly.

16. Meanwhile Peter kept on knocking. Finally when they opened the gate and saw him standing there, they were astonished. 17. He quickly motioned for them to be quiet. Then he described for them how the Lord had brought him out of the prison. "Go and report this to James and the brethren," he said, and hastily took leave of them for a safer place.

MOTIONED. We can suppose that Peter's pounding on the gate didn't get too loud. The way things stood, it wouldn't do to attract too much attention. A search for him could get under way any second. When at last the gate was opened and the brethren saw that it was actually he, they were shocked. It was incredible that he should show up like this when they knew he was under the prison's tightest security. We would have had difficulty believing it ourselves. Very likely they got a little loud in their exclamations, so Peter had to hush them with gestures. It was risky enough just being there. He told them what happened. Then he asked them to get word to another group meeting with James, the Lord's brother. By this time, (A.D. 44), James had assumed a position of leadership in the church. The elders were undoubtedly with him and they would be encouraged by news of his deliverance.

SAFER. Once Peter brought the comforting news of his escape, he left at once for an unknown destination. He made a point of telling no one where he was going, sparing them the risk of being tortured for the information. It was not safe for him in the city, yet there is no reason to believe he fled all the way to Rome per the Catholic tradition. It is pure speculation, of course, but it is not unlikely that he traveled north to the city of Antioch where revival had broken out among the Gentiles. There he would be out of Herod's jurisdiction. Peter was one to go where the action was. It is known that from this period on, the apostles gradually left Jerusalem. Only James remained behind to lead the church. His ascetic life and faithful attendance in the temple made him popular with the people. However history tells us he was finally stoned to death in A.D. 61 by the Jewish rulers at a time when there was no Roman governor on the scene.

"How did Herod react to Peter's escape?"

18. At daybreak there was tremendous confusion among the guards as to what could have become of Peter. 19. Herod ordered a close search made, but he was nowhere to be found. Then he had the guards interrogated and ordered their execution. After that he went down from Judea to spend some time at Caesarea.

SEARCH. Pandamonium broke loose when it was discovered that Peter was gone. No one could believe he had escaped the prison, so an intensive search was made. If he were held in the fortress of Antonia, just N.W. of the temple area, it would have taken some time for a thorough search. When all proved futile, and it was determined that Peter was really gone, the guards were examined. Herod could reach only one conclusion—either the guards were in on the escape or they had been asleep at their posts. Either was a capital offense under Roman military law. He had them tried before a military court and executed. Don't feel that Peter caused innocent deaths. These guards were likely guilty of other matters before God and Herod was His instrument of justice. Herod was so embarrassed he could not fulfill the promised expectations of the Jews, that he left the city and returned to his palace at Caesarea.

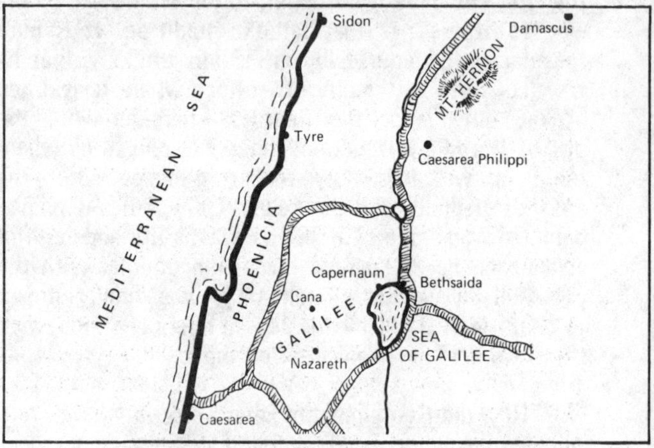

"Did Herod stay in an angry mood?"

20. Herod became furious with the people of Tyre and Sidon. And since these cities depended on the king's country for support, they were eager to make peace with him. They sent a delegation to see him which first contacted Blastus, his personal secretary, and won him over to their side. 21. In that way they secured an appointment with Herod. So on an appointed day, Herod, decked out in his royal finery, took his place on a public throne and began delivering an address to them. 22. Shortly the people began shouting a flattering acclamation, "Why this is a god speaking to us and not a mere man!"

DELEGATION. Herod's pride was hurt by Peter's escape, so he quit Jerusalem in a display of temper. Hoping to save face by holding a great festival in honor of the emperor, he announced a day when the celebrations would be held. At this same time, he became angered with the Phoencian cities of Tyre and Sidon. Since the days of Solomon, these cities had depended on Galilee for food. Having offended the touchy king in a way unknown to us, they sent a delegation to make peace. Finding the king's secretary, they persuaded him (by bribery?) to set up an appointment for them. The king apparently consented to hear them on the same day he set aside for honoring the Caesar.

FINERY. Josephus, the Jewish historian, tells us that Herod set his throne facing the East and sat on it wearing a robe of silver woven with amazing workmanship. When struck by the rays of the sun, it gave the king a resplendent and awesome appearance. From his throne he spoke to the crowd. Apparently the dazzling sight of the king inspired the group from Tyre and Sidon to strike the flattering chant, "This is a god speaking and not just a man!" Herod, who was at least a half-Jew, should have recoiled from such blasphemy. But filled with vanity, he forgot his Jewishness and allowed the people to worship him as devine.

23. And immediately the angel of the Lord struck him with a sickness because he did not refer the glory to God. He was eaten up with worms and died.

SICKNESS. In the heat of pride, Herod accepted honor that was due God alone and was smitten with a terrible disease. Little did he or his cohorts dream that divine retribution was at hand. Immediately after he had accepted the praise, he suffered excruciating pain in his abdomen. He had to be removed from the dais and carried into the palace. Josephus' parallel account of this incident says he died five days later at the age of 54. It was the 7th year of his reign. Had not this awful thing happened, he might have gone down in history as one of the great kings of the Jews. He was popular with the masses. While Josephus gives us the results of the disease, Dr. Luke reports the symptoms.

They seem to describe a ruptured cyst or peritonitis, which corresponds to being worm eaten. No one doubted the act was judgment from God.

"How did God's work fare in contrast with that of His enemy, Herod?"

24. But the Word of God continued to grow and spread. 25. Meanwhile, Barnabas and Saul were able to complete their task at Jerusalem and return to Antioch taking John Mark along with them.

SPREAD. He who had slain James, the brother of John, and had imprisoned Peter, died the death he deserved. The Word of God had multiplied in spite of the fierce persecutions. And now, with the persecutor gone, the persecuted move on with their work for Jesus. We're not sure just when Barnabas and Saul visited Jerusalem. It could have been after the death of Herod when Judea was in the hands of procurators who managed the province for Rome. Not only would it have taken them time to gather a sizeable relief fund, but it would have been unwise for Saul to re-enter Jerusalem while the persecutions were going on. Likely he was still hated by every Hellenistic Jew in the city. Therefore, the relief party may have arrived after the death of Herod.

JOHN MARK. John would be his Jewish name, Mark his Roman name. We know him best as the author of one of the gospels. Modern scholars make him a young cousin to Barnabas. Mary, his mother, is believed to have been either the sister or sister-in-law of Barnabas' father (Col. 4:10). She would be that Mary in whose home the disciples met to pray when Peter was imprisoned. It is likely that Saul and Barnabas stayed with her when they visited Jerusalem with the relief mission. Coming from a wealthy home, Mark would be well educated. No doubt he proved himself a fine assistant and Saul and Barnabas felt he was too valuable to leave behind when they departed for Antioch.

"Has the church action now shifted from Jerusalem to Antioch?"

13 1. Now in the church at Antioch there were prophets and teachers. They were the leaders. Chief among them were Barnabas, Simeon, (who was nicknamed "The Black"), Lucius (from Cyrene), and Manaen (who was raised at court with Herod Antipas), and Saul.

CHURCH. The Lord is now ready to spread the gospel throughout the Gentile world. For that task, He established a new headquarters at Antioch. The Jerusalem church, still bound in Jewishness, is unable to envision a Gentile world won to Jesus. The Lord's appeal to Israel to repent AS A NATION is ended. Consequently it is about the last we'll hear of Peter, since his ministry was to the Jews (Gal. 2:9). It is in the great Gentile church at Antioch that the burden for the Gentiles arises. The final stage of the Great Commission ("unto all the world") is ready to begin. The Antiochian church will send out the first missionaries. It is to this church, not the elders at Jerusalem, that they will report. The Lord's church, which at first was all Jewish, is due to become predominately Gentile.

TEACHERS. The Spirit lists five men as examples of the leadership in the Antiochian church. Barnabas and Saul we already know. The other three, Lucius, Simeon, and Manaen, are named as prophets (preachers) and teachers. Some have speculated that Lucius (a common name) is Dr. Luke, the writer of Acts. But there is no evidence of any connection. He is likely one of the men from the Roman province of Cyrene on the No. African coast who teamed up with those from Cyprus to preach the gospel in Antioch. Simeon may have been the one who helped bear Jesus' cross. Most fascinating is Manaen. Raised in Rome as a foster brother with Herod Antipas (who tried Jesus and slew John the Baptist), he is here seen as one of the leaders. Strange are the ways of the Lord.

2. On a particular occasion, while these men were performing their spiritual tasks and fasting, the Holy Spirit said to them, "It's time now for Barnabas and Saul to be set apart for the work to which I have called them."

SAID. See how the Holy Spirit rather than the apostles is now giving orders directly to the leaders of this Gentile church? The shift to Antioch has been made. One day, as the five mentioned leaders were carrying out their appointed ministries in the church, the Holy Spirit, by prophetic utterance (probably through one of their number), made it known that it was now time for the missionary outreach to begin. The Lord had previously told Saul he would bear His name among the Gentiles. It's time for him to get going. The Antiochian church was called into existence for a definite purpose. That purpose is now becoming clear. Its task is world evangelism. To begin the task, the Spirit orders the release of two of the church's five top leaders. It must have seemed a big loss to the people to let go of its most powerful ministers. Twelve years have passed since Paul was commissioned by the Lord. Now he's finally under way.

3. Then, after fasting and praying, the men of the church laid hands on them and sent them off as missionaries.

FASTING. When the church heard that it was the Spirit's will for them to release Barnabas and Saul, the matter was taken very seriously. Seemingly the whole church began fasting and praying to make sure this tremendous step was being directed by the Spirit. How different from the way Peter seized the initiative when he asked the church to nominate successors for Judas, and then **cast lots** to finalize the choice. In Antioch the Gentiles listened to the Holy Spirit. Fasting is known to increase one's spiritual sensitivity. Only after diligent seeking in prayer was the church convinced of the call. They were not about to give up these two leaders with just a word of prayer.

SENT. Satisfied the Spirit had issued the call, the church formally commissioned Barnabas and Saul for the new venture by the laying on of hands. This, of course, added nothing to their qualifications. They were already Spirit-filled and among the most qualified. It was a ceremonial act whereby the church said, "You are OUR official delegates as well as apostles of the Lord." It was the church's way of **acknowledging** a call God had ALREADY bestowed. A hundred ordination services would be meaningless apart from God's call. Thus we have the first missionary enterprise, born in prayer, coming from a Gentile church. Since it was expected that the One Who had called them would also provide for their needs, no provision was made for their financial support.

"Then the gospel really did spread to the Gentiles from Antioch?"

4. Having been sent by the Holy Spirit, Barnabas and Saul departed from Antioch. After making their way down to Seleucia, they set sail for Cyprus. 5. Arriving at Salamis, they preached God's Word in the Jewish synagogues. With them was John Mark, whom they had taken along to serve as their assistant.

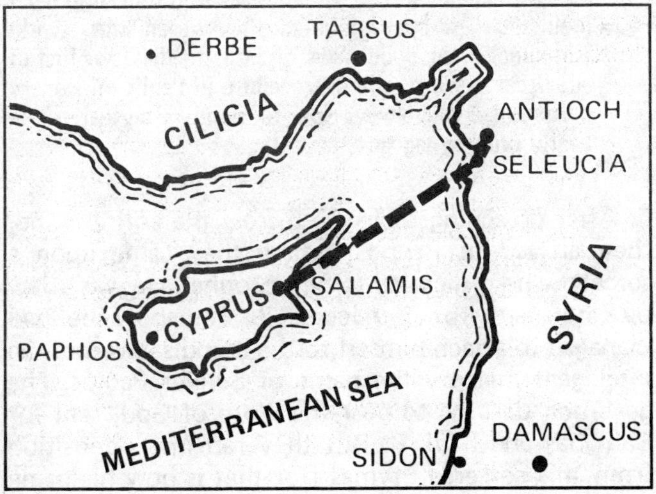

DEPARTED. Likely the two missionaries, accompanied by a group from the church, walked the fifteen miles to Seleucia, Antioch's seaport on the Mediterranean. Needing someone to tend to their secular needs, they took along John Mark. Some sort of a sailboat was available to them and they embarked for the island of Cyprus some 60 mi. out to sea in a S.W. direction. At this time, Cyprus was a Roman province managed by a proconsul. It was a wise place to begin, for the large island of Cyprus was the native home of Barnabas, who at this point seems to be in charge of the expedition. His knowledge and contacts would be useful. Besides there were numerous Cyprian Jews (who had become Christians) who fled to the island to escape the Jerusalem persecutions (Acts 8:4; 11:19).

SYNAGOGUES. Landing at Salamis, the commercial center of the island, they found a Jewish population large enough to require a number of synagogues. While the island consisted mostly of Greeks and Phoenicians, there were many Jews there as well. The synagogues always provided for discussions and invited visiting rabbis to speak. This offered a prime opportunity for the gospel since Paul was a rabbi. So long as the synagogues were open to them, the missionaries made use of them. In fact, it would have been foolish to overlook such an open door as they began their work. Announcing the good news of Jesus to the Jews first of all, became the standard procedure in Paul's missionary pattern. He was always sure of some "God-fearers" in nearly every synagogue.

6. After preaching their way across the entire island, they arrived at Paphos, where they came upon a sorcerer who pretended to be a prophet. He was a Jew by the name of Bar-Jesus. 7. Somehow he had managed to attach himself to the island's governor, an intelligent man by the name of Sergius Paulus. The governor, desiring to hear the Word of God, sent for Barnabas and Saul. 8. But they ran into opposition from this sorcerer Elymas (for that is how his name

should be translated) who was doing his utmost to keep the governor from accepting the faith.

ACROSS. Luke does not report their success at Salamis, neither does he tell how they fared as they preached in town after town while moving across the 400 mile length of the island. Apparently he is not writing a log of the journey. Moving steadily westward, the team reached Paphos, the capitol, a thriving city at the other end of the island. It was also the residence of the Roman governor. When he heard of the preaching of Barnabas and Saul, he was eager to learn what they taught. Unearthed Greek inscriptions confirm the historical accuracy of Luke's statement that Sergius Paulus was indeed the proconsul (governor) at this time.

SORCERER. In the governor's entourage was an unscrupulous Jew named Bar (son of) Jesus (Joshua or Savior) who apparently served as the court magician. It was not uncommon to find a magus of this sort attached to wealthy and powerful homes much as celebrities today look to occult teachers. This man was also a spirit-medium who claimed supernatural power—perhaps even divine powers. Inasmuch as the Roman ruler was a thoughtful man, he sensed there were powers beyond human forces. This would make him vulnerable to the "black arts" of this Babylonian magus (sorcerer), who had evidently gained real influence over him. As a Jew, Bar-Jesus must have been aware of the O.T. prohibition of all forms of sorcery (Lev. 20:27). The sorcerer panicked at the presence of the missionaries. He desperately tried to keep the governor from listening to them, for his salvation would spell the end of the magician's influence. Elymas is apparently a Semitic word for sorcerer. This is the first recorded opposition to the missionaries.

"How will the missionaries handle this type of opposition?"

9. Then Saul, also known as Paul, stared fiercely at the sorcerer. Filled with the Holy Spirit, 10. he said to him, "You fake! You cheat! You son of the devil!

You tricky villain! You are always twisting the truth and opposing righteousness every chance you get. 11. Listen you! The hand of the Lord is going to strike you right now! You will become blind and won't see the sun for a while." Instantly a dark mist fell upon him and he began groping about, begging for someone to lead him by the hand.

PAUL. We come to the first time in Acts when Saul is referred to by his Roman name. From now on he will be known only as Paul. Also an important change has taken place, Paul has apparently assumed leadership of the gospel team. With his Hebrew name dropped, his Gentile name will now be used in connection with spreading the gospel to the Gentile world. Barnabas must have recognized the superiority of his junior partner and graciously yielded the leadership. The Lord was wise in selecting Barnabas, for only someone as unselfish as he would encourage Saul of Tarsus to turn into Paul the apostle. By the time they had reached this end of the island, Paul was the dominant personality. He is the one in charge of this scene with the sorcerer.

YOU FAKE! Here, on this first missionary trip, we have a dramatized encounter of the forces of light and darkness. Satan's man, Elymas, did his best to keep the governor from listening to the gospel. Once Paul saw no progress could be made with this antagonist in the way, there occurred a head-on collision between a Spirit-filled servant of the Lord and a Satan-filled enemy of the gospel. Then it was the Spirit led Paul to make a direct assault upon the powers of darkness. He pronounced blindness upon the sorcerer, performing the only punitive miracle recorded of the apostles. It was an extraordinary action.

BLIND. Perhaps Paul was thinking of the way the Lord struck him with blindness when he opposed the gospel. It served to bring him to his senses, it might do the same for Elymas. God honored Paul's words. The man who blinded others to the truth, now became blind himself. It is fully possible that Elymas was emotionally unstable. Those who dabble in demonism open themselves to this danger. This would account for the collapse of the sorcerer upon meeting the real power of Christ. Far from being a "son of a savior," as his name implies, he was a son of the devil. Shut up to the torment of darkness, he would now be alone with the demons with whom he was so friendly. Likely he was terrified by the prospect.

12. When the governor saw what happened, he was so amazed at the power of the Lord's backing, he became a believer.

BELIEVER. When Sergius Paulus saw his magus overcome by God's power working through Paul, he was deeply impressed. With Elymas removed, he was able to give heed to the gospel. He had already shown a genuine interest in the missionaries, having suspected the work of the magus was based on trickery rather than contact with God. Their message having penetrated his heart, this miracle confirmed it. It is not known that he truly received Christ, but scholars have adduced from ancient writings that members of his family were later known as Christians. Observe how Paul, by himself, would have been no match in this battle against Satan. Elymas could have defeated him. But in partnership with the Holy Spirit, he was more than equal to the task. Thus it is vital that Christians learn to recognize how Satan blinds men to the truth, and equip themselves to deal with him in the Spirit's power.

"With the work in Cyprus finished, did the team return to Antioch?"

13. After leaving Paphos, Paul and his companions put out to sea once more, this time headed for Perga in Pamphylia. There John Mark deserted them and returned to Jerusalem. 14a. From Perga, the two missionaries proceeded to Antioch, a city on the Pisidian border.

PERGA. Flushed with triumph after the winning of the Cyprian governor, Paul is too encouraged to think of returning to Antioch. So he set sail for the mainland of Asia Minor (Turkey). The three missionaries arrived in the town of Perga, located about 12 miles inland from the sea coast. It was distinguished by the presence of the most ancient and sacred temple of the goddess Diana. It is the speculation of many Bible students that in this low lying country, with its marshes and mosquitoes, Paul was stricken with Malaria. This could explain why they didn't stay long. Nothing is reported except the desertion of John Mark, who left them and returned to Jerusalem.

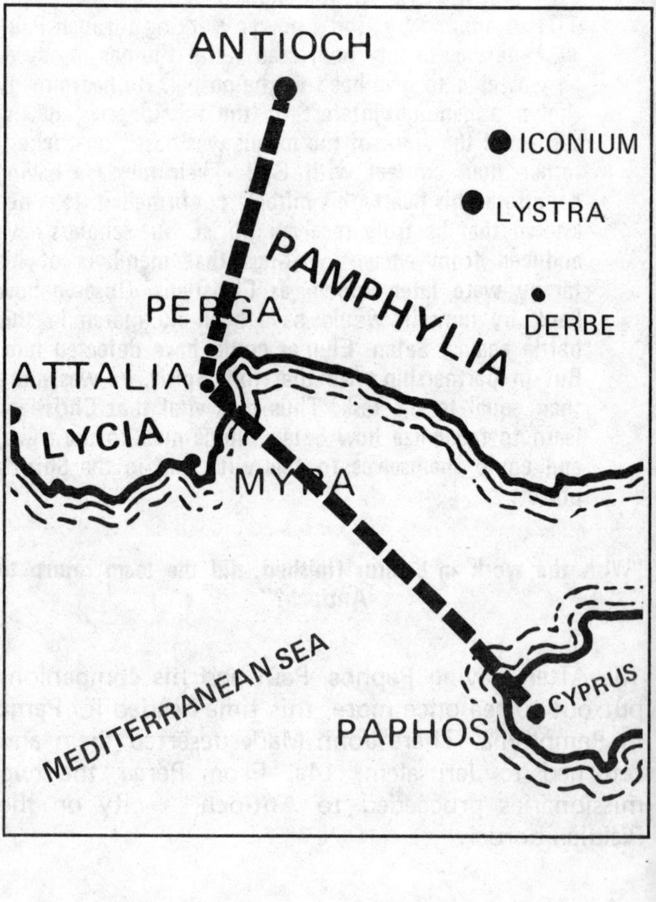

ANTIOCH. Paul and Barnabas moved 90 miles north from Perga to Pisidian Antioch. We now have two Antiochs in our story, the one they left in Syria and this one in Pisidia. The 3600′ altitude would make it a good place for Paul to recuperate, if indeed he did have malaria. Besides, it was the chief civil and military center of that part of Galatia. Paul was particularly anxious to evangelize the Roman colonies strung out along the imperial roads. This would aid greatly in the spread of the gospel. However, to reach this city, the missionaries had to make a difficult journey. It meant climbing the Taurus Mts. and passing through a bandit infested district. That could have influenced young John's decision. It could also be he resented the fact that his uncle Barnabas was no longer the head of the expedition, which we deduce from the words, "Paul and his companions." This Antioch is one of the principal churches to which Paul addressed his Galatian letter.

14b. On the Sabbath day they went into the synagogue and took their seats. 15. After the usual reading from the Law of Moses and a related portion from the Prophets, those in charge of the synagogue passed this message to them: "Brethren, if you have any word of encouragement for the people, let us hear it."

SABBATH. On reaching Pisidian Antioch, Paul headed for the synagogue. He went on a Sabbath, however, for that is when there would be the greatest number of Jews and proselytes gathered for worship and instruction. Also many God-fearing Gentiles, drawn by the teaching of a true and living God, would be there. With a ready-made audience gathered to hear the Word, this was the place to start. Wherever there were Jews, there were synagogues. Each had officials who cared for its affairs and had the privilege of asking whomever they chose to speak and exhort the congregation. As a visiting rabbi, Paul was always certain of an invitation to speak. Thus, whenever he reached a new city, he always went to the synagogues first. When they were closed to him, he went elsewhere.

READING. On this Sabbath, Paul and Barnabas took their places in the congregation. It was the custom, after the prayers had been said, to bring two Scripture passages to the people. The first was read from one of the five books of Moses, the second a portion from the Prophets which had a bearing on the passage from the Law. When that was done, the synagogue officials would ask someone to speak. On this occasion they had taken note of the two visitors and sent word inviting them to address the congregation. This was the opportunity Paul was waiting for. Apparently he developed this practice as he traveled across Cyprus, but only now do we come to his first **recorded** sermon. Note how it is addressed to Jews. Before the account is closed, Dr. Luke will give us summaries of Paul's messages to Christians and pagans. That we hear him speak to a Jewish audience first is consistent with the plan, "to the Jew first."

"This is the first time we'll hear Paul preach, isn't it!"

16. So Paul stood up. After silencing the audience with a motion of his hand, he began:

"You men of Israel, and all of you who fear our God, listen to me! 17. The God of this people of Israel chose our ancestors and made a great nation out of them during the time they lived as aliens in Egypt. Then, with His mighty hand, He brought them forth out of that country. 18. For the next forty years He put up with their unruly conduct during the wilderness wanderings. 19. When He brought them into the land of Canaan, He destroyed the seven nations who inhabited the land and gave it to His people Israel as an inheritance. By now some four hundred and fifty years had passed. 20. After this He appointed judges to rule over them until the time of the prophet Samuel. 21. When they begged Him for a king, God gave them Saul, the son of Kish, a man from the tribe of Benjamin, who reigned for forty years. 22. After God removed him, He set up David as their king saying this about him: 'I have found David, the son of Jesse, to be My kind of man, one who will obey me no matter what I ask of him.' "

LISTEN. Upon receiving the invitation to speak, Paul moved to the pulpit. He gestured for attention and began his address. It is clear his audience consisted of two classes of people: (1) men of Israel (Jews), (2) those who feared God (Gentiles). Starting off much as did Stephen, Paul outlined the history of God's dealing with His people Israel. He began with their deliverance from Egypt, tracing God's faithfulness in dispossessing the 7 nations of Canaan, all of which were mightier than they (Deut. 7:1). Then came the time of the judges, ending with the prophet Samuel. Finally, at their insistence, God gave them kings. First, they had their own choice, Saul of the tribe of Benjamin. Then God replaced him with His own choice, David. Paul ends the historical survey of Israel with King David, since the Messiah came from his line. It is the "Son of David," he wishes to introduce to his audience.

23. "God promised He would bring forth a Savior of Israel from among the descendants of David, and He did. It was Jesus. 24. Just before Jesus arrived, John the Baptist prepared the way for His coming by asking the people of Israel to be baptized to show their willingness to turn from their wickedness. 25. As John neared the end of his ministry, he said this: 'Who do you think I am, the Messiah? I'm not He. You should be looking for the One coming behind me. I'm not even worthy to untie His sandals!' "

SAVIOR. After reviewing the stirring history of the Jewish people, an approach calculated to awaken their sense of obligation to God, Paul reminds them how God promised a Savior (Messiah), Who would come from the line of David. God kept that promise when He brought forth Jesus. But before Jesus arrived,

John the Baptist, acknowledged to be one of the greatest of the prophets, paved the way for His appearance with his baptism of repentance and announcement that the kingdom of heaven was at hand. Paul's audience was familiar with John and his message. So far Paul has touched on two points his listeners would readily admit: (1) the Messiah was promised, and (2) John the Baptist was raised up to prepare the way for His arrival. Now all he has to do is persuade them that Jesus is the One John was heralding.

26. "My brothers, you who are the sons of Abraham, and all of you Gentiles who fear God, we are the very people to whom this message of salvation has been sent. It is for all of us! 27. But those at Jerusalem, blindly following their leaders, didn't recognize Him, neither did they understand the words of their own prophets, though they read them every Sabbath day. Unwittingly they fulfilled those very prophecies when they condemned Him. 28. Although they were unable to establish grounds for the death sentence, they asked Pilate to execute Him anyway. 29. So when they had completely carried out all that the Scriptures said would happen to Him, they took Him down from the cross and laid Him in a tomb."

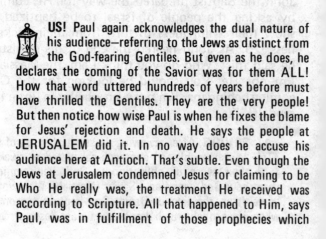

US! Paul again acknowledges the dual nature of his audience—referring to the Jews as distinct from the God-fearing Gentiles. But even as he does, he declares the coming of the Savior was for them ALL! How that word uttered hundreds of years before must have thrilled the Gentiles. They are the very people! But then notice how wise Paul is when he fixes the blame for Jesus' rejection and death. He says the people at JERUSALEM did it. In no way does he accuse his audience here at Antioch. That's subtle. Even though the Jews at Jerusalem condemned Jesus for claiming to be Who He really was, the treatment He received was according to Scripture. All that happened to Him, says Paul, was in fulfillment of those prophecies which give a detailed account of the way the Messiah would be received when He appeared on earth. The way Paul is going about his presentation, it will be hard for his listeners to contradict him, since his message is based wholly on their own Scriptures.

30. "But God raised Him from the dead, 31. and for many days afterwards He was seen by those who journeyed with Him from Galilee to Jerusalem. These same people are even this day publicly witnessing to the truth of His resurrection. 32. And that's why we're here. We've come to tell you the exciting news concerning the promise God made to our fathers. 33a. He has fulfilled that promise for us, their children, by raising Jesus from the dead."

NEWS. Paul shifts from the sad story of Israel's rejection to the triumphant tidings of Jesus' resurrection. For the narrative to end with the death of Israel's Messiah would be sad indeed. But to learn that God had raised the Messiah from the dead and given Israel a SECOND CHANCE, would be the most exciting news a true Jew could hear. Paul backs up his announcement by referring to the many disciples who saw Jesus after His resurrection and who were still alive and testifying. We know that more than 500 of them saw Him at one time in Galilee (1 Cor. 15:6). Paul's language here excludes himself and Barnabas from being among the original disciples or eyewitnesses.

33b. "This is also confirmed by that which is written in the second Psalm:

'You are My own Son, for I have sired You this very day!' (Psa. 2:7).

34. That God intended to raise this Son from the dead, never again permitting Him to face decay, is also clearly stated:

'I will give you the holy and guaranteed blessings which I promised to David' (Isa. 55:3).

35. We find the real meaning of these things established when we turn to another Psalm:

'You will not allow Your Holy One to suffer decay' (Psa. 16:10).

36. Now as for David, this latter passage cannot apply to him for he did undergo decay. After serving the purposes of God throughout his lifetime, he died and was buried with his ancestors. 37. So then it is not David who is referred to here, but Someone Who was preserved from decay because God raised Him from the dead. Only one person fits that description–Jesus!"

WRITTEN. Paul has made a startling announcement, backing it with quotes from the best and most familiar Messianic passages of the O.T. Their combined sense is this: (1) after centuries of waiting, God brought forth the awaited Messiah, Whom He calls His Son (Psa. 2:7). (2) However, God promised David that one of his descendants would be the Messiah, and that promise was confirmed long after David had died (Isa. 55:3). (3) Further, it was promised the Messiah would be a RESURRECTED Person Who arose before his body could experience any decay (Psa. 16:10). Now many Jews believed that King David himself was to be raised and returned to the people as the Messiah. But Paul, arguing as did Peter at Pentecost, says the Scriptures couldn't refer to David since his body had already suffered corruption. David was still in his grave. Only one Person, therefore, met all the requirements of these prophecies–Jesus, Who identified Himself as the Son of God. He alone returned to life BEFORE His body could suffer any corruption.

"What did this really mean to Paul's listeners?"

38. "Now then, my brothers, hear this! Complete forgiveness of all your sins is offered you through this man Jesus! 39. Do you understand? I'm saying

that everyone who believes in Him is totally forgiven of all his sins. This is something the Law of Moses cannot do for you, since it does not provide justification from all sins."

COMPLETE. Paul's audience received shock after shock. Now they hear him announce total forgiveness for ALL sins through faith in Jesus. The Gentiles must have stared at each other in amazement. If what Paul was saying was true, it meant they didn't have to be circumcised and become Jews to be justified in God's sight! Paul didn't even mention water baptism or godly living as requirements for salvation. He preached faith in Christ—period. Here, in his first recorded address, we find Paul stripping the gospel of its Jewishness. How the audience must have stared dumbfounded at this rabbi. Here was a man trained under Gamaliel, telling Jews in their own synagogue, that a man their rulers crucified in Jerusalem can do for them what the Law of Moses could never do for them—make them perfect in the sight of God! Paul has seemingly crystallized his message of grace which he later expounded in Romans and Galatians.

MOSES. The Jews must have been dumbfounded to hear a rabbi speak of the failure of the Law. Neither Peter nor Stephen had hinted at such a thing. This was something brand new in gospel preaching. Paul boldly says the Law of Moses is inadequate to justify a person, but faith in Christ fully justifies both Jew and Gentile in the sight of God. Paul's words here might appear to be saying that there is some justification under that Law, but that is not the case. Paul is merely contrasting the COMPLETE forgiveness found in Christ, with the PARTIAL MERCY offered under the Law. There was mercy under the Law, but never justification. While there were some sins for which the Law provided mercy, in no way could the Law make a sinner righteous.

"What if Paul's listeners reject his words about Jesus?"

40. "Beware brethren, that the dire pronouncements uttered by the prophets don't apply to you. Recall their warning:

41. **'Behold you scoffers. Consider this and perish! I am doing a great wonder in your day. And it is such a wonder that if anyone described it to you, you wouldn't believe him' "** (Hab. 1:5 LXX).

WARNING. Paul ends his message by warning his listeners not to turn a deaf ear to his announcement. Doing so could bring divine judgment. He backs his warning with words from the prophet Habakkuk, who warned Israel, prior to the Assyrian invasion, that unless she heeded God's Word she would suffer an unbelievable judgment. She did. She went into captivity. Similarly Paul cautions his audience that turning from the news of Christ could place them under the same prophetic threatening of God. Drawing from the verse he selected, we understand him to be saying that the judgment falling upon rejectors will be so terrible people will not believe its description. It will be incredibly awful—HELL!

"How did the people react to Paul's message?"

42. As Paul and Barnabas were leaving the synagogue, the people implored them to come back on the next Sabbath and repeat the message. 43. Once the meeting had broken up, many of the Jews and godly Gentiles who were in the audience accompanied Paul and Barnabas, who continued speaking with them urging them to press on in the grace of God.

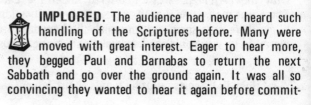

IMPLORED. The audience had never heard such handling of the Scriptures before. Many were moved with great interest. Eager to hear more, they begged Paul and Barnabas to return the next Sabbath and go over the ground again. It was all so convincing they wanted to hear it again before committing themselves one way or the other. Another group, consisting of both Jews and proselytes, couldn't wait until the next Sabbath. They followed the two missionaries out of the synagogue, bombarding them with questions. The grace of God was really working in their hearts, as they displayed great interest in the news of Jesus. Paul and Barnabas urged them not to slacken in their quest to know the truth.

44. The following Sabbath nearly everyone in town turned out to hear their message about the Lord. 45. But when the Jews saw the crowds, they were filled with jealousy and began contradicting him and defaming him with blasphemous words.

CROWDS. During the week, news of Paul's preaching spread throughout the city. On the next Sabbath it seemed the whole town had thronged to the synagogue to hear what the new missionary had to say about the Word of God. By now, the Jewish leaders were becoming envious of Paul's success. While many Jews did welcome the gospel, the majority of them would be unhappy to see salvation offered to Gentiles on an equal basis with Jews. They were offended when Paul by-passed the Jewish requirements, saying all that mattered was faith in Christ. So they spoke out against him, attempting to refute his message. When this was unsuccessful, they became angered to the point of cursing him. Their words likely included the name of Jesus, making them blasphemous.

"Surely Paul would have a strong answer for those Jews."

46. But Paul and Barnabas were unflinching in their stand. They became even more bold and replied, "We were obliged to share this great news from God's Word with you first, but now that you have rejected it, thereby condemning yourselves as unworthy of eternal life, we turn to the Gentiles."

OBLIGED. Paul and Barnabas didn't trifle with the stubborn Jews. Both were familiar enough with Jewish history to know how futile that was. Yet they carefully fulfilled the obligation "to the Jew first." Why? The Lord made it clear the Jews were to have the first chance at the gospel. They were the greatest sinners. They crucified the very One for Whom their nation was raised up to bring into the world. The offer of "to the Jew first," manifested the loving genius of the gospel by giving them a chance to repent and be forgiven. However, if the Jews didn't want the salvation available in their Messiah, then it was to be offered to all others who did want it. Modern Christians should profit from this example. Often a long, fruitless waste of precious time is squandered on hard hearts—some of them relatives.

TURN. Once God's free gift of eternal life had come into the world, it was not to become the victim of the Jews' "dog in the manger" policy. If His people, the Jews, didn't want it, it was to be offered directly to those who did—the Gentiles. Thus Paul quickly announced his turning to the Gentiles of Pisidian Antioch. Here we meet for the first time the missionary policy that became standard procedure throughout his journeys. In every new town he went first to the synagogues. But when the local Jews, as a body, rejected the gospel, he then preached to the Gentiles in that same city. His words here do NOT mean that he would never again preach to Jews, only that in Antioch he would not again preach in the synagogue but to the Gentile populace.

47. "For this is what the Lord intended when he commanded us:

'I have appointed you to be a light unto the Gentiles, that you should show the way of salvation to the entire world.' " (Isa. 49:6).

US. Paul quotes a passage from the prophet Isaiah that applied first to Israel, but was actually fulfilled in Christ. Yet, the only way Jesus could be the "light" to the Gentiles was for His servants to carry His Word to them. With Christ operating as the Holy Ghost, and working THROUGH His ministers, Paul and Barnabas take the verse as applying to themselves. They feel they are following the orders of the indwelling Christ when they present Him (the Light) to the Gentiles. So it is out of obedience, rather than an offended nature, that they turn from the Jews. As soon as their announcement was made, they undoubtedly dramatized it by moving down the aisle and out of the synagogue.

48. When the Gentiles heard this, they rejoiced and gloried in the message of the Lord. As many as were appointed to eternal life, believed it. 49. And the Word of the Lord spread far and wide throughout the whole region.

GLORIED. While the Jews of Pisidian Antioch resented the idea of unrestricted salvation for Gentiles, the Gentiles were thrilled and delighted. Suddenly they were free of the synagogue and every Jewish requirement. As a result many of them departed from organized Judaism to form Gentile churches of their own. We can assume that Paul lost no time in helping them get started. Now they had God's Word for themselves, and gloried in it. It set them free from the burdens of legalism. It appears from vs. 49 that Antioch became an evangelistic center from which the Word radiated to the surrounding region.

APPOINTED. Some expositors make vs. 48 read, "And as many as were disposed to eternal life, believed," but the Greek clearly means destined, chosen, or enrolled. There is nothing to fear from the predestinarian ring of this verse, for it simply means that God knew ahead of time (and marked down) those who WOULD believe. The redemption program is based on man's FREE WILL response to God's revelation. Predestination pertains only to the fact that God FOREKNOWS those who WILL believe the gospel. He makes His plan on that basis. God never violates human freedom for it would defeat His purpose. Everything He seeks from man must be freely given. Loving God, for example, must be a freewill act, or it is not love. Therefore, "appointed to eternal life," refers to God's election of people who had ALREADY chosen Him as it took place in His foreknowledge.

"How did the Jews react to the success of the gospel in Antioch?"

50. But the Jews, using their influence, stirred up hostility among the proselyte women in the social circles. They in turn aroused the leading men of the city. Finally, such a mob was raised up against Paul and Barnabas they were forced to leave the territory. 51. So they shook the dust off their feet in protest against them and went on to Iconium. 52. Meanwhile, the new converts at Antioch continued to be filled with joy and the Holy Spirit.

HOSTILITY. Determined to get rid of Paul and Barnabas, the Jews enlisted the help of some of the wives of the city officials. These would be wives who were also attached to a synagogue and subject to the influence of the Jewish leaders. They were induced to turn their husbands against the missionaries. Wherever Paul went throughout the Roman world, he met with this kind of opposition from the Jewish leaders. The only exceptions were at Philippi and Ephesus. Forced to leave the city, they "shook the dust off their feet," a gesture commended by the Lord when His disciples left an inhospitable place (Lu. 9:5; Matt. 10:14). The action was directed more against the Jews than the town itself. It meant they were through with them for good. It was the custom of Jews to be careful not to bring any dust to Jerusalem from Gentile communities, hence the expression, "shake off" dust.

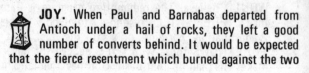

JOY. When Paul and Barnabas departed from Antioch under a hail of rocks, they left a good number of converts behind. It would be expected that the fierce resentment which burned against the two missionaries would continue, in some measure, against the new disciples. Thus, their lot was anything but comfortable. However, far from being discouraged by the expulsion of the men who had brought them the news of Christ, they were filled with joy. This abiding joy was firm evidence of the Lord's presence within them. Nothing but the awareness of Jesus' Ghost (Holy Spirit) could have compensated them for the loss of their teachers and social standing. Thus they were truly converted to Christ and not merely to the two men who were suddenly taken from them. Suffering and persecution are unable to rob true Christians of holy joy, for it is impossible to take the Holy Spirit from God's people. Thus JOY was concrete evidence of their salvation. No SIGNS of any kind are reported.

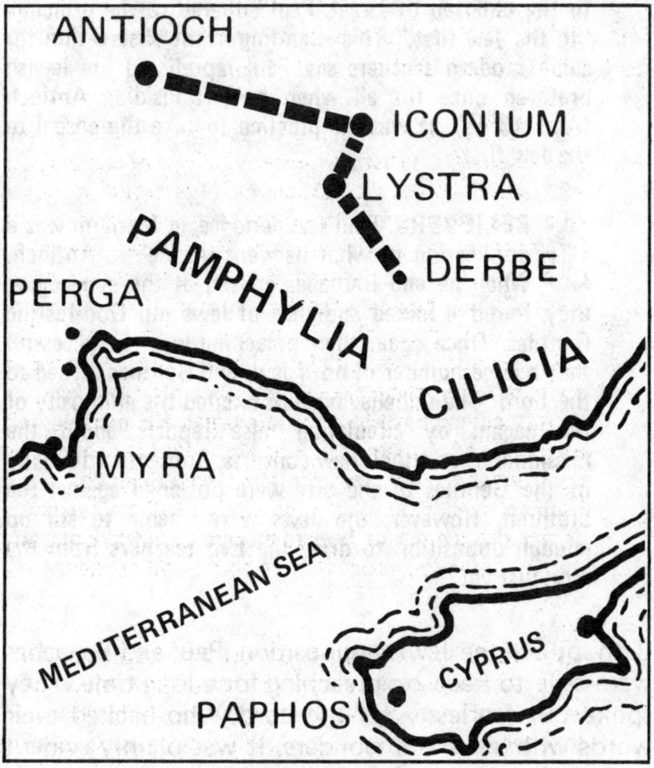

14 1. When Paul and Barnabas reached Iconium, the same thing happened. They went first to the synagogue where they preached the gospel so convincingly, a large number of both Jews and Gentiles became believers. 2. But as before, the Jews who shunned the message stirred up the Gentiles, seeking to poison their minds against the brethren.

ICONIUM. Far from retreating in discouragement, the two missionaries pushed deeper into Gentile territory. Moving eastward from Antioch, they traveled 90 miles along the Roman military highway to Iconium. The town, known today as Konya, contained many Greeks, a few Roman soldiers, and an old established Jewish colony. Following the same procedure, they went first to the synagogue to proclaim the gospel to the children of Israel. Paul adhered to the principle "to the Jew first." This is an important observation for some modern teachers say Paul repudiated his Jewish brethren once for all when he left Pisidian Antioch (Acts 13:46). It was his practice to take the gospel to the Jew first.

BELIEVERS. Paul's experience in Iconium was a duplication of what he went through in Antioch. When he and Barnabas arrived at the synagogue, they found a mixed audience of Jews and God-fearing Gentiles. Once again their preaching was so successful that a large number of both Jews and Gentiles turned to the Lord. The unbelieving Jews excited the animosity of the pagans by circulating false reports about the missionaries and their new converts. Consequently many of the Gentiles in the city were poisoned against the brethren. However, the Jews were unable to stir up enough opposition to drive the two teachers from the city, just yet.

3. In spite of the Jewish opposition, Paul and Barnabas were able to keep on preaching for a long time. They spoke out fearlessly for the Lord, Who backed their words with signs and wonders. It was plainly evident

that the Lord Himself was ministering to the people through His servants.

LONG TIME. The unbelieving Jews began to slander the Christians, but it was a long time before the opposition became serious. Seemingly the Lord had an appointed number of souls He meant to save before the apostles had to leave the city, and as always He has the means to frustrate His enemies. In this case, He enabled His preachers to perform many public miracles which powerfully appealed to the Gentiles. This retarded the rise of opposition in their hearts. We can assume many were saved before there were any miracles at all. The apostles preferred NOT to work physical miracles, knowing the **real** miracle was the work God did in hearts with His Word. But in this case, public miracles were needed to counter the activities of the Jews and allow the missionaries to stay in town long enough to finish their work.

HIMSELF. The apostles laid their hands on the sick and people were healed. But it is vital to see that it is the indwelling Lord Who performs the actual miracle. The preachers were NOT the authors of health, neither did any life-giving power reside in them. It is Jesus Who heals. As in the days of His flesh, when He spoke the Word of life and healed the sick, so here is He doing it again—THROUGH Paul and Barnabas. While the miracles did accomplish the necessary delay in the persecution of the apostles, they also served: (1) to certify the indwelling presence of the Lord within His servants, (2) as SIGNS which validated the Word of grace as the missionaries spoke to the city. Miracles seemed to have played a big part in the success of the gospel in Iconium. However their role must always be subordinate to the real miracle produced by God's Word. They serve a supportive function only throughout the book of Acts. While miracles are great attention getters, they cannot produce the faith needed for salvation.

4. The result was the townspeople became divided in their opinion about them. Some sided with the Jews,

others with the apostles. 5. When a mob of both Jews and Gentiles, with the consent of the leaders, was set to move against them, thinking to stone them, 6. Paul and Barnabas got wind of it. Hurriedly they decided to take refuge in the Lycaonian cities of Lystra and Derbe, and the adjacent countryside. 7. From there they continued to preach the gospel.

DIVIDED. After sufficient time had passed for the apostles to accomplish their work, the Lord allowed the suspicion sown by the Jews to come to fruition. It reached the place where the city was divided, part holding with the Jews, part with the preachers. But that is the nature of the gospel, it divides cities and families (Lu. 12:51-53). When God was ready for His missionaries to move on, He permitted the storm of persecution to gather so that the precious gospel seed would be blown further into Gentile territory. When the apostles got wind of the planned assault, they wisely fled before the Iconium mob could carry out its intentions. The devoted missionary found it wiser to flee a town than remain to die a martyr. Moving southward, they passed the boundary marker into the Lycaonian area of Galatia. The good news of Christ had now moved 18 miles further down the same military highway to the town of Lystra. The apostles spent no time complaining of their bitter lot, but cheerfully continued the work God had given them. They expected God's Word to do its work every place it was sown.

"How did things go for the apostles at Lystra?"

8. One day at Lystra Paul noticed a man with crippled feet who had never once walked in all his life. He had been lame from birth. 9. He was sitting there listening to Paul preach, when something about him arrested the apostle's attention. It struck Paul the man had the faith to be made well. Studying him intently, 10. the apostle called to him with a loud voice, "Stand up!" At once the man sprang to his feet and started to walk.

LAME. We don't know where Paul preached in Lystra. It appears there was no Jewish population, therefore no synagogue. That meant he had to take to the streets in a wholly pagan town. That's not easy when there is a language barrier. So Paul had a difficult time gathering a crowd. This time he had no ready-made audience with a familiar language and understanding of the Scriptures. Yet there was one man who listened to him, the lifelong cripple. He couldn't walk away. As he listened, God's Word penetrated his heart and went to work. Paul noticed the effect it was having on him. In time he discerned the man had the faith to be healed. Now he had a way to gather a crowd. So he shouted with a loud voice, "STAND UP!" People turned to look. When they saw the cripple leap up and walk they were electrified. Paul used a MIRACLE-MAGNET to draw the crowd he needed. There's no hint that he put on a healing campaign. He merely used this one incident as an opening wedge to preach the gospel to this pagan city.

11. When the crowds saw what Paul had done, they began to shout in their Lycaonian dialect, "The gods have come down to us in human form!" 12. Barnabas, they decided, was the Greek god Zeus, and Paul they called Hermes, because he was the spokesman.

GODS. When the Lystrian crowds saw the instantaneous healing of the cripple, they were stunned. To their pagan minds there was but one explanation—their gods were visiting them. As do primitive peoples everywhere, the Lystrians associated the miraculous with divinity. Their wild shouts were not understood by Paul and Barnabas who didn't know the Lycaonian dialect. They had no idea they were being welcomed as gods from heaven. That gods might appear in human form was a common notion of those times. The Roman poet Ovid tells how Jupiter and Mercury (the Latin names for Zeus and Hermes) once visited the earth in the shape of men and were received as guests. Even more stimulating is the fact that their visit was supposed to have occurred in this very region. This would explain the delirious joy of the Lystrians.

ZEUS-HERMES. Zeus, the mightiest of all the ancient gods, was considered to be the father of all other gods and men. He was known as Bel in Babylon, and Osiris in Egypt. Hermes was the herald or spokesman for the gods. According to the myth, he accompanied Zeus on his visits to earth, and was regarded as the god of eloquence. It is thought that Barnabas was a man of grand bearing and imposing appearance, hence the heathens considered him to be Zeus. Paul, because he was the chief spokesman, and perhaps the more animated of the two, they regarded as Hermes. These superstitious people accepted the healing of the cripple as clear evidence they were being visited by these two gods. To their minds everything fit the myths of Zeus and Hermes perfectly.

13. The priest of Zeus, whose temple was located at the approach to the city, brought oxen and wreaths of flowers to the gates where he and the townspeople prepared to offer them as sacrifices to the apostles.

SACRIFICES. The city was wild with joy over the thought that Zeus himself had come to be among them. His temple stood outside the city gates to protect the town, but the great god was now in the midst of his people. Surely they were now safe from all enemies. More than that, Lystra was a farming community. It was located on a barren plain that was waterless and treeless. But Hermes, who was also the god of food distribution, was in their midst as well. He would be able to guarantee plentiful harvests. What greater thing could happen to a city that was defenseless and struggling to survive, than a visit from such gods! The people were ecstatic with joy. They rush to prepare sacrifices and feasting hoping to appeal to the natural talents of their gods, who in turn could put an end to all of their problems. Are they much different from those who receive Christ today and expect Him to miraculously solve all of their problems?

14. But when Paul and Barnabas finally grasped what the people were about to do, they tore their clothes and rushed shouting into the crowd.

GRASPED. Unfamiliar with the Lycaonian language, it was some time before the missionaries guessed what the people were up to. It is possible that the oxen were driven to the door (gates) of their dwelling, there to be sacrificed. Not until they saw the sacrificial wreaths about the necks of the animals, did the apostles realize they were to be the recipients of divine worship. Filled with horror and astonishment, they began tearing their clothing and raced shouting into the crowd. The tearing of clothing, mentioned here for the last time in the N.T., was a Jewish gesture of horror at some act of blasphemy. Sickened by the idea, the apostles hasten to repudiate it as vigorously as possible. Likely the fate of King Agrippa was still a vivid memory.

15. "Stop!" yelled the apostles, "What are you people doing! We are mere men like yourselves. We have come to bring you the good news that you can now turn from worshipping empty idols such as these and worship the living God Who made heaven and earth and the sea and everything in them. 16. In the past He patiently allowed the Gentile nations to go their own way without interference from Him. 17. At the same time, though, He has never left them without some kind of a witness to Himself. Why the very rain from heaven and the harvest seasons, which supply food and gladness to your hearts, are generous reminders of Himself to this world." 18. Even with such remarkable words as these, the apostles just barely succeeded in keeping the crowds from sacrificing to them.

STOP. Satan moved in on the missionaries with no ordinary temptation when he inspired the Lystrians to worship them. They could have reasoned, "After all, these poor souls are ignorant of God and we do stand in His place. Accepting this worship now would allow us to minister with more authority. We could help them better." How often is the premise applied today, that the end sanctifies the means? The apostles would have none of it, but protested with as much grief and energy as possible. They refused to bring the sin of idolatry upon themselves or the people by tolerating such an act. Denying any deity, they put themselves in the same class with their audience, suggesting they too suffer, and die like all men. Such words were meant to awaken hope of deliverance. A Christian never benefits from the tribute of praise.

WITNESS. Paul is here speaking to a strictly Gentile audience. The God of the Scriptures is unknown to these people. To the Jews, to Whom He was already the One true God, Paul could speak of the promised Christ (Messiah). But to the Lystrians, Paul first had to open the BIBLE OF NATURE and declare its Creator. The use of the masculine pronoun (he) in Greek hints that Paul pointed toward the temple of Zeus when he said we have come to help you turn from empty idols. The Lystrians were amazed to hear him say there was only one God Who made heaven, earth, and the sea. They had a god for each realm. Proof that He was alive was the administration of rain, for it first comes up from the sea into the sky, and from there is distributed upon the earth. It takes a living administrator to do that. Rain (water) is God's gift to men, a perpetual miracle testifying to His goodness and presence. Though Gentiles have been indifferent to God, says Paul, He has provided a sufficient testimony in nature so as to leave them without excuse (Rom. 1:22ff). With such fascinating words Paul just barely dissuaded them from their attempted sacrifice.

"Then was Paul able to preach freely in Lystra?"

19. Shortly some Jews, who had followed them from Antioch and Iconium, arrived on the scene. They were so successful in turning the crowds against Paul, that they stoned him and dragged his body out of the city, supposing him to be dead.

STONED. How long did the apostles' popularity last? Only as long as it took their enemies to reach Lystra after them and turn the crowds against them. The reaction was instant. Honored as gods in one hour, they were regarded as criminals the next. Such is the fickle nature of popularity. How worthless it is. Unable to tempt the missionaries with worship, Satan turned to violence. He used the vicious Jews who walked over 100 miles to do their dirty work. Paul learned of Galatian fickleness the hard way. Later, when writing to them, he said, "Oh you foolish Galatians, who has bewitched you?" (Gal. 3:1). With his admirers turned foes, Paul was stoned. Thinking him dead, they dumped his body outside the city. When Paul writes, "Once I was stoned," this is the occasion he has in mind (2 Cor. 11:25).

"Wow! Was Paul really dead?"

20. But as the band of newly won converts stood around looking down at him, Paul arose and re-entered the city. The next day he and Barnabas left for Derbe.

AROSE. We're not told how Barnabas escaped being stoned. He may have been in another part of the city when the mob rampaged. In any event, it was Paul who felt the rocks. Before long he fell unconscious. The townspeople, believing him dead, dragged his body outside the city and dumped it beside the road. Hours later, when the crowds had disappeared, and with only a small group of disciples on the scene, Paul regained consciousness. Some think he was actually dead and was raised by a miracle. If so, Luke does not describe it that way, neither does Paul make that claim any place. What is miraculous, though, is Paul's indomitable spirit. Bruised and bloodied he went right back into the town that stoned him. Some Gk. texts say it was at night. If Timothy saw this event, he was 15 at the time. Lystra was his home. He was among those embracing the gospel. The genuineness of their salvation is seen in the fact that they did not forsake the gospel though their leader was supposedly slain.

21. When they had preached the gospel in Derbe and had made many disciples in that city, they returned to Lystra and to Iconium and to Antioch. 22. There

they poured fresh encouragement into the believers that they might persevere in the faith. Further, they reminded them that the road into the kingdom of God was paved with many hardships. 23. Then, with much fasting and prayer, Paul and Barnabas appointed elders for them in each church. After that they committed them unto the Lord in Whom they had placed their trust.

DERBE. As quickly as Paul could locate Barnabas, the two were on their way to Derbe, 30 mi. south of Lystra. Now known as Zosta, this frontier city had a synagogue. Here they labored completely unmolested. Apparently the whole synagogue was converted. How varied have been God's workings in the missionaries on this Galatian tour. In Antioch they were expelled without stoning. At Iconium they escaped upon learning of a plot against them. At Lystra Paul was stoned and left for dead. Yet Derbe presented no opposition at all. It's never all bad for the Christian. God always provides relief. Yet, Paul was faced with another kind of test here. Derbe was only 160 mi. from Tarsus, his home. He could have elected to return to Syrian Antioch via the Cilician Gates (mountain pass), but God's man wouldn't quit Galatia without checking on the churches he had established. So he and Barnabas made a U-turn and walked back over the route they had come.

ELDERS. Behold the courage of this man Paul! What devotion to Jesus' call! Leaving Derbe, a scene of huge success, he returned to Lystra where he was stoned. One scholar notes that new magistrates had been installed in all the cities where the pair had gone. The new administrations would not be hostile to the missionaries. The Lord could have easily arranged that, and it would help. In the cities they sought to put the churches on a solid basis by appointing elders. The term "elders" includes all church officers. Their tasks were no doubt patterned after the Jerusalem church. It is possible these elders were converted Jews or proselytes, giving them the advantage of Jewish training in the Scriptures. However, Paul would certainly make that secondary to being filled with the Spirit.

HARDSHIPS. Paul's final words to the disciples in each place had to do with the tribulations they should expect as Christians. The NT takes for granted that suffering is the norm for God's people, the pathway to glory (Rom. 8:17; 2 Thess. 1:4; 2 Tim. 2:12). Paul bore the scars of that truth in his body. The record of missionary endeavor in any century is one of toil and sacrifice and death. As someone has said, "When we cease to bleed we cease to bless." Those standing vigorously for Christ will pay a price, even in our time. Those urgently seeking to launch out for Jesus are often hindered by their own churches. The tribulation Christians suffer now is as real as any of Paul's day, only its forms are more suited to our times. Believers can become trapped in the down draft of comfortable living, or hooked on the things of this world. It's still hard to live for Christ.

24. Then they crossed the Pisidian frontier into the province of Pamphylia, 25. arriving at Perga. After preaching their message there, they went down to Attalia, 26. where they caught a ship sailing for Antioch. Thus they returned to the city where they began their journey and had been committed to God for the work they had now achieved.

RETURNED. After installing officers in the church at Antioch, the missionaries headed south over the Taurus Mts. to the coast for the return trip home. They re-visited Perga where they first landed upon arriving in Asia Minor. For some reasons unknown to us, they didn't preach there on that occasion. Now that is rectified. Then comes news that a ship bound for Antioch in Syria is due to depart from Attalia. So Paul and Barnabas hasten across the Lycian border to that nearby seaport. The ship took them directly to Selucia bypassing the Island of Cyprus. From this Antiochian seaport, they walked the 15 or so miles up the Orontes River to their home base at Antioch. In completing this first missionary journey, the apostles had covered more than 1400 miles and were gone for two years or longer (A.D. 45-48).

"What happened in Antioch on the return of the missionaries?"

27. When they arrived in Antioch they summoned the members of the church together to tell how God had worked through them and confirm the fact that God had definitely flung open the door of faith to the Gentiles. 28. Then they stayed on with the believers at Antioch for a long time.

TELL. Now that the first missionary circuit has been completed, Luke ties the story together. It began with the apostles prayerfully committed to God and sent forth by the Antiochian congregation. Now the prayers of that church have been answered. The results, in addition to those individual cases of conversion on the island of Cyprus, were at least four Christian churches established consisting mostly of converted pagans. The focus of the report, however, is on God, not on the sufferings or sermons of the missionaries. The church was surely overjoyed, for the prayers of the people made possible the success of the mission. Now they are no longer the ONLY Gentile church in existence—a much more comfortable feeling. Without the prayer backing of the Antiochian church, God may not have used the missionaries at all. Luke appears to be stressing the role of the local church and its prayer-support behind this first missionary journey.

DOOR. Of particular joy to this Gentile church was the unchallengable demonstration that God had thrown open the door of the kingdom to Gentiles. This first journey provided more confirmation that Gentiles did not have to become Jews in order to be saved. Further, it proved that NO ceremonial requirements of any kind were necessary. The door to the kingdom was entered by faith in Christ and nothing else. Not only was there an absence of any laying on of hands and baptisms, but very few miracles were required. Gentile hearts proved to be fertile ground for the Word of God. The Antiochians were not the only ones interested in the spread of the gospel in Cyprus and Asia Minor. The Jerusalem church (wholly Jewish) was concerned. It seemed certain the world-wide church would soon become more Gentile than Jewish. It is estimated that Paul and Barnabas remained with the Antiochian disciples for a year or more.

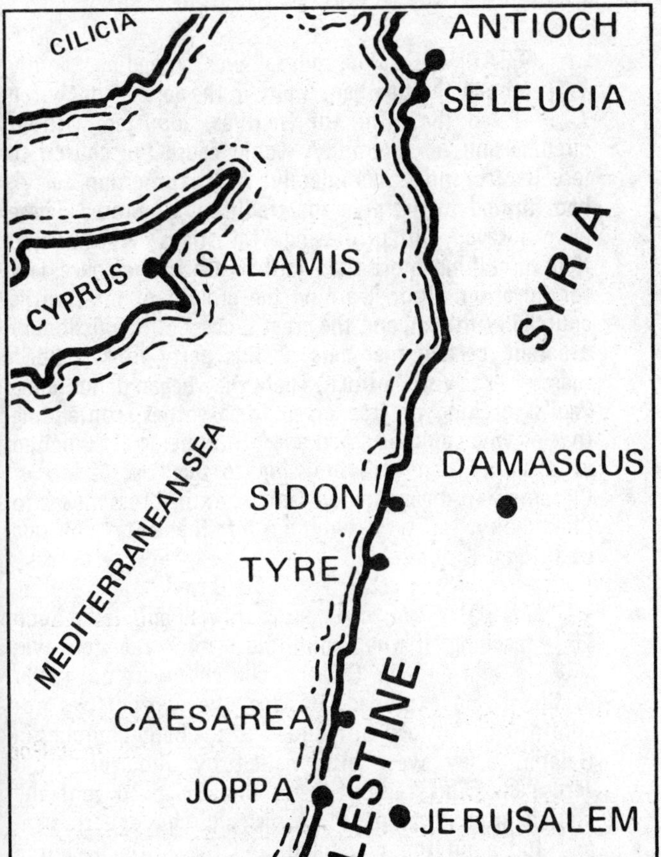

15

1. During the time Paul and Barnabas were at Antioch, some men showed up from Jerusalem and began teaching the brethren the Jewish tradition, "You cannot be saved unless you are circumcised according to the Law of Moses." 2. Their teaching stirred up a great furor with Paul and Barnabas in the midst of the controversy. Finally it was decided that Paul and Barnabas, accompanied by certain of the brethren, should visit the apostles and elders at Jerusalem and get the matter settled.

TEACHING. The gospel was spreading rapidly among the heathen. Many in the Jerusalem church feared the influx of Gentiles, admitted without circumcision or ceremony, would cause the church to lose its Jewishness completely. A "circumcision party" had formed to preserve the traditions of Moses. These were unsaved, but professing "Christians" who insisted that something more than faith in Christ was necessary for salvation. Upon learning the growth of the Gentile church at Antioch, and the great success of its missionary program, certain members of this party took it upon themselves to visit Antioch. There they began denouncing Paul's teaching of free grace for Gentiles, contending that no one could be saved apart from being circumcised as a fleshly sign of submission to the Law of Moses. Circumcision meant to Judaism, what the cross means to Christianity. It was symbolic of the entire Mosaic tradition.

FUROR. We can guess how Paul felt. Such teaching, if true, would mean his 2 year tour was in vain and his Galatian churches were not really in Christ. He exploded. Besides, the conflict was not confined to Antioch but spread to the baby churches in Galatia. They were also visited by Judaizers from Jerusalem. This red-hot issue threatened to split the church into two camps: the Jewish churches at Jerusalem and Judea on the one hand, and the Antioch church and her Asia Minor satellites on the other. It is possible that Paul wrote his letter to the Galatians (the new churches) at this time, for they would be shaken by such teaching. One can feel Paul's rage as he attacks the false teachings of the Judaizers in his letter to the Galatians. Luke is silent about that letter.

SETTLED. The controversy broiled for over a year. A Jew-Gentile split seemed imminent. Something had to be done. The Antiochian church took the initiative sending Paul and Barnabas, along with some other responsible members, to see if the matter couldn't be settled at Jerusalem. It would be a shame if Paul had to spend a lot of his time defending his work when he could be reaching more Gentiles. A clear cut statement was urgently needed. It should be noted that Peter was living at Antioch when the Judaizers arrived. He had to be publicly rebuked by Paul for separating himself from the Gentiles to eat with the Judaizers (Gal. 2:11). They would not eat with Gentile Christians whom they regarded as still unclean. Peter knew better, but his action confirmed the claim of the Judaizers. Therefore he was rightly rebuked by Paul in public. Apparently he returned to Jerusalem before Paul's party departed to visit the apostles.

3. So the congregation saw them off on their journey to Jerusalem. Inasmuch as the route took them through Phoenicia and Samaria, they visited the brethren along the way explaining to them in detail how salvation was coming to the Gentiles. This news was joyfully received by the Christians there.

JOURNEY. The Antiochian church knew a great deal was at stake in the forthcoming meeting at Jerusalem. The entire congregation apparently formed an honor guard to escort the delegates from the city, indicating the importance the church attached to the mission. The natural route to Jerusalem would take the caravan through Phoenicia and Samaria. In a manner consistent with his enthusiastic spirit, Paul visited all the churches enroute, telling them of the great success of their missionary trip among the Gentiles. Since these churches were themselves established by Hellenistic Jews who believed in Jesus, they were thrilled to hear that God had flung wide the door of salvation, that Christianity was no longer Jewish.

"Will those at Jerusalem feel the same way?"

4. On their arrival at Jerusalem the Antiochian delegation was officially welcomed by the church. As soon as they were greeted by the apostles and elders, they gave a full report of the way God was using them to reach the Gentiles. 5. But then some "converted" Pharisees came forward to protest the report, saying, "It is mandatory that all Gentile converts be circumcised and compelled to observe the Law of Moses."

WELCOMED. Word traveled ahead of the caravan so the Jerusalem church knew the Antiochian delegation was on its way. The leaders were all on hand to greet the brethren when they arrived. It was an official greeting and the church was gathered to hear what the delegates had to say. Paul and Barnabas delivered the same glowing report that they gave to the churches enroute, but they didn't get the same joyous response. The rank and file Jewish Christian was not happy to see Christianity become a Gentile movement. It is likely that even the apostles and elders were reluctant to see Judaism fade away. But if salvation is really by faith plus nothing, then there was nothing to prevent the entire Gentile world from coming to Christ. In that event, Christianity's Jewish beginnings would be lost in the shuffle. So it wasn't exactly a warm welcome that awaited the delegates.

PHARISEES. It was easy for Pharisees to embrace Christianity. For them salvation was merely a matter of **adding** the idea that Jesus was the Messiah to what they already believed. Thus they were inclined to feel that Christianity was nothing more than a new party formed INSIDE Judaism; that it in no way canceled the Jewish customs. It was from these "converted" Pharisees that the circumcision party (Judaizers) arose. Unwilling to see Judaism die out, they adopted a legalistic idea of salvation. They insisted that no non-Jews could be saved without submitting to circumcision and observing the Law of Moses. It was the more zealous ones of this group who stirred trouble in Antioch and the new churches of Galatia. Here, on their home grounds, they would be more outspoken and forceful in their demands. The conference was headed for a showdown on the question: can Gentiles be saved without becoming Jews?

6. Then, the apostles and elders who had scheduled this meeting for the sole purpose of considering this matter, threw it open for discussion. 7. But after a great deal of debate back and forth, Peter arose to address the convention:

"Brethren, is this not something which was already settled by God in the early days? Was it not by my lips that He chose to preach to the Gentiles that they might hear the gospel and believe it? 8. They made no confession of any kind, yet God, Who reads the hearts of men, saw their faith and gave them the Holy Spirit just as He did to us. 9. He canceled any differences between us and them by cleansing their hearts by faith."

DEBATE. We can only guess about the debate that ensued. Surely it was heated. The teams were likely divided off, with the Judaizers on the one hand and the Antiochian Gentiles on the other. Since their opinions were diametrically opposed, the debate was animated and hot. After observing the confusion created by the conflicting views, Peter decided to step in and end the bitterness being generated. In his heart he knows what God wants. It's time to redeem himself from the blunder he made at Antioch. He rises to his feet to announce a principle that will lead to the right solution. He is going to ask his Jewish brethren (his remarks are aimed at them), to think back to the conversion of Cornelius and his household. The principle which will solve this matter lies there.

ADDRESS. By asking His brethren to go back some 10 years to the Cornelius affair, He means to show how God has ALREADY made known HIS will in the matter. He points out three things which unmistakeably show God's intention: (1) The salvation of those Gentiles at Cornelius' house was God's idea in the first place. (2) God bore witness to the salvation of the Gentiles by giving them His Holy Spirit. He couldn't be mistaken about their eligibility for salvation, since He could read their hearts. (3) After God had cleansed their hearts by faith, there could be no difference between Jewish and Gentile Christians, for the outward circumcision of the Jews merely typified the inward circumcision of the heart (Rom. 2:29). The receipt of the Spirit accomplished the inward cleansing. An important principle emerges from Peter's message: observe the direction God is taking and work with Him.

10. "How is it then, that you dare to question God's judgment in this matter by seeking to burden the Gentiles with a yoke which neither we nor our fathers were able to bear? 11. By now it should be clear to all of us that we are saved by the grace of the Lord Jesus, the same as they are."

QUESTION. Peter makes a penetrating observation: if God cleansed the hearts of the Gentiles at Cornelius' house by faith alone, requiring no ritual, why should we Jews seek to impose the burdensome Law of Moses on Gentiles God is saving now? Apparently many believed the Cornelius affair was simply a SPECIAL CASE and not a NEW DOOR God was opening. But with Gentiles all over coming to Christ, the incident proved to be a SIGN POST indicating a new move (Phase III) on God's part. God is saving Gentiles, says Peter, apart from any Jewish ritual and we'd better go along with Him. To add circumcision and the rabbinical traditions where God has required none, amounts to questioning His right to save people by grace. Besides, he says, since we know from experience that we can't keep the Law anyway, are we not also saved by grace just as they are? Of course we are.

YOKE. At this time in history the accumulation of rabbinical tradition had become unbearable. The rank and file Jew groaned under the heavy burden of the Mosaic Law. When Jesus invited His hearers, "Take My yoke upon you," He was contrasting life lived by grace against one which sought righteousness through trying to keep all the Jewish rules (Matt. 11:29,30). Even those who claimed to fulfill all the requirements of Judaism knew no real peace of heart (Matt. 23:4). In saying that "neither we nor our fathers" could keep the Law, Peter renounces the whole Mosaic system as no longer obligatory. If no one can really keep the Law, it cannot possibly be the means of salvation. Consequently, he says, all of us are saved by grace alone. What wonderful words to come from Peter as we hear him for the last time in the book of Acts.

"How did the audience react to Peter's statement?"

12. Upon hearing those words the entire crowd became silent. Then they quietly listened to Barnabas and Paul as they told of the signs and miracles God had done through them among the Gentiles.

LISTENED. Peter's words were so arresting the crowd sat in tranquil silence. The debate was over. Further argument would clearly be against the revealed will of God. At this point, Barnabas and Paul are invited to speak. Barnabas first, because he is better known, having been generous with these brethren in the past (Acts 4:36). The missionaries surely told of their work both in Syrian Antioch and in Galatia, emphasizing how the Holy Spirit had filled the hearts of the Gentiles in exactly the same manner as He had filled the Jewish Christians. These reports confirmed what Peter said about God saving Gentiles without any observance of the Law. Thus the hearers were further impressed that Gentile salvation was a work of God and that Christianity, stripped of all Jewish ritual, was acceptable to Him. Note that nothing is said of Titus being presented to this group, since Luke is more interested in reporting the settling opinion than giving details of the arguments presented by either side.

"How was the matter finally settled?"

13. When they had finished speaking, James arose to present the concensus of the meeting:

"Listen to me, brethren. 14. Simeon has told us what happened when God first began favoring the Gentiles to take out from them a people who would bear His name. 15. The whole idea of Gentile salvation squares with all that the prophets have said, as summarized by the prophet Amos:"

JAMES. After Paul and Barnabas had finished, James stood up and claimed the attention of the audience. What he has to say would be important. He was more than a pastor, he was the bishop of the Jerusalem church. Also he was a strict observer of the Law. The "circumcision party," no doubt considered him the chief exponent of their position. But if they expected him to support the Jewish view of salvation, they were in for disappointment. He chose, instead, to declare himself in full agreement with Peter, announcing that all the prophets agreed with that position too. In support of his statement he will quote the prophet Amos. This James is the Lord's brother. He ministered to the Jerusalem church until he was stoned to death in A.D. 61 on orders of the high priest.

16."'After this, says the Lord, I will come back and restore the fallen house of David; from its ruins I will rebuild it and raise it anew: 17. So that the rest of mankind may find the Lord, that is to say, even the Gentiles who are called by My name. 18. The One Who says these things is the Lord, Who reveals things even as He has known them from the beginning.' "

RESTORE. James is quoting the prophet Amos from the Septuagint, the Greek version of the Hebrew O.T. In its primary sense, the passage has to do with the restoration of the temple and royal house of David after the Babylonian captivity. But James uses it in a secondary sense, seeing the house of David restored through the Son of David (Jesus). When the Lord was raised from the dead, God was rebuilding the house of David from its ruins. To provide His Son with a spiritual nation, God gathered together a people consisting of both Jews and Gentiles. The Amos passage definitely speaks of Gentiles being claimed by God (Amos 9:12). The final words (vs. 18) James inserts into Amos' quote. He allows that God knew from the beginning He was going to save the Gentiles, but only now is the eternal decree coming to pass.

19. "Therefore, in my judgment, we should not impose any of our legal burdens on those Gentiles who are turning to God, 20. but instruct them, in writing, to refrain from associating themselves with anything offered to idols, to keep themselves from immorality, to avoid eating the meat of strangled animals, or eating blood in any form. 21. For after all, the Law of Moses has been preached in the synagogues for a very long time now, and in every city his words against these things are read aloud every Sabbath."

JUDGMENT. James' proposal is far different from what the Judaizers wanted. Announcing what must have been the majority opinion, he states that all attempts to impose circumcision and the Mosaic traditions on the Gentiles are to cease. Thus the Holy Spirit made His will known. The Gentiles were asked to abstain from (1) idolatry, (2) immorality, (3) the eating of strangled flesh, and (4) the eating of blood in any form. These four specifics were not related solely to the Mosaic Law. They had a higher priority than the Levitical rules, for the O.T. declared those who did such things would be cut off from God's people. All that James asks is that the Gentile Christians refrain from those things which by their **very nature**, were inconsistent with a life lived unto God, or were **forbidden** by God Himself.

REFRAIN. 900 years before the Mosaic Law was given, God forbad the eating of blood in ANY form (Gen. 9:4). He wanted blood drained from the animals as soon as they were killed. Consequently those strangled in snares, dying with their blood still in them, could not be eaten. Also taboo was the pagan practice of mixing wine with animal blood and drinking it as a delicacy. With Pagan standards of morality extremely low in those days, James wants Gentile converts to abandon their old ways and adopt the higher Jewish code of relations between the sexes. Gentiles were further asked not to eat the meat of animals sacrificed in pagan temples. It was the custom to sell the surplus meat in the market place. To the Jewish mind, the eating of such meat was the same as worshipping the idol. So James asks that the Gentiles abstain from eating such meat as a concession to the "weaker" Jewish brethren who are not yet free from their food laws. The meat itself is not evil, neither is the eating of it, as Paul later advised the Romans (Rom. 14:14ff.).

SYNAGOGUES. It is clear from James' words that the first Jewish Christians did not forsake the synagogue system, even though they met in their own fellowships on Sundays. It is also likely that the Gentile converts joined them. Why? There was no N.T. as yet, and the Sabbath school was the logical place to learn more about God. With the legalistic requirements removed from the Gentiles, this posed a knotty problem. In the Asian and European synagogues, there was a big gap between the freedom Gentiles enjoyed and the strict codes by which Jewish lives were regulated. That's why James felt it necessary to impose some conditions on Gentiles for the sake of Christian unity. It would be rough to have Gentiles flaunting their liberty in the face of Moses' teachings while at the same time attending the synagogues. It would only produce resentment. James is in no way appeasing the "circumcision party" with his proposal, but offering practical rules necessary for unity in the church.

22. Then it was decided by the apostles and elders, with the whole church in agreement, to choose delegates from among their own number and have them accompany Paul and Barnabas on their return trip to Antioch. Accordingly they selected Judas Barsabbas and Silas, two leaders in the church, 23. and sent the following letter with them:

"We, the apostles and elders and brethren at Jerusalem, send greetings to our Gentile brothers in Antioch, Syria, and Cilicia. 24. We hear that certain people from our fellowship have come among you, challenging your salvation and troubling you with their teachings. We want you to know that they had no authorization from us to do such a thing. 25. After meeting together to consider this matter, we unanimously agreed to pick some delegates from our group and have them come to you in the company of our beloved Barnabas and Paul. 26. These are men who have staked their lives on the name of our Lord Jesus Christ. 27. We therefore are pleased to commend to you Judas and Silas, who will confirm, in person, the things written in this letter."

AGREEMENT. James' words found favor with the conference and the Jerusalem church yielded in the matter of imposing Jewish rites on Gentile converts. How thrilled Paul must have been to have it all settled in his favor—and in writing. The letter was a good idea, for the Gentile Christians were widely scattered and the letter insured their getting the news in its pristine form. Today that letter stands as a Christian Bill of Rights, speaking against those legalists who try to enslave modern believers with some form of law. Paul was grateful for this confirmation of his ministry. The delegates accompanying Paul and Barnabas could report the feelings of the Jerusalem church to the Gentile brethren at Antioch. From there the communication would radiate to the satellite churches in Cyprus and Asia Minor, which may have been started by Paul during the silent years prior to his call to active duty by Barnabas.

28. "It pleases the Holy Spirit and us to announce that you are not to be burdened with legal requirements other than these essentials which cannot be avoided: 29. that you are to abstain from meat which has been offered to idols, meat with its blood still in it, and meat which has been strangled. Beyond that, if you keep yourselves from immorality, you will have fulfilled your part. Farewell."

PLEASES. In vs. 27 the Jerusalem church was pleased to send Judas and Silas (later known as Sylvanus and companion to Paul) to Antioch. But in vs. 28 we find the Holy Spirit is pleased to join in the announcement of Gentile freedom from Jewish rules. The Lord Jesus, operating as the Holy Spirit, was able to express Himself through the willing hearts of the Jerusalem assembly. His thoughts became theirs, so that the judgment expressed was as much His as theirs. This is a tender letter, not one of ecclesiastical arrogance imposing decrees on others. The spirit is one which sets men free from the yoke of ritualists and the prejudices of bigots. It was truly done in the name of Jesus. The tone indicates the Jerusalem church regretted having to mention even the four specifics needed for Christian unity. The brethren at Jerusalem seem to want the Gentiles to enjoy their freedom in Christ. That indeed is the work of the Holy Spirit.

"How did the Gentile Christians react to this decision?"

30. So the party took leave of the Jerusalem brethren and went down to Antioch. When they had assembled the entire congregation, they delivered the letter to them. 31. So great was the encouragement it brought, the believers broke out in great rejoicing as soon as it was read. 32. Then Judas and Silas, prophets in their own right, preached long messages, encouraging the brethren still more and establishing them in the faith.

33. Their ministry was so appreciated, it was some time before they could get away to return to those who had sent them. 34. (Omit). 35. But Paul and Barnabas stayed on in Antioch teaching and preaching God's Word with many others helping them.

ENCOURAGEMENT. It was a happy party making its way back to Antioch. The problem had been resolved. The official letter is in their possession. Upon their arrival in the Syrian capitol, the whole church is assembled. The letter is read. Great relief sweeps over the congregation. Its warm tone thrills the Gentile Christians. Then Judas and Silas, themselves inspired preachers, brought more words which heightened the joy of the Gentiles. The visiting preachers were so appreciated, the assembly was reluctant to let them return to Jerusalem. But they had to get back with their report. So they departed with the good wishes of the Antiochian church. Verse 34 is not found in the most ancient mss., having been inserted into the text about the 5th or 6th century. With the circumcision matter settled, Paul and Barnabas threw themselves into the work of teaching and edifying the saints. In the meantime, the missionary call burning within Paul won't be denied for long.

36. After some time had passed, Paul approached Barnabas with a suggestion. "Shouldn't we go back," he said, "and see how our brothers are doing in those cities where we preached the Word of the Lord?" 37. Barnabas agreed, but wanted to take John Mark along with them. 38. However, Paul was determined that someone who had deserted them in Pamphylia was not worthy to go with them now. 39. So a sharp disagreement occurred between them and they parted company over it and went their separate ways. Barnabas took Mark with him and set sail for Cyprus, 40. while Paul chose Silas to be his new companion. Then, after the brethren had commended him to the keeping power of God's grace, 41. Paul

traveled through Syria and Cilicia bringing fresh encouragement to the churches there.

DISAGREEMENT. Barnabas was happy with Paul's suggestion for a return visit to Cyprus and the churches they started in Asia Minor, but he wanted to take along his cousin, John Mark. Paul said no. Both were stubborn about it. Possibly both were right, but a wonderful friendship came to an end because of it. In reporting the incident, Luke allows us to see how great men, who are also great friends, can be penetrated by Satan. It must have shocked the church to see these spiritual giants part company. What a testimony to the devil's power in the church. After this great victory, Satan moved to the attack. Christians must always be on their guard after they have experienced a nice success in Christ! Of course God exploited the evil, ending up with two missionary teams instead of one. But the ugly scar remains. Barnabas and Mark went to their native Cyprus while Paul returned to his native Cilicia.

SEPARATE. The Spirit had indeed said, "Separate unto Me Barnabas and Saul," but now they had separated **from** each other. After being made fast friends in the Spirit, they each go their separate ways—all because of this dispute over Mark. The compassionate Barnabas was for giving Mark another chance, hoping perhaps, to salvage him. Paul, on the other hand, didn't want to risk another washout. Had Paul yielded it would have cost him nothing. As it was, he lost a dear friend. Had Barnabas yielded, he would have had other chances to help his cousin. As it was he deserted his best friend. Both men were the losers. Since Luke doesn't appear to take sides in the dispute, perhaps we shouldn't either. However, it seems the Antiochian church sides with Paul. Only he was committed to the Lord's care. Barnabas now disappears from the N.T. Tradition says that he went on to a successful ministry in Cyprus and possibly Egypt. He died as a martyr for Christ.

SILAS. After the split, Paul had to find a new missionary partner. He was apparently impressed with the inspired preaching of Silas, one of the two prophets who came down from Jerusalem. He was a Jewish Christian from the Jerusalem church and could help Paul in disarming Jewish prejudices. Also he was a Roman citizen and could travel freely in Gentile lands. Since he was named in the official letter from the council, his credentials were top notch. He also spoke Greek. Paul either sent for him to come from Jerusalem or he returned on his own. In any event, he makes himself available to the Lord as Paul's companion for the second missionary journey.

16 1. From there, Paul moved on to Derbe and Lystra. Here he greeted a young disciple by the name of Timothy. Timothy's mother was a Jewish Christian, but his father was a Greek. 2. The lad had earned a fine reputation as a Christian among the believers of Lystra and Iconium, 3a. and Paul wanted him to join their party and travel with them.

MOVED ON. With Barnabas returning to the island of Cyprus, Paul elected to go north by land and visit the churches of northern Syria and Cilicia. They were the ones named in the official letter from Jerusalem. They needed to hear the decree which freed them from all Jewish ritual. Taking the land route to Asia Minor gave Paul an opportunity to visit his home in Tarsus, the capitol of Cilicia. He hadn't seen his family for ten years. We can assume he didn't spend much time visiting relatives. He doesn't appear to be a family man. Besides he was anxious to press westward to the churches of Asia Minor and share the Jerusalem letter with them. Crossing the Taurus Mts. by way of the historic pass (the Cilician Gates), the missionaries followed the road that led them to Derbe and Lystra. They are now approaching the towns in the opposite direction from their first trip, hence they are named in the reverse order.

TIMOTHY. At Lystra, Paul ran into a young man converted on the first journey. He may have been in the group that gathered about Paul's seemingly lifeless body when he was left for dead. Young Timothy had grown into a fine Christian with a good reputation as a disciple of Christ. Paul became fond of him. He looked on him as a "son," as he later calls him (2 Tim. 1:2). The child of a Jewish Christian mother and a pagan father, he had been well trained in the Scriptures. It occurred to Paul that this young Christian might be the right person to join them and serve in the same capacity that John Mark filled on the first missionary journey. Also, it seems Paul needed someone to minister to him as a personal attendant, perhaps in connection with his illness. In any event, Timothy's parents have no objection to his going.

3b. Since it was common knowledge that Timothy's father was a Gentile, Paul had him circumcised out of consideration for the Jews living in the region. 4. Then as they moved on through the various cities, they shared the Jerusalem letter with the Gentiles, asking them to observe the decisions made by the apostles and elders. 5. They found the churches fairly well established in the faith and growing in numbers every day.

CIRCUMCISED. With a letter in his pocket freeing Gentile believers from the Jewish rite of circumcision, Paul nonetheless circumcizes Timothy. Why? He was a half-Jew whose pagan father apparently forbad the ceremony. To bring him on the team without circumcision would offend those Jews Paul wanted to reach. Knowing Timothy was raised as a Jew, the Jews of that region would expect the operation to be performed. It would definitely cause trouble if it wasn't. Paul very much wanted Timothy on the team. So, following the principle of expediency, he performed the minor surgery. We must note that it was done for practical reasons only, NOT to fulfill the Law. Neither did Paul consider himself bound by his own rules, but felt free to bend those rules when the circumstances justified it (1 Cor. 6:12). Timothy was already raised under the Law. It was purely a matter of avoiding needless offense to the Jews and Jewish brethren. Paul was one to avoid giving offense. So Timothy became a special case. With Titus, though, it was a different matter. He was wholly Gentile. Consequently, Paul refused to circumcize him. In one case it was expedient to circumcise, in the other it wasn't. Paul's entire case for Gentile liberty was based on what he did with Titus. It wasn't with Timothy. In his letter to the Galatians he forbids Gentile circumcision. To them it would have meant that faith in Christ was not sufficient for salvation.

SHARED. As the apostles went from city to city, they read the decrees of the Jerusalem council which freed Gentile converts from Jewish rites and submission to the Law of Moses. Yet it appears they were faithful in asking them to observe the food laws and higher moral code as James had stated. Paul had probably given his word he would do this and here we see him keeping that word. The passing along of these rules undoubtedly paved the way for unity in the Jew-Gentile fellowships. Yet the need for these rules must have relaxed very quickly. We do not find Paul imposing them on the Gentiles in any of his letters. He does not even refer to them when he discusses the food question in his letters to the Romans and the Corinthians.

ESTABLISHED. In telling us that the churches of Asia Minor, founded on Paul's first missionary journey, are now established and flourishing, Luke gives us an exciting report. Phase III of the Lord's program is successfully underway. Jesus has done what He set out to do. He returned in the Spirit to operate as the Holy Ghost and build His church through His disciples. He said it would be carried out in successive stages: first in Jerusalem, then Samaria and finally the whole Gentile world. Luke has been careful to tell us when each phase was accomplished. Now he reports the

Gentile phase as well established and growing. All that remains is fanning out from this terrific start until the whole world is covered with the gospel. The next big thing to happen in history will be the destruction of Jerusalem and the subsidence of Judaism. After that, Christianity will emerge as the great religion of the world.

"Where does the Lord want His missionaries to go with the gospel next?"

6. After that, they made their way through the Phrygian-Galatian region, because the Holy Spirit had forbidden them to preach the gospel in Asia. 7. Then when they had passed through Mysia, hoping to enter Bithynia, the Spirit of Jesus stopped them again. 8. So they continued along the Mysian border until they reached Troas.

FORBIDDEN. After leaving Lystra (Timothy's home) the missionary party crossed the border into another part of Phrygia to visit Iconium and Antioch, cities evangelized on Paul's first trip. From Antioch it would have been natural for them to continue westward to preach in the great cities of Asia. Paul was most anxious to go to the great city of Ephesus. However, the Holy Spirit, speaking perhaps through a prophet at Lystra, told them they were NOT to preach there. This is NOT the Asian continent as we think of it today, or even the rich peninsula now called Asia Minor. It was a Roman province occupying the western portion of Asia Minor (modern Turkey). It had a number of large cities, chief of which was Ephesus. Barred from moving westward, where would they go? To the south was malaria country. They'd come from the east. That left only the north open to them.

STOPPED. Traveling northward along the eastern border of Mysia (see map below), the party came to the Bithynian border. They were all set to enter Bithynia (a province along the Black Sea) when the Lord again halted them. Since He is here referred to as the "Spirit of Jesus," we may assume it indicates some manifestation more closely associated with His indwelling presence. It is interesting to find the Lord, operating as the Holy Ghost, referred to as the Holy Spirit in one verse and then called the Spirit of Christ in the next. It may be intended to show the different methods of communication He used, but one thing is sure—they are one and the SAME Spirit. One can see the error of distinguishing too sharply between the Holy Ghost and the Lord operating in the Spirit, by comparing these two verses.

TROAS. The missionaries don't know it yet, but the Lord wants them to go to Europe. They are not to spend any more time preaching in Asia, but go as quickly as possible to Macedonia. Thus it was the Lord Who blocked their advance whenever they purposed to go in the wrong direction. While they have covered quite a bit of ground, they have not preached in any of the cities. Stopped once more at the Bithynian border, there was nothing to do but go westward. At last they came to the Aegean Sea. From there they traveled down the coast to Troas. This was an important city built a few miles south of the ruins of ancient Troy. It was a regular port of call for ships traveling between Asia and Macedonia. Now the Lord had His missionaries where He wanted them. From here ships could easily take them to Europe.

"Now that Jesus has gotten His missionaries to Troas, how will He lead them to Europe?"

9. During the night Paul had a vision in which he saw a certain Macedonian standing there pleading with him. "Come over to Macedonia," the man was saying, "and help us." 10. Paul quickly grasped the meaning of the vision and we set about at once to leave for Macedonia. We were satisfied that God had called us to preach the gospel there.

VISION. No sooner did the missionaries arrive in Troas than the Lord made known His will by means of a night vision. In the preternatural communication Paul sees not an angel but a man from Greece. He is begging them to bring the gospel to Macedonia. To this point, Paul has been in the dark as to why he was forbidden to preach in Asia. Now he's very glad he waited on the Lord and followed orders, though it undoubtedly seemed like a wasted journey at the time. The Lord wants him in Greece as quickly as possible. That's where he is to do his preaching. This vision climaxes an extraordinary series of spiritual communications the Lord has used to get His servants to Europe. Obviously Paul was very sensitive to the promptings of his indwelling Lord. Without hesitation the party sets sail across the Aegean Sea for Macedonia.

WE. It is evident that Dr. Luke joined the party here at Troas. The first of the "WE" sections in Acts begins here. Isn't it interesting how he inserts himself into the story with so little fanfare? From here on he will be Paul's companion and personal physician. The apostle suffered some chronic infirmity which apparently required frequent medical attention. So Luke gave up his practice to care for the apostle on his journeys. Some think Luke is the man Paul saw in the vision and that Jesus used him to clothe the Macedonia call.

COME OVER. This distance from Troas to Macedonia on the opposite side of the Aegean Sea was a little over 100 miles. Four centuries earlier it had been the center of Greek power under Philip and Alexander the Great. Since 146 B.C. it had been a Roman province. Along with Achaia to the south, the two provinces constitute modern Greece. In this lay many great Gentile cities. They would be Paul's targets. Raised in Tarsus, which was "no mean city" itself, Paul was a city man. He was at home in the midst of teeming traffic. It was Paul's strategy to win the great cities, knowing the gospel would radiate from them to the surrounding areas. After Paul establishes the church in the great cities of Greece, he will have completed a giant arc of which Ephesus is the center.

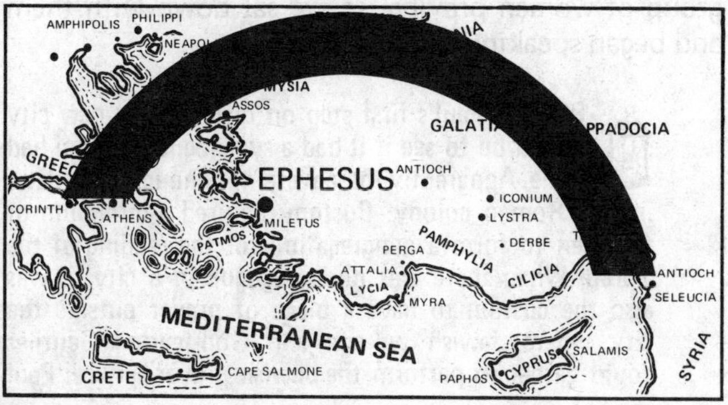

11. So we put out from Troas setting a straight course for Samothrace. The next day we landed at Neapolis. 12. From there we went directly to Philippi, a leading city in the first district of Macedonia and a Roman colony. We spent a few days here to make plans.

PHILIPPI. The second part of the missionary journey gets under way with four people in the party. Good winds speed them to Samothrace, an island 38 miles off the Samothracian coast. It was small, serving as a hideout for criminals and weird religious cults. The party didn't tarry here but moved right on to Neapolis. This was the seaport for Philippi 10 miles further inland. Philippi is Paul's target. Named for Philip of Macedon, it was the site of a famous battle in Roman history. Luke notes that Philippi is not only a first rate city, but also a Roman colony. A colony was an extension of the city of Rome established on the soil of another country. The residents of these colonies were thus citizens of Rome with the local government based on Roman law. This will be the first great city in Europe to hear the gospel from the missionaries. Macedonia was divided into four districts. Amphipolis, not Philippi, was the chief city of this district.

"Were they able to make any converts in Philippi?"

13. On the Sabbath day we went outside the city gate and walked along the riverside where there was supposed to be a place of prayer. Here we found a group of women praying, so we sat down with them and began speaking to them.

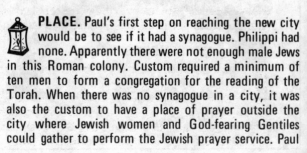

PLACE. Paul's first step on reaching the new city would be to see if it had a synagogue. Philippi had none. Apparently there were not enough male Jews in this Roman colony. Custom required a minimum of ten men to form a congregation for the reading of the Torah. When there was no synagogue in a city, it was also the custom to have a place of prayer outside the city where Jewish women and God-fearing Gentiles could gather to perform the Jewish prayer service. Paul and his friends were told of such a place. Usually it was a light structure, often open to the sky. Water from the river was used for the washings connected with the worship. On the Sabbath (which indicates he was still seeking Jews and proselytes) they found such a group gathered by the side of the Gangites River, less than a Sabbath's day journey from the city. Knowing the gospel liberated women as well as Gentiles from Jewish discrimination, Paul joined the group and began telling them of Jesus.

14. One of those listening to us was a God-fearing woman named Lydia, a dye merchant from Thyatira. As she sat there weighing Paul's words, the Lord moved on her heart and she responded to the message. 15. Then she and her entire household were baptized. After that, she insisted that we remain with her for a time. "If you honestly believe I am a true believer in the Lord, come down to my house and stay with me." So persistent was she, that we finally yielded.

MERCHANT. Among those listening to Paul that day was a prominent business woman. She was a Gentile proselyte (God-fearer) whose home was Thyatira, a city noted for its purple dyes. She no doubt had an establishment at Philippi large enough to accommodate guests and receive her wares from Thyatira. Since Thyatira had a Jewish colony, it is likely she became a God-fearer there. Her principle business was dye making, but she likely produced purple cloth as well. The ancients highly prized the Thyatiran tints which ran from rose-red to sea-green. It would appear that Lydia was a widow and had no family, otherwise the text would have presented her as a housewife rather than as a business woman.

RESPONDED. Luke wants us to remember that it is the Lord Who touches people's hearts, not merely the words of His servants. There is no way for any preacher to reach into someone else's heart. That is Jesus' part in the program. We speak, and He bears witness. He is the One building the church, even though He does it through His servants. Paul had not spoken long when Jesus touched Lydia's heart. She responded to become the first European convert. The first organized missionary effort in Europe began with the winning of a woman. Years later Paul will send a letter to the church at Philippi. The chances are it began in this woman's house. It is precious to note how the gospel honors women.

"Who was the next convert in the city of Philippi?"

16. On one occasion, when we were on our way to the place of prayer, we encountered a slave girl who was possessed by a divining spirit. Her owners were getting rich off of her affliction by using her as a fortune teller.

GIRL. The next person we see Paul deal with is a demon-possessed slave girl. Her owners were exploiting her satanic bondage to make money. Luke's choice of words in the Gk. text indicates she was regarded as a voice (oracle) of Apollo, the god of divination. Either the clairvoyant spirit in this girl used her speech organ so that she gave out involuntary utterances (spiritist medium), or else she was a psychic and perceived the information. In any event, the inhabitants of Philippi believed she was inspired by Apollo and would pay large sums to have her tell their fortunes. Demons do have the power to reveal some useful information. The slave girl was owned by shrewd masters who played upon the credulity of the people. They used the girl's unfortunate "gift" to build their own fortunes. Actually such a thing is NOT a gift, but a liability instead.

17. This girl began following along behind Paul and the rest of us shouting, "These men are servants of the Most High God. They have come to tell us how we can be saved." 18. When she had carried on like this for many days, Paul finally became so irritated that he turned around and said to the spirit within her,

"In the name of Jesus Christ I command you to come out of her!" And the spirit came out of her that very moment.

SHOUTING. Day after day, as the missionaries journeyed from Lydia's house to the place of prayer, the slave girl would tag along behind shouting her unsolicited testimonials to the crowds. As the evil spirits which met Jesus truthfully acknowledged Him for Who He was, so does this spirit truthfully identify Paul and his companions (Mk. 1:24; Lu. 4:41). Her words, "Most High God," meant to the pagans the "Supreme God." Among the pagans, salvation was the object of many prayers made to their "savior gods." Many of the mystery cults which flourished then promised salvation to their initiates. But Paul didn't need the testimonial of an evil spirit. To accept it would be to enter into league with the demon. To openly deal with it meant antagonizing the forces of hell. Paul knew what was at stake if he acted against the demon.

COMMAND. In time the girl's shrill crying got to Paul. He decided to risk open war with Satan. In a burst of irritation, he wheeled about and spoke directly to the demon. In Jesus' name he ordered the spirit to come out of her. That name on the apostle's lips carried the same authority as Jesus Himself. But not because Paul had power within himself. He didn't. The indwelling Lord chose to back His servant. As a result the evil spirit obeyed at once. Modern exorcists do not get instant results, but agonize and debate with demons for hours. It can be assumed that the girl became tranquil and clearheaded. Before that she was raving, now her behavior was evidence of God's power at work in her. If the girl was saved, then we have a second convert who was also a woman. But what a contrast between these two—one a devout woman seeking God, the other a demon-possessed slave.

"Surely the girl's owners didn't take kindly to that?"

19. When the girl's owners saw what happened, they realized that any hope of further wealth through her

fortune telling was gone. So they seized Paul and Silas and dragged them before the city officials in the main square. 20. There they made them stand before the Roman judges while they charged, "These men are Jews and they are disturbing the peace of our city. 21. They are advocating customs which are not lawful for us, as Roman citizens, to accept or observe."

SEIZED. Paul had no choice but to refuse the patronage of hell. He had to deal with the demon. And his action was correct. The Lord apparently wanted to save the girl. It was Jesus Who actually cast out the demon, not Paul. He could neither heal nor deal, for all such work is performed by the indwelling Holy Ghost. The subtle part of the scene is that the demon spoke the TRUTH. But demons do that. People can be led into dangerous error by the messages from demons. Unfortunately their spirit-messages are true when it suits their evil purpose. Paul, however, was not deceived and went on the offensive. Note that he did NOT resort to prayer, but turned and dealt directly with the demon. The devil retaliated with angered men. He always uses men. He has no other means. So the apostles were seized by rough hands. From then on the missionaries could expect serious opposition in Philippi. They had triggered the wrath of hell.

CHARGED. Once the girl's masters beheld her new behavior, they knew their lucrative business was gone. They felt an unwarranted attack had been made on their property rights (the girl). So they had the missionaries arrested and charged—not for destroying their profits—but for disturbing the peace with illegal religious activities. Note how they are charged as JEWS, not as Christians. Apparently the Philippians felt there was no difference. At this time the Jews were in special disgrace having been banished from Rome. They were also forbidden by strict Roman law to propagate their religion among Romans. So the two missionaries were arrested as wandering Jews, charged with illegal proselyting in a Roman Colony. Since Luke was a Gentile and Timothy but a half-Jew, they were not arrested.

22. Shortly the crowds joined the attack against the missionaries. Then the judges stripped them of their robes and ordered them beaten with rods. 23. After they had suffered many blows from the wooden whips, they were thrown into prison and the jailer ordered to keep them under close guard.

BEATEN. The Macedonian call wasn't so intriging now. The Philippians, at least, were not begging for gospel help. The opposite was true. The public sided with the masters of the slave. The judges, eager to please the people, proceeded to order punishment without trial. The citizens of Philippi considered it outrageous that wandering Jews should damage two Roman citizens. They were determined to teach them a lesson. The magistrates summarily stripped off their clothes and turned them over to the lictors for whipping. The lictors were inferior officers of justice who carried out the orders of the magistrates. They could inflict both corporal and capital punishment. As symbols of their office they carried bundles of rods (corporal) with an axe (capital) in the midst of them. It was with these rods that the missionaries were beaten. The blows were delivered with such haste, there was no way for the victims to protest that they were Romans.

24. Inasmuch as he had received such strict orders, the jailer threw them into an inner cell and secured their feet in stocks.

SECURED. The jailer wasn't about to take any chances with his charges. Likely he was a retired soldier. One of the purposes of the Roman colonies was to provide a place of settlement for those veterans who had served their time in the military. He could be expected to carry out his orders in the strictest fashion. He was not concerned with the comfort of these Jews. Accordingly he threw them in the inner prison which was probably underground and dark and unventilated. And he didn't stop with that. He also secured their feet in stocks. Now they couldn't possibly get away. So there they sat, bruised and bleeding. Gone were their clothes and their possessions too. But that meant little to this jailer who is going to be the third person in Philippi reached by the power of Christ.

"Wouldn't that cause the missionaries to be disheartened?"

25. Around midnight Paul and Silas were praying and singing praises to God while the prisoners listened to them. 26. Suddenly there was a violent earthquake. It was so strong it rocked the foundations of the prison. All the cell doors flew open and every man's chains were loosened.

EARTHQUAKE. If Satan expected his assault on the missionaries to dampen their spirits, he was in for disappointment. Though their bodies were bleeding and aching in the stocks, their spirits soared heavenward. They chatted with the Lord and filled the prison with their hymns of praise. Those walls had never heard such sounds before. So loud were they, the prisoners throughout the jail heard them. Then God let go with an earthquake that cancelled the work of the devil. The cell doors flew open and the anchor pins slipped out of the walls. Even the stocks were broken. No one was hurt, everyone was free. It was indeed a miracle even though Luke is very circumstantial in describing the event.

27. When the jailer awakened and saw the prison doors had been opened, he assumed that all of his prisoners had escaped. He was on the verge of killing himself, 28. when Paul shouted to him, "Hey! Don't do that to yourself! We're all here!"

DON'T. The earthquake jarred the jailer from his sleep. He went at once to see if his charges were secure. When he found the doors all open, he took for granted the prisoners had seized the opportunity to escape. He knew the consequences. His life would be forfeited. To a soldier raised in the discipline of the Roman army there was only one thing to do—kill himself.

Suicide was regarded as a noble act in such cases in those days. Apparently he had come from a well-lighted area and couldn't see too well in the dark. He didn't notice the men in Paul's cell. But Paul could see him and knew what he was intending when he drew his sword. Paul's shout stayed the jailer's hand. It was true. Every prisoner was still there. Apparently the other prisoners had all moved to the missionaries' cell. Something about those men of God had kept them from running away. Perhaps they felt safer with these missionaries who regarded the earthquake as an answer to their prayers.

29. Then the jailer called for lights. Trembling all over, he came running into the cell and fell at the feet of Paul and Silas. 30. After he had led them out, he said to them, "Sirs, what must I do to be saved?"

OUT. The jailer's awe of the missionaries is obvious. That he fell at their feet indicates he believed they were in some way responsible for the earthquake. Also they were responsible for the fact that all of his prisoners were still present. After returning the others to their cells, he escorted Paul and Silas outside where he put to them his question, "What must I do to be saved?" Earlier he thought of them as criminals, now he calls them "Sirs." Their dignity and calm amidst an earthquake which came in answer to their prayers, was supernatural. Had not the slave girl identified them with the "Supreme God?" The jailer has no fear for his physical safety. His other prisoners are secure. Paul and Silas did not run. It is spiritual salvation that concerns the jailer. Had he offended the God of these missionaries, a God Whose power had just been demonstrated? It is from the wrath of their God that he wishes to be saved. He was convinced they were protected by their Deity.

31. "Believe in the Lord Jesus Christ," they replied, "for in Him lies salvation for you and your entire household." 32. Then they shared the message of the Lord with him and all the others in his house.

BELIEVE. The jailer asked a direct question. He got a direct answer. He asked WHAT, they replied with WHOM—a person—Jesus Christ. If he wanted to be saved, it could only come about through placing his complete trust in that Person. That was their simple answer. Nothing less would save him, nothing else was needed. Not only the jailer, but his entire family could be saved from divine wrath by the same process—placing their faith in the Person of Christ. Obviously he wanted his whole family to learn about the Lord and be saved. It is quite likely that his home was on the prison compound. If so, it was convenient for him to summon his family that Paul and Silas might preach Christ to all the members of his household together. It is possible they too were impressed by the earthquake.

HOUSEHOLD. Well-meaning Christians take vs. 31 out of context to make Paul say the jailer's family would be saved if the jailer placed his trust in Christ. Then they apply that twisted meaning to their own situation, thinking their faith in Christ somehow guarantees the salvation of loved ones. The practice can only lead to frustration and disappointment. The jailer's faith DID NOT secure salvation for his household. By faith he summoned them to hear Paul and Silas preach about Christ. Each person of his entire household heard the Word and was invited to place his individual faith in Jesus. Those longing to see their loved ones saved, should see that they are confronted with Christ, just as the jailer did. Even that, however, does not GUARANTEE salvation. The salvation program is based on "Whosoever will." God never manipulates a man's will. Yet that's what would be needed if one person's faith could guarantee the salvation of another. Each person must respond to Christ's invitation on his own.

33. And right there, in the dead of night, he took them and washed out their wounds; and immediately afterwards, he and his whole family were baptized.
34. Then he brought them into his house and fed them, while he and his household rejoiced together because all of them now believed in God.

WASHED. We can assume the explanation of salvation occurred in the prison courtyard or some adjacent quarters, for vs. 30 says, "He led them out." There was water there. If not a well, then some kind of storage facility. This water was used to cleanse the deep wounds in the missionaries' backs. Then it was the missionaries' turn to wash (baptize) the new believers. After that the entire party went into the jailer's house where food was set before the apostles. The scene is one of great rejoicing. See how the joy of these new believers appears to be the only outward evidence of their receiving the Holy Spirit. No supernatural manifestations are mentioned. Why? Perhaps because there are no Jews to be convinced by signs. The "fruit of the Spirit" is the normal evidence of salvation. Paul and Silas are still in custody. The jailer has not violated his trust. He was instructed simply to secure them. He can still deliver them on demand. The great change in the heart of the jailer (per his kindness to the apostles) is solid evidence of his conversion.

"How did things work out the next day?"

35. At daybreak the magistrates sent their police officers to the jail with orders to "Release those men." 36. The jailer quickly advised Paul and Silas of the action, saying, "The magistrates have sent word that you are to be released. You are free to go. You can leave in peace if you want to." 37. But Paul said to the officers, "I should say not. They gave us a public beating without any kind of a hearing, and then they threw us in jail—and we're Roman citizens! Now they'd like us to leave quietly. That won't do at all. If they want us to leave peaceably, let them come and escort us themselves."

RELEASE. Apparently the magistrates felt the missionaries had learned their lesson and should be released. It doesn't appear that they had any knowledge of the happening at the prison during the night. Also the earthquake could have caused them some uneasiness in the matter. So the lictors (the officers who beat them) are sent with the release order. Upon receiving the news, the jailer advises his new friends to leave town in peace. He knows by now that they are Roman citizens and could cause trouble if they wished. But Paul wants more than just their freedom. He feels his rights have been violated and insists on humiliating the magistrates. Note that he is not insisting on anything that would advance the ministry, such as his possessions, or an opportunity to continue teaching. It is strange to see a man who fondly refers to himself as the "bondslave of Christ," exalting himself as a Roman. Slaves have no rights. Besides, what will be gained for Jesus through this insistence on civil rights? Satan it seems, moved in very quickly to tempt the apostle after the great victory of faith in the prison. But he does that, as we all know.

"How did the magistrates react to Paul's charge?"

38. The police reported these words to the magistrates. And when they heard that Paul and Silas were Romans, they feared for their lives. 39. So they came in person and apologized to them. Then they escorted them out of the prison, pleading with them to leave the city.

FEARED. The magistrates were shocked to learn that the men they had imprisoned were Roman citizens in good standing—as good, in fact, as the magistrates themselves. They were greatly alarmed for fear of being called to account for the illegal trial and imprisonment of subjects of Rome, an act of treason against the emperor. There is nothing for them to do but proceed to the prison and do all they can to satisfy the prisoners. So they went to the prison and apologized, begging the missionaries to be satisfied with their apology. Then they escorted them from the prison. The magistrates then pleaded with them to leave town. They feared the crowds might take action and bring trouble upon the city. But Paul and Silas don't have to leave. They have not been convicted of any crime.

"Are the missionaries in any hurry to leave the city?"

40. On leaving the prison, Paul and Silas went to Lydia's house where they met with the new believers. After speaking words of encouragement to them, they departed from the city.

DEPARTED. The missionaries show no sign of being in a hurry to leave the city once they are free. Instead they go to Lydia's house, the meeting place for the first Philippian church. Here they find Luke and Timothy and inform them of all that happened. They probably introduced the members of the jailer's household as well. Then they left Philippi taking Timothy with them. We find him in their party at Thessalonica and Berea (Acts 17:14). Dr. Luke doesn't go. He stays behind. Some commentators think Philippi was his home town. Consequently the writing style now shifts back to the third person. We will not see Luke again until Paul returns to Philippi on the third missionary journey.

17 1. They continued their journey through Amphipolis and Appollonia, arriving finally at Thessalonica. Here there was a Jewish synagogue. 2. As was his custom, Paul went there to preach. For three Sabbaths he reasoned with them out of the Scriptures. 3. He expounded each text to show that the Messiah was to suffer and rise again from the dead. "The Messiah," he said, "is none other than this Jesus Whom I am announcing to you." 4. Some of them were convinced and threw in with Paul and Silas. So did a great number of God-fearing Greeks and a considerable number of the leading women.

CONTINUED. The three missionaries moved southwesterly along the Via Egnatia, one of Rome's busiest roads. Thirty miles down that road they came to Amphipolis, where a town still exists. Thirty more miles took them to Appollonia, a great trading center. But in neither city did Paul pause to preach, because there were too few Jews. He was headed for Thessalonica, the largest city in Macedonia. Here there would be many Jews. Unlike most cities mentioned in the Bible, this one has kept its importance and most of its name. It was a wealthy, heavily populated center of commerce. It rose in tiers upon the steep hills behind the city so that it formed a giant amphitheatre facing the Aegean sea. It is called Salonika today.

SYNAGOGUE. As per his usual practice, Paul sought out the synagogue. For three consecutive Sabbaths he preached Christ in this important synagogue. There he sought to prove from the O.T. that Jesus was the Messiah. The force of his argument was that the Scriptures foretold the sufferings and resurrection of the Messiah and that Jesus was the only One Who fulfilled those requirements. The response followed the familiar pattern. Some Jews believed the message, but the bulk of his converts were God-fearing Gentiles. It's significant that a large number of the town's leading women also came to Christ. Paul's method of preaching did not include extracts from literature or philosophy. He quoted the Scriptures, stated his propositions, then argued them from the Word. This method won many converts who solidly united themselves with him and Silas in standing for Christ.

"How did the Jewish leaders react to this?"

5. But the Jews became jealous and conspired with the riffraff of the market place to raise a mob and throw the whole city into an uproar. A great crowd descended upon the home of Jason thinking to seize Paul and Silas and haul them before the city council. 6. When they didn't find them, they dragged Jason and some of the new Christians before the council, shouting, "These men who have caused trouble the world over have now come here, 7. and Jason has harbored them in his house. These people defy the decrees of Caesar. They claim another king, one Jesus."

JEALOUS. The familiar pattern took shape once again. The majority of the Jews would not believe the message and became envious of Paul's success with the Greeks. To stir opposition to the missionaries, they rounded up some idle toughs hanging about the market place and incited them to spread violent and terrorizing talk throughout the city. In time a fearful mob descended on the house of Jason. He was one of those converted and subsequently played host to Paul and Silas. His Hebrew name was Joshua or Jesus, but he used his Greek name, possibly for business reasons. When the mob found Paul and Silas gone (perhaps because of a timely warning), they seized Jason and some other believers in his home. Then they hauled them before the magistrates where they lodged serious charges against them.

HARBORED. Jason and the others were charged with harboring political and religious agitators and accused of introducing a king to rival the claim of Caesar. Jesus was a king, but not One Who sought Caesar's throne. He had one of His own. But the tint of truth was sufficient to make the charges deadly serious. Also, the propagating of any new religion was illegal. By this time, the Thessalonian Jews knew of the missionaries activities in the other provinces of the empire. Because it is mentioned that Paul spent three Sabbaths in the synagogue doesn't mean he was there only three weeks. From his letters, we estimate he was there at least several months and continued his work with increasing success. Apparently he focused much attention on the second coming of Christ (as king), hence the charge of sedition.

8. These words sparked a great rumble through the crowds which in turn had an effect on the magistrates. 9. After requiring Jason and the others to post a peace bond, they let them go.

BOND. After hearing the charges, the magistrates wisely concluded there was insufficient evidence for a trial. Besides, the principal defendants were not available for questioning. So they placed the Christians under a peace bond. It was a wise move. This way they were pledged to guarantee no repetition of the trouble. It is easy to see Satan's hand in this. After three months, Paul is obliged to leave town. If he stayed, it would only cause more trouble and jeopardize the new church. Beyond that, it could bring great hardship upon the new believers should higher Roman authorities have to step in to quell future disorders. Paul didn't want that.

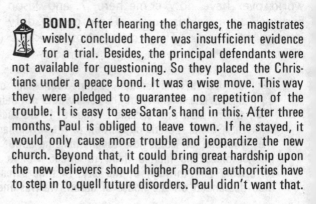

From his letters we learn the church became an "on fire" center for Christ (1 Thess. 1:6-10).

"Did Paul move on from Thessalonica after that?"

10. As soon as it was dark, the brethren hurridly sent Paul and Silas to Berea. As soon as they arrived, they headed straight for the Jewish synagogue. 11. Here they encountered a different breed of Jew than those in Thessalonica. These people were open-minded and received the message with great eagerness. Every day they checked the Scriptures to make sure what they were hearing was really true. 12. As a result, many of them became true believers, as did a fair number of the fashionable Greek women and quite a few men.

BEREA. Under cover of darkness, the brethren lost no time in getting Paul and Silas out of Thessalonica and on the way to Berea. This town, some 60 miles west of Thessalonica, was a quiet place well off the main road. They would be safer here. However, the persecution had not cooled their zeal any. As soon as they discover the synagogue, they resume their work. A surprise awaited them here. They found the Berean Jews to be fair-minded, open to new ideas. They not only listened to the missionaries, they also checked the Scriptures to make sure the statements were true. Consequently many of these Scripture-loving Jews became believers. It was the reverse of the situation at Thess. There the bulk of the believers were Greeks. Here they are Jews, though some of the leading Greek women were also converted. The name of these Bereans has been immortalized in thousands of Berean Bible classes across our land. Not because they harkened to Paul, but because they checked what he taught against the Scriptures. We need more Bereans today.

"How long would the Lord allow them to stay here?"

13. But when the Thessalonian Jews found out that Paul was preaching the Word of God in Berea also,

they came hurrying to excite and stir up the crowds. 14. The believers quickly sent Paul away to the coast, while Silas and Timothy remained behind. 15. Those accompanying Paul escorted him as far as Athens. Then they returned to Berea after receiving instructions for Silas and Timothy that they were to come to Paul as quickly as possible.

JEWS. For once, Paul had the privilege of seeing many of his own people come to the Lord, yet the most discouraging thing he faced was the opposition of the Jews. Once more he is not allowed to do his work in peace. Just as the Jews from Pisidian Antioch and Iconium made trouble for him in Lystra, so now the Jews of Thessalonica arrive to turn the crowds against him at Berea. But the Berean brethren know what to do. They quickly sent Paul with an escort to the coast. We're not sure that he actually boarded a ship. The trip to the coast may have been just a ruse. In any event he reached Athens with those escorting him, the only ones who actually knew where he was. Safely in Athens, he asks his escorts to bare a message to Silas and Timothy upon their return to Berea. They are to come to him at once. Inasmuch as Paul was the real target of Jewish hostility, it was good strategy for him to leave and allow Silas and Timothy to stay behind and ground the new church with more teaching.

"What did Paul do with himself while waiting for Silas and Timothy?"

16. While Paul was waiting for them in Athens, his spirit was agonized at the sight of this great city so full of idols.

ATHENS. While waiting for his two friends to join him, Paul toured the city of Athens. Most people would be overwhelmed by its majestic beauty and architectural magnificence, but not Paul. He saw, instead, the idolatry of the people and their need for God. Likely he was not immune to the aesthetic beauty of the great Acropolis with the Parthenon above it, but it saddened him to think that all that splendor was devoted to heroes and gods. He knew Athens was the leading center of culture and philosophy of the ancient world, yet none of it was dedicated to the true God. For all of its wisdom and workmanship, the city was as pagan as could be. Renowned as the cradle of freedom, the people of Athens had their liberty to consecrate themselves to idolatry. What a waste. None of it could enlighten the human soul.

IDOLS. Ancient writers have said there were more idols in Athens than in all the rest of Greece. The city contained over 3000 public statues, and behind the door of every home was an image of some sort. Entire streets were lined with idols. On one street, a bust of Hermes stood before each house. Every square of the city had a sanctuary for a pagan deity. The King James reading, "Wholly given to idolatry," means the idols of Athens were as "thick as trees in a dense wood." As the apostle moved through the city, his indignation burned hotter and hotter. It grieved him to see all that magnificence dedicated to gods that were demon inspired (1 Cor. 10:20). Note that amongst all the people Paul encountered, the cultured and refined were more inclined to idolatry than any other.

17. So upset was he, that he began reasoning with the Jews and God-fearing Gentiles in the synagogue, and had daily arguments with those he met in the marketplace.

ARGUMENTS. Paul was so stirred by the city's idolatry, he decided not to wait for Silas and Timothy. He began preaching without them. As always, he went first to the synagogue that his fellow Jews might have the first opportunity to hear the gospel. Since no church was started in Athens we conclude they refused him the use of the building and was forced to take to the streets. He went into the marketplace where he found those who would discuss the gospel with him. This was a bold thing for a humble tentmaker to do, for the marketplace (Agora) was the favorite gathering spot for intellectuals in this city of wisdom and learning. This was not a market in the usual sense of bazars and shops. It was the stock market of news. The elite minds of the world gathered in this "wall street" of learning to speculate in ideas. Paul may not have been able to speak their language with the grand style and classic accuracy to which they were accustomed, and thereby invited ridicule. But he was not ashamed of the gospel. He was ready to submit its claims to the keenest minds and brightest intellects of the city. Here he learned first hand how the wisdom of this world is at odds with the wisdom of God (1 Cor. 1:21).

"Did the people of the marketplace listen to him?"

18. While he was speaking in the marketplace, some Epicurean and Stoic philosophers joined the argument. "What is this phony philosopher trying to say?" asked one group. "He seems to be trying to introduce us to some foreign gods," replied the other. This was their conclusion upon hearing Paul mention Jesus and the resurrection.

EPICUREANS. The Epicureans were atheists in that they believed the world was an accident. They believed you were here today and gone tomorrow, so why not enjoy life as much as you can. To them, seeking pleasure was the main purpose of life. They did not deny the existence of any gods, but maintained they were totally indifferent to the affairs of men who were left to find their pleasure as they could. Consequently they were given to gross sensualism. This teaching was founded by Epicurus, who died in Athens 270 years before Christ. He left his home and garden to be used as a headquarters for the Epicureans. It was still maintained at the time Paul visited the city.

STOICS. The Stoics were the opposite of the Epicureans. They were pantheists, claiming God was in everything and everyone. To them, pleasure was not good and pain was not evil. Virtue was its own reward and vice its own punishment. They denied the immortality of the soul, claiming people were swallowed up in the Deity after physical death. Both Epicureanism and Stoicism were attempts to come to terms with life before the advent of Christianity. Modern pagans haven't been able to come up with anything any better. The Stoics were founded by Zeno, in Athens, at the same time Epicurus was founding his school. While these two rival schools of thought were opposed to each other, they did agree that the preaching of this itinerant Jew was probably worthless, but there was something in his words that raised their curiosity.

PHONY. The KJV uses the word "babbler," but the Greek literally means a "grain picker." At first it applied to birds, then beggars who lived off of scraps. Finally it was used contemptuously to describe those who sought to make a living by peddling bits of philosophy they picked up here and there. In those days, philosophers were well paid for sharing their ideas with the public. Paul was branded as a pretender philosopher. They looked down on him, perhaps, because he could not speak their language in perfect cadence. Likely his presence was not very commanding either. Even so, he presented the simple story of Jesus and His resurrection. However, to the prejudiced minds of some of the philosophers present, Paul's words, "Jesus" and "Anastasis" (Gk: resurrection) were taken to mean he was speaking of a new god and goddess. This is why they wanted him examined by the council.

"Did Paul get any further hearing in Athens?"

19. So they took him by the sleeve and brought him before the Areopagus. "Please tell us," said the council, "more about this new teaching you are proclaiming. 20. For you speak of things which are very strange to us and we'd like to know more of their meaning."

AREOPAGUS. Originally this was called the "Council of the Areopagus," but in time the name was shortened to "the Areopagus." This council was the ancient court of Athens which had the power to make all decisions with respect to religion and morals. It was located on a hill just N.W. of the marketplace and was reached by a flight of stone steps which led directly to the judges platform. The judges sat out in the open on seats hewn from rock. The hill was named after the Roman god of war, "Mars." It is also called the "hill of Ares," for that is the Greek name for the same war god. Apparently philosophers of rank could haul strange lecturers before this council to give an account of their teachings. It appears that Paul is not under arrest, but brought here to see if he should be charged with some offense. While Athens tolerated freedom of religion, the introduction of new religions from the East was prohibited. This was the finest place in all of Athens for Paul to speak.

21. It should be noted that the Athenians and the strangers visiting them had no time for anything but talking or hearing about the latest thing in new ideas.

IDEAS. After explaining that the court was interested in examining Paul's new teaching, Dr. Luke turns aside to give us a comment on the Athenians themselves. These people were the victims of their own ears. Their passion for philosophy and new ideas had been developed to such a point, they were no longer interested in that which was familiar. All the Athenians, says Luke, as well as all those visiting them, used all of their spare time going about seeking some novel notion. Not that they wanted to DO anything about the ideas, they just wanted to HEAR them. In that they remind us of our modern sermon listeners. The practice had been going on for centuries. Demosthenes, one of their own orators, said of them 400 years before, "All you care about is going up and down the market asking each other, 'Is there any news?' " To the Athenians, an idea became old the moment they heard it. Just as people today become addicted to drugs, the people of Athens were "hooked" on news.

"Will Paul now preach to this council?"

22. So Paul stood up in full view of the council, and said:

"Men of Athens! I see that when it comes to religion you are scrupulous in every detail. 23. For in the course of my passing through your streets, I was able to examine your fine temples and monuments, and among them I found an altar with the inscription, TO AN UNKNOWN GOD. This God, Who is the unknown object of your worship, is the very One I have come to proclaim to you!"

MEN OF ATHENS! Behold the itinerant tent-maker at the brow of Mars Hill! A crowd had no doubt followed from the marketplace up the steps to the Areopagus. Standing behind him was a mixed multitude of poets, artists, philosophers, and warriors. Before and below him was the city of Athens. Just east was the Acropolis with the Parthenon radiating the glory of ancient Greece. The council was ready. Athens was about to hear its first preaching from the lips of an apostle of Jesus Christ. What a place for an obscure Jew! Then he speaks. "Men of Athens," he shouted in the classic style of Demosthenes whose thunder had often rolled off this very spot. Paul's words came out like those of a consummate orator. The Spirit of God was speaking through him. Thus he was calm, self-assured, and displaying the remarkable dignity which comes when a man knows how to adapt himself to the situation.

RELIGION. Paul began by telling the Athenians that he was impressed with their extraordinary interest in religion. His words were calculated to win their philosophic minds. They were proud of their religious objects, so he was off to a good start. "Scrupulous," can also be translated, "superstitious," as in the KJV; but it is not likely he meant to be critical with his first words. He is too wise for that. Then he mentions seeing an altar to an "unknown god." He cleverly turns the idea around so that the altar itself stood as an Athenian confession of ignorance concerning the true God. In this Paul is doubly shrewd. Not only does it give him a chance to declare Christ, but it also clears him of any charge. He cannot be charged with introducing new gods to Athens when he has come to do nothing more than give them a fuller understanding of that God to Whom their altar was dedicated. Such an approach easily gripped his audience.

PROCLAIM. Proclaim is the right word, for no finite man can define or explain the Infinite God. But proclaiming Him is exactly what the Athenians want. That's the reason for their altar to the "unknown god" in the first place. It's not hard to fathom what they meant by such an altar. So careful were they in worshipping invisible gods, they constructed altars to the "unknown" god for fear of offending a god not yet revealed to them. It should be noted that all men have the religious instinct which works like the needle on a magnetic compass. It points only to the one true God. While few people heed it, it bothers every man that comes into the world (John 1:9). It was this instinct which told the Athenians that no matter how many altars they made to their gods, there was still one God Who existed beyond their worship system. Paul is saying, you do well to worship this Being Who is unknown to you, for He indeed exists. You lack only an idea of His nature and magnificence, and that I am here to declare unto you.

24. "The God Who made the world and everything in it; the God Who is the ruler of heaven and earth, does not live in temples made by men. 25. There is nothing He lacks which His creatures could supply. To the contrary, it is He Who supplies their needs. He is the One Who gives life and breath to men and all else that lives."

GOD. Paul begins to tell the Athenians about the true God. The language he employs would be familiar to any Jew, for his statements resemble O.T. quotes. Yet they are truths which would take away the breath of these pagans. The idea of ONE God Who was absolute, was overwhelming. And since He is that great, it follows He could not be compressed into any man made temple. Paul may have gestured toward the great Parthenon when he said that, for it was dedicated to ALL the 30,000 Athenian gods. His statement that one God created the universe struck hard against the Epicurean philosophy which regarded the universe as an accident, a work of chance. It also countered the Stoic notion that the physical universe always existed, that it was never created. Paul says the world sprang into existence by a decree from the mind of the one true God.

RULER. Not only did the God Whom Paul declares MAKE the universe, He also RUNS it. The world is not a huge machine that manages itself. To the contrary, it is kept in perfect time and harmony because of the relentless activity of its Creator—the one God. Then Paul moves to demolish another pagan idea. Instead of His being dependent on His creatures for worship and service, they are the ones who need Him. The heathen believed their gods needed their services. That's why they made their temples so lavish. They also brought them costly gifts and offerings of food and drink, as if these were necessities of their deities. When Paul says that God is the source of life for all living things, it is implied that He is the One Who supplies all the natural wants of man. Thus the Athenians are taught that God does not need their services—they need Him.

26. "He has created all the races of men from one man that they might inhabit the face of the earth. He determines when people will arrive on this earth and where they shall live. 27. It is His intention that men should seek Him, groping, as necessary, to make contact with Him. However, He is not very far from any one of us. 28. For, you see, it is in Him that we live and move and have our existence. Why some of your own poets affirmed this truth when they said, 'We are indeed His children.' 29. If it is true that we are God's children, then we ought not to think of the One

Who made us as an image of gold or silver or stone, shaped by the skill of men."

CREATED. The Athenians never heard such a lofty concept of any god. Paul shocks them by announcing that the true God not only brought forth the entire human race from one man (they thought the races varied in origin and that they themselves were above all others), but controls the timing of each man's arrival in the world, right down to the very place where he is to be born. That was a breath-taking notion for people itching to hear something new. Then he says the whole point of putting men on earth in the first place was that they might seek the God Who made them. Beyond that, the God of creation is so close they can touch Him, but not with their physical fingers. For the nature of the true God is such that people can live and move in Him and yet not see Him. That, at once, puts Him beyond the physical realm. Therefore, He cannot be contacted by any physical means.

SEEK. It was an arresting thought that all men were to seek God. Cut off from the literal presence of his Creator, man is limited to the five senses. With these he is expected to read and examine the evidence of God in nature and grope after Him by faith. The religious instinct, which causes all men to worship something or someone, was meant to spur man in his groping after God. This is why Paul says all mankind is without excuse (Rom. 1:20). The physical universe shouts, "He lives!" (Dead idols cannot communicate this fact.) Yet, He cannot be found in nature. Nature **speaks** only of His power and existence, revealing nothing about His person. The Bible alone describes God as a Person and tells HOW to get to Him. Man's "groping" is beyond the senses, or by faith. God established the faith-method as the way men should seek Him. If people want to contact Him, it must be with their hearts, not with their eyes or fingers.

POETS. Paul knew the Aeropagus would not attach any importance to the O.T., so he quotes from some of their own poets whose words enunciated kindred truth. Epimenides had written, "For in thee (though he meant Zeus) we live and move and have our being." Aratus and Cleanthes had said, "We are indeed his children." So if a man actually lives and moves within his god, he degrades himself to make a statue or altar to worship some god of his own manufacture. The very nature of man, says Paul, the fact of our high origin in God, argues against such idolatry. We debase ourselves when we stoop to worship that which is less than ourselves. Paul is often criticized for quoting from pagan philosophers in his message. But his point in quoting those poets was to show that even their own philosophers realized the foolishness of trying to confine the divine nature in some kind of a temple or adequately represent him with an idol. While these philosophers were non-Christian, their statements tended to confirm Paul's claims for the true God.

30. "In times past, God overlooked man's ignorance of Himself, but now He commands men everywhere to turn to Him, 31. because He has set a day in which He will judge the world on the basis of what it has done with a Man He appointed. It will be a righteous judgment, for He has furnished proof to all men concerning this Man by raising Him from the dead."

OVERLOOKED. Paul's message now shifts from those things which men could know by way of NATURAL revelation (the bible of nature), to that which can be learned only from the WRITTEN revelation (the inspired Word). Thus he moves his hearers from the known to the unknown. He is done with reasoning about the knowable facts of God and brings them to the the gospel. He says that God overlooked (not "winked at" as in the KJV) the fact that men remained ignorant of Him in those days when Deity had to be discovered in nature. Of course they were still GUILTY for they had the means of knowing. Even though God saw the wickedness of men in those times, he did not destroy the creation. Instead, he exercised great forebearance. In His mercy, He let it pass. But those days are gone, says Paul. A change has occurred in God's dealing with man.

A MAN. We have here a greatly shortened summary of what Paul actually said, but it is clear he is speaking of Jesus. Now that God has come in Person, revealing Himself through "a Man" the situation is different. No longer will God tolerate man's ignorance of Himself. With the advent of Christ there is even less excuse for not knowing Him. Consequently all men will be judged, not on their ability to read and believe the evidences of God in nature, but on the basis of what they do about "this Man." Since God Himself has appeared on earth, men are now **commanded** to turn to Him, whereas before they were merely **expected** to do so on the strength of the natural revelation. God can overlook the former ignorance because of Jesus' finished work, but there is no way for Him to overlook the sin of ignoring Christ. The remedy for **all** sin is in Him alone.

JUDGMENT. Paul moves to the most awesome event facing mankind—the day of judgment. This was totally unknown in Greek philosophy. Such information could only be acquired by divine revelation. Paul declares that the date has been set and the Judge will be none other than "a Man" who was born on the earth, died, and rose again. Because God has given the world such a clear revelation of Himself through this Man, and certified all He said by raising Him from the dead, He now COMMANDS people to repent, i.e., turn from their evil and their idols, to the true and living God. News of a man raised from the dead would be amazing, for neither the Stoic nor Epicurean philosophies considered such a thing possible. That was the most unsettling truth they heard. Paul's closing words are, Repent! Turn to God for the judgment is ahead! There's nothing philosophical about that, it's pure Bible!

"How did these Athenians react to Paul's bombshells?"

32. Now when they heard Paul mention the resurrection of the dead, many in the crowd began to laugh in derision, but others said, "We'd like you to tell us more about this matter at another time."

33. So Paul left the assembly. 34. However some of them joined with Paul and went on to become believers. Among them was Dionysius, a member of the Areopagus, and a woman named Damaris. There were some others besides.

DERISION. Paul wasn't able to finish his message. For when he mentioned the resurrection of Jesus, the crowd exploded in derisive laughter. To this point, he likely held his audience spellbound. He had handled himself with great skill, careful not to offend. He approached the gospel with oratorical grace and godly wisdom. But with the mention of Jesus' resurrection he reached the dividing point. The results were what one might expect when the world's wisdom clashes with the wisdom of God. Here in Athens, the capitol of the world's wisdom, the majority scoffed at such an idea, some wanted to learn more, and a few believed. Paul apparently sensed the futility of continuing his address. Since he was not charged with anything, he was free to leave the assembly.

BELIEVED. Paul's work was not entirely unfruitful. He reached Dionysius, a member of the 12 man panel making up the Areopagus. A woman named "Damaris," also heard him somehow in Athens and became a believer. Then there were some others. However, there is no evidence that a church was started in Athens. It just wasn't a good place for the gospel. Some have dubbed Paul's work here a failure, but success in God's eyes has to do with faithfulness, not the numbers who respond to the invitation. I think he was an outstanding success. He reached the best spot in Athens for declaring the gospel. There he did a masterful job. The failure was on the part of the Athenians, not Paul. It is not fair to say he relied too much on human wisdom simply because he quoted the Greek poets. True, he used it to approach the Greek mind, but it is not his fault if the preaching of the cross is foolishness to the Greeks (1 Cor. 1:18). No method of preaching can overcome that obstacle. It has to do with the HEART of the listener, not the SKILL of the preacher.

18 1. Paul left Athens after this and went to Corinth.

CORINTH. Leaving Athens, a city of loungers and leisurely speculators, Paul moves 45 miles south-westerly to a town that bustles with business—Corinth. This was a famous Gk. city. It had two great ports, one facing Europe, the other facing Asia. It was the meeting place of nations for traffic, a department store of the world. It swarmed with tradesmen and travelers. A wide open city, it was famous for its wealth and vice. The temple of Aphrodite with its thousands of priestess—prostitutes gave license to sensuous revelry. The "Corinthian girls," were harlots. To be classed as "a Corinthian," meant one was wholly given to dissipation and debauchery. Because it was a world merchandise center, it had a large Jewish colony. Corinth was to the Jews commercially, what Jerusalem was to them religiously.

2. Here Paul met a Jew named Aquila who was born in Pontus. He had only recently come from Italy with his wife, Priscilla, for Claudius had expelled all Jews from Rome. Paul paid them a visit, 3. and because they were tentmakers, the same as he, he stayed with them and they worked together at their mutual occupation.

TENTMAKERS. When Paul reached Corinth, he thrilled to its great evangelistic possibilities. With so much commerce passing through the place, the gospel could rapidly spread from here throughout the world. But he had to eat. And since he was alone, he needed to provide for himself. He had a trade. All Jewish lads were raised to know a trade. Paul's was that of a tentmaker. Having come from Cilicia, a province specializing in the manufacture of goat's hair cloth, he had the skill of making items such as tents and curtains. So he went to the market place where he would be certain to find other Jews of the same trade, perhaps even from Cilicia. The various trade guilds always collected in groups in the bazaars. This would not be the first time Paul worked at his trade. He did so at Thessalonica (1 Thess. 2:9). Here he met Aquila.

EXPELLED. Life for a man like Paul would be unbearable without close companions, so God provided Aquila and Priscilla. Their friendship would be comforting until he could be rejoined by Silas and Timothy. Besides, he needed someone in the midst of his dejection after leaving Athens so frustrated. His new friends came to Corinth as a result of the Jewish expulsion from Rome under an edict of Emperor Claudius issued in A.D. 49. That order did not apply to Jews who were Roman citizens, for they were regarded as Romans, not Jews. We're not told whether they were saved before they met Paul. It is likely they brought their faith with them from Rome where their activities may have contributed to the expulsion order. Regardless of their background, they have come to Corinth, a good place to pursue their trade. All travelers needed tents. Here God gives Aquila and Priscilla to Paul to become his friends for life.

"Did Paul preach first in the synagogue as usual?"

4. In addition, he went into the synagogue every Sabbath, and with his convincing arguments, sought to persuade both Jews and Greeks.

PERSUADE. For six days a week Paul labored at his profession, but on the Sabbath, he went into the synagogue to hold disputations with the Jews and God-fearing Greeks. We can judge his style and attitude from one of his letters: "When I came to you, it was not with the excellency of speech or of wisdom. . . for I determined not to know anything among you save Jesus Christ and Him crucified. And I was with you in weakness, and in fear, and in much trembling" (1 Cor. 2:1ff). He had just seen how the human wisdom of Athens failed to bring her people to God. It would be even more useless here in this city of sin. Thus Paul declares the simple gospel of Jesus' death for sin. His method of discussion is also known to us. He opened the O.T. Scriptures to the prophecies referring to the Messiah and there substituted the name of Jesus.

5. But when Silas and Timothy arrived from Macedonia with financial relief, Paul was able to devote himself full time to preaching and explaining to the Jews that Jesus was the Messiah. 6. However, when they turned against him and began blaspheming the name of Jesus, he vigorously shook the dust from his garments and said to them, "Your blood be on your own heads. I am now clean. From here on I will preach to the Gentiles."

ARRIVED. When Silas and Timothy came to Paul some weeks later they brought him not only the warmth of their companionship, but a gift of money from the church at Philippi (Phil. 4:15). You recall they had stayed behind in Macedonia while Paul was in Athens. Since it was Paul who was the target of Jewish hatred, it was he who had to be hustled out of town. They completed their follow-up work and were now able to join the apostle. Relieved of the necessity of making a living, Paul could now preach full time. The Gk. text indicates he felt a great pressure to bring the gospel to this city. So, for the time being at least, he was able to answer the burning within him and reach those about him with the gospel. It is known, however, that for the most part of his 18 month stay in Corinth, he made his living with his own hands. But now he is free of that burden and concentrates his first efforts on the Jews.

TURNED. Paul found the Corinthian Jews no more receptive than those of Athens. Yet he persisted in arguing with them until they became so openly hostile to the Lord he knew any further effort would be futile. So he gave up on them. This time, we note, he was not driven from the synagogue, but forsook it voluntarily. As he did, he performed a gesture similar to the one he made at Pisidian Antioch. He removed his outer cloak shaking the synagogue dust from it to express his disgust and signify that he was through with the Jews. Undoubtedly he felt revulsion at their slanderous use of Jesus' name. They knew what it meant. They had often shaken off Gentile dust before entering their synagogue. Feeling his responsibility to the Jews is now discharged, he practically places a curse on them while announcing that he was taking his message to those who would appreciate it, the hated Gentiles. How that must have infuriated the Jews.

7. With that he left the synagogue and moved his ministry to the house of a God-fearing Gentile who lived next door. The Gentile's name was Titius Justus. 8. Then Crispus, the leader of the synagogue, became a believer in the Lord as did all of his household. And many Corinthians who listened to Paul also believed and were baptized.

HOUSE. Paul did a startling thing. He opened a Christian center right next door to the synagogue. He had won the landlord to Christ who in return offered his house to Paul. Now he could hold teaching sessions right under the Jews' noses. It must have been very unsettling to the Jews to have the headquarters of this heretic adjacent to their synagogue. Then to make matters worse, Paul successfully led the synagogue ruler to the Lord. He also shifted to the new center. To have **Gentiles** flocking to Paul in a building next door to their synagogue must have been especially irritating. Today it would be like having a cult establish its ministry next door to your church and begin weaning away your members. It is likely that Titius Justus was head of a Roman family in Corinth and a man of influence. The success of Paul in this home was sure to bring the Jews to the boiling point in time.

"Didn't Paul see how all this was building to an explosive situation?"

9. Then one night the Lord spoke to Paul in a vision. He said to him, "Don't be afraid any longer! Speak out fearlessly! Don't let anyone silence you! 10. I am with you and no one will be allowed to harm you. There are a lot of people in this city who belong to

Me." 11. So Paul settled down and remained in Corinth a year and a half teaching the people the truths of God.

AFRAID. As Paul's success mounted so did the danger to his life. The rage of his opponents became more obvious with each passing day. It no doubt suggested to him that he might soon have to leave Corinth, even as he had left other cities in the past. But then he had an encouraging experience. Right when the situation appeared to be the most critical, he had a vision of the risen Christ. The Lord told him to continue his work and gave him two good reasons for taking heart: (1) he would be afforded divine protection, (2) and he was guaranteed great success. The Lord said He had many people in this sinful city marked out for salvation. It is not at all unlikely that this vision occurred at that moment of which Paul spoke when he said, "I was with you in weakness and in fear and much trembling" (1 Cor. 2:3).

SETTLED DOWN. Assured of both protection and success, the apostle remained among the Corinthians 18 months. Until the vision occurred, he was desperate to complete his work. The vision taught him to relax, knowing no one could close the door of opportunity until God was ready for him to move on. Because of Dr. Luke's mention of the procounsul Gallio in the next verse, we are able to date this interval in Paul's life with some accuracy. His 18 months at Corinth probably stretch from the Fall of 50 to the Spring of 52. From an inscription found in central Greece, it appears that Gallio took office in July, 51. This is the most precise dating of events in the book of Acts. Gallio ruled over Southern Greece (Achaia). It was during his 18 months at Corinth that Paul wrote his two letters to the Thessalonians. In the next five years he will not journey about so much trying to establish new churches. Instead, he will spend most of his time consolidating the work in two great Christian centers, Ephesus and Corinth. It was from Ephesus that he wrote to the Corinthians.

"Did the Lord really shield Paul from harm?"

12. But when Gallio became the governor of Achaia, the Jews made a concerted attack upon Paul. They seized him and brought him before the governor's court for judgment. 13. "This man," they said, "is urging the people to worship God in a way that is against the law." 14. Paul was all set to defend himself, but before he could say a word, Gallio turned on the Jews. "Listen you Jews," he said, "if some kind of a crime or violation had been committed, I'd be inclined to hear your case. 15. But since it has to do with your own opinions and personalities and your own law, you'll have to take care of it yourselves. I refuse to get involved in such matters." 16. With that he ordered them out of his court.

SEIZED. The Lord promised no harm would come to Paul, but He didn't promise him immunity from attack. The aroused Jews, thinking a new governor would decide against Paul in order to win favor with the large Jewish colony, seized Paul and brought him before Gallio. But they misjudged their new governor. He refused to hear the case and peremptorily dismissed the Jews from his court. This was fortunate for Paul. A decision by the governor of a province would no doubt have been upheld in all the Roman provinces and would have seriously changed Paul's ministry. For once the efforts of the Jews to silence Paul backfired. Previously when he turned from the Jews to the Gentiles, the Jews were able to stir the crowds against him and have him charged with a public offense. Yet this was the first time he was hauled before the governor of an entire province. Jesus kept His word. Paul's ministry was safe.

GALLIO. Likely the Jews mistook Gallio's gentle nature for weakness. His younger brother, the author Seneca, described him as gentle, tactful, modest, and amiable. "No mortal," he said, "is so pleasant to everyone as is Gallio." Gallio also had his brother's passion for justice. So when he dismissed the charges of the Jews as being superficial, he was actually upholding the Roman law of freedom of religion. Paul was all set to show that he was proclaiming the true faith of the Jews' ancestors, but it wasn't necessary. Gallio judged the matter as wholly Jewish and threw the case out of court. Had it been a matter of breaking the law, he would have taken it up. His sense of justice would have demanded it.

"That was an unexpected turn of events, wasn't it?"

17. Then the pagans seized Sosthenes, the leader of the synagogue, and began beating him in full view of the court. Yet Gallio remained indifferent to the whole affair.

BEATING. Inasmuch as the hearing was held in open air, the crowds could watch the proceedings. They saw how irksome the Jews were in pressing their charges. They particularly noted the noisome way in which Sosthenes took the lead in persecuting Paul, now declared an innocent man. The governor's attitude toward the Jews must have triggered their anti-Jewish feelings. The mob set upon Sosthenes in full view of the tribunal. Gallio apparently couldn't care less. He no doubt figured the interest of justice was well served by such an action, so he did nothing to halt the anti-Jewish demonstration. Seemingly he cared nothing for religious matters and concluded the beating of Sosthenes might cure the Jews of attempting to use his court in such a high-handed way.

SOSTHENES. It is quite probable that Sosthenes is the same one mentioned in 1 Cor. 1:1. If so, he was converted to Jesus and became a member of the Corinthian church. In that case he was highly esteemed by Paul for he wrote, "Paul...and Sosthenes our brother unto the church of God. . ." We can't be certain as to his identity for the name was not uncommon. Luke is especially anxious for us to see how wonderfully the Lord kept His word to Paul. Even those who would persecute him were themselves persecuted. It was fortunate for the gospel that Gallio acted as he did. An important governor, whose brother was a favorite at the Roman court, his ruling no doubt would have served as a precedent for other Roman governors. Thus, for a period of at least ten years, Christianity enjoyed the same protection under the law as did Judaism.

"Did Paul leave Corinth shortly after this?"

18. After this incident Paul stayed in Corinth for some time. Then taking Priscilla and Aquila with him, he said goodbye to the brethren and set sail for Syria. In Cenchrea he had his hair cut for he had taken a Jewish vow.

LEAVE. Inasmuch as Gallio's decision gave Paul official liberty for his ministry, it was hard for him to leave Corinth, even though he had been there for 18 months. This was a problem church, the only one in the N.T. where the "gift of tongues" was in evidence, and the one which caused him the most heartache. So he stayed on a while longer, perhaps a month or two. Yet he had a longing to get back to Syria for he had been away from Antioch a very long time. Taking Priscilla and Aquila with him he went to Corinth's eastern seaport, Chenchrea. Here he could easily catch a ship for Syria, but he would have to go by way of Ephesus since they were the two great mercantile capitols of the world. Inasmuch as these two towns faced each other on opposite sides of the Aegean Sea, Paul was destined to put in at Ephesus for a short time before continuing on to Syria and Palestine.

VOW. While awaiting a ship at Cenchrea, Paul had his hair cut to signify the completion of a Jewish vow. Apparently he had taken this vow sometime earlier, perhaps about the time when he was really concerned for his physical safety (1 Cor. 2:3). Again he may have thought to seal the Lord's promise of safety by reverting to the old Jewish custom of taking a deliverance vow. Since he was a Jew, there was nothing wrong with the act, however, it did obligate him to go to Jerusalem. Every vow under Jewish law required a trip to Jerusalem (Num. 6:1-21). He was now **legally** bound to make an offering in the temple. This was surely a mistake for the apostle of Gentile freedom, for he had no business in the city of Jerusalem.

"How will Paul be received in Ephesus?"

19. On arriving at the port of Ephesus, Paul parted company with Aquila and Priscilla. Then he went by himself into the synagogue to debate with the Jews. 20. They were very interested in his message and asked him to stay and teach them, but he had to refuse. 21. Feeling he couldn't spare the time, he hurriedly sailed from Ephesus. However, before leaving, he promised them, "I'll come back and see you again, Lord willing."

HURRIEDLY. Note the accelerated action. Luke is not in the party so his report covers a lot of ground fast. There is always more detail in his account when he is an eyewitness to the events. Paul and his companions part company soon after they walk the four miles inland to the heart of the city. Aquila may have been headed for his home in Pontus, or he could have been eager to see about opening a branch office in this bustling city. Paul wants to try out the gospel on the Jews, so he heads for the synagogue. A surprise awaited him. Not only were they receptive, they wanted him to stay and tell them more about his message. But he had to refuse. He felt obliged to get to Jerusalem to complete the final requirement of his Nazarite vow. The KJV reading, "I must by all means keep this feast, etc.," is not found in the best texts and should be omitted. It is to Antioch that Paul is eager to return. He is anxious to report the results of his journey to the church that sponsored him and prayed for his success. You can feel the haste Luke builds into the next verses.

EPHESUS. This great city straddled the trade route from Rome to the east. It's port was navigable for seagoing ships. It ranked third in importance after Alexandria in Egypt and Antioch in Syria of the eastern Mediterranean cities. Besides its great markets, theaters, and gymnasiums, the city boasted the temple of Artemis, the seventh wonder of the world. Because of its sanctity and wealth, this temple was the center of eastern banking. Many kings deposited their fortunes here for safekeeping. The traffic through the city was equal, if not surpassing that of Corinth, making it an outstanding place for the gospel. When Paul saw this great city, he knew it could become another Gentile headquarters. The goddess Artemis, (identified by the Romans with their goddess Diana) was worshipped with sex rites, as was Aphrodite of the city of Corinth. Ephesus was also a sex-city.

22. As soon as Paul landed at Caesarea he hurried up to Jerusalem. After paying his respects to the church there, he went down to Antioch, 23. where he spent

some time. Then he left Antioch and set out on another journey making systematic visits to the churches throughout Galatia and Phrygia, strengthening the disciples as he went.

LANDED. We next find Paul at Caesarea, the Roman built port from which one went up to Jerusalem. He hastily went to the sacred city to fulfill his vow-obligation, and while there, greeted the Christian brethren. But he didn't stay long. Jerusalem wasn't a healthy place for him. Besides he was anxious to return to Antioch (Syria) and tell the Gentile church all that happened since he and Silas set out on what we call the second missionary journey. The Antiochian Christians must have been thrilled to hear that the gospel was so solidly established in Europe. When they sent Paul, they thought he was simply going to revisit the Galatian churches and strengthen them. Now they hear the exciting news that Jesus has churches in Europe also.

JOURNEY. See with what few words Luke tells of Paul's visit to Jerusalem and his return to Antioch. And then, before we know it, we're back on the road with him again. This would have been a good place to start a new chapter, for the beginning of this third missionary journey surely marks the beginning of another adventure in the life of Paul. Luke is not along and his account is painfully scant. We don't even know who Paul's companions are. Neither are we sure he revisited every church, but we think he did. Leaving Antioch, his home base for his travels, he again takes the natural land route and sets out for the churches of Asia Minor. This time the Lord does not place any road blocks in his way. The path is clear for him to go to Ephesus. After the fine reception he got in that great city, we can be sure he is making a beeline for those Jews who showed an interest in the gospel. If he could get a church started in Ephesus, it could be the headquarters for all the churches of Asia Minor.

"What will Paul find when he gets to Ephesus this time?"

24. In the meantime, a Jew by the name of Apollos had come to Ephesus. He was a native of Alexandria and a very learned and eloquent man. He was extremely well-grounded in the Old Testament Scriptures and able to present them convincingly. 25. Somehow he had received instruction concerning the way of the Lord, and what he preached and taught was accurate as far as it went. However, his understanding of Jesus was limited to those things taught by John the Baptist.

APOLLOS. While Paul was making his way to Ephesus, a remarkable Jew had shown up in that city. He was Apollos, a native of Alexandria, Egypt. Luke interrupts his story of Paul to tell of this fascinating Jew. He was a disciple of John the Baptist, or as expressed in the Greek text, he knew "only the baptism of John." When the Baptist was alive, he had many disciples, not all of whom turned to Jesus and were saved. Some were scattered throughout the Jewish colonies of the world before they could learn of Jesus' death and resurrection and receive the Spirit. As a result they remained John's disciples. Apollos was one of these. We're not told just how he came in contact with John the Baptist's teaching. Perhaps someone brought it to him in Egypt. Being a gifted scholar and familiar with O.T. prophecy, he had no trouble believing John's message concerning the coming of the Messiah. He believed it was his duty to get out and tell the news, "The Messiah is coming! Repent and be baptized for the remission of sins!"

26. While he was in the synagogue, preaching John's message so boldly, Priscilla and Aquila were in the audience and heard him. They were able to take him aside and explain the way of God to him more accurately.

EXPLAIN. Fortunately Aquila and Priscilla were present when Apollos spoke in the synagogue. They were impressed with his sincerity and eloquence as he declared the repentance message of John the Baptist. Because he was a humble man, they made friends with him. Accordingly they were able to fill him in on the events of Christ and Pentecost and the salvation experience. They had no trouble winning him to Jesus. The text doesn't indicate whether or not he was baptized again. It was surely worth the trouble it took for Aquila and Priscilla to deal with him, for Apollos went on to become one of the most outstanding preachers of the gospel. Some scholars feel he wrote the Epistle to the Hebrews.

ACCURATELY. How marvelous that these godly Christians cared enough to take this defective young preacher aside and see that he was saved and properly instructed. It is also precious to think that Apollos was humble enough to sit at their feet and learn. He could have used his great skill to argue against the truth, but he didn't. One wonders how many more, like Apollos, were scattered through Asia and Egypt knowing only the "baptism of John." Such people would have no atonement for their sins, no personal triumph through Jesus' resurrection, no High Priest as their Advocate, no indwelling presence of the Holy Ghost (Jesus), and certainly not the joy of God's power in their lives. The only message they knew was "repent and be baptized," to prepare the WAY of the Lord. Paul is going to meet some of these "John" disciples when he reaches Ephesus. There he will introduce them to the second half of John's message—receive the Lamb of God. They had fulfilled the first half of John's message, i.e., "repent," but they failed to "believe" on the One coming after John (Jesus), consequently they were unsaved.

27. Then it occurred to him to go across to Achaia. The Ephesian Christians, eager to sponsor him, wrote to the Corinthian disciples asking them to welcome him. His visit to Achaia brought great reinforcement to those, who by God's grace, had become believers. 28. With irresistible arguments he powerfully refuted the Jews in public, demonstrating from the Scriptures that Jesus is truly the Messiah.

VISIT. Shortly after Apollos was saved, he had a desire to go across the Aegean to visit the Christians in Achaia. According to one good text, he was invited there by some Christians who heard him in Ephesus. In any event, the little group of believers in Ephesus gave him all the encouragement they could, providing him with a letter of introduction to the church at Corinth. On reaching that city, Apollos proved himself a powerhouse for God. He not only strengthened the believers in the church, but he held public debates with the Jews in which he refuted their counter-arguments against Christianity. With great authority he showed from the Scriptures that Jesus fulfilled all the Messianic requirements, and he did it with such force the Jews couldn't deny his claim that Jesus is the Messiah.

IRRESISTIBLE. There is no doubt that Apollos was one of the greatest forces for Christ in that day. Luke devotes more space to him than to Silas or Timothy, both of whom were closer to the doctor and meant more to him personally. This was due to the large place Apollos occupied in the church later on. Also, Luke is going to report Paul's encounter with some of Apollos' converts in the next chapter. In one place Paul speaks of the great preacher as watering seed which Paul, himself, had sown (1 Cor. 3:6). Because of his unique method of handling the Scriptures, he was extremely popular and an "Apollos" party was formed around him. If this party functioned in opposition to Paul, the apostle doesn't mention it in any of his letters, for he warmly speaks of him as a "fellow-laborer" (1 Cor. 4:6).

19 1. While Apollos was in Corinth, Paul completed his journey through the inland region of Asia and came to Ephesus. There he ran into a number of converts, 2. whom he asked, "Did you receive the Holy Spirit when you became believers?" "No," they replied, "We haven't heard of the Holy Spirit being given to anyone yet."

CONVERTS. By the time Paul got to Ephesus, Apollos had crossed over to Greece. He missed Apollos, but he did run into a group of twelve men who were also followers of John the Baptist. They may have considered themselves as part of the Christian community, but they more likely were a small fellowship by themselves. In spite of their profession, it didn't take Paul long to recognize they weren't converted to Christ. The same defect existed in them as was in Apollos before he was instructed by Aquila and Priscilla. Inasmuch as Luke tells the story of Apollos so completely, it seems almost certain that these were some of Apollos' converts **before he was saved.** Paul is suspicious enough to check on their salvation experience by asking two revealing questions. How they answered would indicate whether or not they were born of the Spirit.

RECEIVE. The question Paul asks first is NOT as it appears in the King James version, which suggests that receiving the Spirit is a second experience which comes sometime AFTER salvation. This, of course, cannot be, for there is no way to be born of the Spirit apart from receiving the Spirit. The Greek text clearly shows that Paul wants to know what happened WHEN they believed, not after. There's no question about that. His point is: if they were believers in the full gospel of Jesus Christ, they SHOULD HAVE received the Spirit the moment they opened their hearts to Him. Inasmuch as the Holy Spirit and the Spirit of Christ are one, no one can be saved apart from receiving the Spirit of Christ into his life (Rom. 8:9b).

GIVEN. Most Bible texts make it appear that these converts never heard of the Holy Spirit. But this would be impossible, since one could not be a disciple of John the Baptist and not know of the Spirit. John said repeatedly that the Messiah would baptize in the Holy Spirit (John 1:33). It was an important part of his message. Their reply is in the sense of John 7:39 where it says, "the Holy Spirit was not yet given." What these men did not know was that Pentecost had already occurred and the Holy Spirit had come to indwell believers. Since Apollos was ignorant of this fact, it appears certain these were his converts. They are not exactly isolated, living as they do, in the great city of Ephesus, so their conversion must have been recent. They could be called "disciples" in the sense that they believed all they heard ABOUT Christ, but they hadn't received Him, neither did they have fellowship with Him. As such, they are examples of the difference we find between believers (professors) and receivers (possessors) in Christianity today.

"What was Paul's other question?"

3. "Well then," said Paul, "on what basis were you baptized?" "We were baptized according to the teachings of John," they replied. 4. Then Paul said to them, "The baptisms John performed were outward tokens of turning from evil, but he also told the people they were to turn to the Person Who was coming after him, that is, they were to place their trust in Jesus." 5. When they heard this, they were baptized in the name of the Lord Jesus.

WHAT BASIS. Once he learned these "disciples" had no experience with the Spirit, Paul next asked about their baptism. Apparently they considered themselves disciples on the basis of some baptism and Paul is curious to know what kind. To his mind, only those who meant business for Christ were baptized and it was accompanied by some evidence of receiving the Spirit. When they said they had received John's baptism, he knew they had misunderstood John's message. They had grasped only PART of what John's baptism was all about. As did Apollos, they supposed John's baptism indicated the turning FROM evil only. Had they understood John correctly, they would have also known that his baptism meant turning TO the One coming after him, that is, Jesus.

BAPTIZED. On the day of Pentecost many of the Jews who turned to Christ had to be rebaptized. They had received John's baptism, and may have repented of their sins, but they did NOT turn to Christ **when he appeared.** Thus they were not really prepared for Him. John's message was not merely REPENT, but repent and get ready to RECEIVE. Obviously their baptism did NOT prepare them to receive Christ, and was therefore insufficient. Yet preparation for Christ was the real purpose of John's baptism. Peter made it plain they would have to be rebaptized BEFORE they could receive the Spirit (Acts 2:38). Now these "disciples" of Apollos have to be rebaptized for the same reason. Once they understood the true meaning of John's baptism they submitted gladly and Paul rebaptized them.

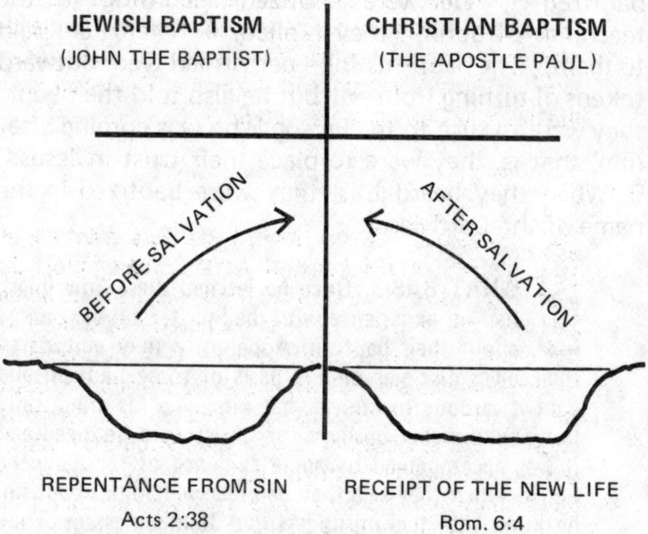

TWO SIDES OF THE SAME COIN

"Then were they saved after they were baptized?"

6. After this Paul laid his hands upon them and the Holy Spirit came upon them. Then they began speaking with tongues and making prophetic utterances. 7. In all, there were about twelve men in this group.

HANDS. For the second time in Acts the laying on of hands is followed by the receipt of the Spirit. It first occurred in Samaria when Peter and John laid hands on the despised Samaritans who had misunderstood Philip's baptism. In their case there was also a lack of evidence of salvation (see under Ch. 8:14-16). Philip, like Apollos, apparently didn't fathom the Spirit's operation well enough to produce genuine disciples. So Peter and John checked to see if the Samaritans received the Spirit when they believed. This scene at Ephesus seems to be a parallel. Paul is correcting the confusion created by Apollos' earlier teaching. After they are rebaptized, their hearts are ready to receive Christ. One by one they receive Christ's Ghost as Paul ministers to them. In no way does the imposition of hands impart the Spirit, even though it occurs simultaneously. The hands dramatize the welcoming of these men into God's family. There were no hands laid on at Pentecost or in the house of Cornelius, you recall.

TONGUES. We've reached the last mention of tongues in the book of Acts. Commentators do NOT agree as to WHICH KIND occurs here. Some feel this is the GIFT of tongues now in operation at Corinth across the Aegean Sea. I feel that ALL cases of tongues in Acts are a SIGN, and those outside this book are the GIFT. This occurrence, I believe, is of the same order as at Pentecost. It was an ENABLEMENT which saw Jesus bringing forth the ecstasy of their hearts in other languages, possibly pure Hebrew. In that case (Ephesians speaking pure Hebrew) the sign would be for Paul. We have already noted how tongues have marked the various stages of the gospel as it spread throughout the world. If Paul had come to think of Syrian Antioch as the capitol of Christianity, that notion is now changed. Ephesus was to become the great center of Gentile Christianity. The shift is made known to Paul by means of Pentecostal type tongues. A similar SIGN POST you recall, marked God's opening of the door to the Samaritans, the Gentiles at Cornelius' house, and once more at Syrian Antioch. Now it had occurred at Ephesus.

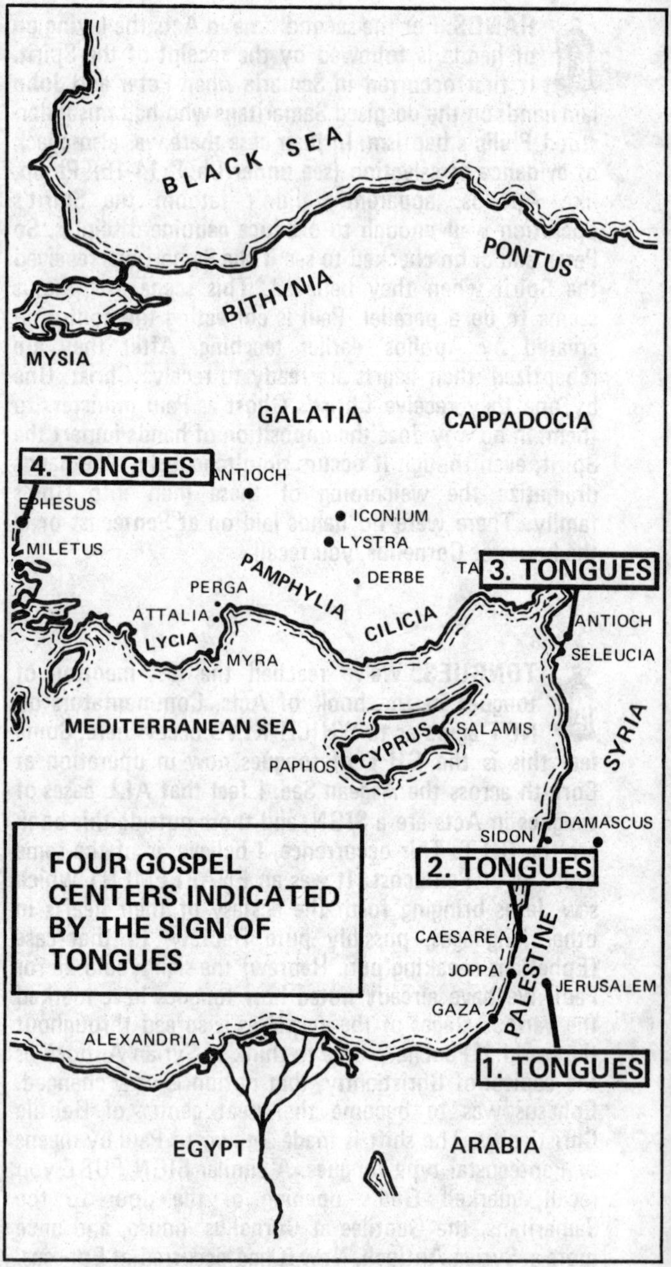
BLACK SEA
PONTUS
BITHYNIA
MYSIA
GALATIA
CAPPADOCIA
4. TONGUES
ANTIOCH
EPHESUS
ICONIUM
LYSTRA
MILETUS
PAMPHYLIA
DERBE
TA
3. TONGUES
PERGA
ATTALIA
CILICIA
ANTIOCH
LYCIA
MYRA
SELEUCIA
MEDITERRANEAN SEA
CYPRUS
SALAMIS
PAPHOS
SYRIA
FOUR GOSPEL CENTERS INDICATED BY THE SIGN OF TONGUES
DAMASCUS
SIDON
2. TONGUES
CAESAREA
PALESTINE
JOPPA
JERUSALEM
GAZA
ALEXANDRIA
1. TONGUES
EGYPT
ARABIA

TWELVE. We're not sure why Luke singled out these twelve men to report their experience. He devoted a lot of space to them, beginning with the story of Apollos who obviously converted them FROM Judaism, but not TO Christ. However, Paul must have met others who were equally confused about water baptism and the Spirit. Our first explanation is that the SIGN of tongues told Paul this was to become the new center of Gentile Christianity. This may have been a part of their prophetic utterances. It is also possible that these 12 men were hereby given to Paul as sub-apostles and would play an important part in the amazing spread of the gospel about Ephesus. Another lesson in this SIGN of tongues is seeing that water BAPTISM and believing ABOUT Christ are not sufficient for salvation. The sign makes it clear that people must know what they are doing when they come to Jesus. This was the great lesson learned by Philip at Samaria and now it is repeated here. The amount of space Luke devotes to this scene tells us it contains a vital lesson—unless men receive the Spirit of Christ, they simply are not saved.

"Did Paul finally get back to the synagogue as he promised?"

8. Then Paul went into the synagogue and for the next three months boldly preached every Sabbath. He argued with the Jews seeking to persuade them concerning the kingdom of God. 9. However, some of them not only hardened their hearts, refusing to believe in the Lord, they deliberately set about to discredit the way of the Lord publicly. So Paul, taking his disciples with him, withdrew from the synagogue and began holding daily meetings in the lecture hall of Tyrannus.

PREACHED. On Paul's first visit to this synagogue earlier, the people were thrilled with his words and begged him to stay. He refused, because he was on his way to Palestine. But now he had returned to keep that promise. So, per his custom of bringing the gospel to the Jew first, his Ephesian ministry began in this synagogue. For three months the Jews listened to him every Sabbath. At the end of that time it became obvious he had accomplished all that could be expected in that place. The leaders became hostile towards him. When they began to slander the Lord openly, Paul decided to abandon the synagogue and find another place to preach. This is quite remarkable when you remember how urgently this church begged him to come with his preaching. Accordingly he rented the lecture hall of a philosopher-teacher by the name of Tyrannus. Nothing is stated to indicate whether or not Paul was able to win him to the Lord.

DAILY. Operating outside of the synagogue, Paul could now preach every day. His first audience consisted of the disciples he was able to bring with him from the synagogue. Likely they met during the siesta hours (11 a.m. to 4 p.m.). The Ephesians did their work in the early morning hours and rested in the heat of the day. It is said of this wicked city, that more people could be found asleep at 1 p.m. than at 1 a.m. Paul used the early hours to work at his trade and lectured during the heat of the day when Tyrannus would be finished with the hall. That Paul's disciples gave up their siesta to join him shows the kind of an example he was. When the Ephesians were resting or socializing, the apostle was taking advantage of the situation to operate his ministry. When we consider that he also used his evenings to visit with the believers and go from house to house winning souls, we get an idea of the energy he devoted to the gospel.

"What could one man do in a city as wicked as Ephesus?"

10. Paul carried on like this for two years, so that all who lived in the province of Asia, both Jews and Greeks, heard the Word of the Lord.

HEARD. Paul continued in the hall of Tyrannus for a full two years, perhaps longer. When you consider how this one man, aware of Jesus' presence within him, took on a city flooded with vice, magic, and witchcraft, and was so successful that all

Asia heard about Jesus, you can't help but marvel at his determination for Christ. Paul stayed on the job in the city, but some of his fellow-workers pushed into the outlying districts of Asia to establish churches at Colosse, Heiropolis, and Laodicea. Asia, of course, is the Roman province in the S.W. corner of what we now call Asia Minor (Modern Turkey). Three years earlier the apostle had been forbidden to preach in this area, now his work covered the entire province with the Word of Christ. The seven churches to which John wrote in the Revelation, were in this territory with Ephesus included as one of the seven. Apart from his letters, the Ephesian program was the most effective of all of Paul's work.

"How is it that one man could be so effective?"

11. And God worked some very special miracles through Paul, 12. so that when even his sweat rags and aprons were brought in contact with the sick, their diseases vanished and the evil spirits came out of them.

MIRACLES. Ephesus could well be called, "Superstition City." Its people lived in a supernatural atmosphere. Under the shadow of the temple of Artemis (Diana), ghostly priests and miracle workers abounded. Between the occult worship of Artemis and the widespread practice of magic, the city was preoccupied with the black arts. This made the residents easy prey to false magicians and vulnerable to demonic penetration. Into this city God brought Paul. The use of miracles would be very important in such a town. As Moses contended with the magicians of Egypt, so Paul accommodated himself to the Ephesian mind. He performed many remarkable miracles in a city that thrived on magic. The text makes it clear that Paul did not have this power in himself. This was God's way of reaching the people through him. His miracles were those of healing and exorcism, that is, healing those suffering corporal diseases and delivering those invaded by demons. Demons and disease brought both mental and physical suffering.

SPECIAL. Had not the Ephesians such great interest in the supernatural, it is not likely that Paul would have resorted to the miraculous. In many places he was thrilled to bring only the Word of God and watch it perform its miracle in the hearts of men. The new birth is the greatest miracle of God. By it, sinners become the sons of God and their destinies are shifted to heaven from hell. However, in those places where man's craving for the supernatural gets out of hand, God is sometimes pleased to meet people at the point of their passion and harness it to the gospel. In Ephesus, Paul's miracles provided a wonderful approach to the mood of the city. It was ever his way to be "all things to all men," so in Ephesus, the supernatural was his point of contact. Without doubt he was probably the greatest "magician" this town had ever seen. Ephesus became the scene of his biggest success.

RAGS. So great was God's power working through Paul, says Dr. Luke, that people were healed at the touch of pieces of material which had been in contact with Paul's body. The sweat rags (handkerchiefs) were common in the warm areas of Palestine, Arabia, and Asia Minor. Paul's apron was worn about his waist as he worked at his trade, while the sweat rag was worn about his head. Healings of this type parallel the case of the woman who was healed by touching the fringe of Jesus' garment (Mk. 5:27-34), or the healing effect of Peter's shadow (Acts 5:15). In such healings, the touch of the items causes the victim's faith to rise to the place where it triggers the healing mechanism God has built into the human body. Jesus explained it as, "Thy faith hath made thee whole." In this city steeped in magic, such healings served to vindicate Paul's ministry. The magicians couldn't match his works.

"The people must have been awed by such miracles!"

13. A party of wandering Jews, who cast out demons in the various towns they visited, took it upon themselves to try the name of the Lord Jesus in their exorcism formula. They attempted to deliver those

who were possessed by evil spirits by saying, "I adjure you by Jesus whom Paul preaches."

EXORCISM. Deception, fraud, and trickery of every kind flourished in the superstitious city of Ephesus. Quick money was to be made off the gullibility of the Ephesians. Consequently the black arts were practiced by many. There were numerous exorcists going about in those days, some renegade Jews among them. They were like sideshow people who undertook to dispel demons by means of charms, spells, or magical words. Jews were especially popular for it was believed they had special power through the name of YHWH (pronounced Yaweh, but erroneously translated Jehovah in many translations). The pagans knew the Jews were not supposed to pronounce this name of the God of Israel, but corrupt Jews ignored the restriction and consequently were in demand as exorcists. When some of them saw the power of Jesus' name on Paul's lips, they were tempted to try it in their magical formula and see if it had any efficacy for them.

14. Among those attempting this were the seven sons of one Sceva, a Jewish chief priest. 15. And the evil spirit in the man they were treating answered back, saying, "Jesus I recognize, Paul I know well enough, but who in the world are you?" 16. With that, the man with the evil spirit sprang upon them and overpowered them with such force that they ran out of the house stripped and bruised.

SCEVA. Among the numerous Jewish exorcists in Ephesus, one group is especially named, the sons of one Sceva, a Jewish chief priest. While there is no record of any Sceva among the chief priests, there is no reason to doubt Luke's accuracy. Of course, he could have picked up the man's title from his sideshow placard where he billed himself as a chief priest. A CHIEF priest would be in great demand in this city for he would be one very likely to know how to pronounce the ineffable name of YHWH. Yet it is not this name his sons use, but the one Paul used–Jesus. In their attempt to imitate Paul, the use of Jesus' name backfires. The man, energized with abnormal strength by the demon, turned on the exorcists with such violence that all seven fled the building naked and wounded.

SPIRIT. See how Luke reports the demon as a person. The spirit is aware of what is going on. He speaks to men as a man, though, as a spirit he must use the victim's speech organ to communicate. As a citizen of Satan's kingdom he would know all about Jesus, even from the beginning. He would also know Paul as one who once served the interests of hell with his war on the church. He would also know those who are true believers in Christ and that these seven men had nothing to do with Jesus. For them, also in Satan's kingdom, to dare to use that dreaded name against him merely infuriated him. Using his victim's body, he took his revenge on these pretenders. A demon, in complete possession of a man, is able to harness the amazing unconscious forces of the human body. This brings home the fact that demons are not only real, but dangerous. In this case, the demon used them to assault the seven who dared to speak Jesus' name against him.

17. The news of this incident spread quickly throughout Ephesus. Those who heard, whether Jew or Greek, were awestruck. Then it was that the name of Jesus came to be regarded with the greatest of respect and honor.

RESPECT. All of the sorcerers and magicians of Ephesus used names in their incantations. It was in the power of some name that they cast their spells. Now the city has felt the power of the name which Paul used in his work–JESUS. Just as the deaths of Ananias and Sapphira brought holy conviction to the church at Jerusalem, so now the experience of the sons of Sceva sent a wave of fear among the Ephesians. Living as they did, in hunger for the supernatural, they have now met a name which is above every name used by the magicians. That name has now been exalted in their midst. Paul has ordered demons out of people, and they have come. In that name, he also commanded men and women to turn to God. With Jesus' name regarded with such awe by both Jew and Gentile, some remarkable results can be expected in this superstitious city. The Ephesians really feared the power of Jesus' name, and when Paul ordered them to turn to God in that name, they took him seriously.

"Wouldn't that have a profound effect on this city of magic?"

18. Then many believers came forward and began confessing their evil practices, giving a full account of their use of magical spells. 19. Many others, who had formerly practiced magic, brought their books and piled them in a heap and burned them publicly. The estimated value of all these books together was 50,000 pieces of silver. 20. So, in this and other ways, the Word of the Lord proved its irresistible power and kept on spreading and growing.

CONFESSING. The people of Ephesus were bored, but the electrifying report of the power of Jesus' name broke the monotony and set the Ephesian minds to thinking about Christ. Apparently a wave of magicians came to Paul to receive the Lord and confess the black secrets of their occupation. Witchcraft depends on the secrecy of its incantations. Should they become known, they lose their power. Thus these people traded their hocus-pocus for the real thing in Christ. The power of the gospel began to surge through many lives. It was the routing of the sons of Sceva that God used to touch off this revival among the magicians. Also, it seems there were many secret believers. The catapulting of Jesus' name to the height of civic glory stirred their consciences and they came forward to confess their part in the magical practices.

BOOKS. When the magicians received Christ, their books of magic were of no further use to them. They wouldn't sell them and damage other lives, though they were worth a great deal of money.

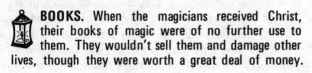

These books (actually scrolls and parchments) contained the secret formulas, incantations which supposedly cured ills and cast out demons. The city was filled with these books. The entire citizenry was involved with the occult. In about three libraries around the world, we have a number of the magical scrolls that have survived. They are full of nonsense and mumbo-jumbo. The superstitious Ephesians spent fortunes on these books. It was the magic capitol of the ancient world. The burning of these books in the public square was an expensive bonfire. The estimated worth was the equivalent of 50,000 days wages. The city must have been shocked at this sight which proved the power of the gospel. Saved men felt it was better to do what was right than to keep something of value.

SPREADING. The black arts business in Ephesus suffered a real blow when so many magicians openly renounced witchcraft. The difference between the power of faith in Christ and the practice of sorcery was so clearly manifest that it opened an even wider door for the gospel. As a result, the Word of the Lord spread everywhere. In one place Paul describes his Ephesian ministry with these words: "A great door has been opened to me. . .and there are many adversaries" (1 Cor. 16:9). Paul went through that door head on. He suffered much more than is recorded here, as we learn from his letters. We owe it to Paul to consider how mightily the gospel prevailed in Asia Minor and Europe because of his untiring efforts. God used the dedication of this one man in a fantastic way.

"What are Paul's plans after this?"

21. When this was all over, Paul purposed in his spirit to go to Jerusalem by way of Macedonia and Achaia. "After I've been there," he said, "I must also pay a visit to Rome." 22. So he sent two of his assistants, Timothy and Erastus, to Macedonia while he himself remained awhile longer in the province of Asia.

JERUSALEM. As the loudest hurricane finally passes into silence, so did sorcery and magic have their last day in Ephesus. With the great new center of Gentile Christianity firmly established, Paul begins to think of new fields of service. He has his eye on Rome. He senses that his indwelling Lord wants him to go there, but for the moment, the Christians at Jerusalem are in great distress. He feels something should be done about it. So he sends Timothy and Erastus to the churches of Greece to raise funds in advance of his coming. They could encourage the churches to have their offerings ready for Paul when he got there. That would allow him to remain in Ephesus a little longer. Once he delivers the offerings to Jerusalem, his plan is to go to Rome. He has no way of knowing the strange route by which he will finally travel to the capitol of the empire, but he's sure he must make the visit. The riot mentioned below occurs while Paul was still at Ephesus.

PURPOSED. Paul also had his eye on Spain, and were not relief needed in Jerusalem, he would have surely gone there via Rome. We know he had no ambitions to develop a work at Rome, for it was his settled policy never to build a work on another man's foundation (Rom. 15:20). But Luke says little of those plans. Paul is already imprisoned in Rome as he writes this account, and it is not certain how it will go with him. But in his letter to the Romans, which he wrote after leaving Ephesus, Paul makes definite mention of his desire to reach Spain. He even asks the Romans to consider helping him on his way (Rom. 15:24). Note how Paul purposed these plans "in his spirit." This is the turning point in Paul's ministry. He is aware now that God does want him to go to Rome. Yet, his own desire to go to Jerusalem, a place he has been ordered away from, will receive the priority (22:18).

"Was Ephesus peaceful after that?"

23. It was right at this time that the rapid expansion of Christianity became responsible for a serious disturbance. 24. It all began with a certain silversmith named Demetrius. He, along with some merchants,

were engaged in the highly profitable business of manufacturing and selling silver miniatures of the temple of the goddess Artemis. 25. He called a meeting of the merchants, together with their allied tradesmen, and addressed them with these words: "Men," he said, "You all know that our prosperity depends on this business. 26. But do I have to tell you what this fellow Paul is doing to us? With your own eyes and ears you can judge how he has succeeded in convincing masses of people that gods made by human hands are not gods at all. And he has done this, not only in Ephesus, but throughout practically all of Asia. 27. I'm warning you, if this keeps up, not only will our business suffer a bad name, but the temple of the great goddess Artemis will become worthless. How would you like to see this magnificent goddess, whom all Asia and the rest of the world worships, stripped of her greatness and become obsolete?"

DISTURBANCE. Before Paul left Ephesus a nasty situation developed. The spread of Christianity was drastically reducing the number of people worshipping the goddess Artemis. This in turn cut into the shrine and souvenir business, which was enormous. People from all over the world visited this 7th wonder of the world at Ephesus. The shrines were miniature temples with a statue of the goddess inside. It provided a means whereby people could continue their worship of the goddess after leaving Ephesus. Many were made of beautiful silver craftsmanship and brought a huge price. A festival was held in her honor each spring. It was probably at the festival of A.D. 55 that this trouble erupted. Artemis is the same as the goddess Diana (Latin) or Cybele. She was supposedly the mother of all gods and men, yet she consisted of nothing more than a meteorite that had fallen from the sky. The black stone resembled a many breasted woman. Symbolizing the bounty of nature, she was regarded as a fertility goddess. Such worship made over a stone, indicates the ignorance and superstition of those times.

DEMETRIUS. This man was likely a wholesaler, who supplied the dealers of Ephesus and shipped his items to cities throughout the known world. When money interests and religion are offended at the same time, it's an explosive result. Demetrius started it by summoning all the people in the shrine-making business and persuading them to stage a mass protest against Paul and his Christian movement. It seems intolerable to Demetrius that the silversmiths, who had the most to lose, should sit by and let Paul's preaching threaten their profitable business. Under the guise of a crusade for Artemis, he feels Paul should be stopped. Not only that, he hints it would be a disgrace to the city if their goddess' glory were permitted to decline. Therefore silencing Paul would also be a patriotic matter. Of course, Demetrius' only concern is the drop in sales of his images. The essence of his appeal is, "This has gone on long enough!"

WORTHLESS. The words of Demetrius tell us something vital. But first consider how one man, Paul, went into one of the greatest cities of the world with its great attraction, the temple of Artemis. And how, in the power of God, he moved against its witchcraft and sorcery and finally the superstitious worship of Artemis herself. But did he wage war against the evil forces directly? No. He preached the gospel, the power of God unto salvation. He was not anti-magic, anti-Artemis, or anti-anything. He was pro-Christ. Spiritual changes occurred in the people as they received the Lord. The changes in the people began to sap the foundation of the pagan systems and they started to totter. The worship of Artemis, which held the Ephesians in awe, declined as men received the Lord. The Word of Christ caused a revolution in men's souls and the evil forces which bound them were broken. In our day, Christians have no need to fight Communism or any other ism directly. They need but see that men experience that spiritual convulsion which snaps the chains of every system that binds men. They all fade away when people experience Christ. Observe how Paul wiped out the magicians (black arts) at the beginning of his Ephesian ministry and had seriously reduced the worship of Artemis at the end of his stay there.

"Was Demetrius successful in making trouble for Christianity?"

28. Upon hearing those words, the crowds were overcome with rage and began shouting, "Great is Artemis of the Ephesians!" 29. Before long their uproar had infected the whole city. Then, in a sudden, concerted move the mob seized Gaius and Aristarchus, Paul's traveling companions from Macedonia, and dragged them off to the theater.

INFECTED. The men of the silversmith's guild were so fired by Demetrius' words, they ran into the public square shouting praise to their goddess. They weren't about to let her become obsolete. They easily infected other Ephesians with their resentment of Paul and his Christianity by saying his work amounted to an attack on their goddess. A mob quickly formed and began staging a demonstration on the great street that led to the huge open air theatre at the end of town. On their way to the theatre, they seized two of Paul's companions, Gaius of Derbe and Aristarchus of Thessalonica (Acts 20:4). (They are referred to as Paul's inasmuch as they are among those accompanying him to Jerusalem with the relief mission). If they couldn't lay hands on Paul immediately, these men would have to do. The mob soon had much of the populace caught up in their enthusiastic resentment. Many commentators feel the festival of Artemis was being held at this time. If so, many visitors would also be in the excited crowd for they had come to worship the great goddess and their effort would be in vain should her glory and preeminence fade.

THEATRE. The ruins of this theatre, where the demonstration was staged, can be seen today. At one time it was an impressive structure, shaped in a semi-circle with tiers of seats ranging up the sloping hillside. It is said to have held as many as 30,000 people, the largest of ancient time. Because it was at the end of the long straight street that ran through the city from the inner harbor of Ephesus, it was easily accessible to the people and the scene of many public gatherings. Among the Greeks, it was common for the people to gather in great crowds and convene themselves as a formal, civic assembly. They were ready to take legal action against Paul and his companions even though the meeting had not been called by the city officials. They show some semblance of wanting to do this legally. To the Greek mind, a large gathering of Ephesians in the theatre constituted a legal meeting.

"How did Paul react to this seizure of his friends?"

30. Paul was all set to rush into the theatre and go before the crowd, but the disciples prevented him. 31. Also, some high-ranking provincial dignitaries, who were friendly toward Paul, sent him a message imploring him not to risk his life in the theatre.

RUSH. It was consistent with Paul's zealous nature to rush to the defense of his friends. On other occasions we have seen him act from emotion rather than wisdom (Acts 9:29,30). Now he is doing it again. It would have been madness for him to have appeared before the excited mob, yet he would have done so had he not been forcibly restrained by the Ephesian Christians. Right at that same moment, however, officers from the Asiarchs (prominent Ephesians, goodwill ambassadors of the cult of Rome and the Emperor) arrived and joined the disciples in preventing Paul from a needless sacrifice of his life. The Asiarchs apparently knew that Paul was a Roman citizen and in no way an enemy of Rome. They sent these officers to dissuade him from making such an appearance. At the same time they were providing him with police protection. The friendliness of the Asiarchs indicates that Rome was not hostile toward Christianity at the time.

"What were the Jews doing all this time?"

32. Within the theatre itself there was great confusion. Some were shouting one thing, others something else, for most of them didn't even know why they were there. 33. Some of the people thought perhaps Alexander was the target of their feelings, since a group of Jews had hustled him to the stage of the theatre. Intending to make a speech in defense of the Jewish position, he motioned for silence with a wave of his hand. 34. But when the crowd saw that he was a Jew, they shouted for about two hours, "Great is Artemis of the Ephesians!"

CONFUSION. A confused mob is dangerous. With such a large crowd milling about in the theatre, anything could happen. Many of the participants didn't know why they were there. They had simply joined the multitude headed for the theatre, anxious to see what was taking place. However, the feelings were all religious. This worried the Jews. They feared the confused hostility of the crowd might turn against them. It was known that they were anti-Artemis, for Jews opposed the worship of all idols and gods other than the God of Israel. The complete disorder of the crowd made the situation threatening. The mood could just as easily become anti-Jewish as well as anti-Christian. The Jews were alarmed by this possibility.

ALEXANDER. The Jews were eager to have it known that they had nothing to do with the present disorder. In an attempt to publicly disclaim any association with Paul and Christianity, they chose Alexander, one of their own number, to be their spokesman. Somehow they managed to have him recognized and brought him to the rostrum of the theatre. Perhaps they saw this as an opportunity to get rid of Paul. However, their real concern at the moment is convincing the excited mob that the Jewish colony is in no way involved in the present turmoil. When he tried to speak, the crowd saw only that Alexander was a Jew. Therefore, he could not be a friend of Artemis. Some no doubt thought he was the real cause of the trouble since he appeared so eager to speak. When he motioned for attention, they shouted him down and for two hours thereafter chanted their praise to Artemis.

"Weren't any of the city officials concerned about this riot?"

35. At last the city clerk was able to get the crowd to settle down. "Men of Ephesus," he said, "everyone knows that our city of Ephesus is the guardian of the temple of the great Artemis and the sacred image which fell from heaven. 36. Since these are facts which no one can deny, why let yourselves be upset by what someone says. The wise thing is to remain calm and do nothing rash. 37. As for these men which you have brought here, they have neither robbed her temple, nor have they spoken of our goddess with blasphemous words."

CLERK. One city official was alarmed by events at the theatre. He was the town clerk, the most important official next to the Roman commander. It was his job to coordinate activities between the city council and the Roman authorities. In free cities, such as Ephesus, the town clerk acted much like a present day mayor. He knew the provincial authorities would hold him responsible if the disorder got out of hand. He was anxious to preserve order lest the Romans impose severe restrictions on the city. His address was therefore intended to calm his hearers by reminding them of the undisputed facts concerning Artemis and her temple. The goddess was not the work of any man's hands, he said, for everyone knows she had actually come down from heaven. The Romans even acknowledged this fact by calling her "Diana of the Ephesians." Diana was the Romans' name for the same goddess.

SPOKEN. In view of these facts, says the clerk, there is no reason for anyone to be uspet or behave in an imprudent manner. It is possible this clerk was also friendly toward Paul. He seems to be in possession of some interesting facts about Paul's friends. Of his own knowledge he certifies that they have not violated the temple of Artemis, neither have they spoken evil of her. This gives us a clue as to the way the Ephesian Christians handled themselves in a city that worshipped a false god. They did NOT attack the goddess. Apparently Paul gave instructions that no one was to assail the goddess of the Ephesians, but to preach Christ and avoid any direct attack on the idols of the pagans. It was enough that people should learn of the new life, which if accepted, would cause the old life to pass away. That wisdom apparently saved the lives of two of Paul's friends. Perhaps modern Christians could profit from Paul's example of exalting Christ rather than investing their energies in various "anti" movements. We're not called to be anti-anything except anti-Satan.

"What about the charges made against the Christians?"

38. "Now if Demetrius or any of his craftsmen feel they have a case against anyone, our courts meet in regular session to care for such matters. Let them accuse each other before a judge. 39. But if you feel this is a matter requiring higher authority, then it should come before the city council. 40. Now there's a good chance that all of us may be charged with riot because of what's happened here today. There is no justification for all this uproar and if Rome demands an explanation, what excuse can we give?" 41. With that he dismissed the crowd and the people dispersed.

COURTS. The essence of the clerk's challenge is why should the whole town get into trouble because Demetrius feels he has a complaint against someone. He should use the courts and seek legal redress, says the clerk, and not involve the citizens of Ephesus in an illegal tumult. Such a thing could put the town in great danger. In this the clerk did not exaggerate. The Romans jealously guarded their territories and watched every appearance of insurrection with a jealous eye. Rome would not hesitate to arraign an entire city on a charge of riot. In this case, the city had no justification for its action. On top of that, it was a capital offense for anyone to take part in a riot. The people listened to the clerk's sobering words. Then he dismissed them and they went home. Paul was apparently ready to risk his life and ministry in an attempt to salvage the situation by himself. But he was to learn that God was not only aware of the problem all along, but had the hidden means for taking care of it. A little later Paul wrote that "civil magistrates were ministers of God to thee for good. . ." (Rom. 13:4). He saw that great principle at work in Ephesus. It is a gift of God where wise government exists.

20 1. When things had quieted down in Ephesus, Paul sent for the disciples. After encouraging them to accept the responsibility of the church, he said goodbye and set out on his journey to Macedonia. 2. As he made his way through the various regions, he brought encouraging messages to the Christians. Finally he arrived in Greece.

GOODBYE. Paul sensed his further presence in Ephesus was a threat to the church, since the hostility was directed against him personally. So he decided to make the trip to Europe he purposed earlier (Acts 19:21). The work was now strong enough to be left in the hands of faithful believers. He waited, however, until the uproar of the silversmiths had subsided, then he took a coastal ship to Troas. Here he expected to meet Titus who was to bring him a report on conditions in the Corinthian church. But Titus wasn't there. So he went on to Macedonia (northern part of modern Greece). It is likely that he went first to Philippi and there met Titus who briefed him on developments at Corinth. As a result of this briefing, he wrote the letter known as "Second Corinthians."

JOURNEY. Luke tells us very little of Paul's experiences in Macedonia. Apparently they were not relevant to the purpose of his account. Thus we must fill in the blanks from Paul's own letters. The above verses cover a period of about nine months. During this time the apostle was extremely busy revisiting the Macedonian churches and establishing new ones.

Rom. 15:19 tells us that Illyricum was evangelized at this time, which means that either Paul or some of his workers got as far west as the Adriatic Sea. Paul was occupied with two great concerns at this time: (1) the spiritual condition of the church at Corinth, (2) the collection of the relief fund which he hoped to take personally to Jerusalem. Luke mentions neither of these things, but they were uppermost in Paul's mind.

3. He stayed in Greece for three months. Then, as he was about to sail for Syria, it was discovered that the Jews had formed a plot against his life. So he switched his plans and decided to go by way of Macedonia. 4. His companions selected for the journey were Sopater of Berea, the son of Pyrrhus; Aristarchus and Secundus from Thessalonica; Gaius of Derbe; Timothy and two friends from Asia, Tychicus and Trophimus. 5. These now went on ahead and were waiting for us at Troas.

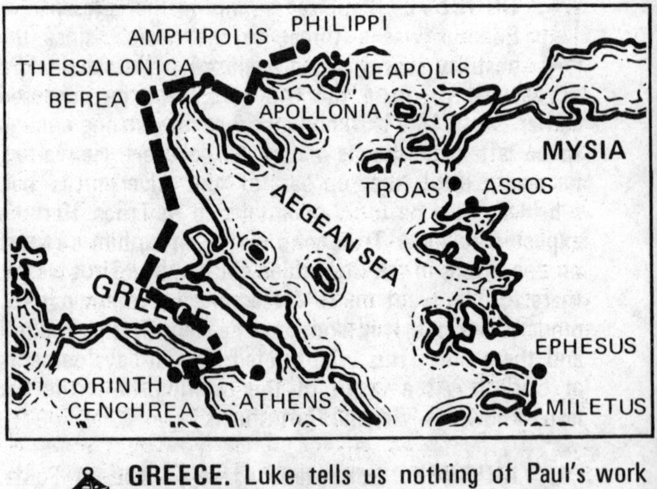

GREECE. Luke tells us nothing of Paul's work in Greece (Achaia). No doubt Paul spent most of the three months at Corinth and had a far better time than expected. Apparently his letters had cared for most of the church's problems before he got there. The Corinthians endured special difficulties because of the immoral and idolatrous nature of their city. It was the sin capitol of the world. Consequently the question of marriage arose, as did the role of women in the church. Then there were matters of the communion, the eating of meat previously offered to idols and spiritual gifts exercised by unrestrained people. Paul had written about these things (1st Corinthians), but when party strife caused his authority to be challenged, he wrote a more harsh letter to set things in order (2nd Corinthians). Finding the church rather orderly on his arrival, Paul was able to concentrate on his fund raising program. He even found time to write his epistle to the Romans, the most profound of all his letters.

PLOT. Paul's heart was all wrapped up in the relief offering he was bearing to Jerusalem. It was an obsession with him. He felt it would draw the Jewish and Gentile churches closer together. It was Gentile money he was carrying. Even though he knew the Spirit really wanted him to go to Rome, he was determined to take this gift in person. After that, he would do what God wanted him to do. That's why he wrote to the Romans. He hoped his letter would suffice as a substitute until he could get there. With the funds all gathered, Paul and his chosen companions prepare to sail to Troas, and from there to Jerusalem. But word comes of a plot against his life by some fanatical Jews aboard the same pilgrim ship. Likely they meant to kill him and dump his body overboard. It was decided that Paul's friends would continue aboard ship while he would slip away and go on foot. His friends were to wait for him at Troas while he made the circuitous journey back around through Macedonia.

COMPANIONS. In those days it was not uncommon for a leader to abscond with collected funds. So Paul, lest anyone think he sought personal profit, arranged for two things: (1) that all offerings be gathered before he arrived in each city, (2) that the churches (if they desired) could send their offering to Jerusalem by the hand of their own representative (1 Cor. 16:1-3). Consequently their party contained men from Macedonia, Gaius and Timothy from Galatia, Tychicus and Trophimus from Asia (Ephesus?). Paul would represent Corinth. Since it took so long for Paul to go through Macedonia on foot, he got no further than Philippi when the Passover arrived. Now the group would have to try and reach Jerusalem by Pentecost. The "us" in the text tells us that Paul was rejoined by Luke at Philippi. Apparently he agreed to go along as the representative of the generous Philippian church. The story will become richer in detail as Luke writes the rest of Acts from his diary notes. Note that verses 1-5 cover the period of a year. Dr. Luke was not along, therefore, the details are quite skimpy.

"Did Paul escape the would-be assassins?"

6. As soon as the Passover celebration ended, we sailed from Philippi and five days later we arrived in Troas. There we spent a week.

TROAS. Paul remained in Philippi for the seven days of Passover ceremonies. The Passover itself took place on the 14th of April and was immediately followed by the "days of unleavened bread." Paul and the Gentile Christians of Philippi celebrated this feast together. The year was 59 A.D. Then he and Dr. Luke boarded a ship for Troas where the other members of the party would be waiting for them. Having successfully eluded his enemies, Paul felt there was no need to continue on foot. The trip took five days. Because of the prevailing winds, it took longer to go from Philippi to Troas than in the opposite direction. It must have been hard for Paul to see the days slip by with the feast of Pentecost only two months away. To have to wait another seven days in Troas before he could secure passage to Jerusalem must have been agonizing. However he would put the time to good use. There were local Christians who could be strengthened.

"Did anything unusual happen at Troas?"

7. On Sunday evening we gathered for the fellowship meal. Paul was speaking and he continued until midnight because he expected to leave the next day

8. There were many lamps burning in the upper room where we were assembled, 9. and a young man named Eutychus was sitting on the windowsill. As Paul's preaching went on and on, the lad got sleepier and sleepier. Finally he dropped off completely and fell the three stories to the ground. When they picked him up, he was dead. 10. But Paul went down and threw himself across the lad. Then, picking him up in his arms and holding him close, he said, "Don't be alarmed, his soul is in him."

MEAL. Apparently a church had been organized at Troas with regularly scheduled meetings on the "first day of the week," as the Gk. text reads. This is the first clear evidence in the N.T. for the practice of Sunday worship. Other references merely imply it (1 Cor. 16:2; Jo. 20:19,26). The fellowship meal (love feast) would also include the communion. Since Paul's party had booked passage on a coastal vessel leaving in the morning, this was to be Paul's last night with them. The seven days of vs. 6 are now passed. The meetings were apparently held in the evening. Many of the believers would be slaves, and it was difficult for them to meet in the daytime. No doubt there were many long prayers, as also were Paul's discourses. Midnight came and he was still going strong. The church didn't bother with clocks in those days.

LAMPS. The meeting was held in an upper room, the third floor of a large family home. It was common, in that part of the world, to have a shop or storehouse on the first floor, live on the second and reserve the third for gatherings and special occasions. The third floor was always the most lavish and the choice place in the oriental home. Since oil was plentiful and cheap in this region, it was possible to have many lamps and torches. As the evening went on, the air in this upper room became heavy with smoke. A young man, who had perched himself on a window ledge, dropped off to sleep. As his body shifted, he rolled off the sill and fell the three stories to his death.

DEAD. Dr. Luke was likely the first to examine the body. Note that it is the physician who writes, "he was dead." In an action similar to that of Elijah (1 Ki. 17:21), Paul handled the body and announced the boy was alive. He did NOT say, "He is still alive." He couldn't. The boy was dead. He simply said the boy is alive. Paul wished to make no display of miraculous power, for this death was his own fault. He had pushed the service (justified or not) beyond the proper limit. The lad was not to blame. So the indwelling Lord indicated to Paul that while he was to restore the boy, he was also to MINIMIZE the miracle. Thus, while the evening was interrupted, things got back to normal quickly. Paul was able to bring to the brethren those things he felt they should have before he left. How many modern ministers would be willing to hush such a miracle for the sake of exalting the message of Jesus? In God's eyes, the miracle of lives changed by His Word is far greater than raising the dead. God can easily raise the dead, but shaping freewill creatures after His likeness is very hard.

"Did the church settle down after that?"

11. Then Paul went back upstairs again. After he had broken the bread and eaten, he resumed his discourse. It was dawn before he finished and finally left them. 12. As for the boy, he was taken home alive, much to the great comfort of everyone.

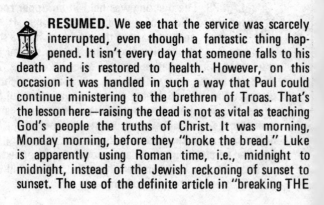

RESUMED. We see that the service was scarcely interrupted, even though a fantastic thing happened. It isn't every day that someone falls to his death and is restored to health. However, on this occasion it was handled in such a way that Paul could continue ministering to the brethren of Troas. That's the lesson here—raising the dead is not as vital as teaching God's people the truths of Christ. It was morning, Monday morning, before they "broke the bread." Luke is apparently using Roman time, i.e., midnight to midnight, instead of the Jewish reckoning of sunset to sunset. The use of the definite article in "breaking THE bread," refers to the communion. After the Lord's supper, they enjoyed their fellowship meal. It was daybreak before Paul finished his dialogue with them and said goodbye. His companions on this trip had already gone down and boarded the ship. Perhaps Paul stayed behind longer to make sure the lad was fully restored to health.

"Did Paul get to the boat in time to sail the rest of the way with his party?"

13. In the meantime we had gone on ahead and boarded the ship and set sail for Assos. Paul was to come overland and join us there. Actually he had planned to do this, wanting to go that far on foot. 14. So we met him at Assos and took him on board and together we went on to Mitylene. 15. From here we sailed to a point opposite Chios. The next day we crossed over to Samos, and the following day we arrived at Miletus. 16. Paul had decided to by-pass Ephesus, because he didn't want to spend any time in the province of Asia. He was in a big hurry, trying to reach Jerusalem by the day of Pentecost, if possible.

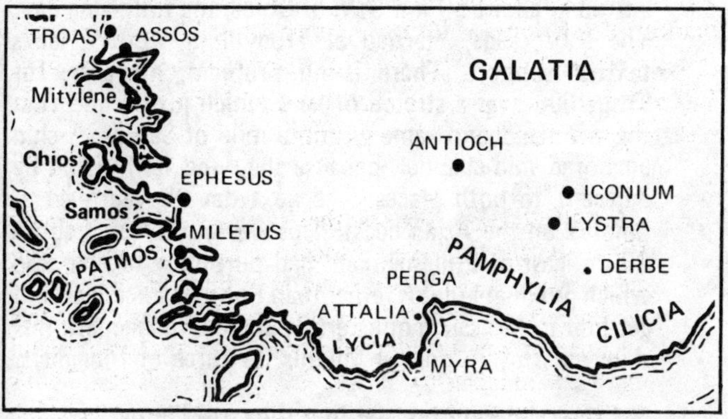

ON FOOT. Paul knew he could walk the 20 miles overland and reach Assos before his companions aboard the ship. The vessel had to go around Cape Lectum, whereas he took the direct route across the cape. Just why he did this after preaching all night, we're not told. It did allow him to spend a little more time with the believers of Troas, but he may have wished to be alone with the Lord. His mind was burdened. He knew he was supposed to go to Rome. The Lord had systematically been taking him along the backbone of the Roman Empire–Antioch in Syria, Ephesus, and then Rome. But he had chosen, instead, to return to Jerusalem and be there when the Gentile money was turned over to the Jewish Christians. So Paul's heart is not as light as it might have been were he already on his way to Rome (Acts 19:21). In his hurry to reach Jerusalem by Pentecost, he will pass up many opportunities to witness. Already he has elected to avoid the province of Asia, the scene of his greatest triumph. In his hurry to leave Assos, Paul left some baggage behind, including his Bible ("especially the parchments")–2 Tim. 4:13.

SAILED. Luke apparently loves the sea. His account contains details of each stop. When Paul boarded at Assos, the little ship went island hopping. The next day they reached the harbor of Mitylene some 35 mi. away. The next day they sailed another 40 mi. and dropped anchor off Chios. They reached Samos, an island about 50 mi. S.W. of Chios, the following day. The KJV reads, "tarried at Trogyllium," but it lacks textual support. There is no problem, however, for Trogyllium was a stretch of land which jutted out from the mainland and came within a mile of Samos. A ship anchored mid-channel (because the wind fell) would be adjacent to both places. The next day they arrived at Miletus on the Asian coast. This was a busy port about 30 mi. east of Ephesus. Paul had purposely taken a ship which put in at Miletus rather than Ephesus since it would get him to Jerusalem quicker. By some arrangement, this ship will stay in port at Miletus for three or four days.

"How did Paul use the free time at Miletus?"

17. However, after our arrival at Miletus, Paul sent a message to Ephesus, summoning the elders of the church to meet with him. 18. When they had come to him and gathered around him, he told them:

"You men are surely aware of my conduct throughout the time I was with you, from the very first day I set foot in Asia right up to this moment. 19. Therefore, you know that I have served the Lord humbly in spite of the heartache and tears I shed amid the trials that came upon me because of the scheming attacks of the Jews. 20. Yet when I was speaking with you, whether publicly or in the privacy of your own homes, did I once hold back anything you needed to hear? 21. To the contrary, I have repeatedly pressed but one message upon both Jews and Greeks—repentance toward God and faith in our Lord Jesus Christ."

GATHERED. So great was Paul's haste to reach Jerusalem, that he refused to stop at Ephesus. But when he found his ship was going to be delayed in Miletus several days, he sent for the elders of the Ephesian church. They traveled the 30 miles to be with him on his last day in port. There he gave them a farewell address calculated to encourage them and at the same time prepare them for what was coming. Paul senses there will be opposition to his teaching and he wants the Ephesian leaders ready for it. Luke was obviously present at this gathering, but he has given us the merest summary of what was said. Even so, we now have a sample of Paul's words to a Christian audience. In the past we have heard him address the Jewish audience in the synagogue of Pisidian Antioch and the pagan audiences of Lystra and Athens.

CONDUCT. Paul's first words are a defense of his manner of life and ministry among the Ephesians. Knowing all sorts of charges will be made against him, he appeals to the personal knowledge of his listeners. He reminds them of the HUMBLE way in which he served the Lord. This is vital since he knows he will later be charged with arrogance and high-handedness with the people. Holding himself up as an example, he asks them to remember his TENDERNESS. He was a man of tender spirit. He wept often. We think of him as a rough and daring man because he boldly charged into danger. But he also shed many tears. His tears were not for himself but those perishing without Christ and those who professed to know Jesus but lived wordly lives. He was TIRELESS in his work, going day and night and from house to house. He showed NO PREJUDICE, for he preached with a whole heart to Jew and Gentile alike. He had but ONE MESSAGE for all, the changed life of the person who exercises faith in the Lord Jesus. These are the things he would have them remember about himself after he has departed.

"Will Paul tell of his plans to go to Jerusalem?"

22. "And now, a prisoner of my own spirit, I am on my way to Jerusalem. I'm not sure what will happen to me there. 23. However, as I go from city to city, the Holy Spirit warns me that imprisonment and suffering await me. 24. But that doesn't bother me, for I am one who counts his work more precious than his life. All I care about is finishing the job the Lord gave me, proclaiming the good news of God's grace."

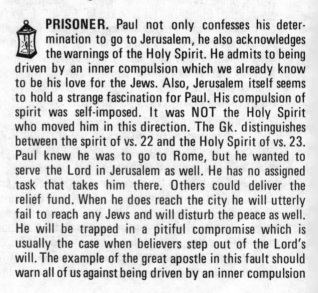

PRISONER. Paul not only confesses his determination to go to Jerusalem, he also acknowledges the warnings of the Holy Spirit. He admits to being driven by an inner compulsion which we already know to be his love for the Jews. Also, Jerusalem itself seems to hold a strange fascination for Paul. His compulsion of spirit was self-imposed. It was NOT the Holy Spirit who moved him in this direction. The Gk. distinguishes between the spirit of vs. 22 and the Holy Spirit of vs. 23. Paul knew he was to go to Rome, but he wanted to serve the Lord in Jerusalem as well. He has no assigned task that takes him there. Others could deliver the relief fund. When he does reach the city he will utterly fail to reach any Jews and will disturb the peace as well. He will be trapped in a pitiful compromise which is usually the case when believers step out of the Lord's will. The example of the great apostle in this fault should warn all of us against being driven by an inner compulsion that leads us contrary to God's will. It's easy for even the most humble Christian to become a slave to his own feelings and ambitions and remain unmoved by God's warnings.

WARNS. Paul was fully aware of the Spirit's warnings. It wasn't as if he didn't realize he was heading for trouble. He probably knew that imprisonment and suffering awaited him. But that didn't faze him. He was used to both. To his mind, self-preservation was a poor motive. Doing a good job for Jesus was all he cared about. So you know Satan would have to use a noble subtlety to reach him. The satanic wile was that he could serve Jesus at Jerusalem as well as any other place. If he gave his life there, what did it matter as long as he was serving the Lord. Tricky? Indeed. Paul knew God wanted him to go to Rome. Should he die in Jerusalem, the will of God would be frustrated. It took something that subtle to reach a man like Paul. The Spirit's warnings will increase as the party goes from port to port, but Paul will brush them off. He will not be detered, for he is already deceived, else why repeat the warnings? It seems almost impious to judge the great apostle, but the lesson in satanic power is too important to miss.

"How will Paul say goodbye?"

25. "So here I stand before you—you among whom I went about preaching the gospel—knowing full well that none of you will ever see me again. 26. Therefore, I must say this: as of this moment, should any of you be lost, I will in no way be responsible, 27. for I have given you the whole plan of God. There isn't anything I have held back from you."

YOU. Paul is speaking very tenderly to the Ephesians here, though his words might seem a little harsh. He knows these will be his last words to them for he is bound on a dangerous journey. He doesn't plan to come this way again. Whether he actually did or not is beside the point. At this juncture, he doesn't expect to see them any more. So it was a solemn moment. How differently we preachers would speak if we knew we were delivering our last words to our people. On this occasion, Paul relieves his conscience, claiming that he has discharged his responsibility to them all. Should any of them be unsaved, it would not be his fault. He has faithfully given them everything essential to salvation. By the "whole plan of God," he means he has not withheld anything they needed to profit in Christ. What an exalted feeling it must have given him to retire from Asia knowing his job was fully done.

28. "Watch out for yourselves first of all, and keep watch over all the flock which the Holy Spirit has entrusted to you as guardians. You are now the shepherd of the Lord's church which He purchased with His own blood."

GUARDIANS. Having relinquished his responsibility to the Ephesians, Paul now passes into the hands of the elders that charge which had been his own. As parents must one day let go of their children, so now had the day come for Paul to let go of his beloved Ephesians. It will be their task to shepherd the Lord's church. To add weight to his charge, and make them feel the responsibility was now theirs, he reminds them the church is none other than that which God purchased with the life-blood of His own Son. He uses the "flock" image. Besides it beautifully pictured the real role of the guardian. Shepherds were always responsible to the owner of the flock and had to render strict account for any who were lost or perished. Note how the shepherds were expected to maintain their own spirituality and keep their lives pure in order to assume watchfulness over others. The word "guardian" is the Greek word for bishops, but here it refers to ALL the elders regardless of any position they might have held within the church. ALL church leaders are "bishops" according to this verse.

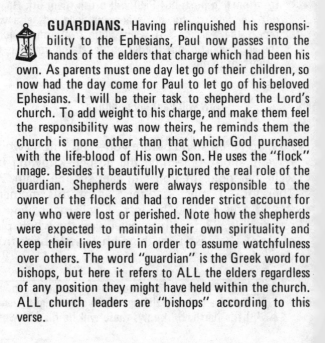

"Was Paul concerned for the future of the Asian churches?"

29. "I'm certain that after I have gone, vicious wolves will come in among you and ravage the flock. 30. From within your own ranks will come heretical teachers who will wean away disciples in order to attract a following. 31. That's why I say keep watch. Bear in mind the three years I spent with you and how I never failed, whether day or night, to counsel each of you, often with tears in my eyes."

WOLVES. Paul glances at the future. He foresees the trends which will develop in the Ephesian church. From his experiences in Corinth and Galatia, he knows that unscrupulous men will invade the church after his departure. They will be false teachers who will seduce the disciples in order to build a following. But even worse, there will be internal enemies as well. From within the bosom of the church will also come heretical teachers who will mercilessly devastate the flock. Therefore, he warns them to be on the alert and watch for these things. His predictions were true, these very things did occur. From the pastoral epistles we gather there was widespread revolt against Paul's teaching throughout the province of Asia. And from John's charge against the church at Ephesus, we see that she did indeed forsake her first love (Rev. 2:4). As did Jesus in the parable of the Good Shepherd, so here Paul pictures the true pastors as shepherds and false teachers as wolves.

COUNSEL. Paul holds himself up to the Ephesian leaders as an example of what a true shepherd should be. He asks them to keep in mind his conduct during his three years among them, particularly how he saw to it that each one was counseled in the truth. Today we call this "follow-up" work. Paul claims to have maintained personal watchcare over each of them. So desperate was he for them at times, that he broke down and wept before them. He is saying that a concern to the point of tears is needed to protect the flock of God. From this we learn how humble and gentle he was among God's people. In spite of his great knowledge and supernatural abilities, he was as though weak in their midst. He acted like a nobody, referring to himself as the "least of all saints." This is the mantle he would pass on to the elders this day at Miletus.

32. "Now I commend you to God and His gracious Word, which not only has the power to build you up, but guarantees your share in the glorious inheritance reserved for all those consecrated unto Him."

COMMEND. While Paul was with them, they could look to him for counsel. But once he departs, they will be on their own. To whom will they look then? To God, even as Paul did. So he commits them to God that they might shift their dependence from Paul to Him and trust Him for leadership and care. How did Paul do this? By prayer. But that's not all. He also commited them to the Word of God. It is no weak instrument, but a powerful and living agency. Those who read and obey it, find themselves headed for a fantastic inheritance. We find three stages to the power of the Word: (1) men are saved by it, (2) they are built-up as they submit to it, (3) by it they are guaranteed, in writing, a fabulous inheritance with all who are dedicated to the Lord. So, even though Paul leaves, they will have the constant presence of the Lord and His Word which they received from the lips of the apostle.

"In what other ways did Paul speak of himself as an example to these leaders?"

33. "I have never once coveted anyone's money or clothes. 34. You are fully aware that with my own two hands I earned enough for my own needs and those of my companions as well. 35. By my example of hard work and helping the poor, I have demonstrated the words of our Lord Jesus when

He said, 'Giving brings more happiness than receiving.' "

COVETED. Paul again reminds them of the example he set for them, this time in the matter of finances. He worked hard to make his own living, and did so with total detachment from any desire for wealth or goods. He had no longing for worldly power. He abandoned all such ambitions when he devoted his life to God. While orientals regarded fine apparel as a mark of wealth, Paul refused to waste any of his earnings adorning himself. Instead he used them to care for his barest needs. Any surplus went to provide for his companions and help the poor. Yet, Paul had a right to be cared for by those he served. God had divinely established that those who preach the gospel should derive their living from the gospel (1 Cor. 9:13,14). Even during his most difficult ministries, both at Ephesus and Corinth, he toiled at his craft so that he could maintain his independence and keep the gospel blameless.

EARNED. While Paul was entitled to a living from the gospel, he refused it and it gave him a marvelous independence. He had far more influence over people than he would have enjoyed otherwise. By his own example, Paul is saying it is a desirable thing for a pastor to be secularly independent of his people. Why else would the apostle be pleased with the work of his hands? Those congregations that feel their pastors are dependent on them often take advantage in dictating what he should teach. The pastor who feels dependent is strongly tempted to cater to the prejudices of his people. Paul seems to be saying that any minister who can work and support himself should do so and remain independent of people. Modern ministers would object, of course, claiming they couldn't do their job if they had to work. Yet, it is interesting to observe what Paul was able to accomplish even though he worked hard for his own living.

GIVING. Paul quotes words of the Lord Jesus which we do not find in the gospels. However, they echo the spirit of His teaching. We gather that it is good both to receive and to give, but one is MORE blessed than the other. It is natural for a person to want to GET for himself. That is, the carnal nature craves power, wealth, and influence. Yet giving is declared the higher function. Why? (1) The man who gives always belongs to himself. No one owns him. The receiver is always obligated to the giver. (2) The man who is constantly acquiring, becomes a slave to material things. The more he acquires, the more bound he becomes. Instead of detaching himself, he becomes a slave to his possessions. (3) God is a giver. The man who gives more and more, becomes more and more like the Lord. Paul cites himself as an example of the Lord's words. In that alone, he gave the Ephesians a terrific example to follow. It is remarkable that Paul should close his lofty exhortation speaking about money. In view of the appeals and abuses seen today, perhaps our generation needs this exhortation more than they did.

36. When Paul had finished his exhortation, he knelt down with them all and they prayed together. 37. The entire group was in tears. Weeping without shame, they threw their arms about Paul and kissed him goodbye, again and again. 38. What saddened them most were his words that they would never see him again. Then they accompanied him down to the ship.

PRAYED. Surely Paul's last words didn't come out easily. He was having great difficulty holding back the tears. As soon as he finished speaking, he dropped to his knees and the others followed suit. We learn from Justin Martyr, years later, that it was the custom of the church to stand for prayer in public places. This kneeling seems to have been occasioned by the strength of his emotions. They all knew they would never see him again. That thought so saddened the elders, they burst forth in abundant weeping. Those tears were proof of the intense regard they had for the apostle. A few years before they didn't know him from Adam, but since then, they had been welded into a spiritual brotherhood by the Holy Spirit. They were really one in Christ, and separation in the flesh was hard to bear. Just as Jesus parted with His friends in prayer, so now Paul says goodbye to his beloved elders, and it hurt. As genuine as this display of affection appears to be, it will be short lived. Before too long, Satan will turn these same tender hearts against Paul (2 Tim. 1:15). Oh, the power of the evil one.

ACCOMPANIED. It was hard for the elders to let Paul go. The text indicates that each took leave of him by embracing him and kissing him repeatedly. The emphatic form in Greek denotes both frequency and tenderness. Men kissing men is as common in the orient as the handshake is to us. Then the moment of parting arrived. The sun was coming up and the winds would begin shortly. So the elders went with him to the dock and saw him aboard. The ropes were loosened. The tide moved the ship out into the channel. As the wind caught the sail, the ship took Paul from their sight for the last time.

21 1. When we had finally torn ourselves away from the Ephesian brethren, we put out to sea and made a straight run to Cos. The next day we reached Rhodes and from there we went to Patara. 2. Here we found a ship that was going nonstop to Phoencia. We went aboard and it set sail immediately. 3. En route, we sighted the island of Cyprus off to our left, but we passed it by as we continued on to Syria. We put in at the port of Tyre for here the ship had a scheduled stop to unload cargo.

TORN. Paul was again on his way, but only after tearing himself from the Ephesian elders. "Torn away," is the fuller sense of the Gk. verb. The prevailing wind out of the N.E. was favorable, so the ship easily covered the 40 nautical miles in one day. The next day they sailed to Rhodes, another island to the S.E. of Cos. The harbor, which had the same name as the island, was marked by one of the seven wonders of the world. A gigantic brass statue of Apollo, so huge that ships could pass between its legs under full sail, straddled the entrance to the harbor. At last they came to Patara. This great port, along with its companion port at Myra, serviced vessels crossing the Mediterranean from Syria and Egypt. Here Paul disembarked the coastal vessel in hopes of finding a faster ship going directly to Syria.

NONSTOP. The missionaries learned of such a vessel which was about to depart. It was headed directly for the Syrian coast and thence to Palestine. This would be ideal. It was an ocean-going ship, rigged for high seas. Now the voyage would be faster. This ship didn't have to hug the coastline, but could cut directly across the Mediterranean, saving considerable time. The distance between Patara and Tyre is about 350 miles. With good winds the trip can be made in about 48 hours. It wasn't long before Paul and his companions sighted the hills of Cyprus off the port beam. Not too many hours past Cyprus, the ship put in at Tyre. This was one of the most famous cities of the ancient world. The vessel may have been carrying grain from the Black Sea or wine from the many islands of the Aegean. In any event it was due to spend seven days in Tyre unloading its cargo. Having gained so much time with a direct crossing of the Mediterranean, the party could afford to wait until the ship was ready to go on to Ptolemais.

"How did Paul use the seven days in Tyre?"

4. Knowing we were to be here seven days, we went ashore and sought out the disciples and spent the week with them. During that time, our hosts, inspired by the Holy Spirit, repeatedly warned Paul not to continue on to Jerusalem. 5. But when the week had passed, we returned to the ship. All the believers, along with their wives and children, came with us to the ship to see us off. And right there on the beach, we all knelt and prayed together and said goodbye to

each other. 6. Then we boarded and the disciples went back home.

WARNED. Determined to make his time count, Paul spent the week with the brethren of Tyre. Apparently a church had been started there, founded perhaps as a result of the persecutions which scattered the believers after the stoning of Stephen. Among the members are some with the gift of prophetic utterance. Through them, the Holy Spirit warned Paul once more that he was NOT to go to Jerusalem. The Gk. text makes it clear that the Holy Spirit impressed them to tell Paul not to go. The rest of the fellowship, now aware of what awaited Paul, did their best to dissuade him. But his mind was made up. He wasn't about to be moved from his plan to hand over the relief fund in person. If the Lord really wanted Paul to go to Jerusalem, it is difficult to understand these repeated warnings. It would be natural for his friends to be concerned for his safety, but warnings from God are something else.

CAME. Paul had never met the Christians of Tyre before. They were strangers to him when he landed. But after spending a week together, they became fast friends. The love which the Holy Spirit gives believers for each other, is quite different from the passing sentiment of the world. When they escorted him to the beach, the sorrow of parting was the same which was expressed at Miletus. Paul appreciated their love for him. He was grateful that they cared enough to warn him. He understood their concern. Jerusalem would be filled with pilgrims observing Pentecost, and they could be stirred against him in fanatical fury. However, he had come to the place where carrying out his inner compulsion to visit the city meant more than his personal safety. We wonder what the seamen thought at the sight of a group of Christians praying together on the beach. It must have been quite a scene.

7. After leaving Tyre, we sailed on to Ptolemais where we greeted the brethren and spent a day with them.

PTOLEMAIS. In O.T. times this port was known as AKKA, but today it is called Acre. In Paul's day it was a Roman colony and bore the name of the first king of Egypt. It was a fine port located some 30 miles south of Tyre. They could have easily walked the distance, but it was more convenient to leave the baggage on the ship and wait for it to take them to Ptolemais. It was the gateway to the interior of Palestine from the sea. For that reason it had been the scene of many wars. Invading armies frequently sought to enter Syria and Palestine by this route. At one time it was the most important harbor along that part of the coast. When the Romans built Caesarea and made it the seat of government, the trade fell off. It too had been evangelized by Greek speaking Christians who fled Jerusalem. This church was another choice by-product of the stoning of Stephen. While their ship sat in the harbor, Paul and his companions sought out the Christians and spent the day with them.

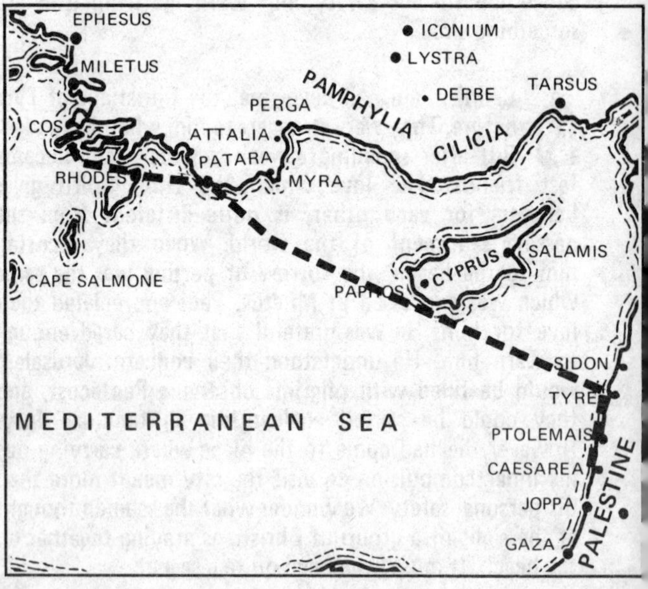

8. We left them and arrived in Caesarea the next day. Then we went to the home of Philip the evan

gelist, one of the original seven deacons, and stayed with him. 9. He had four unmarried daughters, all of whom possessed the gift of prophecy. 10. We had been there several days when a prophet named Agabus arrived from Judea. 11. He took Paul's belt and bound his own hands and feet with it. Then he announced, "Hear what the Holy Spirit says: The owner of this belt will be bound just like this by the Jews of Jerusalem and they will deliver him into the hands of the Gentiles."

PHILIP. The next day they went to Caesarea (perhaps on foot?) to the house of an old friend, "Philip the evangelist." It has been 20 years since we last saw Philip in Ch. 8, but Paul had visited him twice before while passing through the area on his way to Jerusalem. He is referred to as "the evangelist" to distinguish him from Philip of the Twelve. Not only had he been successful in evangelizing the towns of Samaria, but he had also properly cared for the spiritual needs of his own family. He has four daughters with the gift of prophecy who were devoting their lives to the gospel. While the text doesn't say so, it can be assumed that these girls also warned Paul against continuing on to Jerusalem. It is known that Philip and his daughters later migrated to the province of Asia where they spent their remaining days. Eusebius the historian says they lived to a great age and were useful in supplying information concerning early Christianity in Palestine.

AGABUS. Luke includes himself as an eyewitness to this scene with Agabus. It is an important event, for God has sent this man from Judea to deliver His final warning to Paul. This is the same Agabus who predicted, at Antioch, the coming famine in Judea. Using the attention-getting drama of the O.T. prophets, Agabus predicts Paul's arrest and imprisonment at Jerusalem. After the apostle had shunned the Spirit's clear warning as seen in vs. 4, the prophet's demonstration foretold the consequences of his decision to go to Jerusalem. The act of binding himself with Paul's belt was as much a part of his message as the words he spoke. The previous warnings had come to Paul along the way, but this one came by way of a man of God obviously sent to BLOCK his path. Note how Agabus was headed away from Jerusalem at a time when all Jews were flocking to that city. It is important to note Agabus' emphasis: "Hear what the Holy Spirit says," as if God Himself is warning Paul NOT to go to the city. In numerous ways the apostle has already been shown that this city was off limits to him. This was his last chance to turn around and head for Rome. It was the climax of all of God's warnings he had received enroute.

"How did Paul react to God's final warning?"

12. When we heard this, all of us, the local people included, began begging him not to go up to Jerusalem. 13. But Paul remained unmoved. "What do you mean by dampening my spirit with your tears? I am not only ready to suffer prison for the sake of the Lord Jesus, but to die as well." 14. When it was obvious that he was not about to be persuaded, we resigned ourselves to the fact and decided to say nothing more. Our final comment was, "The will of the Lord be done."

BEGGING. When Paul's companions heard Agabus repeat the Spirit's warning, they were even more alarmed. The local believers joined in begging Paul not to proceed to Jerusalem. If Agabus did not understand his prophecy to be a warning to Paul NOT to go to Jerusalem, he would have corrected the disciples as they pleaded with Paul. It is more likely that he joined them in begging Paul to refrain from going. The apostle felt the pressure of their pleas. He knew they were motivated by love, but he viewed it all as an attempt to soften his will. So he asked them to cease. Seeing the invincibility of his will, they stopped trying to persuade him. It was now obvious that he was "bound" and determined to go, even though he had no commission to do anything there for the Lord. Some have likened his situation to that of Jesus when Peter sought to dissuade Him from going to Jerusalem. But our Lord had a mission. He had a job to do there. Paul did not. He was driven by an inner compulsion to present the relief fund in person, that's all.

READY. One has to admire Paul's rugged spirit. It wasn't easy to resist the pleas of his friends. Yet, in his heart, he felt his decision was consistent with God's call on his life. He knew the Lord was building His church through him. He also knew that UNITY was uppermost in the Lord's mind. Had not Jesus prayed, "That they may be one, even as We are one" (John 17: 21). So it wasn't cussedness or stubbornness that impelled Paul. He believed what he was doing was in the Lord's interest. He saw how taking the offering to Jerusalem could WELD the Jewish and Gentile Christians together, and he wanted to be there to see that it did. His error, was committed in the line of duty for Jesus. It wasn't the BEST work that God had for him, but it was definitely a GOOD thing to try to unite the church. To our minds, with the advantage of hindsight, it would have been better had he heeded the Spirit's warning and turned his steps toward Rome. However, the one who wrote Rom. 8:28 will experience its great truth. He will still get to Rome—the hard way. Remember the lesson: the right motive doesn't justify disobedience to the known will of God.

"Where would Paul stay once their party reached Jerusalem?"

15. When it came time for us to leave, we packed all of our things and headed for Jerusalem. 16. Some of the disciples from Caesarea knew of a place where we could stay when we got there so they went along too. Accordingly they took us to the house of Mnason of Cyprus, a believer from the early days of the church. 17. So it was that we arrived in Jerusalem and received a warm welcome from the brethren.

MNASON. Now that they are but 2 days from Jerusalem, the big hurry is over. After spending a few days with their friends in Caesarea, they load their baggage on beasts of burden and head for the city. The offering likely included articles of clothing and other provisions as well as money, so pack animals would be needed. Further, they would need a place to stay once they arrived at their destination. It would have to provide space for their luggage as well as lodging. Apparently some of the Caesareans knew of a convenient place in Jerusalem, so they go along as part of the caravan. On arriving in the city, they are led to the home of Mnason. Not only does he have the needed accommodations, he is also one of the original Jerusalem Christians. Not every Jewish Christian would have been willing to receive the Gentiles in Paul's party. But this man was a Hellenist, therefore more liberal. The brethren with Mnason gave the missionaries a warm welcome. He must have been a dedicated man for he was also willing to let his home become the headquarters of the relief commission.

"After they got settled, how soon did Paul go into action?"

18. The next day Paul had us accompany him while he paid a visit to James. All of the elders of the church were present at this meeting. 19. After the usual exchange of greetings, Paul gave a detailed account of all that God had done among the Gentiles through his ministry. 20. When they heard his report, they gave much praise to God. But they had a discouraging word for him,

"Brother, you can see for yourself what we're up against here. Note the thousands of Jews who have become believers, but who are still vigorous supporters of the Law. 21. Now here's what most of them have heard about you. They've been told that you are teaching the Jews in Gentile countries to break away from the Law of Moses; that they ought not to circumcise their children or follow the traditions."

VISIT. We have reached the great moment for which Paul longed. His desperate rush to Jerusalem was to meet with the elders and present the offering. Paul now has an appointment with James. He was relieved to find them warm and receptive, for he wasn't sure how they would receive him or the offering. The Jews were reluctant to touch anything with a Gentile taint. Then Paul told of all that God had done through him during the five years since they had last seen him (18:22). Since then he had established great Christian centers on both sides of the Aegean, one at Corinth, the other at Ephesus. Then he introduced the representatives from the Gentile churches who had come with him. After that, came the great moment when he presented the offerings. The elders were not only glad to hear of God's grace being showered upon the Gentiles, the offerings were also a big help since many Christian Jews were being persecuted and deprived of their livelihood.

BUT. Then came the blow. Everything was fine with the report and the offerings, but PAUL HIMSELF was the fly in the ointment. If he had stayed away, there would have been no problem and the offerings MIGHT have accomplished the unity he sought. As thrilled as the elders were, they have to tell Paul the hard truth. He, himself, is the real threat to peace between Christians and Jews. The very thing he had come to do, he was defeating by his presence in the city. About that time, Paul must have thought about the Spirit's warnings. As grateful as the leaders are for his sacrifice, it is obvious they feel it would have been better had he not come in person. The city had not changed any toward him. He is still a hot potato. And the last thing the Jerusalem church needed was another disturbance triggered by Paul's presence in the city. The problem is so serious the elders make no attempt to conceal it.

TOLD. Once again Paul was a victim of the Judaizers. Rumors had spread among the Jewish Christians that Paul was teaching the foreign Jews to abandon circumcision and the Law. Of course, it wasn't true. He did, however, teach that circumcision and Law keeping had nothing to do with salvation (Gal. 2:15,16). But he never once said they were displeasing to God. He was well aware that many Jewish Christians retained the old customs as part of their worship. His old enemies from Asia would be in the city for the feast (Pentecost A.D. 59) and they wouldn't bother to make this distinction clear. As a result, Paul was pictured as an enemy of the Law. There were multitudes of Jews who embraced Christ who continued to love the Law. Even the apostles kept the ordinances, participated in the temple worship, and practiced the legal forms of purification. With most Christian Jews retaining their passion for the Law, it was easy for the Judaizers to stir resentment against Paul. He should have anticipated it.

"How does James propose to salvage the situation?"

22. "So now where do we stand in this? For the multitude is certainly going to learn of your arrival. 23. We have a suggestion if you would be willing to consider it: There are four men here who are under a vow. 24. Take them to the temple and join with them in the purification ceremony and pay for their expenses. Then they can shave their heads. By doing that, you will demonstrate to the people of the city that you do conform to the Law of Moses and uphold the ancestral traditions. In that way they will know the things they have been told about you simply aren't true."

STAND. The elders apparently have already given the problem some thought. James is tactful in offering the suggestion to Paul. It is clear, however, that the elders themselves knew that Paul had NOT attacked Judaism and in no way was he the enemy of Moses. They realized he had been misunderstood and misrepresented. Nevertheless, something has to be done about it and they have a suggestion. It should be noted that their suggestion is given to avoid the animosity of the legalistic Christians of Jerusalem. But wasn't this exactly what Peter had done years before when he visited Antioch (Gal. 2:12)? Is Paul prepared to do the same thing for which he rebuked Peter? Of course no one is thinking of that right now. James and the elders are seeking a way to avoid trouble in the city, and to have Paul publicly seen as a pious and observant Jew is the only answer they see to the problem. Without doubt, Paul is in a somewhat compromising situation. If he does this, and word of it gets back, will it not be difficult for the Gentile Christians to understand?

VOW. Anxious to remove the false impression that Paul was anti-Jewish, James and the others propose that he join with four Jewish Christians in discharging a Nazarite vow. This vow was commonly made at a time of personal danger, or because of a disease or accident. The maker of the vow was bound to let his hair grow uncut for a period of time. After that he would offer sacrifices in the temple and cut his hair. Often a poor man could not afford the sacrifices which consisted of a he-lamb, one ewe-lamb, one ram as well as cereal and drink offerings (Num. 6:14ff). It was regarded as a mark of piety for a wealthier person to bear the expenses of such sacrifices on behalf of the poor. The elders recommended that Paul include himself in the ceremony for a few days and then pay all the costs. Having already written to the Corinthians, "To the Jew, I became as a Jew, that I might gain the Jews," this suggestion was not out of line with his feelings. While Paul did try to strip the gospel of all Jewishness, it was never a part of his doctrine that the Jews should abandon their ceremonies.

25. "But as far as the believing Gentiles are concerned, you already have our judgment on that. We sent to them, in writing, that all we required of them was that they should abstain from meat offered to idols, from drinking blood, from eating unbled animals that have been strangled, and to keep themselves from immorality."

GENTILES. James is quick to let Paul know that the suggestion that he participate in a Nazarite vow does not mean they are going back on their judgment of Gentile liberty. They have not forgotten the working agreement which was approved by the Jerusalem council years before. To the contrary, they re-affirm it, repeating all four of the conditions. They have no thought of abrogating any part of it. All they want is for Paul to go into the temple and act like a Jew so that the Jewish Christians will see that he still loves the sacred things of the Law. If he will pay the fees demanded by the priests to release these four men from their vow, and at the same time participate in the vow himself, the elders believe it will conciliate the Judaizers and remove the hostility building toward him.

"Will Paul go along with this suggestion?"

26. Paul bowed to their request. And the next day, after arranging to go through the purification ritual with the four men, took them into the temple. There he gave notice that he would participate in the seven day ceremony at the completion of which he would offer his sacrifice along with the others.

BOWED. It must have been with some reluctance that Paul consented to join the four Nazarites in their purification. It was not that he was against such things. He himself had made a similar vow five years earlier at Cenchrea (18:18). But doing it to please the Jews is a far cry from obeying his call to the Gentiles. Many of the things he had written to the Galatians indicate he had no passion for Jewish custom. Later, when he writes to the Philippians, he will tell them he had come to regard those customs as rubbish (Phil. 3:8). In agreeing to the scheme, some have felt Paul compromised himself. At the very least, his wisdom in doing this is doubtful. There is no evidence it accomplished what he hoped for. Instead it got him into serious trouble. Paul will soon have cause to regret this trip to Jerusalem. It is going to take useful years out of his life and put an end to his public ministry. Apparently his love for the Jews overruled his good sense.

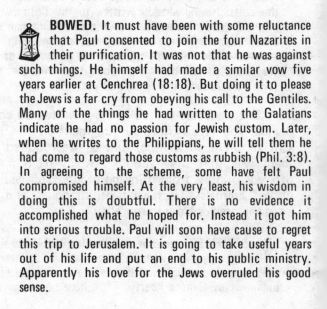

PURIFICATION. The last seven days of the Nazarite vow were ceremonial. It was in these that Paul agreed to participate. This meant he would have to spend a week with the four men, living with them in an inner chamber of the temple set aside for that purpose. First, Paul had to make arrangements with the priests. Once that was done, they could all go inside the temple to begin the seven days of ceremonies. Paul was required to stand with the men as their animals were offered in sacrifice. He also had to be present when their heads were shaved and the hair burned as a peace offering. When all offerings were finished, and the priests satisfied with the fees paid, they could pronounce the release of the four men from the vow. It is quite possible that Paul himself participated in some secondary vow of his own as an act of personal devotion. This would give the appearance that he still loved the Law of Moses. Yet he knew that all such things were fulfilled in Christ and that the ordinances of the Law were nailed to the cross (Col. 2:14-17). Paul should have stood his ground as he did when he confronted Peter in Antioch.

"How long will it be before Paul realizes his error?"

27. When the seven days were almost at an end, some Jews from Asia observed Paul in the temple. Whereupon they began to spread an alarm throughout the Jewish multitude. When a mob had formed, they seized Paul, 28. and started shouting to everyone, "Men of Israel, give us a hand with this man! He is the one who has been going all over telling everybody to despise our people, the Law, and this holy place. What's worse, he has now defiled our temple by bringing Gentiles into it." 29. They jumped to this conclusion having previously seen Trophimus the Ephesian with Paul on the city streets. Now they supposed he had brought him into the temple.

OBSERVED. When the seven days of the vow were almost up, some Jews from Asia (probably from Ephesus) spotted Paul in the inner area of the temple where he was staying. He was well known to many of the foreign Jews from those cities where Paul had stirred up their hatred. Only a few days before they had seen Paul in the company of Trophimus on the streets of Jerusalem. He too was well known as a Gentile from Ephesus. When they saw Paul with the four men taking their vows, they jumped to the conclusion that Trophimus was one of them. The place where they observed Paul was off limits to all Gentiles. To the mind of a Jew there was no worse offense than defiling the temple in this fashion. These words uttered by the Asian Jews were sufficient to inflame the mind of every Jew in the city. It was to be expected that Paul would run into trouble inasmuch as he was out of the will of God.

PLACE. Had the Jews been correct in their charges against Paul, he would be guilty of the worst crimes against Jewish Law. Paul was well known. By now his name was a byword in Israel. To say that he was the one who was preaching against the Law was enough to identify him. But to catch him in the act of bringing Gentiles into the temple was enough to cause a riot. In saying, "Men of Israel," the Asian Jews were appealing to the deep orthodoxy of the Jewish pilgrims who had thronged the city. The place where Paul was spotted was the Court of Women. It was to be entered by Jews only. It contained the temple treasury and various chambers where candidates stayed while completing the Nazarite vow. It was surrounded by a high wall and was reached by a flight of 14 steps. At the bottom of the stairway was the outer court, or Court of Gentiles where any stranger might enter to worship. But at the entrance to the stairs which lead up to the interior of the temple was a sign posted in Greek and Latin warning Gentiles to go no further on PAIN OF DEATH. The mob inside the temple proper incorrectly assumed that Paul had brought Trophimus up those stairs to the sacred interior of the temple.

"Will Paul be able to declare his innocence?"

30. Almost instantly the whole town was in turmoil and people came running together from all directions.

The mob took Paul and dragged him out of the temple and immediately the doors were closed behind them. 31. Just as they were preparing to kill Paul, word reached the commandant of the Roman garrison that all Jerusalem had exploded in a riot. 32. At once he summoned his troops with their officers and swooped down on the crowd. When the mob caught sight of the approaching commander and his forces, they stopped beating Paul.

DRAGGED. When the Jews of Asia shouted for help in dealing with Paul, mob action broke forth so fast there was no way for the apostle to declare his innocence. Word that he was defiling the temple with a Gentile shot through the city like a bolt of lightning. The people were stirred to the core. Those in the inner court lost no time in dragging Paul down the steps to the outer court. As the populace hastened to the scene, it seemed as if all Jerusalem had turned out. The people didn't want to kill Paul on the spot. That would defile their holy place with his blood. So they started dragging him outside the temple. Working as fast as they could, the Levites began closing all the temple doors. They didn't want the sanctity of the temple outraged by a boistrous crowd.

BEATING. Had it not been for the timely intervention of the Roman commander, Paul might not have lasted even a few minutes longer. So, faithful to His promise, God secured the safety of His servant. Word had reached the tribune that the city was in riot. He was already on the alert, for the Romans were particularly jumpy and watchful during the feasts. As soon as he received the news, he signaled some of his centurions to follow him. They raced down the stairs of the Tower of Antonia and charged into the mob. When the crowd saw them coming, if left off beating Paul. The commander didn't have far to go. His quarters were in the castle of Antonia at the N.W. corner of the temple. It was built by Herod the Great as a residence for the Roman governor when he was in Jerusalem. It also served as the barracks for around 4,000 men who were stationed there to keep the city in subjection. With its four towers ranging from 75 to 100 feet high, it was a staunch fortress.

33. The commandant stepped up and placed Paul under arrest, ordering him bound with double chains. Then he began asking the crowd just who this man was and what he had done. 34. Some started shouting one thing, some another, making it impossible for him to get at the truth. So, in the midst of the uproar, he ordered Paul taken into the barracks.

ARREST. Believing Paul to be some sort of a criminal, the commandant didn't hesitate to place him under arrest. Not only had the Jews jumped to a mistaken conclusion about Paul, so did the tribune. Regardless of what Paul had done, his case had to be handled legally and not by a mob. The tribune tried asking the confused crowd about Paul, but it was useless. So he ordered him taken into the barracks for questioning. To make sure Paul caused him no trouble, he cuffed him to two soldiers. Poor Paul. Imagine his feelings about now. It wasn't while preaching in the temple or reasoning in the synagogues or trying to reach Gentiles that he was arrested, but while engaging in an O.T. ritual. Agabus' words must have rung in his ears when those chains snapped on him (21:11). At that moment Paul's public ministry ended. He will never see Spain (Rom. 15:28). The rest of Acts records his trials, his journey to Rome, and closes with him in prison. That's an awful price to pay for trying to appease people with whom he has no business in the first place.

35. By the time they reached the stairs, the mob had become so violent, it was necessary for the soldiers to lift Paul to their shoulders and carry him. 36. Even then the crowd pressed close behind shouting, "Away with him!"

SHOULDERS. Unwilling to forego the pleasure of putting their victim to death, the mob pressed close upon the soldiers hoping to snatch Paul and make off with him through the crowd. The threat was so great it was necessary for the troopers to hoist the apostle to their shoulders. By now they had reached the stairs down which the commander and his men had just come. Paul's intentions had been honorable, but his noble ambition blew up in his face. He was ready to sacrifice himself to bring peace between the Jewish and Gentile believers, but he succeeded only in turning Jerusalem into a riot. Once before God had told Paul, "Hurry up and get out of Jerusalem fast, for they will not receive your testimony concerning Me" (22:18). Yet he had returned in the face of that warning, and many others, and was now under arrest with the crowd shouting, "Away with him!" Once again Paul was sampling the hardness of the Jewish heart. Those were the same words they had shouted after his Master 27 years before.

"Surely Paul would like an opportunity to speak to this large crowd?"

37. As Paul was about to be taken inside the barracks, he said to the commander, "May I have a word with you?" Whereupon the commander replied, "What! Do you know Greek? Then you are not the Egyptian who recently led a band of four thousand assassins into the wilderness?"

WORD. When the soldiers bearing Paul reached the top of the stairs and were about to enter the barracks, Paul spoke to the commander. The tribune was amazed to hear him make such a courteous request in educated Greek. At once he realized he may have been mistaken in his guess about Paul. He had supposed him to be an Egyptian who had appeared in the city earlier and stirred a revolt against Rome. Felix the procurator had sent a body of troops against this Egyptian and his followers, slaying a number of them, but the leader escaped. They were called assassins because they carried knives under their cloaks and stabbed their victims by stealth. Josephus says a number of false leaders appeared about this time. They induced many to become followers on the pretext of overthrowing the Romans. The tribune assumed that Paul was the escaped Egyptian who had now returned to the city for a second try. He interpreted the riot as the people's vengeance upon him for getting the city into trouble with Rome.

"Will Paul get a chance to speak to the people?"

39. "I am a Jew," said Paul, "a citizen of Tarsus in Cilicia, which is an important and honored city. Please, may I have your permission to speak to the people?" 40. The commander consented. So Paul, from this vantage point atop the stairs, gestured with his hands to get the attention of the people. A great hush fell over the crowd. Then Paul began speaking to them in their own Hebrew dialect:

PERMISSION. Paul assured the tribune he was not the Egyptian, but a Jew from an honored Roman city in Cilicia. We don't know why he didn't say he was a citizen of Rome. Tarsus was the capitol of Cilicia and famous for its university. Paul politely begs the commander for permission to address the people. Seemingly it is his fluent Greek that impresses the tribune rather than the rank of his home town. So he grants the permission, hoping to find out what this is all about and get the commotion settled. So Paul, from his elevated platform atop the stairs, gestures to the crowd below him in the outer court of the temple. The people were perplexed by this move. They no doubt are wondering why the tribune allowed it. But it worked. The people became silent. Their attention must have been even more focused when they heard him speaking in Aramaic, their own Hebrew tongue. Aramaic, a mixture of Syriac and Chaldee, was the common language throughout the Mid-East for all who did not speak Greek.

HUSH. Paul's facility with languages stood him in good stead. The moment he spoke to the tribune in fluent Greek, he had the man's complete attention. Then he shifts to Aramaic to win the attention of the crowd below. The mob beneath the tower was a little stunned to see Paul released from the grasp of the soldiers and allowed to speak. What a strange sight. Picture the apostle standing on a projection or balcony well above the heads of the people. See how quickly they settle down when he addresses them in their familiar Aramaic. Moments earlier this was a raging mob bent on beating him to death. Now they stare up at him in rapt silence. Stranger still is the fact that Paul wants so desperately to speak to these people who were so violently opposed to him, even to the point of shouting, "Away with him!"

22 1. "Brothers and fathers, listen to me. Give me a chance to speak in my own defense." 2. When they heard him saying these things in Aramaic, his audience became even quieter.

DEFENSE. Paul's passion for the Jews is astonishing. Moments before he was about to be murdered by this crowd. Now notice the gentleness in his voice. How he would love to win them for Jesus. He spoke to them in Palestinian Aramaic, not only because they would understand him better, but he wanted to win their sympathies by putting himself before them as a fellow Jew. When he says "brethren and fathers" in the mother tongue, the audience becomes even quieter. Whereas shouts of rage rang through the temple area earlier, one could now hear the wind whispering across the courts. Paul has his audience. But it will be the last time he will ever speak to the Jews of Jerusalem. Even so, he shouldn't be here. God had told him to let this city alone. Somehow he thinks the story of his amazing conversion will win their Jewish hearts. Note again how the pureness of Paul's motive does NOT justify his being out of God's will. He will suffer the consequences regardless of his noble intentions.

3. "I am a Jew, born in Tarsus of Cilicia, but raised in this city. I was trained under Gamaliel who thoroughly schooled me in every point of the Law

of our fathers. I was just as determined to honor God in everything as you all are today. 4. I persecuted to the death those who followed in this new way. I chained both men and women, throwing them into prison."

JEW. See how cleverly Paul suits his words to his audience. These people all knew him. He was once famous for his Jewish scholarship and quick advancement, possibly to a place in the Sanhedrin. His name had been a byword in all Jerusalem. Speaking to them in the mother tongue, he seeks to remind them of his former prestige among them. While he had not been born in the land, he was raised in Jerusalem. He had received his training at the feet of Gamaliel, the greatest of all their teachers of the Law. Because of his strict background, he became fired with zeal for God and the Law. So consuming was his zeal, that he became the number one enemy of Christianity, dedicated to wiping out the followers of this new way of life. With these words he hopes to remove suspicion from himself so that he can win them with the story of his conversion. But he is blinded by his ambition. He fails to realize that they will hate him all the more for his defection from that high position in their midst. To their minds he is a traitor.

5. "The high priest and the council of elders can testify that what I am saying is true. For I received letters from them addressed to our fellow Jews in Damascus, authorizing me to travel there as their emissary. So I started out, bent on arresting all the Christians who had fled there for refuge. I was planning on returning them to Jerusalem in chains. 6. While I was on this journey, not far from Damascus, a great light from heaven suddenly flashed all around me, 7. and I fell to the ground. At the same time I heard a voice saying to me, 'Saul, Saul, why are you persecuting Me?' 8. 'Tell me, Sir,' I asked, 'who are you?' And He said to me, 'I am Jesus of Nazareth, Whom you are persecuting.' 9. My companions saw the light, but

of course they didn't understand the voice of the Person speaking to me. 10. So I said, 'What shall I do, Lord?' And the Lord said to me, 'Get up and go into Damascus. There you will be told of the work God means for you to do.' 11. But since the brightness of the light blinded me, my companions had to lead me by the hand as I came into Damascus."

DAMASCUS. It has been more than 25 years since Paul received authority from the elders to arrest Christians in Damascus. Some of those elders were still alive to verify his claim. His mission, though, was to seize only those who had fled Jerusalem in the wake of the persecutions triggered by the stoning of Stephen. He was not to arrest any of the residents of Damascus. His purpose in telling this is to let his audience know that he once felt about Christians as they do. His words have the meaning of, "I was once what you are, a hater of all Christians." But this is merely a prelude. He means to show by the story that he was not simply persecuting Christians, but the Lord Himself. That's the bomb he wants to drop on his audience. If a zealous leader like himself could be wrong about Christ, might not his listeners be wrong also?

LIGHT. After confessing his fanatical zeal for the Law plus his hatred for all Christians, Paul moves to the story of his conversion. He hopes to penetrate them by recounting the event which turned the Christian-hater into a Christian himself. Accordingly he speaks of encountering the light which was so intense it drove him to the ground, and how there were communications between him and the risen Jesus Who appeared in that light. Paul's companions not only saw the light, but seemingly heard what sounded like a voice. At the very least they heard Paul talking to someone they could not see—someone he addressed as Lord. Paul's audience must have shivered when the apostle sent the convicting words, "I am Jesus of Nazareth," crashing down on them from the stairs. For further explanation of the event, readers may refer to Ch. 9 and the insight paragraphs under vss. 3-9. We learn here, however, that Paul's blindness was due to the light. We weren't told that in Ch. 9.

12. "Now there was a certain man in Damascus by the name of Ananias. He was highly respected by all of the Jews, for he was a very devout man who carefully observed every detail of the Law. 13. This man came and stood beside me. He said, 'Brother Saul, receive your sight!' The instant I looked up, I saw his face! 14. Then he said to me, 'The God of our fathers has chosen you as one who should know his will, to see the Righteous One, and to hear words from His lips. 15. This is because you are to be a witness for Him to all men, telling them what you have seen and heard. 16. So now, what are you waiting for? Get up and be baptized, and wash away your sins by calling on His name.' "

ANANIAS. Because Paul is here speaking to Jews, some of the details found in Ch. 9 are left out, yet other things not found in the earlier chapter are included. We pick up some new facts in this account of his Damascus experience. In reporting Ananias' visit, Paul first describes him as a strict and devout Jew. It is assumed that he is a Christian, but Paul is careful not to say so. He meticulously avoids any words that might offend his hearers. Ananias' first act was to serve as God's agent in restoring Paul's sight. Then he commissioned him to declare Christ before all men. Thus Paul was declared an apostle by means of a **Jewish** agency, a highly respected one at that. The words, "receive your sight," translated literally read, "Look up and see." So it was that when Paul looked up (by faith) he actually received his sight.

CHOSEN. When he came to Saul, Ananias already knew that God had ordained the persecutor as His apostle to the Gentiles. Ananias serves as God's representative in the HUMAN ordination. This little, unknown Jew commissioned the great apostle on the basis of three things: (1) Paul has been **chosen** to learn many things concerning God's will which had not yet been revealed, (2) he **saw** the Lord Jesus, though Paul tactfully uses the O.T. name for Messiah ("the Righteous One") to avoid offense, (3) he **heard** Jesus speak to him directly. Paul was DIVINELY ordained on the Damascus Rd., but the SPECIFICS of his new job, i.e., suffering for Christ and declaring Him to the Gentiles, were told to him at his HUMAN ordination by Ananias. See how Paul says "all men," to avoid using the hated name—Gentiles. It was SEEING and HEARING the Lord that made him an apostle. Jesus took control of his life that day. This experience qualified Paul as Judas' replacement. Matthias had no such experience. The latter was not commissioned by the Lord. We never hear of Matthias again (Acts 1:15-26).

BAPTIZED. This is CHRISTIAN baptism, the kind that signifies the cleansing work of Christ already done in a man's heart (see under 19:5). Ananias presses water baptism on Paul as something to be cared for at once. It would be his first ACT of faith. In so doing, he will testify to the cleansing he has received by "calling on His name." Please note, however, that this baptism has nothing to do with OBTAINING salvation. He is already "Brother Saul." This is NOT the baptism of Acts 2:38 to which the Jerusalem Jews submitted PRIOR to receiving the Holy Spirit. Paul ALREADY HAS the Spirit. The Lord established water baptism as the outward ratification of the salvation contract. God's part is to PROVIDE salvation, man's part is to ACCEPT it by faith. Water baptism is a PUBLIC announcement which says, "I accept what God has done for me." It is much like signing a contract. The O.T. ceremony ratifying the contract between God and the Israelites was circumcision. The N.T. ceremony ratifying the contract between God and the believer is water baptism. Many Christians are frozen in their progress because they have not publicly ratified the contract between them and God.

17. "Then one day after I had returned to Jerusalem, I was in the temple praying when I fell

into a trance. 18. Once again the Lord appeared and spoke to me. 'Hurry up,' He said, 'and get out of Jerusalem right now, for the people there will not believe your testimony concerning me.' 19. 'But Lord,' I protested, 'they all know full well how I used to go from one synagogue to another arresting and beating those who believed in You. 20. And they also know that when the blood of your witness Stephen was being shed, I stood there watching, wholly approving the action. In fact, I was in charge of the cloaks of those who stoned him.' 21. But the Lord overruled my protest. He said, 'Go! For I am sending you far away to the Gentiles.'"

TRANCE. Paul's commission, which came by the mouth of Ananias, was to be restated 3 years later when the apostle returned to Jerusalem. After spending those three years in the Lord's wilderness school, he came to Jerusalem. This was his first time back in the city after being saved (Ch. 9:26ff.). On this occasion he entered the temple, no doubt driven to prayer by the hostility of the Jews. It was during this time of urgent prayer that he fell into a trance. The trance is quite different from ordinary prayer. In a trance the usual order of life fades from consciousness while the soul occupies exclusively with the Lord. In this ecstatic state, Paul saw the Lord again. In the vision he was clearly told to leave the city of Jerusalem because the people there would not receive his testimony for Christ. It was made unmistakeably clear to Paul that his ministry was NOT to the Jews of this city, but Gentiles in far away lands. In the Gk. text, the Lord's "GO" is most emphatic.

PROTESTED. Paul argued with the Lord, hoping to talk Him out of the order. He believed that if the Jews could only hear the story of his amazing conversion, they'd face the truth of Christ. It seems to Paul, that the people of Jerusalem, knowing his former hatred for the Christians and his part in the murder of

Stephen, would be favorably inclined to what he had to say. But God knew better. So He summarily commanded him to get out of the city at once. It was then that the other Christians of Jerusalem got wind of the plot against his life and hastily took him out of town. Now here he is, 25 years later, trying to do what the Lord clearly told him NOT to do. Clearly, the Bible was not written to exalt any of its heroes, but to extoll the grace of God. Even though Paul is out of God's will, the Lord still means to use him. He will suffer, spending the rest of his life in prison because of his disobedience to God's clear command. But God's grace will prevail. The apostle finally surrenders. He will write those seven great prison epistles.

"How will the Jews react to Paul's mention of the Gentiles?"

22. Up to this point the crowd had quietly listened to Paul. But when he came to that hated word—Gentiles—they started shouting, "Kill him! A man like that should not be allowed on the earth! It is a disgrace to let such a fellow live!" 23. And because they were screaming and waving their clothes and throwing dust in the air, 24. the commander brought Paul inside the barracks and gave orders for the truth to be beaten out of him by scourging. The tribune was determined to find out why the crowds were shouting such things against Paul.

SHOUTING. Paul managed to hold the attention of his audience all through the story of his conversion. But when he mentioned that hated word, "Gentiles," the crowd exploded. He had implied that since the Jews did not want their inheritance through the Messiah, it would be given to the Gentiles ("dogs" to the Jews). That statement fell like a burning match on the gasoline of Jewish bigotry. The uproar was instantaneous. In every way possible, the crowd began shouting contempt for Paul, demanding his death. To them he was a monster who should be swept from the earth. If rocks had been at hand, both Paul and his soldier escort would have been stoned. Fortunately the courtyard was paved. However, they had to grab something, so they picked up handfulls of dust. Having just said what he did, the crowd was convinced that all the charges made against him were now true. From this point on they would not listen to another word he said. In fact, one reason for the uproar was to keep him from saying anything further.

KILL HIM. Though God had told him to leave this city alone, Paul felt his story couldn't miss in winning the Jews. But he was blinded by his love for his people. So he took it upon himself to try reaching them once more. His mistake provides a vital lesson. It is often thought that when a great leader defects from a religious movement an exodus is sure to follow. This is almost never the case. When a prominent priest, for example, defects from the Catholic church, he is not regarded as someone to follow, but as a traitor. Let a leader come out from Mormonism and will a host follow him? No, the other Mormons hate him for turning against his first love. Paul hoped that the Jews, recalling his former greatness in Judaism, would be impressed by his example. But it was a serious misjudgment of the Jewish mind. Far from producing any wholesale exodus from Judaism, Paul merely stirred up the hatred of the people of Jerusalem. They never forgave him for deserting his high place in their midst. God knew this. That's why He warned Paul not to come to the city.

SCOURGING. When the commander heard the new outburst of rioting, he was determined to get at the truth once and for all. This time he meant to extract it from Paul himself. So he ordered him taken into the barracks for scourging. Apparently he couldn't understand Paul's address in Aramaic and was unable to fathom the real issue between him and the Jews. He supposes Paul guilty of some great crime. So he decided to get to the bottom of it by subjecting Paul to an examination by scourging. Paul had been beaten a number of times according to his own testimony, but he had never been scourged. This was a peculiar form of Roman torture. The scourge consisted of leather thongs, fitted with bits of metal and bone, and attached to a heavy wooden handle so that an awful blow could be delivered. Each blow that landed tore bits of flesh from the victim. It didn't take too many such blows to kill a man. Most who suffered scourging were crippled for life. Paul was ordered stripped and bound for the ordeal, as was his Master before him.

25. And when they had him all stretched out and bound for lashing, Paul spoke up to the centurion standing there, "Is it legal for you to scourge a Roman citizen who hasn't been tried or convicted of any crime?" 26. As soon as the centurion heard this, he went to the commander about it. "What are you doing?" he asked, "This man is a Roman citizen!" 27. Whereupon the commander immediately went to Paul and said to him, "What's this I hear? Is it true that you are a Roman citizen?" "Indeed I am," answered Paul. 28. "So am I," enjoined the tribune, "but it cost me a fortune for the privilege." "Ah," said Paul, "but I am a citizen by birth."

LEGAL. Paul has been stripped of his clothing to expose his back to the scourge. Thongs held his arms fast to whipping posts so that he couldn't escape any of the blows. He didn't mind the bonds, they'd been foretold by the prophet Agabus. But being scourged was another matter. He could lose his life. So he spoke out, mentioning his citizenship. The moment he spoke of being an uncondemned Roman, the preparations were stopped. It was a serious offense against the emperor to scourge one of his citizens. Suddenly the whole garrison felt itself in danger of Roman power. The centurion hastened to the commander who became alarmed at the news and went quickly to Paul about it. No doubt it was hard for him to believe the bedraggled figure lashed to his whipping post was a Roman citizen. The tattered Paul didn't look like a man who could afford the cost of citizenship. He was surprised when Paul said he was a citizen by birth. As such it ranked higher than his own, though it cost him a fortune. It is not clear why Paul was reluctant to declare his citizenship, though we can assume he felt it would somehow hinder his ministry to the Jews if it were known.

CITIZEN. We are not told just how Paul's family came to acquire its citizenship. The mere fact that he was a citizen of Tarsus did not make him one. While it was a free city, it was not a Roman colony. It is a good guess that somewhere along the line, Paul's father or grandfather had rendered a great service to the emperor, some general, or administrator. And the citizenship had been conferred as a reward of merit. It was not uncommon for a person to be able to buy citizenship in those days. The more corrupt emperors saw it as a way to line their pockets, so that in time it lost its distinction. In the present case, however, Paul is able to make use of it to exempt himself from the terrible ordeal of scourging. A man did not have to prove his citizenship on the spot. He needed only to claim it. If he falsely claimed to be a citizen the penalty was even worse. Citizenship meant that one was a citizen of the CITY of Rome itself. Most of the subjects throughout the empire were not citizens of Rome, but of the various provinces. A person with citizenship enjoyed all the privileges of a free man in Rome, no matter in what part of the empire he lived.

"Did the revelation of Paul's citizenship change the situation much?"

29. As soon as they found out that Paul was a Roman, the men who were going to scourge him hurriedly untied him and fled the scene. The commander himself was greatly alarmed when he realized he had ordered a citizen placed in chains.

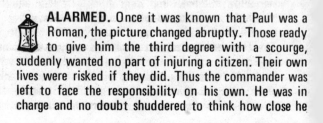

ALARMED. Once it was known that Paul was a Roman, the picture changed abruptly. Those ready to give him the third degree with a scourge, suddenly wanted no part of injuring a citizen. Their own lives were risked if they did. Thus the commander was left to face the responsibility on his own. He was in charge and no doubt shuddered to think how close he had come to ruining his career. Even now things had to be handled very carefully. The matter was far from settled. But what to do? Could he turn Paul lose with an apology, as did the magistrates at Philippi? Hardly. The Jews would surely slay the apostle. In that event the tribune could be charged with failure to protect a Roman citizen. Still, Paul had violated no Roman law. He couldn't be held as a criminal. The whole disturbance was due to some unknown issue between Paul and the Jews. The commander was now forced to conduct a proper investigation and discover the cause behind the riot which had occurred in the temple.

30. Now it became binding upon the commander to get at the bottom of the trouble between Paul and the Jews and find out exactly what it was he was accused of. So the next day he unshackled Paul and ordered the chief priests and whole Sanhedrin to assemble that he might bring Paul in for a confrontation with them.

CONFRONTATION. The commander had tried talking to the excited mob, but couldn't get straight answers. He didn't want to examine Paul any further, for he was an uncondemned Roman. Besides, it was a Jewish matter. Therefore, he would lay the problem before the responsible Jews of Jerusalem. That should shed some light on the situation. So that very night the tribune sent word to the elders of Israel to convene a meeting on the following day at which time he would bring his prisoner down to them. After the Jews had assembled, Paul was released from his chains (seemingly he had worn them during the night) and was brought down to the council chamber. He stood before the elders unfettered. Here he will be allowed to speak to see whether or not there is a case against him which the Sanhedrin should try. The nature of Paul's chains from this point on is rather obscure. It is possible that he wore no chains until Festus replaced Felix, and Felix left Paul bound as a favor to the Jews (Ch. 24:27). Paul seems to have enjoyed considerable freedom during that two year interval.

23 1. Staring intently at the council, Paul said, "Brethren, all of my life I have lived with a perfectly clear conscience before God. It is still clear at this moment." 2. Before Paul could say any more, the high priest, Ananias, ordered some of his attendants who were standing near Paul to strike him on the mouth. 3. "God is going to strike you!" retorted Paul. "You whitewashed wall! You sit there pretending to judge me according to the Law, yet you order me struck in violation of the Law!"

COUNCIL. That the Roman commander could assemble the Sanhedrin, at his own discretion, to try a religious matter, shows how completely the Jews were subject to Roman authority. But now the council has met. Paul is placed before his peers and given a chance to speak in his own defense. He eyes each of the members, watching to see if any will arise to accuse him. Since this is not an actual trial, but an investigation, Paul is allowed to speak first. Is this finally the moment for which Paul has waited so long—a chance to address the rulers of Israel? With his first words, the apostle practically dares the Sanhedrin to find anything wrong with his Jewish conduct since he turned to Christ. His reference to "clear conscience" means he has lived as a true and loyal Jew. It is this remark that offended the high priest, who no doubt felt it was up to the council to make that determination.

STRIKE. Before Paul could finish his first statement, the high priest signaled his attendants standing near Paul to strike the blow. It was customary to treat impudent witnesses in this fashion when they were in contempt of court. A shoe fitted with an iron heel was kept at hand for the purpose. When a witness made an outburst, he was struck across the mouth with the heel of the shoe. It was humbling since the shoe was held in low esteem. It touched the ground. The servants were ready to fire the blow at a motion of the high priest's hand. Josephus tells us that this Ananias was in office A.D. 47-59 and that he was a rascal. He loved violence and so thoroughly disgraced his office with his greed, that his scrooge-like ways became a byword among the people. He had once been deposed for stirring up trouble between the Galileans and the Samaritans. For political reasons, however, he was restored to office by the emperor Claudius. Without realizing it, Paul spoke prophetically concerning the fate of this man. He was later seized by loyalist Jews who slew him because of his pro-Roman activities.

WHITEWASHED. Paul had been through a lot. He'd been assaulted by a mob, spent the night in chains and now this—all for trying to minister to the people he loved—the Jews. Now the leader of his nation silences him with a cruel blow to the mouth, forbidding him to speak further in his own defense. Paul was a man of strong emotion who never once claimed perfection. Apparently he had come to the end of his patience and let fly at the high priest with a charge of his own. He called him a "whitewashed wall," Jewish slang for hypocrite. The metaphor pictures a dangerous, tottering wall that has been made to look like new with a coat of whitewash. This priest was a hypocrite. He was known to be lining his pockets with tithes intended for the common priests. And too, the blow itself was illegal. According to Jewish Law, Paul was innocent until found guilty. The priest violated the very Law he was pledged to uphold.

"How did the council react to Paul's outburst?"

4. Those standing close to Paul were shocked. "Do you dare to insult God's high priest?" they asked. 5. "I'm sorry brethren," said Paul, "I didn't dream he was the high priest. Had I known, I would not have said what I did, for it is written, 'You shall not speak evil of a ruler of your people.' "

INSULT. We don't think Paul meant to be sarcastic, but he could have. There is no way to gather the tenor of his voice from the text. If he meant his words to be biting, then it could read, "I didn't think anyone who spoke as he did could be the high priest."

It is also possible that he didn't recognize the man. This was not a regular session of the Sanhedrin so the high priest may not have been in his usual place nor wearing his robes. Further, Paul might not have known Ananias by sight since his trips to Jerusalem over the past twenty some years were quick visits with the Christian brethren. However, Paul could have seen Ananias during the time he lived in the temple with the four young men whom he sponsored in the completion of their nazarite vow. In any event, he was quick to apologize to those who heard his remark and probably to the high priest as well. His quick submission to the Law was a demonstration of his clear conscience with regard to the Jewish Law.

"What will be Paul's strategy for defending himself in this situation?"

6. Then Paul, noting how the Sanhedrin was divided into Sadducees and Pharisees, resorted to a strategy. He called out sharply, "Brethren, I am a Pharisee as were my fathers before me. I am on trial here today because I am one who believes in the resurrection of the dead!" 7. The moment he said that, the Pharisees and Sadducees began to quarrel among themselves. The assembly became divided into two opposing groups. 8. The Sadducees, you see, deny that there is any resurrection, or angels, or spirit-beings, while the Pharisees believe in all three.

STRATEGY. Paul was in a difficult situation. Of course, he had gotten himself there by coming to Jerusalem in the first place. Now the hostility against him was so great he could no longer defend himself. Further preaching of Christ seemed impossible. Then he hit upon a strategy that might salvage the situation. He called out the fact that he was a Pharisee. Apparently he had noticed how the Pharisees and Sadducees were collected in groups in this non-scheduled meeting. It occurred to him to exploit the bitter and heated issue which existed between them—the matter of the resurrection of the dead. "I'm on trial because I believe in the resurrection," he announced. That started a rumble which quickly divided the council into two camps, pitting the Pharisees and Sadducees against each other. Dr. Luke, who is a Gentile and without much knowledge of such things, explains to his Roman readers in vs. 8 why Paul's words caused the instantaneous division. The Pharisees believed that the hope of Israel was tied up in the resurrection. But the Sadducees denied not only the resurrection, but any existence of people as spirit-beings. They did believe in the Spirit of God, however.

RESURRECTION. Paul wasn't just clever in introducing the matter of the resurrection—he was inspired. It was more than a ruse to get himself out of trouble. He was ready to die for Jesus (21:13). Yet, it does sound strange to hear him declare himself a Pharisee, rather than a Christian. But that was part of the strategy. He was a Pharisee. By making reference to that fact, and the resurrection, he was subtly saying to the Pharisees present, "You also believe in the resurrection. You ought to be helping me instead of hindering what I am trying to do." In this way Paul was killing two birds with one stone. He knew the controversy sparked by his remark would remove attention from himself and fix it on a matter of which Jesus was the center. Now that's ingenious. If things went right, he would not only extricate himself from a tight spot, but be able to speak of Christ. The "hope of Israel" as Paul saw it, was the Lord Jesus, Who less than thirty years previously, had been raised from the dead. It would be easy for him to move from the doctrine of the resurrection to the One Who raised men from the dead and then identify Him as the HOPE of Israel.

"Did Paul's strategy work as he thought it might?"

9. Before long the whole place was in an uproar. Then some doctors of the Law who belong to the Pharisee party came forward and openly sided with Paul. With heated words they protested the charges against him. "We find nothing wrong with this man!" they said, "it is entirely possible that an angel or spirit did speak

to him as he says." 10. The arguing became so intense that the tribune was afraid they would tear Paul into pieces. So he sent his troops into the midst of the fracas with orders to get Paul out of there and safely back into the barracks.

UPROAR. The Pharisees had no love for Paul, but his words had placed them in the position of having to defend him. The Pharisees, doctors of the Law, were not about to let the Sadducees get away with indicting a man for believing in the resurrection. So they moved from their seats and stood behind him. Without meaning to support Paul's testimony concerning the vision, they argued that it was easily possible that an angel or spirit had spoken to him. They were probably looking directly at the Sadducees when they said it. That brought the Sadducee doctors from their seats in response. Paul was caught in the middle. The tribune, who was carefully watching the proceeding, saw that his prisoner was in grave danger. Both factions were trying to seize him. So he ordered his troops to rescue him. This inquiry having failed, Paul had to be preserved for a fairer hearing later on. He was a Roman citizen and entitled to due process.

11. That very night the Lord stood beside Paul and said to him, "Cheer up! For even as you have testified of Me to the people of Jerusalem, so must you also bear witness of Me in Rome!"

BESIDE. The Lord's miraculous appearances to bolster Paul's sagging spirit are most interesting. We don't know how many there were but three are recorded as taking place after his Damascus Road experience. He despaired at Corinth and the Lord lifted him up (18:9). There is the incident before us. A third occurs during his voyage to Rome (27:23). After each appearance He is on top again. Here is a man who did many miracles in the Lord's power, yet there were periods of depression in his own life which he could not handle. We can suppose they were due to satanic attacks. In each instance the Lord is obliged to bail him out.

Without this spiritual rescue, the apostle might have succomed. Even though Paul brought this present circumstance upon himself, God would not allow him to bear more than he could take (1 Cor. 10:13). However, it is interesting to note that God did let him hit bottom before He stepped in to rescue him.

CHEER UP. We can guess how defeated Paul must have felt sitting there in his cell in the castle of Antonia. He must have tortured himself with "What have I done?" He had brought no unity to the church. He had become involved with Jewish customs. He had turned the city to riot. He had even appealed to the Sanhedrin as a Pharisee. Surely he wasn't too proud of that. And now he was at the mercy of Roman officials. What now of his plans to go to Rome? Long before he set himself to visit Jerusalem, he knew the Lord wanted him to go to Rome (19:21). He was very discouraged. Then, as He had done before, the Lord stepped in to encourage His apostle (18:9). Paul couldn't take any more. So the Lord paid him a visit. He told him to cheer up, assuring him he would yet witness in Rome. The effect was magical. From then on Paul is no longer the victim of circumstances but the master. He is in complete charge of things as he trusts the Lord to get him to Rome.

12. In the morning a group of Jews met to form a conspiracy to kill Paul. They took an oath pledging themselves not to eat or drink until they had slain him. 13. There were more than forty of them involved in this plot. 14. The group went to the chief priests and elders with their scheme. "We've bound ourselves with a solemn oath," they said, "not to taste anything until we have killed Paul, 15. and we want you and the council to ask the commander to bring Paul back down for another hearing. He'll do it if you pretend you are going to conduct a thorough investigation and settle the case. Then we'll be all set to kill him before he gets here."

CONSPIRACY. The Jews had Paul in their grasp, but quick action on the part of the commander removed him to safety. That, of course, didn't end the bitterness. A band of forty men, probably of the fanatical political group known as the "zealots," laid plans to slay the apostle no matter what it cost. They swore to neither eat nor drink until the job was done. Then they went to the priests with their plot and secured their cooperation. The plan called for the council to request the tribune to return Paul to their chambers for further inquiry. Then they would spring an ambush somewhere along the way. Apparently the conspirators meant to attack the unsuspecting soldiers in order to get to Paul. They knew he would be well guarded. The act was sure to produce a heavy loss of life, but such was their hatred for Paul. Should their plan fail, relief from such a vow was provided for in the Jewish system. It seems that God, as He often does, is going to permit a testing to come to Paul after the great blessing of the vision.

"How will God deliver Paul from this plot?"

16. Now the son of Paul's sister heard of the planned ambush and somehow managed to gain entrance into the barracks and tell Paul. 17. Then Paul summoned one of the centurions. "Take this boy to the tribune," he said, "he has an important message for him." 18. So the officer, asking the boy to follow him, took him to the commander, "The prisoner, Paul," he said, "asked that this boy be brought to you. Apparently he has an important message for you." 19. The commander then took the boy by the hand and drew him aside that their conversation might not be overheard. "What is it you have to tell me," he asked. 20. "The Jews," replied the lad, "are going to ask you to bring Paul down to the council tomorrow, pretending they want to examine him more thoroughly. 21. But don't listen to them! More than forty of them are lying in ambush right now, jus

waiting to seize him. They mean business for they have taken a vow not to eat or drink until they have killed him. The trap is set. All they are waiting for is your decision." 22. The tribune then dismissed the boy with a strict warning, "Don't breathe a word of this to anyone."

SON. We should ever be amazed at God's resources to deliver us. Out of the blue comes word of a person we've never heard of. He's going to be God's means of saving Paul from this ambush. It is Paul's nephew. How he got wind of the plot we don't know. Perhaps he was a member of the zealot band that hatched the scheme and they didn't suspect his family connection with Paul. If so, he assumed a great risk in carrying the information to his uncle. Again he may have merely overheard the plot and hastened to Paul with the news. Here is an uninfluential, obscure young man who does an important job for God—and he's never heard from again. The Lord has a way of employing apparently insignificant means to accomplish great ends. He has unlimited resources for delivering us from trouble. The lad couldn't have been too young. His words to the tribune reflect more than youthful wisdom.

SUMMONED. That Paul was able to summon a centurion to his quarters and have him escort the boy to the tribune indicates that Paul was held in an honorable custody. As a Roman, he still retained his privileges, even though he was a prisoner. So far he is guilty only of disturbing the peace. In evidence of his privileged status, we see that he not only could receive visitors, but the centurions were obliged to heed his requests. Thus it was that the centurion promptly took the young man to the tribune. Even the commander displayed seriousness. He listened carefully to the lad. Here was one Roman who knew the temperment of the Jewish people. Therefore, he made up his mind at once to do something about it. Having already jeopardized his career by threatening the apostle, he now seems eager to protect him. The nephew was not retained, but permitted to leave with the warning that if he valued his life, he would keep the matter to himself.

23. The tribune then summoned two of his centurions and issued the following orders: "Get 200 fully equipped infantrymen ready to move out for Caesarea by nine o'clock tonight! Along with them, take 200 bowmen and 70 mounted cavalrymen. 24. And see that you provide mounts for Paul. I am holding you responsible for getting him safely to Felix the governor."

ORDERS. The tribune was a man of action. He hastily summoned two of his subordinate officers and ordered them to prepare a military escort. They were to take Paul to Caesarea under cover of darkness. Accordingly he told them to call out 470 men. The Gk. is a little uncertain as to whether there are 270 or 470, but the commander's determination suggests the latter. The force consisted of 200 heavily armed footmen, a small squadron of cavalrymen, and a body of bowmen, more than 10 times the number of reported assassins. It is clear he means to take no chances with his unusual prisoner. In view of the explosive nature of the tense situation, the size of the escort is not excessive. He really didn't know what might happen since he had already seen one huge riot because of this man. In any event, he feels it is his duty to get Paul safely out of the hands of the treacherous Jews. See how extra mounts were provided for Paul. Obviously they intended to run in relays. Likely all this was done as quickly as possible so the party could move out as soon as it was fully dark.

25. And then he addressed a letter to the governor which went something like this:

26. "Claudius Lysias, to his excellency, governor Felix: Greetings!

27. Here is a man who was seized by the Jews. They were close to killing him when I arrived with my troops and rescued him, having learned that he was a Roman citizen. 28. Wanting to know the charge they were making against him, I had him brought down to the Sanhedrin. 29. It was then that I discovered that he had done nothing worthy of death or imprisonment. Their accusations had to do with controversial matters of the Jewish Law. 30. However, since I have been informed that an attempt is to be made against his life, I am sending him to you at once. At the same time I am instructing his accusers to come before you and present their charges."

LETTER. The letter which the tribune wrote to Felix was longer than the verses above. Luke merely gives the gist of it, and how he got that, we don't know. This letter, which was required to be forwarded with prisoners, was part of the Roman system of justice. Interesting is the human way in which the tribune seeks to present himself in the best possible light. Note how he makes it appear that he rushed to Paul's rescue because he ALREADY knew he was a Roman citizen. The truth was, he didn't learn this until he had ordered him scourged. He first supposed the apostle to be an Egyptian traitor. But he doesn't mention that. It's too embarrassing. Then he says he had Paul investigated before the Sanhedrin, and as nearly as he could tell, the apostle was guilty of no crime. The furor was apparently over a theological matter. However, since a plot had been formed against the prisoner's life, Lysias felt it better to send his prisoner to Felix and let him make the final determination. He didn't dare turn Paul loose. The Jews would surely kill him, and then he'd be responsible for the death of a Roman citizen. That was itself a crime against Caesar.

"Was the tribune's maneuver successful?"

31. Carrying out their orders, the soldiers took Paul, and after marching all night, arrived in Antipatris.

32. The next morning, the foot soldiers returned to their barracks in Jerusalem, leaving it to the cavalry to take Paul the rest of the way. 33. Upon reaching Caesarea, they presented the letter to the governor and handed Paul over to him. 34. When he had read the letter, the governor asked what province Paul was from and was told he came from Cilicia. 35. "Very well then," said Felix, "I will hear your case myself after your accusers arrive." He then ordered Paul confined to quarters in Herod's palace.

ANTIPATRIS. The soldiers moved quickly to carry out the tribune's orders. Leaving by nine o'clock, or before, they traveled the 35 miles under forced march to reach Antipatris by morning. This city lay at the foot of the Judean hills. It was built overlooking the plains by Herod the Great who named the city after his father, Antipater. Once in Antipatris, the greater part of the danger was behind them. They were safely through the mountain passes where the possibility of an ambush was the greatest. So the foot soldiers turned around and headed back for Jerusalem where their presence might be needed in case a riot should occur. The Jews could become violent once it was discovered they had again lost their quarry. It was easy for the cavalry to escort Paul the remaining 27 miles to Caesarea. The route stretched across level plains inhabited mostly by Gentiles. Since extra mounts had been provided for Paul, they could move swiftly. Can you picture how Paul must have felt after riding a horse for 72 miles?

CONFINED. As soon as the cavalry reached Caesarea, Paul and the military letter (known as an eulogium) were both given over to governor Felix. The governor read the letter at once. Since it did not state the province of which Paul was a citizen, he asked the question. When he learned that Paul was from Cilicia, an imperial province, he agreed to hear the case. Inasmuch as Felix presided over an imperial court, the matter could be tried before him. The letter was favorable to Paul. So Felix was moved to provide him with an apartment in the governor's palace. It was fortunate that he was assigned nice quarters. They were to be his home for the next two years. He thinks the matter will be settled as soon as his case is heard, but the unscrupulous Felix will cause his imprisonment to be extended. At least, though, he is out of the hands of the Jews and on his way to Rome—the hard way.

24 1. Five days later Ananias the high priest arrived in Caesarea accompanied by some of the elders and an accomplished lawyer named Tertullus. They had come to present their case against Paul to the governor. 2. After Paul had been summoned into the courtroom, Tertullus was allowed to speak first. He stated his accusations against Paul in an address to the governor:

"We owe you so much, your excellency, for it is because of you personally that there is peace in our land. It is entirely due to your great wisdom that so many wonderful reforms have been made to raise the standard of living throughout the province. 3. No matter where we are, most excellent Felix, we feel obliged to acknowledge all the good you have done, and with truly thankful hearts."

LAWYER. We can imagine the fury which raged in the hearts of the Jews when tribune Lysias informed them that he had sent Paul to Caesarea, and that they themselves would have to make the journey to present their charges before governor Felix. The Jews speedily complied with the tribune's order. Not more than five days after Paul reached Caesarea, Ananias and his colleagues appeared on the scene. Paul's keen mind and penetrating oratory, as well as his ability to win audiences with his openness and fairness of speech were well known to the Jews. So they hired a Roman attorney to represent them in the matter. They needed someone familiar with courtroom procedure under Roman law and who could speak Greek fluently. Tertullus is probably a Hellenistic Jew. Again we must assume that far more was said than Luke reports in the few verses he devotes to Tertullus' address.

GOVERNOR. After the death of Herod Agrippa (see 12:23), Judea was once more added to the great Roman province of Syria to be presided over by governors. Antonius Felix was appointed governor of Judea in 52 and stayed in office until 58. Historians describe him as a cruel and lustful man. He was thoroughly corrupt, with a depraved thirst for plunder. His attainment of such a high post came as a result of contacts at Rome. His brother Pallus was a favorite of Emperor Claudius. Antonius and his brother were once slaves, but they had been freed by Antonia, the mother of Claudius. His influence at Rome gave Felix such protection that he felt he could get away with any crime. He often put down rebellions with bloody viciousness and lined his pockets with the proceeds of condemned properties. He even hired assassins to kill the high priest Jonathan. The historian Tacitus describes him as one who "exercised the powers of a king with the mind of a slave."

WISDOM. The silver tongued lawyer was allowed to speak first and present the charges against Paul. But he begins his address with gross flatteries designed to win the favor of the judge. He was an unscrupulous flatterer who didn't hesitate to pervert the truth to accomplish his purpose. It was common in those times to address rulers with flattering language, but Tertullus overdoes it. He praises Felix for bringing peace to the land and for many great reforms which he said helped the nation Israel. The truth was, he had put down some rebellions with terrible viciousness and had merely allowed the Jews to run their affairs without too much interference from him. That was the extent of his kindness. For this lawyer to direct such extravagant words to a man steeped in depravity and hated by the people, disgraced the noble profession he represented. The Jews disgraced their religion in hiring him.

4. "But I must not weary you further. What we ask, Sir, is that according to your customary kindness

you allow us to make a brief presentation of our case against this man. 5. We have found him to be a persistent troublemaker. He is constantly stirring up riots among the Jews all over the world. He is a ringleader of the sect of the Nazarenes. 6. Why he even tried to defile our temple. In fact that is what he was doing when we arrested him. [We were intending to try him according to our Law, 7. but then tribune Lysias stepped in and took him from us with great force, insisting that his accusers appear before you]. 8. Yet, all that is necessary is for you to question the man and you will discover very quickly that our charges against him are all true." 9. At this point the other Jews joined in asserting that the charges were indeed as stated.

CASE. We don't know how long Tertullus went on with his flattery, but apparently he noticed signs of impatience on the part of Felix. He quickly ended with a promise to be brief in presenting the charges. He then cited three specifics against Paul: (1) he was a dangerous pest who caused uprisings among the Jews throughout the empire, (2) he was a ringleader among the Nazarenes, (3) he was caught attempting to defile the temple. The first charge was serious. Should it be proved true, Felix would have to deal with it severely. It was a crime against the emperor. We're not sure what the second charge meant to Felix. The Romans considered Christianity a part of the Jewish religion. As such, it enjoyed the same protection under the law. It was possible the Jews were cleverly trying to divorce Christianity from Judaism so as to remove this protection.

ARRESTED. Tertullus stated the third charge carefully. He did not accuse Paul of taking Gentiles into the temple for that could not be proved. So he says he ATTEMPTED to defile the temple and was seized before he could do it. The portion of the text inside the brackets do not appear in the earliest mss. They are deleted by most authorities. For readers who might be interested, the bracketed portion would show Tertullus twisting the facts so that the Jews appeared to be doing their duty. They were merely maintaining law and order on the temple grounds when commander Lysias stepped in and wrested their prisoner from them with great violence. The glib lawyer is definitely trying to put Lysias in a bad light. He wants it to appear that the Jews were interrupted while making a lawful arrest. Lysias, of course, is not present to defend himself. The other Jews in Felix's court all seemed satisfied with Tertullus' work. They openly agreed with his statement of the charges.

"When will Paul get his chance to be heard?"

10. Then the governor motioned to Paul that it was his turn to speak. Paul arose and began:

"Just knowing, Sir, that you have presided over Jewish affairs for many years gives me a great deal of confidence as I make my defense. 11. No one is going to fool you. You have the means of finding out the facts for yourself. And one fact of which you are probably aware, is that it was no longer than twelve days ago that I arrived in Jerusalem to worship. 12. At no time was I ever found assembling a crowd or arguing with anyone in the vicinity of the temple, or in any of the synagogues, or in any part of the city itself. 13. Sir, it is impossible for them to prove any of the things of which they accuse me."

TURN. Note the fairness and order of this hearing. Contrast that with the treatment Paul received before the Sanhedrin where he was struck on the mouth on the high priest's orders. Under the protection of Roman arms he can now speak to the high priest and elders. True, he is defending himself before Felix, even so it gives him a final opportunity, though indirectly, to address the rulers of Israel at a time when they are forced to listen. Paul does not begin as did Tertullus, with flatteries and extravagant praise. He simply mentions a very important qualification which would allow the governor to render a good decision in this case, i.e., his experience and thorough knowledge of the Jews. It is a form of honest praise. Paul can make a confident defense because the man trying him knows the facts of the case or has the means of determining them.

WORSHIP. After expressing his pleasure in standing before someone qualified to judge the facts, Paul ventured to suppose that Felix knew only 12 days had passed since he arrived in Jerusalem to worship. The twelve days would include the time performing the Nazarite vow in the temple as well as the five days since his arrest. This fact bears powerfully on his case, for: (1) he has not had time to do the things charged against him, (2) his purpose in coming to Jerusalem in the first place was to WORSHIP God in accordance with the customs of the Jews. In other words, he had come to Jerusalem to fulfill the duties of the religion they now accuse him of renouncing. Paul is saying, their charge doesn't make sense. I didn't come to Jerusalem to defile the temple, but to worship in it. Since the whole event lay within the span of 12 days, Felix would have no trouble getting the complete information. Presenting his case on that basis would tend to indicate that Paul was open and honest. Did Paul compromise himself in saying he came to Jerusalem to worship? His primary purpose was clearly to bring the offering.

14. "However I will admit this: I do worship the God of our fathers according to the new Way, as we call it, although they refer to it as a sect. Yet I believe in the Jewish Law and all that is written in the Prophets. 15. Like my accusers, I too cherish our one hope in God and believe in the resurrection of all men, both the righteous and the wicked. 16. It is because I believe these things that I strive, no less than they, to live with a clear conscience before God and man."

ADMIT. Paul replied to Tertullus' second charge that he is a ringleader in the sect of the Nazarenes by boldly admitting that he does follow the new Way. But he denies that it is any kind of a newly formed heresy. All new movements are heretical in the eyes of the old. We do not worship some new deity, says Paul in answer to the third charge, but the ancestral God of Israel. Far from deviating from the vitals of the Jewish faith, I believe wholeheartedly in everything laid down in the Law and the Prophets. Beyond that, Paul said he cherished the one great hope—as did the bulk of the Jewish nation—belief in the resurrection of the dead. By this time in history, the doctrine of the resurrection was a part of Jewish orthodoxy, though the Sadducees, the minority party, didn't accept it. Felix was no doubt impressed with Paul's honesty. He freely admits his differences with the Jews as to the Way he worships God, but maintains his innocence in all matters pertaining to Roman law.

CONSCIENCE. The Jews listening to Paul were shocked by his testimony of a pure conscience. To them it meant he was claiming perfection under the Law. They didn't see how a traitor to Judaism could be ceremonially pure. A clear conscience, as far as the Jews were concerned, meant one had meticulously lived up to all the requirements of the Jewish code. But to Paul the meaning was much deeper. He knew that the conscience was a device planted by God in the hearts of men to guide them with respect to right and wrong. The man who heeds this inner voice becomes strong and powerful within his own person. He is forthright and can look any man in the eye and is usually fearless when opposed by evil. Felix sensed the truth of Paul's claim, for he discerned his great inner strength. What Paul was really claiming was a life free from treachery and craftiness, that he was a person who dealt openly and honestly with all men.

17. "After being away from Jerusalem for a number of years, I returned with a collection of money to aid my countrymen and make certain offerings.

18. I had just made these offerings and had completed my purification ceremony when some men found me in the temple. There was no crowd around me at the time, there was no disorder of any sort, yet I was accused—and by whom? By some Jews from the province of Asia, 19. who ought to be here before you if they have any real charges to make against me. 20. However, since they are not here, shouldn't these people who are here state specifically what it was they found me guilty of doing when I stood before the Sanhedrin? 21. There is no crime, unless they wish to charge me with shouting in their midst. For I did call out this statement, 'It is because of the resurrection of the dead that I am on trial here today.' "

RETURNED. Paul next explains to Felix the purpose of his visit to Jerusalem. Far from coming to the city to make trouble, as alleged by Tertullus, he had come on a mission of mercy and worship. His last visit was four years earlier. On this present occasion he had come to bring relief to his people and participate in the festival sacrifices. Instead of defiling the temple, he had actually gone there to purify himself. He was in a purified state when set upon by the Asian Jews. Since the Asian Jews were the ones who seized him in the temple, they should have been present in court as the prosecutors if they had a legitimate charge to make against him. However, since they are not there, Paul ends his defense by saying that his opponents who were present could themselves state that the Sanhedrin was unable to convict him of any offense, unless it was for his outburst concerning the resurrection. That, of course, was not a crime.

22. Then Felix, who was well informed about the Christians and their activities, adjourned the hearing. "When commander Lysias gets here," he said, "I will decide your case." 23. Then he ordered the centurions to keep Paul under house arrest, but not to prevent

any of his friends from coming to see him or ministering to his needs.

ADJOURNED. Felix was glad for the absence of Lysias. It gave him an excuse for adjourning the hearing without a decision. When the trial started, he no doubt expected to find in favor of the Jews. But after hearing Paul, he was probably convinced he should be set free. He apparently had considerable knowledge of Christianity and knew that the charges against Paul were unfounded. But that posed a serious problem. He didn't dare upset the Sanhedrin by acquitting Paul. He had already offended them enough with his high-handed administration of Jewish affairs. Right at this time Nero had come to power at Rome. And Felix's brother Pallus no longer enjoyed the same influence he had with Claudius. So he had to play it cool.

HOUSE ARREST. With conflicting statements between Paul and Tertullus, Felix could easily postpone his decision on the pretext of waiting for Lysias' testimony. But that left Paul dangling. He was not free, neither was he condemned. Aware of Paul's probable innocence, the governor gave orders that he was to be kept under house arrest. The restraint was relaxed even to the point of receiving visitors and gifts. It is also likely that he was neither shackled nor confined. Felix is shrewd. His ears perked up when Paul spoke of the relief fund. That meant money. Felix thought Paul had access to large funds and wealthy people. He possibly looked for a huge bribe. There were severe laws against bribery, but the greedy Felix no doubt hoped for an offer of money for the release of Paul as we see in verse 26 below. At least he seems to be going out of his way to make things comfortable for Paul.

24. It was some days later when Felix, accompanied by his Jewish wife, Drusilla, thought he would like to hear Paul again. Accordingly he sent for him that he might hear further what he had to say about faith in Christ Jesus. 25. But when Paul began to discuss justice, self-control, and the coming judgment, Felix

became frightened. "That will be all for now," he said, "you may go. I'll send for you again when I can find the time." 26. All along, though, he was secretly hoping Paul would offer him a bribe. That's why he kept sending for him. However, he was also interested in these frequent chats about spiritual things.

HEAR. Apparently Felix was extremely interested in Christianity. He saw in his celebrated visitor an opportunity to improve his knowledge of the Way. Returning from some place within the province, he and his wife Drusilla arranged themselves in an apartment of the palace where they could conveniently send for Paul and learn more of the Christian faith. Drusilla was a Jewess. She was known to be beautiful. She had been married to the King of Emesa, but Felix saw her and connived with a magician to lure her away from her husband and marry him. She was also the daughter of Herod Agrippa I [he beheaded James and imprisoned Peter], and no doubt had heard much about the Christians. Now she had the opportunity to examine one of the chief representatives of Christ close up. This particular interview may have been her idea. Some scholars believe she was fascinated by this man who was spreading the Christian faith throughout the world.

FRIGHTENED. The Greek indicates this was not a formal proceeding, but a private interview. Paul's audience consisted only of this licentious Roman and his profligate Jewish wife. The pair no doubt put questions to Paul, but he was able to turn the conversation to things they did NOT want to hear. Thus he spoke of justice to a corrupt judge, self-control to a man who was wholly self-indulgent, and of the coming judgment to one who needed to be reminded that even as he passed judgment on others, so would he one day stand before the Judge. Felix became alarmed. No one had talked to him like that for a long time. Now he was getting it from a prisoner. So great was the conviction that he ordered Paul back to his quarters, promising to hear more of the matter when he could find the time.

AGAIN. Felix found the time to hear Paul again. In fact he talked with him a number of times after that first interview. But he was never so close to the kingdom as that day when he and his wife heard Paul in their chamber and trembled with conviction. The Lord gave Felix every chance to repent and be saved, but as time went on, his interest turned from spiritual things to securing a bribe. Felix is interesting. Here was a man who was thoroughly corrupt, yet had a sufficient yearning after righteousness to feel shame. He was able to be moved by the truth. But after refusing the way of salvation that first time, it became easier for Felix to resist the Holy Spirit on each subsequent chat with Paul. This process is what the Bible calls "hardening of the heart." Felix observed the great interest the Christians showed in Paul and believed they would make a real sacrifice to secure his freedom. His love of money no doubt overpowered his desire to respond to the gospel.

27. This went on for two years until Felix was finally succeeded by Porcius Festus. Even then he did not release Paul, but ordered him detained in prison, hoping to placate the Jews.

SUCCEEDED. Two full years passed before Felix was replaced by Festus. What happened during that time we don't know. The Holy Spirit covers them with a mantle of silence. We'd like to know what Paul did and what happened to Timothy and Silas? Most scholars think Luke was with him and during that time gathered his material for volume I of this account (gospel of Luke). We do know that Paul had plenty of time to reflect on his ministry. By now he realizes the Lord was right in ordering him to stay out of Jerusalem. He is clearly in this mess for refusing to heed the repeated warnings of the Spirit. It must have been agonizing for him to see time slip by with the job still not done. Even so, he had the Lord's promise, "You will yet bear witness of Me in Rome" (23:11).

PLACATE. After two years had gone by, Felix was summoned to Rome. He was recalled by Emperor Nero over an outbreak between Jews and Gentiles in the city of Caesarea during which he had killed many leaders of the Jewish party. Also it appears that charges had been brought against him for maladministration of his province. Likely the Jews filed these charges because of his abuses and viciousness in handling disorders. When Nero replaced Felix with Porcius Festus, ordering him to Rome, he made no effort to right the wrong he had done Paul. Instead he added to the injustice. In an effort to placate the hostility of the Jews, his last official act was an order that Paul should remain a prisoner. He didn't dare turn him over to the Jews since he was Roman. Were Nero to learn of it, it would go hard with him.

FESTUS. We know very little about Porcius Festus, but he appears to be a better man than Felix. Seemingly he came to his post with a desire to have an honest administration. But he soon found himself in a hotbed of Jewish intrigue. So much turbulence had been created by his predecessor, that he was never able to bring things under control. He didn't last long. Josephus, the Jewish historian, tells us that he died in office after serving only two years. His death was the result of his despair in failing to cope with the plots of the Jews and the disorders sown by his predecessor. He had no real knowledge of Jewish affairs. This put Paul at a serious disadvantage. It was to be expected that the new governor was to do his best to win the favor of the Jews in the hope of bringing peace to the province. This, plus his inexperience in Jewish dealings, placed Paul in an unfavorable situation. This man would not be able to understand that Paul would be done away with if the Jews could get their hands on him.

25 1. Three days after Festus arrived in the
province to take office, he left Caesarea to go
up to Jerusalem. 2. There the chief priests and
other leaders of the Jews availed themselves of the
opportunity to mention their case against Paul. They
urgently begged Festus, 3. as a favor to them, to
bring him to Jerusalem. It was their intention to
waylay Paul and kill him in an ambush.

JERUSALEM. No sooner did the new governor take office than he was off to Jerusalem to see if he couldn't please his subjects with a prompt visit. This would show his desire to cooperate with the Jewish leaders and display his willingness to serve their best interests. This was his strategy for peace in the province. No sooner did he arrive in Jerusalem, however, than he found himself caught in a Jewish plot. The chief priests and other influential Jews had lost none of their bitterness against Paul. They saw in the new governor's inexperience a way to get their hands on the apostle. So they asked him to do them a favor. They wanted him to send to Caesarea and have Paul brought to Jerusalem for trial. They reminded him that governor Felix had done them the favor of keeping him in custody.

AMBUSH. Just as the Jews of Corinth had tried to persuade the new governor of Achaia (Gallio) shortly after he took office, so now do the Jerusalem Jews seek to persuade Festus before he has a chance to get the lay of the land. The fierce and fiery character of the Jews is seen in their persistence to kill Paul. They hope Festus will go along with their reasoning that it would be easier to bring Paul to Jerusalem than have the whole company of Jews make the trip to Caesarea. The Gk. implies they had already laid their plot, that the assassins were even then lying in wait. The trap was set even as the Jews pleaded with Festus. It is possible that some of the zealous forty, who had been frustrated in the earlier attempt, were among those ready to waylay Paul's party as it came to Jerusalem.

"Did Festus go along with this suggestion of the Jews?"

4. But Festus answered, "Paul is safely in custody in Caesarea, and I will be leaving for there myself, very shortly. 5. However, those of you who have the responsibility in this matter are invited to go with

me. If you have definite charges to make against this man, you will be able to present them there."

TO GO. Though Festus was new on the job, he wasn't about to be taken in by the Jews. He refuses their request. He must have suspected something was wrong when they were in such a hurry to try a man who had been in custody for two years. Perhaps he sensed some mischief was afoot and said no. He also explains that he doesn't expect to be in Jerusalem for any length of time. That wouldn't be conducive for a proper trial. Besides, the purpose of his visit was to get acquainted, not get involved in legal matters. He did want to get back to his capitol as fast as he could. As a courtesy to the Jews, he invited the responsible ones to come along with him, promising to hear the case as soon as he got back to Ceasarea.

6. So when the governor had spent a week with them, ten days at the most, he returned to Caesarea. The following day he took his seat in the courtroom and ordered Paul brought before him. 7. When Paul entered the room, the Jews who had come down from Jerusalem stood around him making all sorts of accusations. The charges were serious, yet all of them lacked for proof. 8. Speaking in his own defense, Paul said, "I have committed no crime against the Jewish Law, neither have I defiled the temple, nor yet have I stirred rebellion against the emperor."

ACCUSATIONS. Festus appears to be a man of his word. He stayed only briefly in Jerusalem. True to his word, he convened court on his return to Caesarea. As soon as the Jews saw Paul enter the courtroom, they began making their charges. Judging from Paul's answer, they apparently repeated the same charges that were made before Felix, i.e., crimes against the Law, the temple, and the emperor. Since there were no witnesses, no proof or evidence of any kind, Festus could see the charges were without foundation. All Paul had to do was deny each charge. Luke doesn't go into the details of Paul's defense, so likely he made the same presentation to Festus that he made to Felix. The most serious charge, as far as Festus was concerned, was that of fomenting unrest in the various provinces of the empire. The other charges, the Jewish matters, would not be of particular interest to him.

9. However, Festus had set his heart on doing the Jews a favor, so he asked Paul, "Would you be willing to go to Jerusalem and stand trial before me there?"

WILLING? Now we behold an evil in Festus. He had seen and heard enough to know that Paul was innocent and ought to be acquitted. But for the sake of ingratiating himself with the Jews, he was willing to put Paul through another trial—this time at Jerusalem. Popularity was dearer to him than justice. Since one of the charges was treason against the emperor, Festus would try the case. However, the other matters had no place in a Roman court. Likely Festus meant to clear Paul of the treason charge and let the Jews deal with the other matters. Due to his inexperience, Festus didn't know the viciousness and hatred of the Jews. Had he, he would have realized he was condemning a Roman to his death. Festus was in an awkward position. He knew the Jews couldn't try Paul on treason charges, yet he himself had no business hearing the Jewish charges. This put Paul in an untenable situation.

10. "No!" replied Paul. "I am standing before caesar's own tribunal right now. This is where I should be tried. I have not wronged the Jews, as you very well know. 11. If I am guilty of some capitol offense that deserves the death penalty, I'm ready to die for that. But if the charges these men have brought against me are false, no one has any right to turn me over to them so they can kill me. I demand my privilege as a Roman! I appeal to caesar!" 12. For a moment Festus turned aside to confer with his council of advisers

Then he gave his verdict to Paul. "You have appealed to caesar, to caesar you shall go."

APPEAL. Paul knew he didn't stand a chance at Jerusalem. Festus was a novice in office and the Sanhedrin would exploit his inexperience to achieve its own ends. No matter what Paul thought of Roman justice, he knew that Jewish influence was so great in Jerusalem that Roman justice couldn't be had there. So he made a sudden and unexpected move. He appealed to caesar. We can be sure he thought about it a long time, keeping it in reserve as a last possible resort. The move caught Festus off guard. He turned to his council of advisers. These were high officials of his administration and young political science students learning the ways of provincial government. It was clear to all that Paul was within his rights in making his appeal. Not only that, it solved a knotty problem for Festus. To him this was a way out of a difficult situation. So Festus announced his decision. Paul would go to Rome.

PRIVILEGE. It might be asked why Paul thought he would fare better at Rome than in Jerusalem, especially when the caesar was the young emperor Nero. Right at this time Nero's record as an administrator was very good. He had able men under him who sought to establish a high standard of justice throughout the empire. Paul had been treated well when he appeared before Gallio in Corinth and his confidence in justice at Rome remained strong. So he made the appeal. At Rome, at least, there would not be the overwhelming influence of the Jews. The position of the Jews at Rome was quite delicate. At this time they were out of favor with the ruling authorities. The idea that Paul made this appeal so that he could get to Rome is most unlikely. Paul had been ready to die at Jerusalem, however, he knew by now that his death at the hand of fanatical Jews would be a waste. He had more to gain for Christ by staying alive. Thus we see a real change in his attitude. Whereas he had stubbornly defied God's warnings not to go to Jerusalem with the offering, Paul now preferred to go to Rome and do the work the Lord had for him there.

"How will the inexperienced Festus explain the case to Rome?"

13. After some days had passed, king Agrippa and Bernice arrived in Caesarea to pay their respects to Festus. 14. Inasmuch as their visit extended over many days, Festus had an opportunity to lay Paul's case before the king. "There is a man here," he said, "a prisoner left by Felix. 15. And when I went to Jerusalem to visit the chief priests and elders of the Jews, they denounced him and wanted me to condemn him. 16. Of course, I let them know that it is not Roman custom to condemn a man until he has had a chance to meet his accusers face to face and be given an opportunity to defend himself."

VISIT. King Agrippa II and his sister (wife) Bernice appear on the scene to congratulate Festus on his appointment as governor of Palestine. Festus was happy to see them for they were regarded as authorities on Jewish affairs. The visit was proper since Agrippa ruled the kingdom immediately to the N.E. of Festus' province. Festus was embarrassed. He really didn't know how to draft the charges against Paul, and a bad report would reflect on his conduct in office. When the visit turned into an extended stay, it gave Festus the opportunity to seek their counsel. As the secular head of the Jewish church, Agrippa could advise Festus on the fine points of the Jews' religion. Festus knew Paul was innocent of the treason charge, but he was very confused about the other charges made by the Jews. He was hoping king Agrippa would unravel the mystery for him. Luke devotes considerable space to Agrippa's visit because his judgment will contribute significantly to Paul's fate at Rome.

AGRIPPA. This is Herod Agrippa II the son of Herod Agrippa I who beheaded James and imprisoned Peter. He was only 17 when his father was struck down by God that day when he was giving his speech (12:20-23). He was too young to succeed his father. When he came of age, after being educated at Rome, emperor Claudius gave him the tiny kingdom of

Chalcis, far north of Damascus, and the title of king to go with it. But as he grew in prominence, he was later given the tetrarchy of Philip, the area east and N.E. of the Sea of Galilee. Thus his kingdom joined the land governed by Festus. He was, for the most part, of Jewish blood. He was descended from the Maccabean priest-kings. He had a palace at Jerusalem and frequently made generous gifts to the temple. He was fairly well respected by the Jewish people. His personal life was another matter. He paid no attention to the Law. He was an adulterer, every bit as sensuous and pleasure loving as his sister Drusilla, who was married to the deposed governor Felix.

BERNICE. Bernice was an extremely beautiful Herodian princess. She was the sister of Herod Agrippa II (as was Drusilla, wife of Felix), but they lived together in an incestuous relationship. She had previously been married to her uncle who was also a Herod and ruler of Chalcis. But when he died, she went to stay with her brother who was then living at Rome. When their relationship caused some scandal, she married a second time. But when her brother came to power and was given the title of king, she left her husband and joined him as his queen. She was living with him at Caesarea Philippi when Festus arrived as governor of Palestine. She accompanied her brother when he came to pay his respects. As a Jewess and a Herodian, she would be very interested in Paul. Later she became the mistress of emperor Vespasian. When the public outcry against her was too great, she left him to become the mistress of his son Titus. It was he who destroyed Jerusalem in 70 A.D. A remarkable number of marriages took place between uncles and nieces in the Herod family.

17. "Since the Jews had come here with me I didn't keep them waiting. On the very next day I took my place on the judgment seat and ordered the man brought in. 18. But when his accusers rose to speak, their charges were not all what I expected. 19. Their quarrel with him had to do with things in their own

religion, which centered largely around one Jesus, a dead man, Whom Paul claims is alive. 20. I knew then the matter was beyond me, so I asked Paul if he would be willing to go to Jerusalem to face these charges there. 21. Then it was that he appealed to caesar. There wasn't anything for me to do but hold him in custody until I could send him to the emperor for his decision." 22. Then Agrippa said to Festus, "I've often wanted to hear this man speak." "You shall hear him," replied Festus, "tomorrow!"

CHARGES. When the Jews swarmed about the newly appointed governor, clamoring for Paul's death, Festus supposed the apostle had committed some great crime. But when the charges were aired in his court, he soon realized the whole fuss was over religious questions, matters beyond the concern of a provincial governor. Festus knew he was over his head, that's why he asked Paul if he would be willing to be tried by a more competent tribunal at Jerusalem. There may have been some honesty behind his question, but he was unaware of the viciousness of the Jews and their determination to do away with Paul. Religious matters were trivial to Festus. He regarded himself as a man of the world. Not only was he ignorant of Jewish affairs, he couldn't care less. All he cares about is Agrippa's help in framing the right kind of a charge sheet to be forwarded with Paul to Rome.

ONE JESUS. Festus, ignorant as he was of Jewish affairs, was astute enough to pick up the central issue in the Jews' charges. It seemed to focus on "one Jesus." The remark which Festus makes is one of disrespect. He is ignorant of the Lord. From this we gather that Jesus Himself was the real issue amidst the angry charges made by the Jews. Festus was too ignorant to catch the real significance. But this is not the case with Agrippa. His ears perked up at the mention of Jesus and Paul. The king was known to be a zealous Jew, regardless of his way of life. He had often heard of both of these men. And to think that the outstanding leader of the Christian movement was right there in the palace whets his interest. What may have seemed trivial to Festus, appears as a unique opportunity to Agrippa. He is thrilled to have Festus arrange an audience for the next day.

"Will Paul get an impartial hearing this time?"

23. So the next day Agrippa and Bernice came into the hearing room with great pomp and splendor accompanied by the military commanders and leading citizens of the town. Then, at a signal from Festus, Paul was brought in.

POMP. When the hour for Paul's hearing arrived, Herod Agrippa strode into the audience chamber with all the pomp and majesty for which the Herods were famous. This parade of splendor occurred on almost the very spot where his father, Agrippa I, was stricken by the Lord for his indulgence in pride. With Herod came the five tribunes commanding the military forces garrisoned at Caesarea. Some eminent townsmen were also present. Then Paul is brought in to stand before these plumed dignitaries. How stupid is the pomp of this world. What a fantasy of greatness it represents. These officials were great in their own eyes, the prisoner great in the eyes of God. For a brief moment they stood before one of God's great men. Now they are known only as people who threw away the greatest opportunity of life. How shocked they'd be to see how history has reversed their status, for later generations have venerated their prisoner and pitied them.

24. Then Festus made the introduction:

"King Agrippa, and all of you gentlemen here today, you see before you a man whom all the Jewish people, both here and at Jerusalem, claim should not be allowed to live. In fact they demand his death. 25. But as for myself, I am satisfied he has done nothing deserving of death. However, he has appealed to the emperor and I am obliged to send him to Rome. 26. Quite frankly, though, this creates a problem. What charges shall I send along with him. Actually there is nothing specific I can put in writing to his majesty. That's why I have brought him here before you all—especially before you, king Agrippa. I am hoping that as a result of this examination you may be able to tell me what to put in my letter. 27. It just doesn't make sense to forward a prisoner without indicating some charges against him."

INTRODUCTION. Note how Festus tried to give importance to the matter by alleging that the entire Jewish nation had appealed to him to do away with Paul. Perhaps his exaggeration was inspired by the ostentation and pomp of the Herods. The fact was, only certain of the leaders had cried out against the apostle. In his presentation to king Agrippa, Festus makes two significant confessions. The first is his strong testimony to Paul's innocence. These words may be the first indication we have that Festus really considered Paul to be innocent. After hearing all of the charges aired in his own court, he had concluded that the apostle had done nothing worthy of death. Under Roman justice he should have been set free. Had Festus harkened to his own convictions, he would have realized this and released Paul. That would have avoided the great problem now facing him.

SENSE. Festus' second confession had to do with the official embarrassment he felt now that Paul had appealed to caesar. It was out of Festus' hands. He was bound to send him to Rome to be tried by the emperor. But it was also his duty to specify the charges against him. But that was the problem. He could find no crimes. Had he acquitted Paul, as he was obliged to do after determining him to be innocent, this embarrassing situation would have been avoided. But now what was he to do? He knew there was no way to forward a prisoner without a proper charge sheet. But how could he write such a letter without incriminating himself? He was hoping Agrippa would be able to come up with an answer. He had the right man. There was scarcely a more competent adviser on Jewish affairs than Agrippa. After all, he was the titular king of the Jews with much interest and experience in Jewish matters.

26 1. Then Agrippa said to Paul, "You have our permission to tell your side of the story." So Paul, gesturing his thanks to the king, proceeded with his defense.

2. "King Agrippa, I consider myself fortunate to be able to make my defense before you today and to answer the charges brought against me by the Jews. 3. No one is more familiar with their customs and controversies than you. Therefore, I beg you to be patient and hear me out."

PERMISSION. Festus turned the proceedings over to Agrippa. In a lordly manner, the king gives Paul permission to speak. It was customary for a prisoner to gesture his thanks to the court, so Paul waved his gratitude to the king. It also indicated that it was to the king that Paul meant to address himself. The speech is essentially the same as that which he made on the steps of the castle of Antonia, but the tone and atmosphere will be suited to his audience. It will be a long speech with only a brief synopsis recorded here. Paul begs Agrippa to hear him out. He is sure the king is interested enough to listen to a lengthy statement. Governor Festus will become bored with the whole thing. This Roman has no interest in Jewish affairs.

FORTUNATE. Paul is most courteous as he begins his fifth defense of himself and his faith. He remains poised, unwearied, as he faces this latest of a series of ordeals. He doesn't belittle himself by resorting to flattery. He is not cringing before this monarch. He keeps himself above foolish praise. However, he really was grateful to be before the king. So his opening words are truthful courtesy. His thanks were sincere. Paul's chain may have rattled as he gestured to the king. Likely it was a token chain, symbolic of his house arrest. It was a great advantage for him to be able to speak before Agrippa. Felix and Festus, before whom he had defended himself earlier, knew little of Jewish customs. They couldn't possibly judge Paul in the light of Jewish Law. But it was different with Agrippa. He was a Jew. He lived as a Jew among his own people for a considerable time. As the king of the Jews, he was expert in Jewish customs and doctrines. It would be very clear to this man that Paul had done nothing which violated Jewish Law, let alone be guilty of treason against the emperor.

4. "The fact that my entire life from boyhood on has been spent among my own people in Jerusalem, is well known to the Jews. 5. Having known me for so long, they can testify, if they would, that I have lived as a Pharisee, the strictest sect of our religion. 6. The only reason I am here is because of my hope in the promise which God made to our fathers. 7. Do not our twelve tribes ceaselessly serve God day and night in hope of obtaining this very promise? It is because of this hope, your majesty, that I am being accused by the Jews. 8. What I don't understand is why it is right for them to embrace this hope and wrong for me to do so. Since when is it a crime to believe that God raises the dead? And why does it seem so incredible to men like you that God can do such a thing?"

PHARISEE. After expressing his satisfaction with Agrippa as his judge, Paul made a statement concerning his Jewishness. Though born in Tarsus, he had been sent to Jerusalem at a very early age to be reared in the school of Gamaliel. Thus his life, from boyhood on, was not spent in an obscure province, but in the heart of Jewry. He insists that he was well known by the Jews of Jerusalem. And in addition, known as one of the strictest Pharisees. When it came to observing the Law and keeping the customs of the fathers, the Pharisees were more dedicated than anyone else. Paul had so devoted himself to being a Pharisee, that all of his thoughts and actions were an embodiment of Pharisaism. He was a fanatical Pharisee. So it is NOT for being anti-Jewish that he is on trial, it has to be something else. Then he names that something else—the hope of Israel.

HOPE. Agrippa was not surprised to learn that Paul believed in a Messiah. He knew all Pharisees staunchly believed God would one day keep His promise made to the fathers of the nation centuries ago. It was this hope that gave life and meaning to the whole sacrificial system. So Paul is asking the king, why am I on trial for declaring something that is believed by Jews in general? More than that, look who it is that is accusing me of this crime—THE JEWS THEMSELVES—the very people who believe as I do! Paul made the resurrection of Jesus the central point of his defense because He believed his arrest and trial centered on that issue. But why, he asks, should any Jew be on trial for believing God had kept His promise. This was not just a clever defense. Paul honestly felt that those who shared the hope of a coming deliverer, ought to be thrilled with someone who was raised in vindication of God's promise to the fathers. And who, by His resurrection, demonstrated Himself to be Israel's long awaited Messiah (Rom. 1:4).

9. "There was a time when I thought it my sacred duty to oppose the claims of Jesus of Nazareth with all of my being. 10. And this I did there in the city of Jerusalem. Acting under authority granted me by the chief priests, I threw many of God's faithful ones into prison. When it came time for them to be sentenced to death, I voted against them. 11. Again and again I would go into the synagogues seeking to force them to curse the Lord by torturing them. So great was my rage, that I would follow them into foreign cities to persecute them."

OPPOSE. Paul advises Agrippa that he knows how the Jews feel. He once felt that way himself. At one time he thought it was his duty to frustrate the cause of Christ. Armed with temple authority, he led a ferocious campaign to wipe out the Christians. But he didn't really want to do it by killing them. That only produced martyrs. He preferred instead, torturing them to make them curse Jesus' name. Of course when that wasn't successful, they were killed. It seems the Christians preferred death to apostasy. Numbers of them were put to death. In sketching his terrible persecutions of the saints, Paul alleges how he (1) threw them in prison, (2) voted for their deaths (indicating that more than Stephen was slain), and (3) shouted his hatred against them while they were being executed. This is perhaps one of the clearest statements to the effect that Christians were indeed slain.

12. "It was on such a mission that I was making my way to Damascus with the full authority and commission of the chief priests. 13. And while I was traveling at midday, your majesty, I saw a light from the sky that surpassed the brightness of the sun. It shone all around me and those traveling with me. 14. We all fell to the ground. Then I heard a voice calling to me in the Hebrew dialect, 'Saul, Saul, why do you persecute Me? Isn't it hard for you to go on like this, kicking against the sharp goad?' 15. 'Who are you, Sir?' I asked. And the Lord replied, 'I am Jesus, the One you are persecuting.' "

LIGHT. We've met this wonderful story of Paul's conversion twice before, but this time we gain additional details. Here we find that the light not only shone upon Paul, but upon his companions as well. We observe too that his companions also fell to the earth with him. It is here, and not in the other accounts that we have the Lord's reference to the proverb, "kicking against the goad." Speaking in Aramaic, (the Hebrew dialect), the goad proverb was based on agricultural life. The plowman would carry a goad (long pointed stick to guide the beast) in one hand and steer his plow with the other as he walked behind the oxen. When the ox rebelled against his master and kicked against the goad, he merely punished himself further. The Lord's words reveal that Paul was already half convicted that the Christian cause was true. Very likely the logic of Stephen's arguments had gotten to him and his fury against the church was an attempt to drown the conviction stirring within him. It blossomed into realization when he met Jesus in Person on the Damascus Road.

16."'Get up on your feet! Stand tall! For I have appeared unto you for the purpose of appointing you as My minister and My witness. You are to tell people everywhere what you have seen of Me here today, and other things that I will reveal when I appear to you in the future. 17. I will deliver you from the hands of your own people as well as from the Gentiles to whom I now send you.' "

APPOINTING. The Lord orders Paul to rise from the dust. He is not being punished for persecuting the church. The purpose of this manifestation, as Jesus explains it, is to present him with a divine commission. That was startling. Paul undoubtedly expected to be wiped out. Instead he finds himself appointed as a personal minister of Jesus with the special task of carrying His exciting news to the Gentiles. He is to tell everyone, including the Jews, what he had seen this day, as well as other revelations to come. Simultaneously with his commission, Paul received a guarantee of divine protection whenever his ministry exposed him to danger. In unfolding the story to king Agrippa, Paul has apparently merged the details supplied him by Ananias as well as those things told him by the Lord three years later when he saw Him in the temple (22:12ff).

18. " 'You are to open the spiritual eyes of the Gentiles so that they can receive the truth and turn from Satan's enslaving darkness to God's liberating light. Then, through faith in Me, they will have their sins forgiven and take their place among the people of God.' "

GENTILES. Paul explains the terms of his commission. His ministry is to do four things for the Gentiles: (1) open and awaken their minds to God's truth. This would allow them to distinguish between what was false (darkness) and what was true (light). (2) Then they would be in a position to turn from Satan's enslaving error. The good news was to deliver them from the power of the devil. (3) Once they choose the truth of God, and place their faith in Christ, they receive the total forgiveness of their sins. (4) This act earns them a place among God's own people. The announcing of the news that the Gentiles were to have an EQUAL SHARE of the inheritance of God's people was the unique and startling aspect of Paul's ministry. It is not likely that Agrippa understood the full significance of what Paul was saying with respect to the Gentiles. The truth was almost too startling for his Jewish mind to grasp.

19. "O king Agrippa, how could I disobey that heavenly vision? I couldn't. 20. So beginning with those in Damascus, then in Jerusalem and throughout Judea, the Gentiles included, I challenged men to repent and turn to God. I further required them to prove their repentance by doing those things which characterized a changed life. 21. This is why the Jews arrested me in the temple and tried to murder me. 22. But having been helped by God, I am still alive and able to bring my message to all, small and great alike. Everything about my preaching is in strict accord with the predictions of the Prophets and Moses. 23. They themselves spoke of the Messiah's suffering, and His being the first to rise from the dead, and how He would proclaim the light of salvation to both Jews and Gentiles."

DISOBEY. After describing his confrontation with Christ, Paul tells of his determination to obey the call. How could he refuse a commission that came with such a manifestation of power. In obedience to this commission, he began asking men to repent and back up their repentance with a changed life. He always insisted on good works, though never as the basis of salvation. To him they were the natural consequence of being saved. If no works followed a person's profession of faith, then Paul regarded his testimony as suspect. James called such a profession "dead faith" (Ja. 2:17). It was while obeying this commission, he says, that he was seized by the Jews. But God, faithful to His promise, delivered him out of their hands so that he was now alive to tell the king of the Lord's delivering power. Paul claimed he was spared to witness to all men, regardless of their rank—even a king.

PREDICTIONS. Governor Festus had been in a stew to learn why the Jews wanted to kill Paul. He needed the information for his report to Rome. Paul has now explained why the Jews wanted his life, but the governor didn't understand it. Because of his ignorance of Judaism, Paul's statement didn't make sense to him. But Agrippa knew what Paul meant. The apostle had shown how he had remained completely loyal to the faith of Israel. He had not gone beyond the predictions of the Prophets or Moses. Since Paul had asked the king to hear him out, we presume he brought forth Scripture after Scripture from the O.T. to show that the Messiah was to suffer, rise from the dead, and proclaim salvation to Jews and Gentiles alike. These three matters were often debated by Jews as they tried to unravel the prophecies. This would be common knowledge to the king. Festus must have fidgeted as he sat listening to these boring Jewish questions.

"Will Paul be allowed to finish his presentation this time?"

24. When Paul had gotten this far with his defense, Festus suddenly shouted, "Paul, you're mad! All this great learning has driven you crazy!" 25. "No, most excellent Festus," replied Paul, "I'm not mad. What I am saying is the sober truth. 26. The king knows all about these things. That is why I speak so freely in

his presence. None of this is news to him. It was not in some secret corner that all this happened."

SHOUTED. Festus couldn't hold back any longer. While he was obviously impressed with Paul's learning, it seemed to him that so much education had driven the apostle insane. In ancient times it was believed that too much study could derange a person's mind. Festus is not renouncing Paul as a hypocrite, but as a mad fanatic. Paul answers the governor calmly and with respect. Then he turns to the king to appeal to him directly. He is careful not to shun Festus, but in turning to the king, he obliquely rebukes the governor for his ignorance. It is as if Paul had said, "You cannot understand me, because you are not a Jew. I am not speaking to you, but to the king, for he understands these things." Paul's aim was not so much to flatter the monarch as it was to handle Festus with as much grace and wisdom as possible.

CORNER. The matters of which Paul spoke were known to every Jew. The life and death of the Lord Jesus had received the greatest publicity. His miracles had been heralded from one end of Israel to the other. His resurrection had been amply attested by hundreds of witnesses. And ever since the advent of Jesus, the gospel had been openly proclaimed in His name. The conversion of the apostle Paul was also a matter of notoriety. He was well known before he turned to Christ. What happened to him on the Damascus Road was so extraordinary that it was the subject of universal talk. There was probably not a Jew in the land who didn't know of Paul's changed life. King Agrippa not only knew of these things, he was listening to Paul because he was familiar with them. He wanted to hear the "prime minister of Christianity," who may have also been the top Jewish scholar of the day.

"Will Paul move in on the king in an effort to persuade him?"

27. "King Agrippa, do you believe the Prophets? I know that you do—" 28. Before Paul could say any

more, Agrippa interrupted him, "Do you expect to make a Christian out of me just like that?" 29. "No matter what it took," said Paul, "I would to God that you and all those listening to me today would become as I am, except of course, for these chains."

BELIEVE. Paul deliberately put the king on the spot. He claimed to be a Jew. So Paul shrewdly asked, "Do you believe the Prophets?" It would be hard for him to deny he believed the Prophets. If the king said "yes," he would be backing Paul's words, for the apostle had clearly preached nothing that wasn't found in the Prophets. If on the other hand he said "no," he could no longer claim to be orthodox and would lose his power over the people of Israel. He was in an embarrassing situation. What would Festus and the other Romans think if he consented to believe in this madness? But then what would the Jews think if he denied the Prophets? While Agrippa sweats out the dilemma, Paul is calm. He had the king in a hard place. It was inconceivable to Paul that anyone who knew the Prophets and the historical facts of Jesus would deny the truth of Christianity. What would Agrippa do?

INTERRUPTED. Agrippa couldn't allow Paul to continue. The situation was already too embarrassing. The eyes of the crowd were on him. He couldn't side with Paul, but neither could he deny his orthodoxy. So he wisely made light of Paul's effort. Smiling, perhaps half-laughing, he made a joke of the whole thing. In effect, he said, "Paul, you're trying to make me play the Christian. With just a few words on your part you expect me to side with you. If I did, it would make me out a Christian too. I assure you it will take more than a few words to do that." The KJV reads, "Almost thou persuadest me to be a Christian," but the Greek text will hardly support it. The king is not confessing nearness to a decision. To the contrary, he is resisting the idea that anyone could maneuver him into siding with Christianity that easily. It is also possible however, that underneath it all, he may have found himself a little too close to Christ for comfort.

CHAINS. The power of the gospel is manifested in this scene. It makes sinners feel their weakness and believers feel like conquerors. Even though he is the prisoner and the one in chains, he is nonetheless the master of the situation. The king's lighthearted reply doesn't daunt the apostle a bit. He rises to an even more daring challenge. With the chain dangling from his wrist, Paul makes a sweeping motion with his hand. He said to the king, "I would to God that you and all those listening to me would become as I am." By that, he was saying, "Not only would I like to see you become a Christian, king Agrippa, but all the others in this room as well." This was a bold move. It had the effect of saying that Paul was the only free man in the place, that he alone was in the truth of God. The king didn't dare let Paul continue. There's no telling what he would say next. He was about to embarrass everyone in the chamber.

30. With that the king arose. So did the governor, Bernice, and all those who were sitting with them. 31. When they had drawn aside to a place where they could talk in private, they all agreed, "This man hasn't done anything deserving of death or imprisonment." 32. Then Agrippa said to Festus, "If he had not appealed to the emperor, the fellow could have been set free."

AROSE. Agrippa would hear no more. He really didn't need to. He had heard enough to decide the matter. So he stood to his feet. That signaled the end of the hearing. The rulers and their counselors withdrew from the courtroom to hold a private conference. Regardless of what anyone thought of Paul's teaching, it was clear that he was completely innocent in the eyes of Roman law. So for the fourth time Roman authorities declared him innocent. It was as Agrippa said, he could have been turned loose then and there had he not appealed to Caesar. The appeal took the matter out of the governor's hands and he had to be sent to Rome. We can suppose that Agrippa was able to tell Festus how to word his letter to the emperor. That, of course, was the purpose of the hearing.

EMPEROR. Once again Paul has been declared innocent by a Roman court. However, since his appeal to the emperor had been accepted, it could not be withdrawn. Paul was to go to Rome. All that remained was how to frame the charge letter to be presented to Caesar. One effect of Agrippa's decision might have been to advise Festus to modify his report so that it included the king's decision. Since Agrippa was a favorite in Nero's court, it would enhance Festus' prestige to include Agrippa's decision. Also this could work to Paul's advantage for Agrippa undoubtedly recommended clemency for the apostle. Right at this time (A.D. 59), the official policy of Rome was favorable toward Christians. It could be expected that Paul would have no trouble in being acquitted. It was not until A.D. 62 that any significant policy change occurred and the Romans became hostile toward Christianity.

"Did Paul leave for Rome immediately?"

27 1. Finally the word came that we were going to sail to Italy. So Paul and some other prisoners were handed over to a centurion named Julius, who belonged to the Imperial Regiment.

SAIL. It would seem that governor Festus delayed sending Paul to Rome until there were enough prisoners to justify a detachment of guards to escort them. Again, the delay may have been due to the lateness of the season. Time was running out for navigation on the Mediterranean. It's possible there was difficulty in getting a suitable ship. The ancients considered it risky to sail the Mediterranean after mid-September. By then the equinoctial storms had begun. All navigation was suspended from mid-November until February. We may assume that the voyage was begun about the beginning of September, almost too late for safe navigation. Note how the "we" narrative is resumed.

It has been over two years since we last heard from Luke (21:18). Now he is back in the picture and on board the ship with Paul. While we're not sure where he has been all this time, it is safe to conclude that he was never too far from Caesarea where Paul was held in custody. Many writers think he used the time to gather material for his two-volume history (Luke/Acts).

PRISONERS. Julius, the centurion in charge of the prisoners, was a member of an honored unit probably stationed at Caesarea. The title, "Imperial Regiment," was often bestowed on legionary troops who had rendered notable service to the emperor. Festus no doubt chose this man because he belonged to this select regiment. Julius' prisoners, with the exception of Paul, were undoubtedly condemned men and on their way to battle to the death in the Roman arena. Convicted prisoners were often disposed of in this manner. Julius seems to have been a man of humane character. He recognized that Paul was not the same as his other prisoners. Besides, the charge sheet revealed he was a citizen, uncondemned, and on his way to a hearing before the emperor. Before the voyage is over, Paul will become the dominant figure aboard ship. His insight, courage, and nearness to Christ will command the respect of everyone, especially Julius. It is not impossible that Julius was present at Paul's hearing at Caesarea, along with other Roman officials.

2. We put out to sea in a boat from Andramyttium which was scheduled to stop at a number of ports along the Asian coast. With us was Aristarchus, the Macedonian from Thessalonica. 3. The next day we landed at Sidon where Julius was extremely considerate of Paul, allowing him to go ashore to visit his friends and be cared for.

ARISTARCHUS. The ship which Festus selected was a small coastal vessel out of Andramyttium, i.e., its home port was this town on the Asian coast near Troas. In the process of heading for home, the craft would put in at a number of ports along the way and encounter a larger ship headed directly for Italy. The prisoners would then be transferred to the larger vessel. Paul was permitted to take along two of his close friends, Luke and Aristarchus. This is the same Aristarchus who was seized by the crowd in Ephesus and who accompanied Paul with the offering to Jerusalem. Very likely they traveled as Paul's slaves, rather than as his companions. This also contributed to the respect Paul received for it was a mark of prestige to own slaves. Paul was one who desperately needed friends. His two companions gladly assumed the slave role for the privilege of ministering to him on the journey. We're not sure that Aristarchus went all the way to Rome. He may have been headed home and left the party when the prisoners were transferred to the larger vessel. At least he is not mentioned after that time.

SIDON. The ship didn't go very far out to sea. The captain wanted to stay close to the shore. Had it been earlier in the season, he would have headed directly for the island of Rhodes. But with the winds now coming out of the west, he preferred to hug the Syrian shoreline, staying to the leeward side of the island of Cyprus. The vessel moved along very well. They reached Sidon, some 70 mi. north of Caesarea, the next day. This city boasted one of the finest harbors of that time. At Sidon, the centurion was inclined to show Paul a great courtesy, the first of a number he will receive during the voyage. In the company of a soldier, he was permitted to go ashore and visit the Christians of that city. A church had been founded here during the persecutions that arose after the stoning of Stephen (11:19). Here Paul received all the love and attention they could bestow while his ship was in port.

"Was the journey as swift from here on?"

4. Putting out to sea once more, we sailed under the lee of Cyprus to avoid the headwinds. 5. Then we turned and made our way across the stretch of sea directly off the coasts of Cilicia and Pamphylia and

landed at Myra in the province of Lycia. 6. There the centurion found a boat from Alexandria that was sailing for Italy, and put us on board.

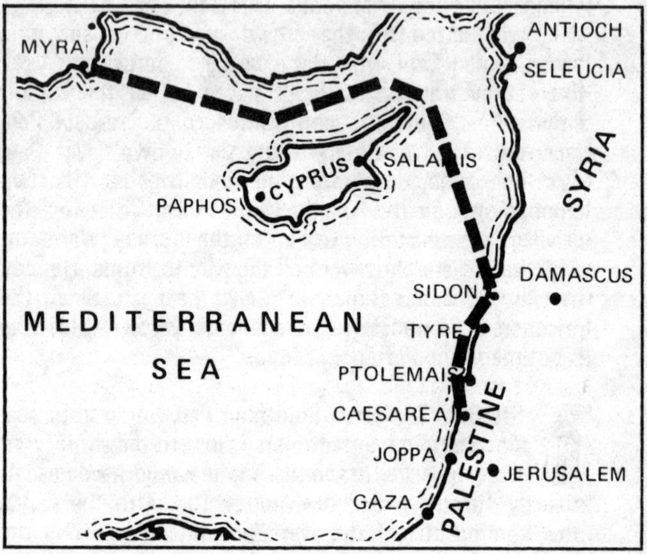

HEADWINDS. Luke loves the sea, you can tell that. He goes into great detail when it comes to nautical matters. At this time of the year, the prevailing winds were out of the northwest. A ship headed for Italy from the Palestine coast would encounter headwinds all the way. When the ship put to sea again, the captain chose to stay on the lee (downwind) side of the island of Cyprus. Then they moved east and north of the island until they reached the coast of Asia Minor. Then they turned westward. From here on it would be difficult and very slow. The ship hugged the shoreline to take advantage of any local winds and the westward ocean current which runs along the coast. By getting into this westward current, they could proceed in spite of the headwinds and finally make it to Myra. Had they not found a suitable ship here, the local winds and current would have allowed them to work their way west as far as Cnidus, but no farther. The ship would have to turn north after that.

MYRA. This fine port was located near the tip of the most southerly region of the province of Asia. A few ruins of the city, two miles inland, are still visible today. The harbor was one of the chief ports for the government grain fleet that plied constantly between Alexandria in Egypt and the bottom of the Italian peninsula. From the land of the Nile, these vessels brought huge cargoes of grain to the people of Rome. Without this fleet, the Romans would have gone hungry. The centurion was delighted to find one of the grain ships in the harbor. It would be fine for transporting him and his prisoners to Italy. On a mission such as this he would be able to commandeer the vessel in the name of the emperor. Some of these grain vessels were almost as large as a modern cargo ship. Ordinarily this craft would have sailed south of Crete directly to Italy, but this late in the summer, it met adverse winds and had to put in at Myra. That was the purpose of this harbor. In those days when there was no compass, mariners had to rely on visual sightings for navigation. The fine harbors and high mountains along the coast of southern Asia were ideal for primitive sailing.

"Wouldn't the winds be pretty bad for westward sailing by now?"

7. From here on it was slow going. After a good many days of difficult sailing, we finally made Cnidus. But the winds kept beating us back so that it was impossible to go any further. We then turned toward Crete hoping to sail under the lee side of the island once we passed point Salome. 8. But even then it was rough. Hugging the coast all the way, we managed to reach Fair Havens, a place not far from the town of Lasea.

SLOW GOING. From Myra, the westward progress of the ship was agonizingly slow because of the strong N.W. wind that was blowing. Finally they reached Cnidus, a distance of only 130 miles. Due to the severe winds, it took "many days." Apparently the winds were so stiff they decided against trying to take the clumsy ship into the harbor. In those days they didn't have rudders on the vessels and relied on huge steering paddles for maneuvering them. Apparently they couldn't negotiate the entrance in the contrary winds. Whatever the reason, they turned southward hoping to find sheltered water along the underside of the island of Crete. After rounding Cape Salome, Crete's eastern most extremity, they hugged the shoreline seeking a protecting cove. But the strong N.W. wind made even that very difficult. At last they came to a small bay called Fair Havens. It is not well known, but it still exists today. The events as described by Luke, have been checked out by seamen experienced in this area and found to be exactly the conditions one could expect in those seas by the end of summer. Luke's account is extremely precise.

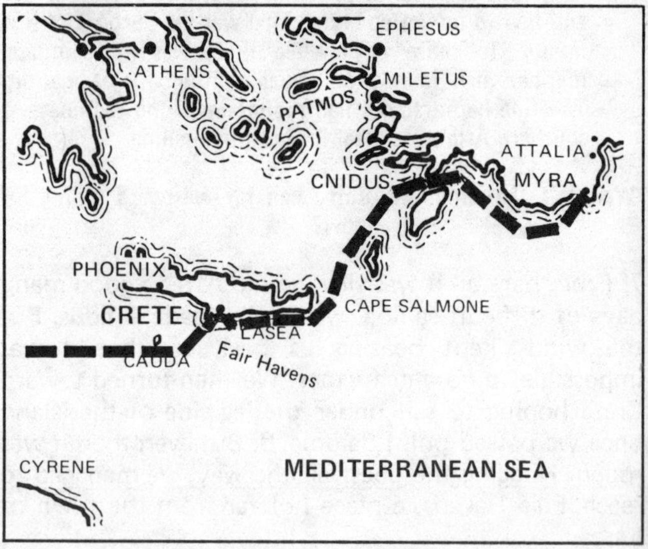

"Will the ship stay at Fair Havens or continue the voyage?"

9. So much time had now passed that it was dangerous to continue the voyage. In fact, it was so late in the year that the Fast was already over. On this account, Paul felt led to warn the ship's officers, 10.

"Gentlemen," he said, "it seems clear to me that if we go on, the ship is certain to be damaged and lose its cargo, and perhaps we'll lose our lives as well." 11. But the centurion was more inclined to heed the counsel of the ship's captain and the owner more than Paul.

DANGEROUS. The delays encountered so far had cost them so much sailing time, that it was now doubtful they could make Italy before the time of open-sea navigation ended. Since the Fast (the day of Atonement) had gone by, it was probably mid-October. To try and reach Italy before mid-November when all sailing ended on the Mediterranean, was terribly risky. The question then was just where to spend the winter and ride out the great storms. Apparently the captain and the crew did not feel that Fair Havens was safe enough. It was exposed to any gales arising out of the east and south. It was at this point that Paul offered his advice. While he was not an experienced seaman, he had been through three shipwrecks and was familiar with the Mediterranean (2 Cor. 11:25).

ADVICE. In his book, "St. Paul the Traveler," Ramsay suggests that a ship's council was held to determine the wisest course to take next. If this is correct, then Paul, because he was an experienced traveler, was invited to attend. If we combine his words here with his words in vs. 21, it does sound as if he is warning a council of ship's officers against continuing the voyage. His advice is to spend the winter in Fair Havens. While this harbor was too open to the sea for safety, Paul's judgment is supported by the fact that there were islands and reefs nearby which gave it some protection. As the emperor's representative, the centurion was the ranking officer on board. The decision was his to make. In this case he deferred to the advice of the captain and the ship's navigator (owner). Apparently he figured their judgment was based on more experience at sea.

12. Since the harbor was not really suitable for wintering a ship, the majority of the officers decided

in favor of putting out to sea again in hopes of reaching Phoenix. This was a Cretan harbor that faced in the direction of southwest and northwest winds. 13. The day came when a light breeze from the south began to blow. It seemed to be just right for taking them to their objective. Satisfied they had made the right decision, they weighed anchor and set sail, carefully hugging the shores of Crete. 14. They hadn't sailed too long when the weather made an abrupt change. Suddenly a typhoon-type gale, which sailors describe as a "northeaster," came blasting from the landward side and caught the ship broadside. 15. It struck with such violent force that there was no way to head the ship into the wind. So we yielded the helm and let the vessel run downwind.

PHOENIX. Some 60 mi. to the west of Fair Havens, was another harbor that was well protected. Luke's description seems to fit the modern port of Lutro, which one nautical expert describes as the "only secure port in all winds on the south coast of Crete." The majority of the ship's council thought it would be better to try and reach this port than take a chance on staying all winter in Fair Havens. Some days later the wind began to blow softly out of the south. The officers felt this was the moment they were waiting for and immediately weighed anchor. After rounding Cape Matala, a threatening promontory a few miles west, they relaxed thinking they were in the clear. With such favorable winds they were sure to make Phoenix in a few hours—they thought.

SUDDENLY. Just when everything seemed to be going so well, the weather made an abrupt change and a furious "northeaster" came blasting down off the high mountains of Crete (7000'), and struck the ship with terrific force. The clouds and the sea churned as the contrary currents of air met. The word Luke uses in Greek can be translated "typhoon." The sailors knew at once it was their old enemy—"Euraquilo!" This expression is compounded from two words: the Gk.

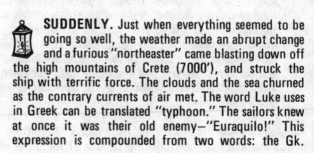

word **euros**, meaning eastwind, and the Latin word **aquilo**, meaning northwind. Hence the word, "northeaster." Such a sudden storm and reversal of wind is quite common in this area. It can swing through the compass points from northeast to southeast, which makes it treacherous. With the wind blowing so fiercely, there was nothing for the crew to do but let the ship run before the wind. It was impossible to turn those ancient ships into gale force winds, or as the original reads, to "look it in the eye." So all command was yielded and the ship was driven at the mercy of the tempest.

"Could they handle the ship in such a storm?"

16. Then there came a brief time of shelter as we ran under the lee of a small island named Clauda. With a great deal of effort we were able to secure the ship's dinghy. 17. Once it had been brought aboard, the crew set to work undergirding the hull with the bracing cables. Fearing they might run aground on the shallows of Syrtis, they dropped the mainsail to slow down the speed with which the ship was being driven before the storm. 18. There was no relief the next day. The ship continued to be tossed by the storm, so they began to jettison the cargo. 19. When it persisted for the third day, they all put their hands to the task of throwing the ship's tackle overboard.

SHELTER. Even with the ship running before the wind it was all the crew could do to keep it under control. Then came momentary relief as the ship passed under the lee of a small island. How they must have scrambled to take care of those things which they couldn't do while buffeted by the full force of the storm. First they took care of the ship's tender (dinghy) which was usually towed behind the craft in fair weather to save deck space. Likely it was filled with water, accounting for the difficulty in getting it on board. Then they took the frapping (bracing) cables, standard equipment on ancient vessels, and passing them under the ship made them taut across the beam. This reinforced the hull against the pounding of the swells. They also lowered the mainsail which caught the gusts and drove the ship along at a fast pace. They feared to go too fast lest they be driven into the shallows (quicksand) off the north African coast which extended between Tripoli and Barca.

JETTISON. The crew did everything possible to strengthen the ship and slow it down, which surely included throwing out the sea anchor. The sea anchor is a huge canvass dish which rides in the water and would serve as a brake against the forward motion of the ship. The big sails had to come down. They would be tattered in the storm. The next task was to lighten the ship so that it would move with the sea rather than pound to pieces against the swells. First to go was the grain cargo. The bulk of it was tossed into the sea. As the storm continued, more drastic measures were needed as a matter of survival. Much of the sailing gear went overboard. The great spar, which held the mainsail to the wind and was almost as long as the ship itself, went over the side. It took all hands to heft it. All of the furniture, freight and extra rigging went into the sea as well. Everything goes when a person's life is at stake. This was now a life and death struggle. It was a test for Paul to be involved in such a struggle when God had already promised to see him to Rome. His faith is being tried once more.

20. Day after day passed and the storm raged with no let up. During that time they had seen neither the sun nor the stars, and all hope of surviving gradually faded. 21. Finally, after no one had eaten for a long time, Paul stood in their midst and said:

"You should have listened to me when I warned you not to sail from Crete. If you had, you would have avoided all this damage and loss. 22. However there is no need to be discouraged. The ship is going to be lost, but not a one of you will lose his life! 23. Last night an angel of the God to Whom I belong and Whom I serve stood before me. 24. 'Don't be afraid, Paul!' he said to me, 'you will yet stand in Caesar's presence. More than that, God has granted you the lives of all those sailing with you!' 25. So men, keep up your courage! I believe God. I'm satisfied that everything will turn out exactly as He has said. 26. But we are going to run aground on an island."

HOPE. Ancient mariners navigated by keeping within sight of land by day and taking their bearings on stars at night. But now ten or eleven days have passed without sightings of any kind. They don't know where they are. Even worse, the ship was undoubtedly leaking badly. The incessant pounding had surely opened seams and it appeared certain they would founder at sea. Consider that these were hardened sailors, men accustomed to the sea. Yet with the incessant fighting to keep the ship afloat and the severe rolling, there was no way to prepare food or find time to eat it. Many were at the point of exhaustion, others were seasick. To work endlessly in the cold and dark and be wet for so long, can sap the courage of even veteran mariners. Thus prisoners and crew alike had given up all hope of being saved alive.

COURAGE! In the midst of this hopeless situation encouragement came from an unexpected source. Throughout the storm Paul had been praying for the safety of all on board the ship. Right when every heart was so dejected and despairing, Paul stood up to announce the word of hope. During the night when his own spirit had apparently despaired of life, Paul received a supernatural revelation by an angel of God. He was told that not only would he survive, but God would spare all of his fellow-travelers for his sake. Likely the apostle thought he would never see Rome and had to be reminded of God's promise. But then notice his human touch. When he says, "I told you so," isn't he rubbing it in a little? Of course his advice was purely human on the former occasion. But this time he is not speaking as an experienced traveler. He now speaks by revelation. No amount of shrewd judgment could have determined there would be no loss of life in this situation. Paul spoke with the assurance of one who had proved God in many trials. He knew by experience that God would keep His Word. How the men must have been cheered by the radiance of the apostle as he said this. What a dramatic scene this must have been!

"How long before Paul's words would be fulfilled?"

27. On the fourteenth night we were still drifting across the Adriatic Sea. About midnight the sailors began to suspect we were approaching land. 28. So they tossed over a sounding line to measure the ocean depth and found it to be 120 feet. A little later they sounded again and this time it was only 90 feet deep. 29. Fearing they might be dashed against the rocks along some rugged coastline, they dropped four anchors over the stern and prayed that daylight would soon appear.

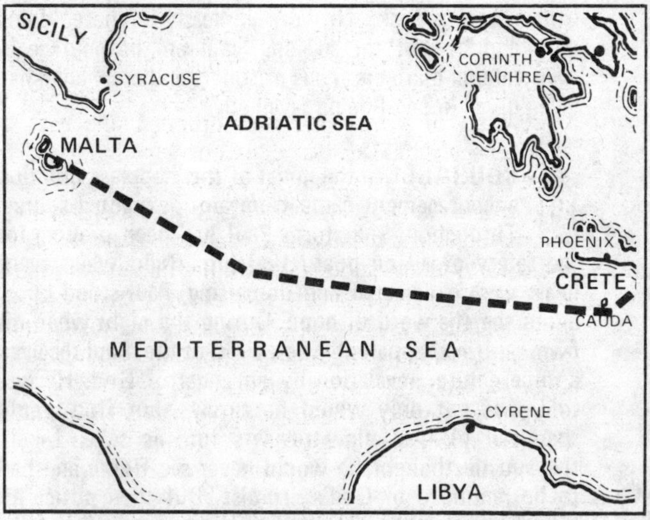

LAND. The ship had been drifting with the storm for 14 days since leaving Fair Havens. Luke reports they had moved across the Adriatic. In those times this portion of the Mediterranean near the tip of Italy, Crete and Malta was known as the Adriatic Sea (also Ionian Sea). Unknown to the sailors, the ship was approaching what is now called St. Paul's Bay on the island of Malta. It was pitch black, but the practiced ear of the lookout heard a new sound above the roar of the wind and the groaning of the ship. It was the boom of breakers upon rocks. Quickly they moved to sound the depth of the water by heaving a weighted line overboard. It measured 120 feet. Some minutes later they sounded again and the waters measured only 90 feet. Such a rapid decrease in depth meant that they were approaching land. They stood a good chance of being carried onto the rocks or foundering on a reef near the land. At 90 feet, the ship's anchors could reach the bottom.

ANCHORS. It was dangerous to proceed any further in the inky darkness. To be pounded against those rocks could mean death for all hands. It is believed by some scholars that the ship actually dropped anchor not far from the entrance to St. Paul's Bay, perhaps only a mile or two away. The hand of God was indeed with them. In those days the vessels didn't have the mammoth anchors we have now, so they had to carry more of them. Thus they dropped four over the stern of the ship. This was done not only to keep them from foundering on rocks, but to wait for daylight when they would try and spot a site which would afford a safe means for escaping to land. Dropping the anchors over the stern was the quickest way to halt the motion of the ship. Had they placed the anchors over the bow, the wind would have swung the ship around carrying them that much nearer to danger. Knowing they were this close to land they were anxious to stop the ship as quickly as possible. The crew's praying for daylight has the idea of wishing for daylight.

30. The crew members had a mind to abandon ship. They were about to lower the ship's tender, pretending they were going to lay out anchors from the bow, 31. when Paul said to the centurion and the soldiers, "Unless these men stay on board, you yourselves will not be saved!" 32. Hearing that the soldiers

quickly cut the ropes holding the lifeboat and let it drift away.

ABANDON. The ship's crew, convinced the vessel could break up at any moment, hit upon a scheme to save their own lives at the expense of the others. Under the pretense of using the tender (shore-boat) to lay out the forward anchors, they planned to steal the ship's boat and escape to land. Somehow Paul perceived their intentions and warned the centurion. Julius acted quickly. Some soldiers standing near the lines holding the boat were ordered to cut them lose, and it dropped into the sea. Paul may not have expected him to take such drastic action. The boat could have been useful in getting people to shore later on. But the centurion was not a seaman. All he could think of was how helpless they would all be if the sailors deserted them. Unfamiliar with navigation, there would be no way for the passengers themselves to handle the big ship when they attempted to beach it in the morning. By now he knew it was best to heed Paul's warnings. So he ordered the little boat set adrift, forcing everyone to stay on board.

33. When day was about to dawn, Paul advised all of them to take some food. "For fourteen days," he said, "you've all been tense and alert and too busy to eat. You have gone too long without food. 34. Now you must eat something. You're going to need it if you are to survive. So relax, not a hair of your heads will be lost." 35. After those warming words, he took some bread. Giving thanks to God in the presence of them all, he broke it and began to eat. 36. Instantly everyone found new courage and began eating. 37. Altogether there were 276 of us aboard the ship. 38. When everyone had eaten all he wanted, they began to lighten the ship by throwing the wheat into the sea.

ADVISED. See how Paul's leadership has surfaced? He's on top of the situation. He's aware of the weakness of the men due to the tension suffered while the ship was tossed at sea. But now the situation is far less desperate. The ship is held at anchor and under control. There will be plenty to do when the sun comes up, but for the moment things are easier. So Paul advises everyone to eat. They are going to need all the strength they can muster if they hope to make land. With the ship more stable, food can be prepared. Assuring them once more that no harm would come to anyone, Paul backed his confidence by taking food. Acting much like the head of a Hebrew family, he gave thanks to God in the sight of them all and began to eat. The rest joined him and took a full meal. Because it was so difficult to feed so many under these adverse conditions, Luke is sensitive to the number of people on board. He gives us the headcount–276.

LIGHTEN. When everyone had eaten his fill, they all went to work to lighten the ship further by throwing out the remainder of the cargo. At the beginning of the storm most of the wheat had been tossed over the side to keep the ship from breaking up due to so much weight in the hold. However, enough had been spared to serve as ballast and provide meals. But now even that had to go. There are numerous accounts describing these Alexandrian grain ships. One of them was 180 ft. in length, 45 ft. across the beam, with a hold 44 ft. in depth. Such a ship would draw quite a bit of water. It was necessary, therefore, to make the ship as light as possible so that it would ride high in the water. The higher it rode, the more easily it would glide up the sand when beached. The further up the beach it came to rest, the easier it would be for the passengers and crew to make their way through the pounding surf.

"Will they try beaching the ship at sunup?"

39. When day broke, they found themselves looking at an unfamiliar coastline. However, they noticed a bay with a sandy beach. Here they planned to beach the ship if they could. 40. So they slipped off the anchors leaving them in the sea. Then they loosed the ropes

binding the large steering paddles. Hoisting the foresail into the wind, they headed for the beach. 41. But the ship ran aground on a low-lying sandbar that separated two bodies of water. The bow was struck fast and the stern began to break up under the violence of the breakers.

BAY. As first light appeared, the crew could make out the coastline of an island. It was the island of Malta, but this portion of it was unfamiliar to them. As it got lighter, they could make out a bay and a sandy beach. Since they appeared to be near an inlet, it seemed worthwhile to try to make the entrance. It would take a lot of skill to negotiate the passage without being swept upon the rocks on either side. In the dim light they couldn't see that another inlet brought currents from another direction. That current carried bits of rock and sand which had been deposited to form a sandbar between the entrance to the bay and the beach. It is possible that sandy shoal was low in the water and was not visible until after they had maneuvered the big ship through the entrance. Their hands would be so full trying to avoid the rocks they may not have even thought of looking for a sandbar.

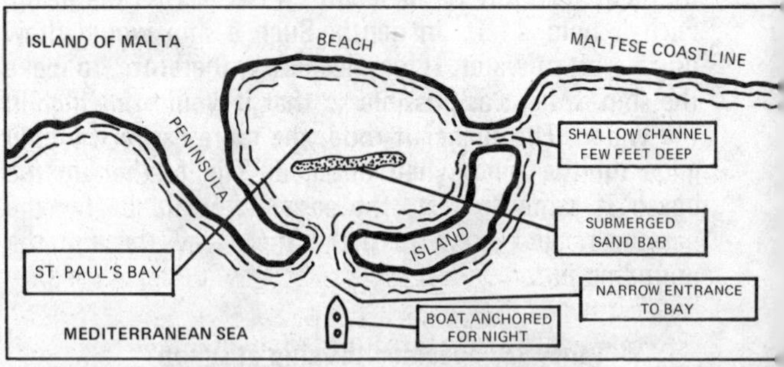

AGROUND. Their plan was good, but it would take a lot of skill to pull it off. They must have done a lot of things fast when they got ready to try for the entrance. While the text lists the events in a different order, they no doubt loosed the great sweeping rudders first of all. Then the small foresail was raised to give direction to the ship. Lastly they cut the ship free of its anchors. They must have felt relieved when the big craft moved through the inlet and headed toward the beach. Then came the surprise. The ship ran upon the sandbar and the bow stuck fast in the mud. The stern was now exposed to crashing breakers which thundered against the massive rear of the vessel. It began to break up almost immediately. Although they were closer to shore, the water was still too deep for wading. The waves were a dangerous threat too. Each person would have to make it to land by whatever means he could find.

"Will all make it safely as God promised?"

42. The soldiers, realizing the prisoners could easily escape in this situation, figured they had better kill them all rather than let any swim ashore and get away. 43. But the centurion overruled their plan since he wanted to bring Paul through safely. Instead, he gave orders that all who could swim should jump overboard and make their way to land. 44. The rest were to follow as best they could by clinging to planks and other pieces of the ship's wreckage. So it was that all of them got ashore safely.

KILL ALL. Isn't it strange that after passing through such a desperate voyage together, the soldiers would even think of killing their companions in suffering? Common misery usually tends to produce common sympathy. Yet here they are planning the cold-blooded murder of those who had done them no harm and had experienced the same trials as themselves. Such was the nature of Roman discipline. It had been drilled into these men that regardless of the circumstances, they would pay with their lives should any of their charges escape. They were used to killing people. Life was cheap to them. The simplest solution, to their minds, was to kill all the prisoners. That way they could be sure none would escape. This was a new threat for Paul.

OVERRULED. The centurion was too grateful to Paul to let anything like that happen to him. Besides, he wasn't really guilty of anything. He was merely being escorted to trial. So Julius gave orders that all of them, prisoners included, were to get ashore. Thus the saving of these lives must again be credited to Paul. They are spared because of him. The centurion could have easily exempted Paul since he was uncondemned, yet he chose to spare them all. It would appear that he was influenced by Paul's prophecy (28:24). Those who could swim were ordered to dive overboard and head for land. The remainder were to get there any way they could. It is possible that rafts were quickly fashioned by tying beams together. Regardless how it was done, they all managed to make it safely. God had said that no lives would be lost, only the ship. His Word to Paul was fulfilled on the shores of the island of Malta. It is well to note that the fulfillment of God's promise was NOT without human effort. These people endured hunger, cold, exhaustion, and the loss of their possessions in the wreck. Plus, they had to make it to shore on their own. But isn't it true that we all still have to do our part even in the face of God's promises?

"Was the island inhabited?"

28 1. Once we were safe on land, we found we were on the island of Malta. 2. The natives welcomed us with extraordinary kindness. They even built a fire for us because we were wet from the rain and shivering in the cold.

MALTA. Likely the members of the crew were familiar with the island of Malta, but they didn't recognize this part of the coast. The island is not big, only 17 mi. long and 9 mi. wide at the broadest point. Though we call it Malta, it was named "Melita" (meaning refuge) by the Phoenician sailors who often found it to be a haven. The inhabitants were descendants of the Phoenicians and Carthaginians and spoke a dialect of the semitic language. In the Gk. text, Luke calls them "Barbarians." He means by that they did not speak

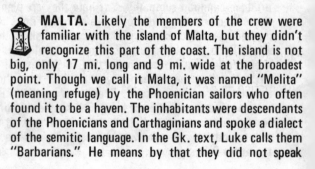

Greek. They were certainly not barbarian in their hospitality. Paul's experience with languages was so widespread he was able to communicate with them. The Maltese natives took pity on the shipwrecked men and received them most kindly. When they saw them shivering in the continuing rain, they hurridly built a large bonfire and invited them to come and warm themselves. That fire must have looked awfully good to the wet survivors.

3. Paul had gathered up an armful of sticks and was putting them on the fire when a viper came out because of the heat and fastened on his hand.

VIPER. The apostle was not one to sit around when there was work to be done. The fire had to be fed. So he busied himself gathering wood to keep it going. Apparently he had scooped up a bundle of brushwood with a poisonous snake mingled among the sticks. Because of the cold, the serpent was in a dormant state. But when the wood was laid on the fire, the heat quickly stirred it to life. It moved fast enough to grab Paul's hand as he arranged the wood. Luke says the serpent fastened on his hand. The Greek word he uses is one which medical writers employ to describe a poisonous bite. From what we know of the viper's jaw and the function of its poison glands, plus the attitude of the natives, it seems clear that God miraculously stayed the normal effects of the bite and saved His servant from a painful death. There are no snakes on Malta today, though one was killed near this same spot in 1820.

"What did the natives think of this event?"

4. Seeing the snake hanging from Paul's hand, the islanders began saying to each other, "This man has got to be a murderer! He may have escaped the sea, but justice is not going to let him live!" 5. But Paul shook the snake into the fire and suffered no ill effects at all. 6. Nonetheless the natives continued to watch him carefully. At any moment they expected to see him swell up and drop dead. But after waiting

a long time and seeing that nothing unusual happened to him, they changed their minds and began declaring he was a god.

WATCHED. When the snake fastened itself on Paul's hand, the apostle momentarily raised his arm. The natives got a good look at the dangling reptile before Paul shook the creature into the fire. They were sure he was a goner. They knew the symptoms of a poisonous viper bite. Enormous swelling occurs almost immediately after which the victim falls to the ground in convulsions and dies. The natives waited for the poison to take its effect. In their superstition they interpreted the event as a special sign. Pagan mythology held that "divine justice" (the goddess Nemesis) finally caught up with escaped criminals in the end. Thus they figured Paul must have been a very great criminal to be bitten by a serpent after having escaped the wrath of the sea. However this supposition was probably reinforced by the fact that he still had chains on his hands.

CHANGED. But as the natives watched and nothing happened to Paul, their minds shifted to the other extreme. The same superstition which led them to conclude he was being punished by divine vengeance, now led them to suppose he was a god. Pagans always associate the miraculous with God. The speed with which they could pass from one notion to the other is an example of the instability of the human soul when it is not grounded in God's Word. So for the second time, Paul is received as a god. We can be sure he denied it just as vigorously here on Malta as he did in the town of Lystra. Isn't it interesting that primitive people have no trouble believing a god can take on human form and walk among men. How different from the unbelieving spirit of our age. Yet people of our time are ready to associate ANY miracle with God. We can assume that once Paul became the center of attention on the island, he took advantage of it for the Lord's sake. It would have been most natural for him to use their mistaken notion about him to tell them of the TRUE God.

"How did Paul serve the Lord on this island?"

7. In the immediate vicinity were some plantations belonging to the chief magistrate of the island, a man named Publius. He invited us to stay with him as his guests. For three days he entertained us royally. 8. It so happened that Publius' father was the victim of recurrent attacks of fever and dysentery, and on this occasion was again confined to his bed. Paul went to see him. After praying for him, he laid his hands on him and healed him. 9. As soon as this happened, all the rest of the sick people on the island came to him and were healed. 10. So grateful were they, they loaded us down with gifts. When it came time for us to sail, they brought aboard all the supplies we needed.

PUBLIUS. Luke now introduces us to the magistrate of the island, a man named Publius. He was a Roman. Since Malta was a province of Sicily, he served under the governor of Sicily. His estates joined the place where the shipwrecked men had come ashore. As a matter of protocol, Julius paid his respects to the magistrate. In the process of their discussion, the snake incident was sure to come and Julius would also tell him of Paul's help at sea. Accordingly Publius invited Paul and his companions (Luke and Aristarchus) to spend a few days as guests in his home. This was a great kindness for they had no place to stay and needed time to find lodging. The magistrate was well paid for his kindness. God will not allow Himself to be any man's debtor. At this very time, Publius' father was having another attack of Malta fever, a disease still common on the island. Paul went to the man and prayed for him and he was healed. The laying on of hands in this case was obviously to help the man release his faith in the Christ of Whom Paul spoke. The sense of touch has the power to do this. Since Paul was a prisoner, his credentials may have still been suspect. So God gave him the credential of miraculous power. This tells us God meant to do a work on the island. Miracles were very useful as attention getters.

REST. The news of this healing spread quickly throughout the island. Anyone suffering an infirmity was brought to the apostle. Likely he preached every day and the Lord continued to heal the different ones. Luke apparently assisted in some way, for he reports they "loaded US with gifts." However his medical supplies went down with the ship. For three months Paul labored with the people and they kept him so well supplied with gifts or "honors," that he didn't have to work to eat. The gifts probably consisted of food and clothing and other useful items replacing those lost in the wreck. When it finally came time to leave, the islanders showed still more gratitude by giving them everything they could think of for their comfort on the remainder of the voyage. Undoubtedly a solid work was established on the island. One writer who lived on the island speaks of St. Publius' church located not ten minutes from his house.

"Did they leave as soon as the winter season passed?"

11. Three months later we boarded the Castor and Pollux, a ship out of Alexandria that had wintered at the island, and set sail for Italy.

SHIP. The three months were probably November, December, and January. With the return of warm winds out of the west in February, the seas were once again open to navigation. The many ships which had wintered at the main harbor of Malta (some 8 mi. S.E. of the spot where Paul's ship was wrecked) could now resume their sailings. The centurion visited the busy harbor where he found another of the great corn ships from Egypt. Luke seems to be fascinated by the fact that it was named after the twin sons of Zeus (Jupiter) whose images were carved on the prow as a figurehead. These twin brothers were regarded as the patrons of navigation and were the favorite gods of seamen. Julius was no doubt relieved to be able to secure passage for his men and prisoners on this large vessel. They'd be on Italian soil in a short time.

12. Our first stop was Syracuse where we spent three days. 13. Then after we had circled to pick up the wind, we made for Rhegium. The following day a south wind sprang up and we reached Puteoli in two days.

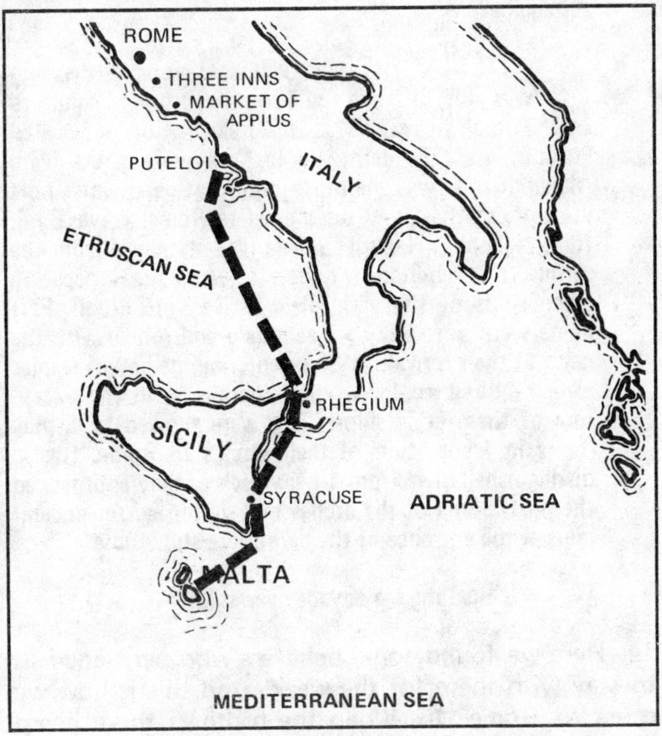

SYRACUSE. The Castor and Pollux weighed anchor and headed for the great port of Syracuse on the island of Sicily. The distance of about 100 miles was made in one day. But here the ship had to stay in port for three days, probably because their nice south wind had failed. We can assume that Julius permitted Paul to go ashore during this time, and if so, he made a beeline for the Jewish colony. After three days the wind came up again, but this time it seems to have been a N.W. wind. By tacking, the ship managed to put in at Rhegium (now Reggio) at the toe of the Italian boot. From here it was only 6 or 7 miles across the Strait of Messina to Sicily. With the wind so unfavorable, the captain didn't dare take his ship through the strait. He decided to wait for a better wind. It came the next day. A good wind from the south allowed him to pass directly through the strait without any dangerous zigzagging.

PUTEOLI. The wind was so favorable the ship was able to make the 150 miles from Rhegium to Puteoli in two days. This great harbor, now called Puzzoli, was the terminus for the grain ships from Alexandria. It was the most important deep water port in southern Italy, and the closest to Rome. It was 8 mi. from Neapolis (Naples) and derived its name from the springs that abounded there. It was a great occasion when ships of the grain fleet arrived in Puteoli. Fast boats were sent out to meet them and return with the news of their arrival. All ships entering the bay of Naples were required to lower their topsails, with the exception of these grain ships. They were allowed to display theirs in recognition of their service to Rome. It also distinguished them from other vessels as they approached the port. Some of the arches that supported the ancient piers at the entrance of the harbor are still visible.

"Is the long sea voyage over at last?"

14. Here we found some believers who persuaded us to stay with them for the week. And this is how we came to Rome. 15. When the brothers there heard we were on the way, they came as far as the Market of Appius and Three Inns to meet us. When Paul saw them he thanked God and was filled with new courage.

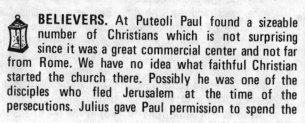

BELIEVERS. At Puteoli Paul found a sizeable number of Christians which is not surprising since it was a great commercial center and not far from Rome. We have no idea what faithful Christian started the church there. Possibly he was one of the disciples who fled Jerusalem at the time of the persecutions. Julius gave Paul permission to spend the seven days with the believers there. Apparently that time was needed to get a response to a dispatch sent to Rome and outfit his soldiers with new equipment to replace that lost in the wreck. It was mandatory that all military units enter Rome in full regalia. Since there was also a large Jewish colony here, we can be sure Paul worked among them too.

MEET US. The Appian highway, one of the great Roman roads of southern Italy passed within a few miles of Puteoli. It was built by Appius Claudius Caecus who laid out the famous road from Capua to Rome in 312 B.C. Another well built road, the Campanium Way, connected Puteoli with the Appian Way. It was along this road that Paul and the others proceeded toward the capitol. Upon hearing of his arrival in Puteoli, the brethren at Rome set out on this road to welcome the apostle. One party waited for him at Three Inns, which was thirty miles from Rome. Another party made it to the market town of Appii Forum, 10 miles further. It had been three years since Paul had written to the Romans and he didn't know how they would receive him. Now his heart is warmed by their effort in coming this distance to greet him and escort him to the city. It gave him new courage to face the work he was to do for Jesus in that great city. It wasn't easy for the famous apostle to show up in chains. The warmth of this welcome really lifted his spirit.

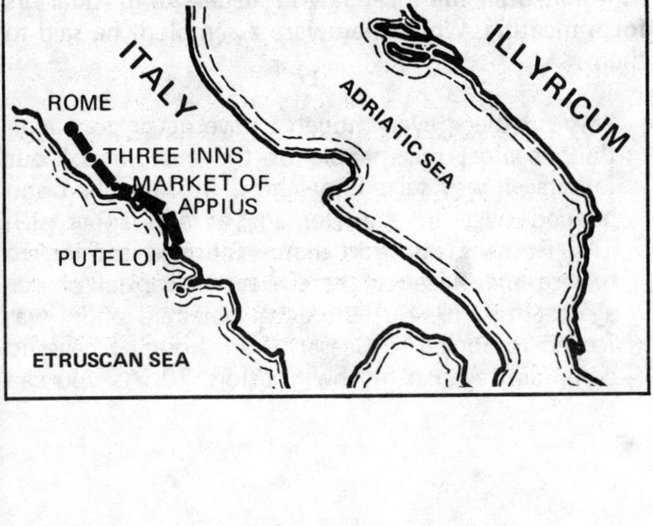

16. Once we were in Rome Paul was allowed to have his own residence which he shared with the soldier in charge of him.

RESIDENCE. When the column reached Rome, the prisoners were turned over to the captain in charge of the emperor's bodyguard. However, Paul was not confined in the garrison along with the other prisoners inasmuch as he was uncondemned and not destined for the arena. He was even allowed to have his own house. Yet he wasn't free. A soldier, to whom he was lightly chained, was detailed to guard him. This great favor was probably due to the letter which king Agrippa drafted for procurator Festus. Paul's position was no doubt further enhanced by the intercession of the centurion Julius. We assume the Christians of Rome provided the means. As a shipwrecked man and destitute prisoner, Paul had no funds on his person. It is believed he was not allowed to leave his quarters to visit the synagogues or work at his trade, but he was able to write letters to friends in other cities and counsel those who came to see him. It was during this time that he wrote his prison epistles. Note that the "WE" has been dropped. While Luke was nearby for much of the imprisonment, he was unable to serve as an intimate companion.

17. Just three days after his arrival in Rome, Paul summoned all the local Jewish leaders to his quarters for a meeting. When they were assembled, he said to them:

"My brothers, even though I have never done anything against our people or the customs of our fathers, I was seized by those in Jerusalem and handed over to the Romans as a prisoner. 18. The Romans questioned me and had a mind to release me because there was no capital charge against me. 19. But the Jews objected and I was forced to appeal to Caesar, even though I have no complaint against my own nation. 20. As you can see, I am a prisoner. This is why I asked you to come that I might talk with you and explain that it is because of the hope of Israel that I am wearing this chain."

SUMMONED. Bearing in mind the exhaustion and privation Paul suffered, we marvel that he moved so fast to begin his ministry in Rome. Only two days are spent getting settled in a place to live. It's doubtful that he took a day to relax. On the third day, he summoned Rome's leading Jews to his quarters. The invitations were probably carried by Luke, Timothy, or Demas, who were known to be with him. Other friends had perhaps also traveled to Rome once they knew their beloved Paul was headed there for trial. The Jews of Rome had heard of Paul. He was a chief topic of conversation among Jews everywhere. They were obviously prejudiced against him. They knew of his stand for Christ and opposed it. They were glad for a chance to gloat over the fact that he was a prisoner. However, their curiosity, if nothing else, would bring them out to hear the man who had so greatly aroused worldwide Jewry.

EXPLAIN. Paul was anxious to overcome the prejudices of the Roman Jews. They knew he had arrived as a prisoner and had appealed to Caesar. He felt he may have already been slandered by messages from Judea and wanted to set the record straight. He sought to clear the air on four accounts: (1) he was not a prisoner because of any crime against the people of Israel or their customs, (2) he had appealed to Caesar as a matter of self-defense since the Jews at Jerusalem had protested his release when the Romans found him innocent of any capital crime, (3) he had no counter charges to bring against his own countrymen, (4) and the real reason he was a prisoner was because he believed in the Messiah as predicted by the Hebrew Scriptures. When he says the "hope of Israel," he means Israel's hope in the Messiah and the resurrection of the dead. Of course Paul believed those Scriptures were already fulfilled in the person of Jesus.

"Did the Roman Jews accept Paul's explanation?"

21. "We have not received any letters about you from Judea," they said, "neither has anyone from Jerusalem come here with a report or comment that discredited you in any way. 22. But as far as this sect that you belong to, everything we hear about it is bad. However, we'd like to hear from you what your own views are."

LETTERS. The Jews denied receiving any word from Jerusalem with **specific charges** against Paul. Neither had anyone been sent to Rome to press any kind of charges against him. This was probably true. If so, it means there would be no accusers when it came time for Paul's trial. The leaders of the Sanhedrin, realizing they were unsuccessful before Festus and Agrippa, undoubtedly figured they had even less chance of a conviction before the emperor. Likely they dropped their action completely, not wanting to be involved in the prosecution of a Roman citizen who appeared to be winning the favor of Roman justice. Thus, no official or unofficial word came to Rome in advance of Paul's arrival. The Jerusalem leaders probably wished the whole thing would die down. The local Jews were anxious to appease the Roman authorities inasmuch as the threat of expulsion hung over them. While the edict expelling all Jews from Rome had been rescinded, the possibility of persecution was very real. Consequently they would like to avoid offending Paul since it was obvious he had now won a favorable place among the Romans. For a prisoner to have his own residence was proof of that.

YOUR VIEWS. While the Roman Jews knew of no charges from Jerusalem, they certainly knew about Paul and the movement he was helping to spread throughout the empire. From their words it sounds as if they didn't have any direct knowledge of Christianity, but this can hardly be the case. They were keenly aware of the church at Rome. It was already in existence when Paul wrote to the Christians there in A.D. 57. In that letter he praised the saints for the fact that their faith and zeal were known everywhere (Rom. 1:8). So it must have been in existence for some time. These Jewish leaders were playing it cool. They didn't want to reveal their true feelings about Christianity for fear of offending Paul. They show some open-mindedness in wanting to hear his message and why he had dedicated his life to this new sect. It was good politics to conceal their true attitude until Paul had declared his. Consequently a day was set when they would return to hear him at length.

"Did the Jews actually come back at a later date?"

23. So a date was set and on that day large numbers of them returned to the house where he was staying. He spoke at length from the Law of Moses and the Prophets laboring to show the real nature of the kingdom of God and convince them about Jesus. They listened to him from dawn to dusk.

LISTENED. When the appointed day came, the Jewish leaders flocked to Paul's house. The place was packed. He now had the kind of an audience for which he had longed. It appears he had all the time he wanted. His preaching covered the whole range of Jewish Scripture. We could wish that we had the text of what he said, but God has not even allowed us a summary. Therefore, we must infer an outline on the basis of his other messages and letters. Accordingly he spoke first of the kingdom of God. That was wise. This was the one common ground between him and his listeners. It was the great hope in the heart of every Jew. Undoubtedly he reviewed how the kingdom was based on the atonement and the arrival of the promised Messiah. Then he surely brought forth the key passages which unfolded the humiliation and suffering of the Messiah. His audience would give him no trouble to this point, but when he began to link the rejected and crucified Jesus of Nazareth with the atonement, the atmosphere changed.

AT LENGTH. Paul took his time, preaching from dawn to dusk. We can be sure that the meeting turned into a debate as soon as he began to show

how Jewish prophecy was fulfilled in the person of Jesus. The prejudice of the Jews would surface quickly. From then on the discussion was hot and heavy. It isn't hard to picture how Paul behaved as the Jews challenged his words. He loved these people. There must have been plenty of tears as he made impassioned pleas to them. They were the first thing on his mind when he began his work in Rome. And here he is, though abused by Jews wherever he went, begging them to behold Jesus as their Messiah. For all that he had suffered at their hands, he could have justly ignored them and dealt with Gentiles only. But his heart's desire and prayer to God was that Israel might be saved. Now he has the entire day to say all that was in his heart.

24. A few were convinced by what he said, the rest were not. 25. Unable to come to any agreement among themselves, they left Paul's house, but not until he had given them these parting words as a warning:

> 26. " 'Go to this people and tell them, you will listen and listen, but never understand; you will look and look, but never see. 27. The heart of this people has become insensitive, they have covered their ears and closed their eyes. They are afraid they might see with their eyes and hear with their ears and their minds be forced to accept the truth. In which case they'd turn to Me,' says God, 'and I would heal them' "

28. "So now let it be clearly understood," said Paul, "that God has made His salvation available to the Gentiles as well as to you. And if you won't accept it, they will!" [29. These words sent the Jews from his house vigorously arguing among themselves.]

AGREEMENT. Once more Paul has offered the gospel to the Jews. And once more, for the most part, they have rejected it. A few of his listeners were convinced of the truth, but the bulk of them remained unpersuaded. The same familiar pattern of

God's grace being met with Jewish prejudice emerged in Rome as it had everyplace else. Thus the book of Acts, while it traces the spread of the gospel among the Gentiles, also clearly records its stubborn rejection by the Jews. Ever mindful that the Jewish people, as the custodian of God's revelation were entitled to hear the message first, Paul sought them out wherever he went. But now that the Jews of Rome have also indicated their disinterest, he feels at liberty to devote himself to the Gentiles. He knew from experience that they would receive the Word warmly. To this day, there is one thing the Jews are agreed upon—they don't want anything to do with Christ. Verse 29 appears in brackets since it is not found in most Mss.

WARNING. We have come to the last recorded instance of Jewish rejection in the Bible. As he had done at Pisidian Antioch and Corinth, Paul ends the interview with a warning taken from the prophet Isaiah. God had cautioned the ancient prophet not to expect the Israelites to harken to his teaching. The best he could hope for was that his work would harden the hearts of the people still further. We must note that God does not deliberately harden anyone's heart. He does deliberately send His Word to men, and that Word **automatically** hardens the hearts of those who DON'T WANT IT. Like the rain which brings out that which is ALREADY in the ground, God's Word brings out that which is already in the human heart. Thus the ministry of Moses, which was said to have hardened Pharoah's heart, could have just as easily SOFTENED the heart of another. Paul warns the Roman Jews that his words have served to make their hearts harder. In that, they are just like their fathers to whom Isaiah originally said these things.

"Was Paul able to go on with his ministry at Rome?"

30. Paul spent the next two full years in Rome at his own expense, welcoming all who came to see him. 31. There he was completely free to preach the kingdom of God and teach the truths of Christ as boldly as he wanted.

SPENT. All during the time Paul waited for his case to come to trial, he was permitted to live in his own rented quarters. He continued to be chained to a soldier and was not allowed to go anyplace. It would appear however that he found great favor with the Roman officials who were not the least interested in hindering his work. From his letter to the Philippians we learn that Paul considered the time spent here to be extremely fruitful. Not only did he win his guards to the Lord, but men and women from the palace as well. Luke happily closes his account with the gospel blazing away in the heart of the Roman empire for two full years. The story of the church which exploded into being at Jerusalem doesn't end with the chief apostle in Rome. The Lord Jesus continues to raise up men like Paul, who are ready to do His will. And He is just as eager to work through them as He was through His apostle.

TWO YEARS. Luke's mention of Paul's two years at Rome is very strategic. It is probably the strongest clue as to whether or not he was released. We are rather certain that he died a martyr, but it was very unlikely that his death occurred at the end of these two years which Luke says were so favorable. While Luke doesn't say so, his words imply that no one came from Jerusalem to press the charges against Paul. The Sanhedrin probably considered it unwise, knowing the Romans resented the Jews using their courts to prosecute religious offenders. Since the charges were weak and unsubstantiated in the first place, the ruling Jews most likely decided to let the matter die by default. Scholars familiar with Roman Law feel the case was probably thrown out of court after the statutory period for filing the complaint had expired. Two full years would have been sufficient to accommodate the entire procedure. Had Paul been executed at the end of the two years, it would be hard to understand why Luke didn't mention it when he spoke of the two years. He's been a very honest and straightforward historian all through the account.

TRADITION

The earliest historians explicitly state that Paul was released and undertook further missionary labors. Clement, Caius of Rome, Dionysius, Tertullian, Origen, and Eusebius all insist that he was set free after his first imprisonment and continued to minister to the churches before he was rearrested at Rome. Tradition says that after he was convicted, he was led some three miles outside the city where he was beheaded on orders by Nero in A.D. 64 or a little later. Inasmuch as he was a Roman citizen, he was not crucified as Peter is reported to have been. A church bearing his name marks a spot along the Ostian Way where his decapitated body is supposed to have been laid to rest.

Besides the testimony of these historians, it would seem from Philippians 1:25 and Philemon 22 that Paul himself expected to be set at liberty. When we come to his pastoral epistles (1 and 2 Timothy and Titus), the history of Paul as reported in them has no natural place in the book of Acts. Because they contain things which would have been unknown to Paul, some modern scholars deny that he wrote them. Either the matters they mention (advanced church organization and encounters with gnosticism) happened AFTER the events reported in Acts, or they simply aren't true. Nearly all scholars accept them as true.

A supposed sequence of events following such a release would be a return to Asia, Greece, and Crete, then back to Rome to comfort the Christians who were suffering.

CONCLUSION

It is important to think of the book of Acts as a sequel to the gospels. In the gospels we see our Lord in action BEFORE His resurrection. But in Acts, we see Him in action AFTER His resurrection. In our study we have seen Him keeping His promise to return and be IN His disciples. The day of Pentecost marked the beginning of the church for that was the day He returned as the Holy Ghost to indwell His people. The Ghost is Jesus in spirit form. (See the discussion of the Holy Spirit as Christ's Ghost in the introduction.) Consequently the book of Acts abounds with supernatural phenomena with the Lord Jesus Himself the greatest miracle of them all.

If we find the supernatural birth of the Lord astounding, our spiritual birth is even more so. We receive eternal life as the God of Glory comes to live within us. By means of His omnipresent Spirit, the Ghost of Christ actually takes up residence in our hearts. From then on, anything can happen as His divine power and presence are displayed in our lives. In the earliest days, the Lord's presence in His people was certified by signs and wonders. That way the experience could not be challenged by Jews who believed that salvation came through the sacrificial system. Today, His presence is certified by the **changed lives** of those whom He indwells.

The book of Acts is merely chapter one of the story of those who have received Christ and obeyed His orders to "Go!" It tells of their faithfulness to Him and His faithfulness to them. They obeyed and He backed their obedience with power. But other chapters are being written as men and women of all ages receive Him and the miracle of His presence radiates from their lives. The final chapter will be written when the whole world bows at the feet of our precious Lord Jesus and honors Him as King of Kings and Lord of Lords.

1982 edition

ABOUT THE AUTHOR. . .DR. C. S. LOVETT

Dr. Lovett is the president of **Personal Christianity,** a fundamental, evangelical interdenominational ministry. For the past 31 years he has had but one objective—**preparing Christians for the second coming of Christ!** This book is one of over 40 of his works designed to help believers be **prepared for His appearing.**

Dr. Lovett's decision to serve the Lord resulted in the loss of a sizable personal fortune. He is well equipped for the job the Lord has given him. A graduate of American Baptist Seminary of the West, he holds the M.A. and B.D. degrees conferred *Magna Cum Laude.* He has also completed graduate work in psychology at Los Angeles State College and holds an honorary doctorate from the Protestant Episcopal University in London.

A retired Air Force Chaplain (Lt. Colonel), he has been married to Marjorie for over 40 years and has two grown daughters dedicated to the Lord.

OTHER **Lovett's Lights**
ON THE NEW TESTAMENT YOU WILL ENJOY...

No. 538—LOVETT'S LIGHTS ON ROMANS with Rephrased Text—By C. S. Lovett ▪ 468 Lights, illustrated with drawings, graphs and paintings, 432 pages, paperback, book size 5¼" x 8¼"

No. 526—LOVETT'S LIGHTS ON JOHN with Rephrased Text—By C. S. Lovett ▪ 588 Lights, 336 pages, paperback, illustrated with paintings, size 5¼" x 8¼"

No. 541—LOVETT'S LIGHTS ON HEBREWS with Rephrased Text—By C. S. Lovett ▪ 279 Lights, 352 pages, paperback, illustrated with drawings, paintings, graphs, book size 5¼" x 8¼"

No. 530—LOVETT'S LIGHTS ON GALATIANS, EPHESIANS, PHILIPPIANS, COLOSSIANS, 1 & 2 THESSALONIANS with Rephrased Text—By C. S. Lovett ▪ 370 Lights, 240 pages, paperback, illustrated with drawings and maps, book size 5¼" x 8¼"

LOVETT'S LIGHTS BOOKLETS

(pocket-sized 3¾" x 5¾")

No. 209—LOVETT'S LIGHTS ON FIRST JOHN with Rephrased Text—By C. S. Lovett ▪ 24 pages, reduced type, 2 colors, illustrated, instruction folder.

No. 511—LOVETT'S LIGHTS ON PHILIPPIANS with Rephrased Text—By C. S. Lovett ▪ 32 pages, reduced type, 2 colors, illustrated, instruction folder.

No. 505—LOVETT'S LIGHTS ON JAMES with Rephrased Text—By C. S. Lovett ▪ 32 pages, illustrated, reduced type, 2 colors, instruction folder.

All of Dr. Lovett's works are available from:

PERSONAL CHRISTIANITY
Box 549,
Baldwin Park, California 91706

SINCE 1951
HELPING CHRISTIANS "PREPARE FOR HIS APPEARING"